AF522520

INDIA AND THE EUROPEAN UNION
Trade and Non-Tariff Barriers

INDIA AND THE EUROPEAN UNION
Trade and Non-Tariff Barriers

Swapan K. Bhattacharya

AAKAR BOOKS

INDIA AND THE EUROPEAN UNION
Trade and Non-Tariff Barriers

First Published, 2005

ISBN 81-87879-22-X

Published by
AAKAR BOOKS
28-E Pocket-IV, Mayur Vihar Phase-I, Delhi-110 091
Phone : 011-22795505 Telefax : 011-22795641
E-mail : aakarb@del2.vsnl.net.in

Typeset at
Arpit Printographers

Printed in India on behalf of M/s Aakar Books by
Arpit Printographers, B-7, Saraswati Complex,
Subhash Chowk, Laxmi Nagar, Delhi-110 092
Phones : 09350809192, 22825424

This volume is dedicated
to the
sacred memories
of my
father *Sambhu Charan Bhattacharya*
and his
sister *Rani Chakraborty*

Preface

The Treaty on European Union (Maastricht 1992) is the culmination of a series of treaties establishing the European Community. The initiative started with the Treaty of Paris, which set up the European Steel and Coal Community (ECSC) in 1951. The European Economic Community (EEC), the first of its kind, came into existence due to the Treaty of Rome in 1957. The EEC, which started with the six countries viz. Belgium, the Federal Republic of Germany, France, Italy, Luxembourg and the Netherlands, now becomes an enlarged Union of 25 states with the inclusion of 10 erstwhile socialist states on 1 May 2004. Newly accessed members are: Cyprus, the Czech Republic, Estonia, Hungary, Latvia, Lithuania, Malta, Poland, Slovakia and Slovenia. The accession treaties, signed in Athens on 16 April 2003, allow the people of the new member states to vote and to stand for election, on the same terms as all other EU citizens, in the European Parliamentary elections in June 2004. In another crucial decision in December 2004, the Union will decide whether to start talks on the accession of Turkey. Copenhagen European Council sets 2007 for the accession of Bulgaria and Romania with the European Union if they fulfill conditions of accession.

An enlarged European Union appears with plenty of opportunities for India. As we know, the EU is India's single largest trading partner in both exports and imports and this trend has been growing over the years. Recently, India has a favourable balance of trade with the EU. An enlarged union means more demand for Indian goods in the European market. EU is now a single market with a single European act and single port of entry. Also a 450 million population is going to generate huge demand for goods and services once their per capita income increases due to several measures related to economic and industrial development. The EU's regional policy is based on financial solidarity because much of the budgeted amount will go to less prosperous states and social groups. For the 2000-2006 period, these transfers will account for one-third of the Community budget or 213 billion Euros. As much as 70 per cent of the funding goes to regions, whose development is lagging behind. They are home to 22 per cent of the population of the Union. A percentage of 11.5 of the funding assists economic and social conversion in areas experiencing structural difficulties. Eighteen per cent of the population of the Union lives in such areas and 12.3 per cent of the funding promotes the modernization of training systems and the creation of employment.

India's trade potentiality to the European Union will enhance due to simplification of procedures, harmonization of rules, harmonization of sanitary and phytosanitary standards (SPS) and technical barriers to trade (TBT) and other technical barriers. Earlier trade with these ten countries was guided on bilateral basis, which will be now converted into a vast single European market. However, this process is not without its negative spillover effects. New forms of NTBs are to emerge in the European market to restrict imports from India. Most important forms of NTBs are growing as per standards followed by European Union. Earlier these ten countries did not follow such stringent standards, but once they become members of the EU, they have to. Secondly, though quota system in the textile trade will be abolished on 1 January 2005, it will remain in the picture for the entire 2004, which will certainly dampen interests of our exporters of textiles and garments.

This book basically analyses the effects of the reduction of EU's tariff and non-tariff barriers on India's exports. Though the Uruguay Round of multilateral trade negotiations stipulate 38 per cent reduction in subsidy on EU's agriculture, agricultural subsidies in some major agricultural items will remain at a very high level even after that. Tariff equivalents of agricultural subsidies are very high for major agricultural goods. Despite the fact that the level of average tariffs is very low in the EU, the extent and gravity of non-tariff barriers are very high. EU is a growing market for India, but this potentiality has been marred by the labyrinthe of NTBs erected by EU on its imports from India. The EU is India's vast market for agricultural goods but the potentiality does not get fully exploited because of the high level of protection. The book analyses the entire gamut of EU's tariff and non-tariff barriers to India's exports.

Indo-EU trade has many dimensions and the spectrum of trade includes not only different composition of goods but also new areas of services including software, IT, health, education, accounting, legal, tourism, insurance etc. The importance of trade in services has been accentuated in the era of globalization since the onset of World Trade Organization on 1 January 1995. The last chapter discusses different dimensions of Indo-EU trade during WTO regime. On several occasions, both India and the European Union have been at loggerheads in the dispute settlement panels of the WTO on several contentious issues. In this chapter, we have discussed in detail the non-tariff barriers existing both in India and in the European Union. There is no gainsaying the fact that extent and gravity of NTBs in both these countries will be reduced once all agreements of the Final Act of the Uruguay Round of multilateral trade negotiations are implemented on 1 January 2005. There has been apprehension in the trade policy communities that developed countries will emerge with newer form of NTBs under some pretext or other.

In writing this book, I gratefully acknowledge contributions of Sam Laird of WTO, Richard Blackhurst and several other experts in the trade policy division of the WTO, Ramiro Guzman and several other experts in the NTM division of UNCTAD. For clarity on the subject, I got immense help from Amb. S. Narayanan, India's erstwhile permanent representative to the WTO and several other officials of the Mission of the European Union in Geneva. I gratefully acknowledge their help in this regard. I also express my deep sense of gratitude to Professor H.S. Chopra, the then Head of the West European Studies division of the Centre for American and West European Studies, School of International Studies, Jawaharlal Nehru University, for supervising my doctoral work. I am immensely grateful to the EU Delegation Library and its staff for providing me all necessary information/documents pertaining to Indo-EU trade. Without their cordial help, it would have been impossible to write this book. I got immense benefit from discussions with Dr. O.P. Sharma, Advisor, International Trade Division, Planning Commission. In India, he is one of the noted experts on European economy due to his long attachment with the study of the subject both in Brussels and in India. I gratefully acknowledge his contribution in writing this book. Finally, I must thank Professor R.K. Jain, Chairperson, Jawaharlal Nehru University-European Union Studies Programme for giving me the grant to publish this book. Last but not the least, I deeply acknowledge the support and tolerance extended to me by my son Sourabh Kanti Bhattacharya and daughter Sarmistha Bhattacharya while writing this book.

Swapan K. Bhattacharya

Contents

Chapter 1

European Community: India's Major Trading Partner

The United Kingdom s Entry into the EC in 1973. Instrument of its Accession and the Joint Declaration of Intent (JDI).

The European Economic Community (EEC) came into existence as a result of the signing of the Treaty of Rome in March 1957. The EEC was the first trading bloc created under the image of a newly born transnational organization, basically targetted towards the development of its member states by promoting trade among themselves, through elimination of internal barriers. This motive became evident during the 1960's, when Britain described it as "common market". The EEC completed its transition period on 1 July 1968, one and a half years earlier than the period stipulated in the Treaty of Rome. It emerged as a powerful single entity capable of pursuing its own growth as well as rendering help to developing countries to improve their interaction with it and its member states, in the economic domain by increasing transactions both ways.

The initial objective of the formation of the EEC was the establishment of customs union with a Common External Tariff (CET) for the six founding member states viz. Belgium, Luxembourg, France, Italy, Germany, and the Netherlands. The Treaty also laid down the directive that after the transitional period was over, all the trade policies of the Community, would be harmonized and that competence to act in this regard would be transferred to the EEC. On 1 July, 1968, the EEC Customs Union and the CET became operational. In 1973, after prolonged negotiations, Denmark, Ireland and the United Kingdom gained admission as full members of the EEC. The custom duties of these new members were finally harmonized with CET on 1 July 1977. As such, it was in the mid-1970s that the EEC felt the necessity of extending economic co-operation to the developing countries in the area of political economy, so as to strengthen its position in the global commercial diplomacy.

The Indo-EEC cooperation began in 1962, when India established its diplomatic relations with the European Community (EC) in Brussels. The relationship received a boost in 1973, when the UK became a member of the EC along with Denmark and Ireland. These three countries became members of the EC through Instrument of Accession with effect from 1 January 1973[1]. The six member Community increased to a nine member-union, thereafter expanding its regional trading bloc. Even though in the late 1960s, the three communities, the European Coal and Steel Community (ECSC) set up in 1951, the EEC and the EURATOM in 1957, were managed institutionally. Yet the Treaties which were instrumental to their establishment, continued to be operational in the legal service. However, in pursuance with the Joint Declaration of Intent (JDI) in 1972, the EC and the UK undertook a special programme for developing trade relations with the developing independent Commonwealth countries in Asia. The participating countries were India, Pakistan, Sri Lanka, Malaysia and Singapore. According to the Treaty of Accession, the UK, Denmark and Ireland gave commitment to get the Treaty ratified in their national Parliaments before 1st January, 1973[2].

Conditions of the Treaty of Accession

The Instrument of Accession stipulated some pre-requisites to be fulfilled before new members would become full members of the Community. Basically, the new member states were to follow the common and harmonized rules on all matters related to their economies. Through the Instrument of Accession, they had given a commitment to reduce trade barriers both in tariff and non-tariff forms within the specified time schedule. The commitments, as enshrined in the Instrument of Accession, were as follows :

- *(i)* The new members had given commitments to accede from the date of accession to all agreements concluded by the original member states relating to the functioning and activities of the Communities.
- *(ii)* The new members undertook to accede to the conventions provided for in Article 220 of the EEC Treaty and to the protocols

on the interpretations of those conventions by the Court of Justice signed by the original members.

(iii) The new members were treated on par with the original member states in respect of declarations, resolutions and other positions taken by the Council. Moreover, it was also binding for the new entrants to honour all agreements concerning establishment of the European Communities, adopted by the common agreement of the member states.

(iv) The new members were required to honour all agreements and conventions entered into by any of the Community members concluded with one or more third states or with an international organization or with a national of a third state.

(v) The new members were required to accede to all internal agreements, concluded by the original member states for the purpose of implementing the agreements and conventions.

(vi) The new members had given commitments to adjust their policies relating to international organizations and agreements to which one of the Community members or member states is also a party.

As a transitional measure, the UK along with the other new members had pledged to liberalize the trading regime by reducing or if possible by altogether removing tariff and non-tariff barriers. All members including UK, emphasized the importance of free movement of goods. This was the main objective behind the formation of the Customs Union in 1968 which meant that there would not be any customs duty on interstate transactions of goods.

Besides reduction of tariffs, another significant aspect of liberalization was the elimination of quantitative restrictions on trade. According to Article 42 of Chapter 2 of the Act, all member states were asked to abolish quantitative restrictions on trade that had been followed since the early sixties under different programmes. Moreover, equivalent effects of such restrictions were also scheduled to be abolished by 1st January, 1975[3]. All these arrangements were thought of for member states as a precondition to be the members of Customs Union.

Though Article 42 of the Treaty of Accession, stipulated removal of all quantitative restrictions between the member states by 1 January 1975, exceptions were granted to member states for a period of two years on exports of waste and scrap material of iron and steel falling within Common Customs Tariff (Heading No. 73.03)[4]. For Denmark, the period was three years and it was five years for Ireland. In order to implement the Treaty of Accession, the new member states had to progressively adjust their State monopolies to the free market economies of commercial character within the scope of Article 37(1) of the EEC Treaty, so as to ensure that by 31 December, 1977, no discrimination existed between nationals of member states regarding the conditions under which goods were procured and marketed. The original members had to follow the same obligations, as the new member states[5].

There is no gainsaying the fact that under Customs Union, all the member states have removed tariffs on many items in inter-state transaction over the years. But non-tariff barriers in the form of technical standards, fiscal and physical barriers have stayed on in the national laws of the member States. The members of the EC have harmonized rules and regulations relating to standards, codes and policies for Intra-Community trade but there have still been considerable discrepancies within the Community.

Reviewing the progress of the tariff reductions commitment as agreed to by the UK, Denmark and Ireland as a precondition to gaining admission to the EC, there seemed to have been no perceptible progress in that area. As a result, India's deficit with the EC had increased tremendously, due to accelerated industrialization and upgradation of technologies of production in India during the early seventies, which accelerated the pace of import of equipments, and the know-how from France, Federal Republic of Germany and Italy. Indo-EC trade during the seventies is shown in **Table 1.1.** India pressed for tariff reduction to which the six countries had agreed to, in the course of their negotiations on Britain's entry into EC. As a

TABLE 1.1 : Indo-EC Trade during 1970s

(Rs. Crore)

Year	*India's Exports to the EC*	*India's Imports from the EC*	*Trade Balance*
1973-74	594	704	–110
1974-75	699	868	–169
1975-76	819	1044	–225
1976-77	1392	1008	384
1977-78	1391	1518	–127
1978-79	1573	2073	–500
1979-80	1682	2120	–438

result, the EC lowered its tariff on a number of items, including bulk Tea. After prolonged diplomatic efforts, "The Six" also agreed to provide zero-duty tariff quotas for handloom fabrics and handicrafts. On the other hand, India agreed to limit its export of jute and coir products to agreed figures. The six agreed to suspend their tariffs partially with regard to these commodities. Later on another self restraint agreement on cotton textile was also concluded[6].

Joint Declaration of Intent[7]

In order to enhance economic co-operation with the former Asian colonies, the EEC and the UK were credited for concluding a Joint Declaration of Intent (JDI) in 1972. Through JDI, annexed to the final act of the Treaty of Accession, the EC had committed to extend and strengthen its trade relations with the Asian countries of the Commonwealth, especially in seeking solution to the trade problems that arose due to Britain's accession to the Community.

JDI constituted the EEC's Community's trade and development policies towards Sri Lanka, India, Malaysia, Pakistan and Singapore. It was basically a long-term perspective for development policies of the Community towards South and South-East Asian countries[8].

From among the developed political collectivities, the EC was the first to have granted (in 1971) the Generalized System of Preference (GSP) facility to India, the first among the Asian countries, aimed at encouraging export of manufactured goods of poor Asian countries. In addition, the EC also sought to strengthen bilateral economic cooperation with the Commonwealth countries of Asia. Apart from extending GSP facility, the EC also undertook to examine, from the date of Britain's accession, the problems of trade of Asian developing countries (Sri Lanka, India, Malaysia, Pakistan and Singapore). Apart from extension of the GSP facility to manufactured goods, the EC also extended tariff benefits to these countries through the Most Favoured Nation (MFN) scheme[9].

Though GSP was aimed at encouraging manufactured exports of developing countries in general and India in particular, it was not very successful in achieving its goal simply because of its structural rigidities. GSP separated goods into different categories, according to the degree of their sensitivity in the EC market. Most sensitive items were excluded from this facility. In most cases the entire gamut of non-sensitive items were included in the GSP list. As a result, most of India's quotas on textiles and apparels remained unutilized over the years[10]. Until recently, agricultural and processed foods were not included into the GSP list. This benefit has also been constrained by enabling and graduation clauses.

There is no gain saying the fact that the Treaty of Accession and its several Protocols/Declarations were biased in favour of the associated countries (i.e. ACP countries under the Lome Convention). EC entered into 13 separate agreements with different groups of countries extending preferential treatment. Though, other developing countries were given GSP facility, ACP countries were formally treated as more than GSP beneficiaries and given better facilities such as those of STABEX and SYSMIN, under the Lome Convention. From that point of view, JDI was discriminatory to the non-members and non-associated countries like India and other South Asian countries. Another serious allegation against the Treaty of Accession/JDI was the narrow legal, administrative and financial framework of the EC to discharge its commercial responsibilities towards the affected countries[11].

Despite the many odds, JDI had many positive aspects which were conducive to the growth of exports of developing countries with the EC. This was the first time when the Community gave much importance to the economic development of developing countries of the Asian region after realizing their problems of trade and development. JDI set the spirit of a dynamic relationship between the EC and the Asian developing countries. It was the first organized effort to strengthen economic/trading relations between India and the EC. The EC extended GSP facility as well as MFN benefits to India[12]. Under the shield of JDI, GSP coverage to India improved over the years and it was extended to other member states. JDI also set the basis for strong Indo-EC cooperation in areas of technology, scientific knowledge, industrial development and better access of Indian commodities to the EC market.

II (a) Indo-EC Commercial Cooperation Agreement (CCA) of 1974, renewed as Commercial and Economic Cooperation Agreement (CECA) in 1981.

The Commercial Cooperation Agreement (CCA) was signed by India and the EC on 17 December 1973 and came into force on 1st March 1974[13]. It was the first ever trade agreement by the EC with any Asian developing country. Both sides consciously felt the need "to consolidate, deepen and diversify their commercial and economic relations to the full extent of their growing capacity to meet each others requirement on the basis of complementarity". This agreement provided the basis for improving economic cooperation between the two countries on a historical basis, spreading over trade, investment, technology transfer and finally the establishment of joint ventures in both collectivities as well as in the third country markets. CCA was enforced first for five years with the provision for automatic renewal unless disrupted by any contracting party[14].

The CCA also extended MFN facility to India in principle in accordance with the provisions of the General Agreement on Tariffs and Trade (GATT) and also emphasized the promotion and diversification of both way trade on the basis of comparative advantage and mutual cooperation. This mutual exclusive relationship is *sine qua non* for accelerating economic growth of an underdeveloped economy like India where foreign trade sector is still premature to face international competition. An Indo-EEC Joint Business Commission was setup to provide institutional support for augmenting two way trade based on complementarity and cooperation between the two democratic collectivities. A Trade Promotion Programme was undertaken at the behest of India-EEC Joint Business Commission with the object of increasing the Community's assistance for India's participation in European trade fairs, visits of Indian delegations to the member countries and vice-versa. Another salient feature of the agreement was the preparation of a report on Joint Project Planning by Smallman Consultant Ltd. to identify the areas of cooperation between these two parties. This agreement also provided for special sectorial agreement between India and the EC on jute, coir and cotton textiles[15].

The CCA between India and the EC cited a model which inspired the non-associated developing countries of the subcontinent to strengthen economic cooperation among themselves through mutual cooperation. These non-associated countries were Bangladesh, Sri Lanka, Pakistan and Nepal. These agreements marked an important beginning of the implementation of the Joint Declaration of Intent annexed to the Treaty of Accession of the United Kingdom to EEC[16].

Functioning of the CCA had all along been reasonably[17] satisfactory which is revealed from the fact that since 1973-74, India's exports to the EC had been increasing satisfactorily both in value as well as in volume terms. Since 1973-74, India has been importing mainly capital goods, engineering goods, machinery (both electrical and mechanical), chemicals and sophisticated instruments machineries, etc., as a move to strengthen its industrial base. On the other hand, India's export basket has constituted jute, tea, textiles and garments, diamond, raw leather and leather manufactures, oil cake, tobacco, carpets, coffee etc. One of the largest import items in India—the raw diamond from Belgium is re-exported after substantial value addition to the EC member states as well as elsewhere[18]. There had been a strong apprehension that India's exports to the west European countries might get hampered owing to UK's accession to the EC, for it had been the traditional and most important trading partner of India on account of historical trade links. But this apprehension got plummeted when India's exports to EEC increased from Rs. 609 crore in 1973-74 to Rs 1392 crore in 1976-77. This steady growth of India's exports was uninterrupted except in 1977-78, when this upward movement was arrested temporarily. Since the conclusion of the CCA, India's exports have been increasing reasonably well, and its imports have surpassed its exports resulting in a chronic balance of trade deficit. EC's imports from India which were worth $806 million in 1973, increased to $2501 million in 1980. On the other hand, EC's exports to India, which were $832 million in 1973, escalated to $3200 million in 1980. As a result of this, tremendous surge in Indian imports, trade deficit, which was $26 million in 1973 rose to $699 million in 1980[19]. This is shown in Table 1.2.

TABLE 1.2 : Indo-EEC Trade

(Unit in Million US dollars)

Year	*India's Exports to the EC*	*India's Imports from the EC*	*Trade Balance*
1973	806	832	– 26
1976	1573	1254	319
1977	1873	1584	289
1978	2045	2370	– 325
1979	2503	2750	– 247
1980	2501	3200	– 699

The CC Agreement provided a solid basis for Indo-EC economic cooperation. On India's request, the EC set up an Action Defining Committee (ADC) which had its first meeting in New Delhi in 1977.

The meeting identified three major areas for intensifying cooperation: new energy sources, environmental research and remote sensing management of scientific and technical information. The CCA did not have adequate room for such cooperation and the initiative was made on personal institutional levels. Indian scientists and policy makers took part in three conferences on solar energy organized by the Commission. A joint coal gasification study was begun in 1978, and scientists from both sides visited the facilities already available in the EC and India. The EC had been making a major contribution to India's food need. Through Food Aid Programme, it took part actively in Operation Milk Flood-II, an ambitious project which helped about 10 million families through increased production and marketing of milk, though operation flood has been subjected to some criticism as well[20].

In 1975, India was plunged into a serious balance of payment crisis due to exorbitant rise in oil prices. The EEC allocated about 40 per cent of the direct aid under the "Cheysson Fund" to India. The aid amounted to $75 million out of a total available fund of $187 million[21]. Besides, India received a substantial allocation of fund from the UN Emergency Fund, to which EC's contribution was $63 million. Under the technical aid programme of EC to developing countries, India received 20 per cent of the total allocation, which was used to combat drought, to construct warehouses for storing foodgrains and fertilizers and to build shelters for the use of cyclone and flood affected people. From the Special Action Fund initiated in 1978, India alone was allocated $50 million of the total $430 million, out of which a sum of $45 million was provided for the Agricultural Refinance and Development Cooperation for lending to farmers, training, etc., and $5 million provided to rural electrification[22].

Some broad conclusions have, therefore, emerged from the review of the operations of the CCA :

Firstly both India and the EC have made concerted efforts to gain the fruits of the agreement. As a result, the contracting parties were able to establish a strong link between trade and cooperation. Besides trade, cooperation had also extended to conservation of natural resources, energy related technology, environment protection and its improvement.

Secondly though in some areas, cooperation was indepth and results were quite enthusiastic, in general, EC's efforts to make it a success was lacklustre simply because of its lack of spontaneity and thrust. This was because of EC's structural and functional limitations. Though bilateral relations between India and some member states of EC were quite encouraging, in general, one cannot say that western Europe was very keen on intensifying its economic relations with India[23].

Thirdly since the conclusion of CCA in 1973, India has been trying to intensify its economic relations through increase in trade. Though exports had gone up significantly between 1973 and 1980, imports had also increased substantially and kept on surpassing exports every year. The situation had become so worse that in 1980, India's trade deficit with EC shot upto $ 699 million from merely $26 million in 1973. This adverse balance of trade situation was due to a growing protectionism in EC during seventies. The Commission resorted to several non-tariff barriers to its cheaper imports from developing countries. Therefore, in spite of India's constant endeavour to increase its exports, it could not achieve much success because of growing protectionism in the EC[24].

Protectionism in the European Community has been evident from the First Oil Shock of 1973. The trend got aggravated during the Second Oil Shock in 1979. The seventies were characterized by growing protectionism in the EC. The first MFA was concluded in 1974 and it was reviewed thereafter for the fourth term ending on 31 December 1994. Apart from quantitative restrictions on exports of textiles and garments, other non-tariff barriers were marketing regulations, health regulations, phytosanitary regulations, import levies and other bilateral agreements restraining exports of textiles and garments[25]. Two oil shocks in the European economy were followed by demand recession. It was also found that growth in productivity was much less than the growth of wage to the workers which led demand side recession. This problem of demand management got aggravated because the European capital goods industry became obsolete in the seventies. Therefore, the output of low capital intensive sector became incompetent and faced less demand. This was the basic reason why EC took recourse to such protectionist measures to protect its ailing domestic industry from foreign competition[26].

After the expiry of the CCA, India and the EC decided to start fresh negotiations with a view to arriving at a new agreement in the light of the experience gained till then. After prolonged negotiations, India and the EC agreed to conclude a new agreement which was concluded on 23 June 1981, known as Commercial and Economic Cooperation Agreement (CECA)[27]. The main objectives of this new agreement were: *(i)* developing commercial relations and intensified economic cooperation, *(ii)* giving a new dimension to the mutual relationship between India and the EC; *(iii)* strengthening economic relationship based on mutual cooperation and comparative advantage; *(iv)* pursuing economic cooperation in an evolutionary and pragmatic manner; *(v)* reaffirming determination to expand mutual trade for achieving wider economic and social objectives as an important instrument for strengthening international cooperation, *(vi)* augmenting international economic cooperation commensurate with human, intellectual and material resources.

The CECA endorsed the MFN (Article 2) treatment as the basis of trade between two countries. Both the contracting parties agreed to honour their commitments given in the GATT. Both parties affirmed their faith on free trade and agreed to extend each other the height of maximum degree of liberalization to the products of each other, which they used to offer to a third country. CECA emphasized the commercial exchange between two countries (Article 4). In order to do this, it was decided to rely on frequent interactions between economic operators of both sides, which included sending trade delegations, promoting visits by persons, arranging trade fairs in both collectivities and facilitating free movement of persons for developing industrial technical and commercial contacts. The agreement emphasized the need for bilateral cooperation in identifying the areas of joint ventures in production, trade and marketing.

In areas of industrial cooperation (Article 5), the agreement laid down principles of joint effort in R&D activities, joint research in areas of energy and environment and a smooth process of technology transfer between the two parties. All such cooperation policies were in conformity with their laws. As regards investment, the EC agreed to extend direct concessional transfer as well as institutional and other source of finance to India suited to its policy framework in favour of non-associated countries. Protection of investment was a crucial area of cooperation, but foreign direct investment (FDI) flow into India had been severely constrained by intricate rules and regulations which existed in India than. After much deliberations and clarifications it was decided that both sides would take steps to promote mutually beneficial investment which was consistent with their laws and policies.

Both parties felt the need for a Joint Business Commission (JBC) (Article 10) as an effective mechanism for monitoring the implementation evaluating of its progress. The Joint Commission was given the task of studying the impact of trade barriers, viz. tariffs and non-tariffs, on adoption of the trade pattern and marketing structure so as to fulfill the objectives of the agreement. A new private mechanism known by the nomenclature "Joint Business Council" (JBC) was set up to act as a catalyst to promote Indo-EC economic and commercial cooperation. The JBC was also required to monitor the Community Fund earmarked for the implementation of the agreement. The Commission was also empowered to mandate a specific subcommission or an Expert Group to study all specific issues that came in the way of implementation of the agreement and to suggest suitable measures which would be binding on the respective governments[28].

The CECA was concluded on 23 June 1981[29]. The new agreement extended the horizon and scope of its economic and commercial cooperation. The Commercial Cooperation Agreement of 1973 continued up to 1980. CCA was the first of this kind of cooperation agreement between India and the EC. In spite of adverse international economic scenario due to two successive oil shocks, India's performance on the export front was relatively well. Between 1973 and 1980, India's exports to the EC increased by 210 per cent, on the other hand, imports also grew remarkably by 284 per cent. The compound growth rate of India's exports was also relatively better which was 17.55 per cent against the import growth of 21.22 per cent during the same period.

Though CECA was much diversified than CCA but its performance on the external front was quite lacklustre during this period. CECA was concluded in June 1981 and continued up to 1994 when it was replaced by the Cooperation Agreement on Partnership and Development (CAPD)[30]. During CECA, exports grew only 9.54 per cent at compound rate whereas import growth was 7.97 per cent from 1980 to 1993. One interesting feature during this period was that exports growth was higher than import growth. This was quite contrary to what happened during CCA.

The percentage change in India's exports over the corresponding period of the previous year was 2 per cent in 1980 but rose to a phenomenal level of 20.6 per cent in 1993. Similarly percentage change in India's imports over the previous year, which was 5 per cent in 1980 also rose to 18.8 per cent in 1993. India's exports to the EC were 1799 million ECUs in 1980, which increased to 5,882 million ECUs in 1993. On the other hand, India's imports from the EC at 2298 millon ECUs in 1980 had increased to 6,229 million ECUs in 1993. As aloways, trade balance was in favour of the Community. India's trade deficit with the Community which was 499 million ECUs in 1980 rose to the peak level of 3,196 million ECUs in 1986, declining to 2905 million ECUs in 1989, but reducing to an all time low of 348 million ECUs in 1991. If success is measured in terms of growth rates, certainly CECA does not deserve kudos, but India has been much successful in reducing the trade deficit with the EC over the years. The entire picture is shown in Table 1.3 showing per annum trend in Indo-EC Trade (1980-2000).

When one reviews the operations of the CECA in terms of trade between India and the EC, one could easily observe that India has not been able to realize its economic potential for exports to the member states of the EC. Though the Commission has been the major trading partner of India, sharing about 30 per cent of its exports and imports, the existing level of Indo-EC commercial and economic exchanges are far below their acutal potential. Both way Indo-EC trade was no more than 1.11 per cent of EC's external trade in 1992.

One plausible reason may be the inability of the Indian exporters to conform to the European specifications and fast changing market trends. To satisfy European quality standards and maintain strict delivery scheme had also been difficult for many of the small-scale exporters from India. In order to capture the European market, quality is the most important determinant rather than cost-competitiveness. In India, we often neglect quality aspect and tend to give greater importance to the price factor[31].

The second major reason for failure to utilize the full potential of India's exports to the EC seemed to have been the emergence of neoprotectionism in the form of labyrinthine non-tariff barriers (NTBs). Textile is India's single largest export item, constituting more than one-third of its total exports. But the irony is that the entire basket of our textiles and apparel exports has been under strict quantitative restrictions in the EC operated through Multifibre Arrangement (MFA). Not only is the NTB coverage ratio higher than in India's exports to the EC, but average weighted tariffs are also exorbitantly higher in the NTB-affected items. Nearly 50 per cent of

TABLE 1.3 : Trends of Indo-EC Trade since 1980

(Value: Million ECUs)

Year	*EU's Exports (FOB)*	*% change over previous year*	*EU's Imports (CIF)*	*% change over previous year*	*Total trade*	*Balance of Trade*
(a)	*(b)*	*(c)*	*(d)*	*(e)*	*(f)*	*(g)*
1980	2298	5.00	1799.00	-2.00	4097.00	499.00
1981	3363	46.00	1880.00	4.00	5243.00	1488.00
1982	3991	19.00	2572.00	37.00	6563.00	-1479.00
1983	3823	-5.00	2196.00	-15.00	6019.00	-1627.00
1984	4629	21.00	2905.00	32.00	7534.00	-1724.00
1985	5560	20.00	2672.00	-8.00	8232.00	-2886.00
1986	5705	3.00	2395.00	-12.00	7876.00	-3196.00
1987	5678	-0.50	2761.00	15.00	8439.00	-2917.00
1988	5673	0.00	3256.00	18.00	8929.00	-2318.00
1989	7085	24.90	4180.00	28.00	11265.00	-2905.00
1990	5997	-15.30	4541.00	8.64	10538.00	-1456.00
1991	5219	-13.00	4757.00	4.75	9976.00	-463.00
1992	5244	0.50	4877.00	2.52	10121.00	-367.00
1993	6229	18.80	5882.00	20.60	12111.00	-348
1994	7053	12.91	6913.00	18.74	13946.00	-1406.00
1995	9943	40.97	7794.00	12.74	17737.00	-1648.00
1996	9895	4.80	8588.00	10.19	18483.00	1307.00
1997	10208	3.16	9465.00	10.21	19673.00	743.00
1998	9539	-6.55	9790.00	3.43	19329.00	-251.00
1999	10344	8.43	10020.00	2.34	20364.00	324.00
2000	13303	28.60	12341.00	12.16	25644.00	962.00
2001	12610	-5.20	12914.00	4.64	25524.00	-304.00
2002	12867	4.77	12984.00	0.54	25851.00	-117.00

* Figures from 1996 onwards are expressed in Euros.

India's exports to the EC are exposed to EC's NTBs. Various quotas have also been binding constraints to India's exports[32]. EC's variable levy is another example of NTBs, which puts an effective barrier to Indian agricultural exports. India is principally an exporter of low value added labour-intensive items which do not have free access to European market. Textiles, leather, jute, diamonds, precious and semi-precious stones, etc. are some of the examples.

II (b) Indo-EC Cooperation Agreement on Partnership and Development, 1994

The thought and action to improve the economic and commercial cooperation between India and the EC was initiated on 17 December 1973 through the conclusion of the Commercial Cooperation Agreement followed by Commercial and Economic Cooperation Agreement on 23 June 1981. In 1994, these agreements were replaced by Cooperation Agreement on Partnership and Development (CAPD)[33]. This new agreement is a modified version of the two erstwhile agreements and is in response to India's economic reforms, which were initiated in July 1991. The new cooperation agreement has maintained the objectives, as enshrined in the CECA, and emphasized upon the need for environmental protection and sustainable management of natural resources. In the new agreement, the EC has extended MFN facility to India in continuation of the earlier agreement. The new agreement has emphasised the highest degree of liberalization in conducting trade between the two contracting parties by eliminating trade barriers.

Trade in goods has been the central issue for discussion in all bilateral negotiations, but, this is for the first time that, both the parties have agreed to promote trade in services in a mutually exclusive way[34]. Regarding customs duty, both the contracting parties have agreed (in accordance with law) to exempt goods admitted temporarily to their territories for subsequent re-export unaltered from duty, tax and other charges. This may also be for goods which re-enter their territories after processing in the other member states which may not be sufficient for the goods to be treated as originating from the territory of that contracting party.

Recently there has been a spate of anti-dumping cases in the EU. A host of India's export of textiles has been subject to EU's anti-dumping duty. In the new agreement, the EU becomes more flexible in dealing with anti-dumping cases arising from India. As regards anti-dumping and anti-subsidy investigations, every party has agreed to examine in detail the submission of the other and will inform the interested parties concerned of the essential facts on the basis of which decision is to be taken. Before imposing any anti-dumping duty, the contracting parties would do their best to evolve a mutually acceptable constructive solution to the problem.

The new cooperation agreement basically works in three broad areas indicated below :

(*i*) improving the economic environment in India by facilitating better access to EU's know-how and technology;

(*ii*) facilitating contacts between economic cooperation and other measures designed to promote commercial exchanges and investments; and

(*iii*) reinforcing mutual understanding of their respective economic, social and cultural environment as the basis for effective cooperation.

Besides other conventional areas of economic cooperation, this agreement has given much emphasis on the importance and upgradation of the protection of intellectual properties in India[35]. Ineffective protection of IPR is the main deterrent factor for inadequate flow of FDI into India. European companies are highly skeptical about transferring their state-of-the-art technologies to India in anticipation of getting it pirated. Especially in areas of patents India has to reform a lot. Presently India is having the process patent system in areas of drugs and pharmaceuticals and agro-chemicals. The present system in India is not at all conducive to higher investment unless the inventions made in these areas are well protected through product patent. In order to upgrade our patent regime, the EU has agreed to provide training to Indian personnel and help Indian technical institutions to introduce courses on IPR study.

The new Agreement has also extended its area of operation to some new horizons. These are : Conservation of depletable energy, doing extensive research on development of non-conventional energy and finding out suitable methods for saving and efficient use of energy. This agreement also stresses the need of protecting the environment. In order to protect natural resources, both the countries have pledged to work together on water, soil and air pollution, community afforestation and sustainable management of natural resources etc. Apart from these areas, the CAPD pledges to extend cooperation in all conventional areas of socio-economic activities of the two countries.

The new Agreement (CAPD) has been formulated in the light of India's move towards liberalization. Since 1991 India has entered into a new era of economic development through liberalizaion of policies and procedures in almost all spheres of economic activities. Taking advantage of a liberalized regime, economic transactions both ways have increased substantially. Such an increase in economic cooperation is not only evident in augmenting trade but also, Europe's response to Indian economic reforms has been encouraging which is revealed from the fact that it has shown an increasing flow of FDI from Europe coupled with the increasing number of joint ventures and technology transfer agreements.

Another important provision of this agreement is the dismantling of all barriers on trade. As a part of the New Economic Policy, India has already liberalized its trade sector through drastic reductions of tariffs from its imports[36]. Though the EC's response is not very encouraging in this area, but as per its commitment given to WTO, it is expected that it will relent on its protectionist attitude over the years[37]

EC'S GSP AND ITS MODUS OPERANDI

In spite of strong opposition from the developed countries, UNCTAD-I adopted **General Principle-VIII**, which recommended that developing countries should be granted preferential access to the developed countries without any reciprocity. Realizing the need for diversification and expansion of exports, the UNCTAD also passed a resolution (A.III.5), favouring the least developed countries', (LDCs)[38] argument of preferential market access to the industrialized countries.

The resolution 21(II) enunciated as below spelt the objectives of the generalized, non-reciprocal, non-discriminatory system of preferences favouring developing countries including special measures extended to least developed nations:

(a) to augment export earning,

(b) to promote industrialization, and

(c) to accelerate rate of economic growth.

A Special Committee on GSP was constituted at its fourth session for implementing the resolution, It recommended :

(1) preference-giving countries, (while reviewing the GSP), would give maximum attention to the need of developing countries in respect of tariff preferences;

(2) enforcement of safeguard mechanism would be an exceptional case and be decided on only after taking due account of the interests of developing countries,

(3) additional measures were suggested in favouring least developed among the developing countries; and

(4) rules of origin should facilitate in achieving GSP benefits.

Factual evidence shows that LDCs could not extract much benefit from preferential arrangements because two-thirds of total export earnings of developing countries are composed of primary commodities which enter developed countries on MFN basis[39]. Therefore, extension of preferences means encouraging export of small manufacturing sector which also attracts higher duty. The intention behind the extension of GSP facility to LDCs was to promote long-term industrialization rather than merely a short-term objective of higher export earnings. Granting preferential treatment creates price effect of the importable which can be split into income effects and substitution effects in micro economic terms. In international economics, increase in preferences has trade creation and trade diversion effects too. To explain these effects it requires quantitative analysis which is discussed hereafter.

In spite of having such growth perspectives, GSP has failed to achieve its desired goals because it has not strictly adhered to the principles as agreed upon in the UNCTAD. In UNCTAD, preferences were slated to have been implemented under 16 different schemes. All schemes are yet to be generalized because preferential tariffs have not been extended to many products of interest to developing countries. It hardly covers even half of all dutiable imports from the beneficiary LDCs[40]. Despite this fact, some of the schemes have introduced reciprocal relationship with the developing countries. Some are also discriminatory in the sense that some LDCs have neither been given complete status of beneficiary countries nor preferential treatment for their exports. In spite of this fact, the "rules of origin" principle contains many complex and demanding requirements that prohibit the access of preferential treatment to the exports of developing countries. GSP started with much fanfare, but uptil now[41] (i.e., GSP has been revised on 31 December 1994, and data available to us upto 1992) it covers only a quarter of the dutiable imports from developing countries which clearly deviates from the path of "mutually acceptable" principles as adopted in the UNCTAD.

In recent years, a substantial improvement has been noticed with the list containing few exclusions. During successive revisions, agricultural products have been brought under the purview of preferential treatment. Some countries have been "graduated" from the preferential schemes and, on the other hand, unlimited duty free entry has been granted to some developing countries under many schemes such as ACP countries under Lome's Convention.

Though the GSP scheme has been improved significantly over the years, even now it covers only a small portion of the total exports of developing countries in general and India in particular. An UNCTAD study[42] shows that from 1970 to 1980, there has been a six-fold increase in total exports to beneficiary countries, while imports from beneficiaries just about trippled. The nature of production as well as exports of developing countries have now been shifted in favour of processed manufactured goods which attract higher duties than finished manufactured items. An indication shows that preferential treatment may have helped the imports of GSP covered products which grew twice as fast as dutiable imports during the 1980s.

Rationale for GSP

Since the inception of GATT in Geneva in 1947, developing countries have been continuously ignoring two fundamental principles i.e. 1), non-discrimination, and (2) reciprocal trade liberalization. LDC's basic argument was that "equal treatment among unequals is unfair[43]. In all multilateral fora, LDC's have not only been advocating for nondiscriminatory trade but also insisting for special and differential treatment (S and DT) favouring them.

Preferential tariff helps developing countries in two ways as observed by Langhammer and Sapir (1987), i.e.[44]

- (*i*) due to reduction in MFN tariff (or preferential tariff) exports of developing countries would become cheaper and thus it will generate trade due to income effect; and
- (*ii*) it has also substitution effect because exports of developing countries will enjoy certain benefits over those of developed countries.

Therefore, preferential tariff has strong spill-over effect. LDCs favour preferential tariff rather than MFN tariff cut because "preferential treatment on exports of developing countries would help the industries of (these) countries to overcome the difficulties that they encounter in export markets because of their higher costs" **(Prebish 1964)**[45]

Whatever may be the form of concessions (either MFN tariff reduction or the preferential treatment), most of the manufacturing goods exports are still outside the ambit of tariff concessions. In fact, markets of the developed countries are protected by higher tariffs on items in which developing countries have comparative advantage.

This trend continues even after eight rounds of multilateral trade negotiations held under the auspices of GATT.

Though the question of "generalized non-reciprocal and non-discriminatory" system of preferences had been discussed comprehensively in the UNCTAD-I in 1964, yet these principles were accepted only in the meeting of UNCTAD-II in 1968 and finally in 1971. It (UNCTAD) empowered developed countries to implement their GSP schemes by waiving the MFN principle of Article 1, of the General Agreement for an initial period of 10 years and could be renewed subsequently. The contracting parties of GATT adopted the principle of "differential and more favourable treatment, non-reciprocity, and fuller participation of developing countries"[46]. This was one of the outcomes of the Tokyo Round in 1979.

The preferential treatment extended to developing countries is commonly known as "enabling clause", which grants the exception to MFN clause and provides the legal basis for GSP to continue beyond the initial period of 10 years without contravening Article-1. Due to its legal base, GSP is binding on contracting parties of GATT which is not the case with the MFN clause. The "enabling clause" (as it is bound by GATT provision) enables developing countries to upgrade their economies within the framework of GATT after fully utilizing the preferential benefit. This also provides "graduation clause" which empowers developed countries to phase out GSP facilities extended to LDCs after the latter's graduation into the advanced stage of economic development. Recently, newly industrialized countries (NICs) are set to be graduated from the preferential benefits. This is done according to the New GSP scheme of the EU which was announced on 31 December 1994. The new scheme replaces quantitative restrictions to trade which EU is bound to phase out according to its commitment given in the WTO. Singapore has recently graduated to the status of a developed country.

Implementation of the GSP Scheme

The entire gamut of GSP operation mainly rests on several schemes adopted by the different preference-giving countries, viz, Australia (1966), Austria (1972), Bulgaria (1972), Canada (1974), EC (1971), Finland (1972), Hungary (1972), Japan (1971), New Zealand (1972), Norway (1971), Poland (1976), Sweden (1972), Switzerland (1972), USSR (1965), and the USA (1965). Erstwhile GDR had no tariff, therefore, no GSP, but extended other benefits to the developing countries[47]. Australia and USSR introduced preferences in favour of developing countries before the agreement on the GSP.

Almost all member states (currently 120) of the Group-77 are beneficiaries of such preferences. Among non-members which have been included as beneficiary countries are Bulgaria, China, Hong Kong, Israel, Taiwan and Turkey. The Democratic Republic of Korea has been excluded from both schemes. In addition to it, a host of other countries are also excluded from this scheme on political ground, especially by the USA. Among the beneficiary countries, LDCs (Least Developed Countries, viz. Bangladesh, Bhutan, Maldives, Nepal and some poor countries of Sub-Saharan region) receive better preferential treatment under GSP than other developing countries.

According to declared principle, all manufacturing exports of developing countries get duty-free treatment, but, developed market economies, from time to time, have imposed numerous restrictions on their import of sensitive products in which LDCs have comparative advantage. Trade in clothing and textiles may be mentioned in this connection. By enforcing so many quotas and ceilings on imports from developing countries, they (DCs) have virtually stopped growth of exports of most sensitive items from the former countries. GSP was originally envisaged for augmenting exports of manufactured goods of developing countries. Initially export of agricultural items was outside the ambit of such preferential treatment. But the constraints have progressively been removed and increasing number of food products are being included in the GSP eligible lists. In case of export of food products, the potentiality is severely constrained by NTBs rather than GSP tariffs.

Preferential benefits under GSP vary from country to country depending upon their socio-economic conditions. The limitations of preferential treatment are in different forms in different countries. In the USA, a country can get duty-free GSP treatment in a given year for a product on the basis of "competitive need criteria". In Japan and EC, preferential imports are subject to annual quantity limits, such as tariff quota, ceilings or maximum country accounts. Of late, developed contracting parties (i.e. USA and the EC) have introduced "graduation clause" under which competitive developing countries are debarred from getting preferential treatment on the ground of improved economic conditions. Besides, "competitive need criteria,

GSP", imports are subject to escape-clause (rules) of GATT which empowers the preference granting countries to stop imports on the pretext of injury/threat to domestic producers. Apart from that, a GSP-eligible product is granted preferential access if it satisfies two conditions, viz. (i) directly imported from beneficiary countries and (ii) substantially produced or processed in the beneficiary countries.

Structure and Operation of the EC's GSP Scheme and India

The EC's GSP scheme in India has been working in three major areas, viz, agriculture, textiles and industrial goods. In the industrial sector, a host of manufactured and semi-manufactured items are included in the GSP scheme of the EC. Most of the GSP-covered items have been enjoying either duty free treatment or minimum duty. The rationale behind such preferential treatment is to let India develop its industrial base as well as manufactured exports. This system is non-discriminatory and non-reciprocal. and is in addition to MFN facilities.

In textiles, total exemption from duty is granted to India because the entire gamut of trade is guided by the MFA system, settled bilaterally between India and the EC. Ceiling and quota arrangements are applicable for preferential imports by individual countries. According to quota system, higher duty is applicable automatically when value of exports exceeds the quota. But in case of ceiling, duty is enforced after negotiations. The EC has never charged higher duty in case of exceeding ceiling limit.

In agriculture, a list of products is drawn up and the items included in the list are determined from time to time. EC is quite flexible in reduction of duty and even in some cases complete exemption is also permissible subject to the exigency of the situation. No quantitative ceiling has been fixed except for five products in which case overall quotas are expressed in tonnes (two types of canned pineapple, instant coffee and two types of tobacco). The preferential treatment is granted according to the nature of products, i.e. sensitive and semi-sensitive items.

Since the adaptation of the EC's GSP scheme in 1971, India has increasingly been enjoying this benefit in all of its manufacturing exports either in the form of zero-duty or in the form of quota/ceiling. Initially, agricultural products were not included in the scheme but afterwards food products were included in the preferential list. The GSP treatment is not the same for all goods. It depends on the nature of goods, i.e. sensitive, semi-sensitive and in general category. The categorization of Indian items under the EC's GSP is as follows :

INDIAN ITEMS UNDER GSP[48]

A. GSP : Non-Sensitive Items

— frog legs
— shrimps
— other crustancas
— okra
— mangoes
— pepper
— castor oil
— vegetable oils
— saddlery
— electrical equipment
— dump trucks
— car parts and engine etc.
— jute products and jute materials

B. Non-GSP Items

— walnuts
— ginger/paprika
— rice
— groundnut and oil seed
— vegetable products
— linseed/castor oil
— oil cakes
— low kips
— radio receivers
— imitation jewellery

C. GSP : Sensitive Items

— Silk (Ch.-50)
— Wool, fine & coarse animal hair, yarn and woven fabrics (Ch.-51)
— Cotton (Ch.-52)
— Other vegetable textile fabrics, paper, yarn and woven fabrics of paper yarn (Ch.53)
— Man-made filament yarn (Ch.-54)

— Man-made staple fibre (Ch.55)
— Wadding, felt and non-wovens, special yarn, twine cordage, ropes and cables and articles thereof (Ch.-56)
— Carpets and other textile floor coverings (Ch.-57)
— Special woven fabrics, tufted textile fabrics, lace, tapestries, trimmings, embroidery (Ch.-58)
— Impregnated, coated, covered or laminated textile fabrics, textile articles of a kind suitable for industrial use (Ch.-59)
— Knitted or crocheted fabrics (Ch.-60)
— Articles of apparel and clothing, accessories, knitted or crocheted (Ch.-61)
— Articles of apparel and clothing, accessories, not knitted or crocheted (Ch.-62)
— Other made of textile articles, sets, worn clothing and worn textile articles, rags (Ch.-63)

Trade in textiles is controlled by the MFA, a bilateral system outside of the GATT framework. GSP facilities have also extended to the items covered by MFA. Preferential (GSP) treatment have been given mainly to three types of products, viz, (a) agricultural goods, (b) textile items, and (c) industrial goods. India is amongst the few developing countries in Asia which are given extensive GSP coverage to its exportables to the EC. The entire spectrum of Indo-EC GSP is shown in following table.

Table 1.4, depicts total imports of the EC from India covered by GSP and its actual utilization during the eighties. It further shows that India's exports to the EC during the eighties grew at an annual compound rate of 10.29 per cent, of which non-dutiable exports grew at 7.5 per cent annually, where rate of growth of dutiable exports was only 7.88 per cent during the same period. GSP applies to the dutiable portion of exports. Also shown is that GSP coverage ratio (i.e. ratio of the total value of exports eligible for GSP to the total exports) had been declining significantly over the years.

In 1981, 73.08 per cent of India's total exports to the EC were eligible for the latter's preferential (GSP) treatment, it declined to 57.38 per cent in 1982 and 70.54 per cent in 1990 but slightly increased to 74.76 per cent in 1992. This showed that EC's GSP scheme was not successful in promoting Indian exports which, on the other hand, implied that EC's GSP scheme had not been popular in India over the years, whatsoever the reasons[49].

The picture of actual utilization is even more dismaying. In 1981,

TABLE 1.4 : Total EC Imports from India Received GSP Benefits ('000 ECUs)

Year	*Total Imports from India*	*Non-Dutiable*	*Dutiable [3=1-(2+5)]*	*Exports Covered by GSP*	*Received GSP benefits*	*GSP Covering Ratio (4/1x100)*	*% of GSP received to the GSP coverage (5/4x100)*	*% of GSP received to total imports (5/1x100)*
	1	*2*	*3*	*4*	*5*	*6*	*7*	*8*
1981	1880013	598751	678915	1373935	582347	73.08	42.39	30.97
1982	2571749	1178549	772663	1475719	620537	57.38	42.05	24.13
1983	2196424	841595	667613	1501705	687216	68.37	45.76	31.29
1984	2905352	1179443	984049	1734644	741860	59.70	24.77	25.53
1985	2672323	940405	751739	1787038	980179	66.87	54.85	36.68
1986	2405672	704009	811484	1794151	890192	74.58	49.62	37.00
1987	2761651	695356	938400	2265682	1127895	82.04	49.80	40.84
1988	3188436	885713	862728	2208832	1439995	69.27	65.20	45.16
1989	4180338	1231532	1157302	2713437	1791504	64.91	66.02	42.86
1990	4542304	1148899	1383433	3204458	2009972	70.54	62.72	44.25
1991	4757636	1168192	1407902	3378064	2181542	71.00	64.58	45.85
1992	4878303	1026904	1606585	3647274	2244814	74.76	61.55	46.02

Source : Commission of the European Communities, *Eurostat* (Various Issues, Brussels).

42.39 per cent of the items covered by GSP beneficial actually, i.e. actual utilization ratio (i.e. ratio of total value of items actually to the total value of items eligible for GSP treatment) was 42.39 per cent in 1981, which increased to 61.55 per cent in 1992. This trend implied that, over the years India had been trying its best to improve its GSP utilization. 1984 was the worst year in respect to GSP utilization when the ratio dropped to 24.77 per cent from 45.76 per cent in the preceding year. But this disappointing performance in GSP utilization has improved significantly in the latter years. The entire phenomenon has been clearly depicted in the Table.

Now let us come to one of the important aspects, i.e.. how much of India's total exports had actually received GSP benefits from 1980 to 1992. Notwithstanding several concerted efforts to improve actual utilization of the EC's GSP facility, actual utilisation has been low because until now (i.e. 1992) it covered barely half of India's total exports to the EC. In 1981, approximately 31 per cent of India's total exports to the EC received GSP benefits, reduced to the lowest level in the next year when this ratio plummeted to 24 per cent. But it has improved in the successive years and finally reached 46.02 per cent in 1992. From Table 1.4, it is quite evident that performance in GSP utilization is better than GSP coverage ratio over the years. During the same period compound growth rate of GSP utilization was 14.76 per cent, whereas in case of coverage ratio it was 9.87 per cent which meant less and less items were covered by GSP.

Agricultural Exports Receiving GSP Benefits

Agricultural exports from India were covered by the EC's GSP only during the eighties. GSP benefit extended to agriculture excluded items in raw form. Exports of agricultural goods receiving GSP benefits did not contain entire basket, GSP given only to those items which are in processed and manufactured form. Food products and processed food items constitute a very negligible portion of the total exports of agricultural items. Table 1.5, shows that out of total agricultural exports eligible for the EC's GSP, the actual exports which received GSP benefit were significantly low and this had been the case over the years. In 1981, out of total exports eligible for GSP treatment only 8 per cent were agricultural, which declined to 6 per cent in 1992. This downward trend implies that in the total GSP basket, importance of agricultural items has been diminishing significantly over the years. This may be due to the fact that we are exporting agricultural items in raw form rather than in processed or value added form. The compound rate of growth of agricultural exports eligible for the EC's GSP was only 5 per cent.

In 1981, out of total exports receiving GSP benefits only 12.55 per cent were from agricultural goods which dropped to 7.72 per cent in 1992. This clearly indicates that not only was the contribution of agricultural sector to the total GSP coverage as well as utilization low but it has also been declining significantly over the years.

Despite all such odds, GSP utilization ratio (i.e. the ratio of agricultural exports which actually received GSP to the total amount of agricultural exports eligible for GSP) has improved significantly during the eighties. GSP utilization in agricultural exports was around 68 per cent in 1981 which escalated to 77 per cent in 1992 : this implied that agricultural sector had optimally utilized GSP benefit. On the other hand, the time series trend shows that in 1980 agricultural goods received GSP benefits were 4 per cent of India's total exports which plummeted to 3.55 per cent in 1992, and this is shown in Table 1.5.

Textile Exports Receiving GSP Benefits

The whole gamut of India's textile trade has been under the Multifibre Arrangement (MFA). And it has been subject to artificial barriers, which include (i) quota, and (ii) ceiling. Following the definition, quota is the maximum absolute amount beyond which higher rate of tariff will be imposed automatically. In case of ceiling it is the minimum absolute level. If exports cross the ceiling limit then negotiations will be started between contracting parties to determine the modalities so as to what rate of tariff is to be enforced, the extent of which, in most of the cases, depends on the degree of sensitivity of the item. This means tariff mechanism is not automatic. Therefore, ceiling is more acceptable to developing countries than quota in respect of restrictiveness.

The EC's GSP scheme is very restrictive to Indian exporters of textiles and garments. Because none of the items in the very-sensitive category enjoys duty free treatment. On the contrary the average (wtd) rate of tariffs on textiles and garments is more than double as compared to average tariffs to other items. **Table 1.6** shows that, out of total exports covered by the EC's GSP, 50.73 per cent were only from textile items in 1981, which remained more or less at the same level even in 1992 (i.e., 50.59 per cent). But the most significant feature

TABLE 1.5 : Total Agricultural Imports from India under GSP Benefits ('000 ECUs)

Year	EC's Total Imports from India	Total GSP Coverage	GSP Coverage: GSP coverage by the agrl. sector	GSP Coverage: % of sect coverage to total (3/2x100)	Total GSP received	GSP Received: GSP recd. by the agrl. sector	GSP Received: % of total coverage to total GSP recvd. in agrl. (6/5x100)	% of GSP recvd to the GSP coverage in agrl. sect (6/3x100)	% of GSP received to total imports (6/1x100)
	(1)	(2)	(3)	(4)	(5)	(6)	(7)	(8)	(9)
1981	1880013	1373935	108113	7.87	582347	73133	12.55	67.64	3.89
1982	2571749	1475719	127531	8.64	620537	92283	4.87	72.36	3.59
1983	2196424	1501705	149547	9.96	687216	98277	14.30	65.72	4.47
1984	2905352	1734644	188172	10.85	741860	114926	15.49	61.07	3.96
1985	2672323	1787038	149607	8.37	980179	101607	10.37	67.92	3.80
1986	2405672	1794151	157339	8.77	890192	88317	9.92	56.13	3.67
1987	2761641	2265682	164758	7.27	1127895	105067	9.32	63.77	3.80
1988	3188436	2208832	178043	8.06	1439995	132171	9.18	74.23	4.14
1989	4180338	2713437	220762	8.14	1791504	156193	8.72	70.75	3.73
1990	4542304	3204459	168535	5.26	2009972	134149	6.67	79.60	2.95
1991	4757636	3378064	214561	6.35	2181542	171681	7.84	80.01	3.61
1992	4878303	3647274	226300	6.20	2244814	173410	7.72	76.63	3.55

Source : Commission of the European Communities, *Eurostat*, (Several Issues, Brussels).

is that its utilization ratio has been declining over the years in spite of the increasing trend in general. In 1981, out of total exports receiving GSP benefit, 49 per cent were from textile items and this had declined to 41.74 per cent in 1992.

Contrary to the previous trend, GSP utilization ratio (i.e. the proportion of total textiles exports which received GSP benefits to the total exports receiving GSP benefits) had been improving over the years from 41 per cent in 1980 to 51 per cent in 1992. Improved utilization ratio implies that Indian textile exporters have been getting better market access to the EC. Improved market access implies that increasing number of Indian exporters have been enjoying facility of duty free treatment extended by the EC to their exports. Finally, in 1981, GSP benefits enjoyed by the textile sector were 15 per cent of the total exports which increased to 19 percent in 1992.

Industrial Exports Receiving GSP Benefits

The rationale behind the introduction of the EC's GSP scheme was to encourage developing countries for production as well as exports of manufactured items with high value addition. This means there have been increasing export substitution rather than export promotion. The conventional wisdom says that developing economies are characterized by surplus labour and less capital and that is why manufactured goods which they produce are more labour intensive and have relatively less capital content. Due to this structural problem, the items which they produce are not internationally competitive except in some areas of handicrafts and works of art. Unless they are given some form of preferential treatment they cannot enter into the markets of the advanced industrialized countries. Due to technological excellence and scale economies, products produced by the developed ones are qualitatively much better. On the basis of this logical fallacy developed countries have offered preferential treatment to exports of manufactures of developing countries to enable them to face more competition in their markets. This preferential access is in the form of duty-free treatment to the manufactured products or reduction of the ratio of duties comparable to the non-beneficiary countries.

The above phenomenon was evident from the general trend of India's exports of industrial goods to the EC. During the eighties, growth rate of GSP coverage was higher in the industrial sector compared to others. The industrial sector registered a phenomenal

TABLE 1.6 : Total Textile Imports from India under GSP Benefits ('000 ECUs)

Year	EC's Total Imports from India	*GSP Coverage* Total GSP Coverage	GSP coverage by the text. sector (3/2x100)	% of sect coverage to total	*GSP Received* Total GSP received	GSP recd. by the text. sector	% of total coverage to total GSP recd. in text. sect (6/5x100)	% of GSP recd to the GSP coverage in text. sect (6/3x100)	% of GSP received to total imports (6/1x100)
	(1)	(2)	(3)	(4)	(5)	(6)	(7)	(8)	(9)
1981	1880013	1373935	697018	50.73	582347	284699	48.89	40.85	15.14
1982	2571749	1475719	670067	45.41	620537	255436	41.16	38.12	9.93
1983	2196424	1501705	646993	43.08	687216	354426	51.57	54.78	16.14
1984	2905352	1734644	764098	44.05	741860	374118	50.43	48.96	12.88
1985	2672323	1787038	815035	45.61	980179	413509	42.19	50.73	15.47
1986	2405672	1794151	745678	41.56	890192	372373	41.83	49.94	15.48
1987	2761651	2265682	1071714	47.30	1127895	436039	38.66	40.69	15.79
1988	3188436	2208892	1184872	53.64	1439995	673056	46.74	56.80	21.11
1989	4180338	2713437	1398536	51.54	1791504	770660	43.02	55.10	18.43
1990	4542304	3204458	1624866	50.71	2009972	848602	42.22	52.22	18.68
1991	4757636	3378064	1710545	50.64	2181542	961536	44.07	56.21	20.21
1992	4878303	3647274	1845197	50.59	2244814	937134	41.74	50.79	19.21

Source : Commission of the European Communities, *Eurostat*, (Several Issues, Brussels).

growth of 10 per cent against 9.86 per cent in textiles sector and 5 per cent in case of agricultural exports. Disregarding growth phenomenon, GSP coverage ratio in industrial exports is fairly high but slightly less than that of textiles exports. In 1980, 41 per cent industrial items were covered by GSP benefits, which shot up to 43 per cent in 1992. Though the magnitude is insignificant, the growing trend proves that increasing volume of India's industrial exports has been subject to EC's GSP programme over the years.

Despite the fact that the growth of GSP utilization in industrial products is significant (i.e. 13.64 per cent during eighties), its contribution to the total benefits received had been increased over the years. In 1981, as much as 38.62 per cent of total exports that received GSP benefits were from industrial products and this increased to 46 per cent in 1992.

Though the significance of industrial sector to the total benefits actually enjoyed has been declining over the years, the GSP utilization ratio of industrial products had shown an increasing trend during the eighties. In 1981, utilization ratio (i.e. GSP benefits enjoyed by the industrial exports to the total industrial exports eligible for GSP treatment) was around 40 per cent which increased to 66 per cent in 1992. This was a marked improvement over the years. Finally, GSP benefit enjoyed by the industrial sector was 11 per cent of the total exports in 1981 which increased to 21 per cent in 1992. The entire GSP operation of these categories is shown in Table 1.7.

The ECs New GSP Scheme and its Implications for Indian Exports

The EC's GSP scheme has been a 10-year phenomenon. On completion of the first 10 years, revision took place on 1st January, 1981 which was followed by a mid-term revision on 1st January, 1986. The next revision was delayed because of a stalemate in finalizing the Uruguay Round of Multilateral Trade Negotiations. But finally the EC Council at a meeting held on 19th December, 1994 approved the new GSP Scheme which entered into force on 1st January, 1995[50]. The scheme, only covers industrial products and was valid for 4 years (1995-98). It is clear from the new scheme that the existing GSP scheme for agricultural products was rolled over for 1995. The list of beneficiary countries also remained unchanged with the addition of South Africa only. Presently as many as 147 developing countries have been enjoying GSP benefits extended by the EC.

TABLE 1.7 : Total Imports of Industrial Products from India under GSP Benefits ('000 ECUs)

			GSP Coverage			*GSP Received*			
Year	*EC's total imports from India*	*Total GSP coverage*	*GSP coverage by the indl. sector*	*% of sector coverage (3/2x100)*	*Total GSP received*	*GSP recd. by the indl. sector*	*% of total coverage to total GSP recd. in indl. sector (6/5x100)*	*% of GSP recd. to the GSP coverage in indl. sector (6/3x100)*	*% of GSP received to total imports (6/1x100)*
	(1)	*(2)*	*(3)*	*(4)*	*(5)*	*(6)*	*(7)*	*(8)*	*(9)*
1981	1880013	1373935	568304	41.36	582347	224935	38.62	39.58	11.06
1982	2571749	1475719	678121	45.95	620537	234819	37.84	34.63	9.13
1983	2196424	1501705	705165	46.96	687216	234513	34.12	33.26	10.68
1984	2905352	1734644	782374	45.10	741860	252816	34.08	32.31	8.70
1985	2672323	1787038	822396	46.02	980179	465108	47.45	56.56	17.40
1986	2405672	1794151	843537	47.02	890192	429502	48.25	50.92	17.85
1987	2761641	2265682	1029210	45.43	1127895	586789	52.02	57.01	21.25
1988	3188436	2208892	846084	38.30	1439995	634168	44.04	74.95	19.89
1989	4180338	2713437	1094139	40.32	1791504	864651	48.26	79.02	20.68
1990	4542304	3204458	1411057	44.03	2009972	1027221	51.11	72.80	22.61
1991	4757636	3378064	1452958	43.04	2181542	1048925	57.10	72.19	22.05
1992	4878303	3647274	1575777	43.20	2244814	1034270	46.07	65.63	21.02

Source : Commission of the European Communities, Eurostat, (Several Issues, Brussels).

The entire basket of imports covered by GSP has been segregated into four groups, the details of which have been annexed to the Main Scheme. In the new scheme, GSP quotas and ceilings have been abolished and all items have been categorized under four major groups depending on the sensitivity viz. very sensitive, sensitive, semi-sensitive and non-sensitive. Very sensitive items attract the highest rate of duty 85 per cent of the common external tariffs (CET) of the EC under MFN and thus getting a waiver of 15 per cent only. The "sensitive" category attracts a duty rate of 70 per cent and is thus eligible to get 30 per cent waiver of the MFN tariffs. "Semi-sensitive" items are subject to 35 per cent tariff, obtaining 65 per cent waiver of the MFN rate. Non-sensitive items are excluded from the duty list.

Eighteen least developed countries like Bangladesh, Bhutan, Nepal, Myanmar, etc., are continuing to get full duty free treatment for their exports to the EC market. Five Andean group countries, viz. Colombia, Venezuela, Equador, Peru, Bolivia and Central American Common Market (CACM) countries like Costa Rica, El Salvador, Guatemala, Honduras and Nicaragua continue to enjoy duty free access to the EC market, provided they continue their efforts to combat drugs. Outside of the GSP regime, products of many other countries from EFTA, ACP, the Maghreb and Mashreq regions, Central and East European countries, Israel, the Baltic countries, Turkey, Cyprus, Malta, etc. get concessional or duty-free access to EC under preferential bilateral trading arrangements such as a common market, customs union, free trade or association agreements[51].

In the revised GSP scheme, the EC has introduced "Graduation Clause" which means more advanced developing countries are excluded from the GSP facilities with a view to imparting more and more facilities to the poor countries. The graduation clause is both "product specific" and "country specific". The main features of the graduation clause are :

(*i*) The graduation clause is supplemented by "solidarity mechanism" which applies to beneficiary countries whose total exports of an item exceed 25 per cent of the value of total imports of that product into EC from all beneficiaries of GSP, they would be excluded from GSP in that particular item w.e.f. 1st January, 1995.

(*ii*) Current GSP beneficiaries with a per capita GNP in excess of US $6000 will be entitled to only 50 per cent of the GSP benefit from April 1995 to 31 December 1995. With effect from 1 January 1996,

GSP benefits are totally withdrawn from these countries. The targeted countries are: Hong Kong, Singapore, South Korea, Saudi Arabia, Oman, Brunei, Quatar, United Arab Emirates, Kuwait, Bahrain, Libya and Narau.

(iii) Those countries with less than $6000 per capita GNP, would continue to enjoy GSP benefits in sectors in which they have attained a high degree of trade specialization and would be entitled to only 50 per cent of the GSP benefits in these sectors with effect from 1 January 1997.

(iv) The EC has decided that preferential access for individual beneficiary countries will be stopped with immediate effect if it is proved that operation of the graduation mechanism has resulted in providing certain beneficiary countries with greater access for specific products than available to them under the existing GSP scheme.

(v) The GSP benefit would be completely withdrawn from 1 January 1999.

Instead of GSP scheme, the EC is going to introduce "Special Incentive Scheme" with effect from 1 January 1999. Under this scheme EC will extend additional preferences to these GSP beneficiaries that make a written request and provide evidence to the effect that they have adopted and effectively implemented the provision of ILO Convention No. 87 and 98 concerning freedom of association and protection of the right to organize and bargain effectively and of the ILO Convention No. 138, concerning minimum age for admission for employment; furthermore, tariff preferences will be given to those countries that strictly adhere to social and environmental clauses.

Implications of EU's New GSP Scheme for Indian Exports

Before the introduction of new scheme, India was one of the largest beneficiaries of the EC GSP scheme. GSP utilization ratio of Indian goods to the EC market has been very low over the years[52]. In 1981, 30.97 per cent of its total exports received GSP benefits in the EU market, of which 3.9 per cent was from exports of agricultural products. In 1990, GSP utilization ratio increased to 44.25 per cent of which 2.95 per cent were from agricultural exports, 18.68 per cent from textile exports and 15.66 per cent from industrial goods exports.

India feels concerned about the new GSP scheme, because she will be graduated from the GSP facility with effect from 1 January 1997 due to its specialization in textiles, garments and leather which are considered as very sensitive in the EC market. Moreover, the EC's GSP scheme will cease to be operational w.e.f. 1 January 1999. Textiles is the only major group whose prospect is uncertain in the EC market after the removal of GSP facility. Not only have textiles been put into the very sensitive category of the GSP list but also all these items have been under stringent MFA quota as well. Though GATT prescribes 6 per cent growth in all quota items (HS category 50-63) but in fact, EC's permissible growth has been only 0.5 to 2 per cent over the years[53]. In spite of stringent quota, the EC has also enforced complicated structure of NTBs. Apart from non-transparent barriers, average (wtd) rate of tariffs of the quotas affected items has been consistently high. Against the average duty of 3-4 per cent (of the rate of customs tariffs), these items will bear levies between 15 and 20 percent. A simple reduction of MFN tariff by 15 per cent (7 per cent after 1st January, 1997) will not help Indian exports in a very significant way. At least in the next four years, India would not be the major player in the EC market.

Another area of concern is that under the Uruguay Round tariff reduction commitments, developed countries pleaded to reduce tariffs on all manufactured goods by 38 per cent. But under the new GSP scheme, the EC has agreed to reduce only 15 per cent on textile items. Even for highly sensitive items this reduction will be only 12 per cent[54].

According to the revised GSP scheme, India ceased to enjoy GSP facilities from 1 January 1997. Under the new provision, the countries having per capita income less than $ 6,000 will continue to enjoy GSP facility in sectors which are highly specialized and will get only 50 per cent of the GSP benefit. This means that in "very sensitive" and "sensitive" categories India will get only preferential benefits of 7.5 per cent and 15 per cent respectively. Even this preferential treatment was withdrawn when India was "graduated" w.e.f. 1 January 1999. Through Council Regulation (EC) No. 2501/2001 on 10 December 2001, a new GSP Scheme came into force from 1 January 2002 to 31 December 2004. The European Community has adopted a new Generalised System of Preference (GSP) to foster sustainable development. The new Regulation complements and fully incorporates the recent "Everything But Arm (EBA) initiative in favour of Least Developed Countries (LDCs). The EBA provides for duty and quota-free access to 49 LDCs. The new GSP is for the period 2002-2004. The salient features in the new GSP Scheme are :

(*i*) Simplification and attractiveness
(*ii*) Better targetting and adoptability.

With more than € 5 billion of preferential imports to the EU, India is ranking second among the users of the EU's GSP.

In the years to come, the social and environmental clauses will dominate in the trade policy commitments of the developed countries[55]. These countries have already started thinking to link social clauses with the trade preferences given to developing countries. The EC and USA are very much vocal about it. In the new GSP scheme, The EC has already linked GSP facilities with improvement of labour standards, human rights treatment and protection of environment. The EC has already achieved a considerable amount of success in garnering support from other developed countries. In the new GSP scheme, the EC has already declared a special system of incentives in the form of additional tariff preferences to those GSP beneficiaries that would effectively implement the social and environment standards. This is an ominous trend to a developing country like India, where labour and environmental standards are at a sub-optimal stage. Though at this moment, these issues are not discussed at WTO, but there is apprehension that developed countries will push these issues at the bilateral level while granting tariff preferences.

Another area of reservation is that in the new system, preferences will not be given to those items which are under anti-dumping and anti-subsidy investigation/measures unless it is shown that the said duties are based on a price reflecting the preferential tariff arrangements granted to the countries. This measure poses a real threat to India's textile exporters in the the EC market because a host of our textile products have been under anti-dumping investigations[56]. Under the pretext of dumping, EC may initiate anti-dumping investigation on these items in which India has strong competitiveness and can scrap preferential treatment[57].

Application of "safeguard" is another danger for Indian exports to the EC. On the ground of material injury to the domestic industry, developed countries are given a free hand to enforce "safeguard" or "transitional safeguard" (GATT Article XIX) on any competitive product imported from developing countries. The new scheme will also have a safeguard clause analogous to the provision of GATT to cope with significant unexpected imports of a product which cause or threaten to cause serious difficulties to a "community producer" of the like or directly competing product. In such cases, common customs tariff duties may be reintroduced on that product at any time at the request of a member State or on the Commission's own initiatives.

In the new GSP scheme, the EC wants effective protection of environmental standards through the enforcement of International Convention on Environment (Agenda 21). For this purpose the EC intends to apply special incentive arrangements initially for tropical wood products from forests, which are sustainably managed in conformity with International Tropical Timber Organization (ITTO) standards. It is also understood that the margin of additional incentives being considered under these conditions may be 20 per cent of the MFN tariff. Implications of this measure to India are not quite clear. Undoubtedly this measure will discourage consumption of forest products. But this is a grey area.

NOTES

1. "Document concerning the Accession to the European Communities of the Kingdom of Denmark, Ireland, the Kingdom of Norway and the United Kingdom of Great Britain and Northern Ireland" *Official Journal of the European Communities*, (Brussels), no.1., sp. ed., 27 March 1972.
2. *Ibid*, n. 1, p. 974.
3. Ibid n. 1 p. 1036.
4. Ibid n. 1 p. 1036.
5. Ibid n. 1 p. 1037.
6. H.S. Chopra and K.B. Lall, "The EEC and India", in K.B. Lall, Wolfgang Ernst and H.S. Chopra (eds;), "*India and the EEC* (New Delhi : Allied 1984), p.12.
7. Ibid n. 1 p. 4.
8. "Joint Declaration of Intent, on Development of Trade Relations with Ceylon, India, Malaysia, Pakistan and Singapore in Documents concerning the Accession of The European Communities" *Official Journal of the European Communities*, (Brussels), 27 March 1972, p.1294
9. Ibid n. 6 p. 13.
10. Swapan K. Bhattacharya, "Transition from MFA to WTO : Prospects for the India's Trade in Textiles and Garments" in K.R. Gupta (ed;) "*World Trade*", (New Delhi, Atlantic Publisher), 1995, pp.240-311.
11. S.S. Saxena, "The EEC, GSP and the Third World" in K.B. Lall, H.S. Chopra (eds;) and "*The EEC and the Third World*", (New Delhi, 1981), pp.137-162.
12. GSP is the benefit unilaterally extended by the European

Community to India, but old developed contracting parties to GATT are committed to extend MFN facility to developing countries without any reciprocity. MFN facility is now given both in goods and services, see "Final Act" of the Uruguay Round of Multilateral Trade Agreement, World Trade Organisation, Geneva, 1994.

13. Commission of the European Communities, *Commercial Cooperation Agreement*, (Brussels, 1973).
14. (a) Ibid n. 6 p. 13.
    (b) K.G. Ramanathan, "Indo-EC Trade Under CCA" Ibid n. 6 p. 140.
15. Ibid n. 13. p. (CCA).
16. Commission of the European Communities, *"Joint Declaration of Intent of the Development of Trade Relation with Ceylon, India, Malaysia, Pakistan and Singapore", in the document concerning the Accession to the European Communities, Official Journal of the European Communities,* No. 1.73, Spl. ed. 27 March 1972, p.1294.
17. K.G. Ramanathan, "Indo-EC Trade under CCA" - in K.B. Lall, Wolfgang Ernst and H.S. Chopra (eds;) "*India and the EEC*", (New Delhi, 1984), p.142.
18. Ministry of Commerce, Govt. of India, *Annual Reports 1973-74,* (New Delhi).
19. Ministry of Commerce, Govt. of India "*Annual Reports, 1973-74* ", (New Delhi).
20. Chopra, H.S. and Lall K.B., Ibid n. 6, p.15.
21. Ibid n. 6, p.16.
22. Ibid n. 6, p.16.
23. Commission of the European Communities, Ibid n. 13.
24. Alexander J. Yeats, "*Trade Barriers Facing Developing Countries : Commercial Policy Measures and Shipping,* (London, McMillan, 1979) p.132.
25. UNCTAD, "*Non-Tariff Barriers Affecting the Trade of Developing Countries and Transparency in the World Trading Conditions* (TD/B/940), (Geneva, UNCTAD) February 1983.
26. The World Bank, "*World Development Report*", (Washington), 1987, pp.143-146.
27. Commission of the European Committees, Ibid no. 4.
28. S.S. Saxena, "European Economic Community and India" in K.B. Lall, H.S. Chopra and Wolfgang Ernst (eds), *India and the EEC*, (New Delhi, Allied) 1984, pp. 73-74.
29. Commission of the European Communities, Ibid no. 9.
30. Commission of the European Communities, *Cooperation Agreement on Partnership and Development*, (Brussels), December 1994, pp.24-35.
31. Anne Weston and Vincent Cable, *South Asia Exports to the EEC; Obstacles and Opportunities.* (London, Overseas Development Institute, 1979), pp.159-161.

32. To know details about the NTB-Coverage ratio of textiles and its average rate of tariffs, see calculation in Chapter-V. Cf. Swapan K. Bhattacharya, "*The Growth of Non-Tariff Barriers in Indo-US Trade*", paper presented at the ICRIER Seminar under USAID Project, (New Delhi), 1994.
33. Official Journal of the European Communities, Ibid no.30.
34. This is the outcome of the Uruguay Round of Multilateral Trade Negotiation, where, for the first time, trade in services has been given the status of a separate negotiating group.
35. IPR is a major issue between India and the EC. FDI flow from EC to India has not grown satisfactorily due to lack of effective protection on IPR. To know in details about this, see
    (i) Swapan K. Bhattacharya, "Intellectual Property Rights : Implications for Indian Industries" *Backgrounder prepared for ASSOCHAM*, (New Delhi), October 1995.
    (ii) __________, "Final Act of the Uruguay Round of Negotiations : The Proposed sui genris system for India", in B. Bhattacharya and A. K. Sengupta (eds;) "*Trade in Agriculture : The Uruguay Round and After*", Indian Institute of Foreign Trade, 1994, pp. 211-242.
    (iii) __________, "Patenting Biotechnology and Micro-organism : Indian Position in the Post Uruguay Round in K. R. Gupta (ed;) *World Trade Organisation and India*, Atlantic Publisher, (New Delhi), 1996, pp. 83-111.
36. Cf. Swapan K. Bhattacharya, "Rationalisation of Tariff Structure of Consumer Goods Imports in India", paper presented at the USAID Seminar on a "*Policy Implements to Trade and FDI in India*", Indian Institute of Foreign Trade, New Delhi, 1995.
37. Cf. World Trade Organisation, "*Uruguay Round : The Final Act*", Chapter on *Agreement on Tariff*, pp. 23-85, WTO, (Geneva), 1994.
38. Craig, R. McPhee, "*Evaluation of the Trade Effects of the Generalised System of Preferences*". TD/B/C.5/87, UNCTAD, Geneva, Jan. 19, 1984 p.3.
39. To see the composition of the India's exports and the importance of different group, see Swapan K. Bhattacharya, "*Export Performance of India : A Sectoral Analysis*", ICRIER Discussion Paper No. 60, New Delhi, 1990.
40. Calculation of GSP coverage is done by the author covering period from 1981 to 1992, which is shown in the latter part of this chapter.
41. Commission of the European Communities, "Official Journal of the European Communities." (Brussels), Dec. 1994, pp. 9-28.
42. Ibid n. 38. p.3.
43. Sam Laird and Andre Sapir, "Tariff Preferences" in Andrezj Olechowsky (ed;), "*The Uruguay Round; A Handbook of the Multilateral Trade Negotiations*", (Washington), 1987, p. 101

44. R. Langhammer and Andre Sapir (1987), "*Economic Impact of Generalised Tariff Preference*", (London, Gower), for the Trade Policy Research Center.
45. See Prebish, Raul, "Towards a New Trade Policy for Development : Condensation of Report" *UN Review*, 11 April 1964, pp. 11-14, UNCTAD (Geneva).
46. UNCTAD (1968), "*The Kennedy Round Estimated Effects on Tariff Barriers*", (TD/6/Rev.1), (New York), United Nations.
47. Sam Laird and Andre Sapir, "*Tariff Preferences" in The Uruguay Round : A Handbook of the Multilateral Trade Negotiations", The World Bank*, (Washington, 1987) p. 102.
48. This list is prepared as per the classification done in the Indo-EC textile accord in December 31, 1994, Cf. Commission of the European Communities, Official Journal of the European Communities, Brussels, December 1994, p. 9-22.
49. For reasons for failure of the GSP utilisation, see Vincent Cable and Anne Weston, South Asia Exports to the EEC : Obstacles and opportunities, (London : Overseas Development Institute, 1979), pp. 159-162.
50. (*a*) Commission of the European Communities, *Official Journal of the European Communities*, (Brussels), 31 December 1994, pp.9-27.
    (*b*) Mission of India to the European Union, "EU's New GSP Scheme: A Guide", February 1, 1995, (Brussels), pp. 1-8.
51. For detail description of the EC's New GSP Scheme, see, "Official Journal of the European Communities", Brussels, 31 December, 1994, No. L348/9. pp. 9-27.
52. (*a*) Swapan K. Bhattacharya, "EC's Non-Tariff Barriers and GSP; Implications for India", *International Industry Annual* , (New Delhi), 1990.
    (*b*) Swapan K. Bhattacharya and Vijaya Katti, "EC's New GSP Scheme: Areas of Concern for India", *Business Line*, (New Delhi), 9 October 1995, .
53. O.P. Sharma, "Textile Quotas During MFA-II" Economic and *Political Weekly*, (Bombay), September 29, 1984, pp. 1711-1716.
54. World Trade Organisation, "*Submission of Tariff Reduction Schedule by the EC*", Vol. 19, WTO, (Geneva), 1994.
55. Swapan K. Bhattacharya, "GATT, the WTO and Social clauses", *International Industries*, Annual, (New Delhi), 1994, pp. 69-77.
56. See tables containing information on tariff and non-tariff barriers for 1988, 1992, 1993 and 1994 in Ch.4.
57. Swapan K. Bhattacharya, "WTO and Agreement on Antidumping Duties : The CAsse of Indo-US Trade" in P.K. Banerjee (ed), *Indo-US Trade and Economic Cooperation*", (New Delhi) : IIFT, 1996, pp. 209-236.

Chapter 2

EC Shaping up as a Single European Market

EUROPEAN "SCLEROSIS" IN THE EARLY 1980s: REMEDIAL PERSPECTIVE

Background

The eighties were dominated by growing protectionism in Western Europe, which was the consequence of increasing obsolescence in the European industry coupled with less profitability as a result of higher real wage compared to its productivity[1]. This neo-protectionism was in the form of non-tariff barriers in addition to customs tariffs. In fact, neo-protectionism had started to surface from the second oil shock in 1979. Protectionism has always been anti-competitive in the sense it does not allow free imports, which causes domestic price of competing goods to rise due to inelastic demand for their imports[2]. This kind of demand causes wide difference between demand and supply price. Restrictions induce importers to get lower price whereas consumers are forced to pay higher price due to supply constraint. The difference between the demand price and supply price is the quota rent, which is enjoyed by the traders of the country that enforces protectionist measures[3].

Competitive policy is characterized by free movement of goods and services without any barrier. Despite the fact that tariffs have been reduced significantly over the years in the industrialized economies, the emergence of non-tariff barriers has endangered trade prospects of developing countries in general and India in particular to the Western hemisphere. It is estimated in several studies that tariff-equivalent of non-tariff barriers is well over 100 per cent in agricultural goods as well as textiles and garments[4]. A USITC study shows that average (wtd) tariff in the US market ranges from 15 to 20 per cent but the tariff equivalents of quotas in textiles vary from 80-100 per cent over basic level tariffs[5]. Therefore, the horror of protectionism engulfs the trade prospects of most sensitive items of India in which it has comparative advantage.

Several studies on protectionism show that the EC is more protectionist than the USA and Japan[6]. The root of protectionism may be due to growing obsolescence of several traditional labour-intensive industries like textiles. In textiles, the EC has been facing tough competition from the Asian countries including India. In order to protect its domestic industry, EC has enforced stringent quotas on textile imports since 1961 under short-term and long term arrangements (STAs & LTAs) and thereafter under the Multifibre Arrangement (MFA). This type of restriction is certainly anti-competitive. Where competitiveness weakens, protectionism flourishes.

For the last 15 years, developed countries have been witnessing increasing use of protectionist measures coupled with the international economic insurgency through the oil-price buoyancy. This exogenous factor is basically responsible for economic sluggishness in the Western countries. The situation became so critical that (as observed in 1970, 1973 and 1975) the economic cycle which was the major business cycle in US history percolated to western Europe as well. In the later half of the 1970s, inflation during slack period was more than that of peak season by 8.4 percentage points. Before that (i.e. in the first half of 1970s) inflation was basically used as a tool of demand management. During that period an increase in prices of raw materials induced high inflation and low output. This was the basic reason for supply shocks[7].

Besides the two oil-shocks in the 1970s, another major influencing factor for "Eurosclerosis" in the early eighties was increase in real wages proportionately much higher than the productivity in the European industry. The result of such ominous trend was the fall in profitability, increase in unemployment which kept investment in a relatively stagnant position. Furthermore, oil price hike resulted in increased obsolescence of the capital stock. This growing obsolescence in capital stock was the major reason of supply side weakness, because the structure of capital stock got increasingly obsolete at a new factor price. The phenomena of supply-side weakness, growing unemployment and increasing obsolescence in capital stock led the western countries to be more protectionist in their trade policies.[8]

"The Second oil shock" in 1979 caused a major setback to European economies which was further exacerbated by the imposition of high interest rates in the USA and over-valuation of its dollar. US allies did not take this step casually and they exerted pressures upon it to lower its interest rates and also to devalue the US dollar so as to restore the parity between US dollar and other major currencies. According to a European analyst, western Europe suffers in export competitiveness in relation to Japan particularly in two areas:[9]

(i) Japan produces high quality labour-intensive manufactured goods;
(ii) There is a significant lack of complementarity between these two economies. As a result, the EC produces many of the same type of the manufactured goods as Japan does. And since Japan is more competitive than the EC, the former always maintains export surplus over EC and United States[10].

Degree of competitiveness of any country depends on many factors. Until now no reliable criteria have been formulated on the basis of which we can measure the degree of competitiveness. It is a term which is relatively determined by various socio-economic factors. The World Economic Forum, a Switzerland based organization has been publishing *World Competitiveness Report* since 1980. This report is now recognized to be the world's leading study, ranking the competitiveness of nations. So far it has covered 49 countries[11].

THE COCKFIELD REPORT 1985 : OUTLINING THE PROCESS OF THE EUROPEAN UNION[12]

Introduction

The programme of single economic market of the European Community was a grandiose one. The idea of internal market gathered momentum in 1968 through the creation of customs union and in December 1992 with the emergence of the Single European Market, the largest trading bloc in the world then composed of 12 and now 15 developed countries of western Europe. The factor which seems to have expedited the completion of the internal market was the emergence of other regional trading blocs, like NAFTA, ASEAN, APEC etc. In order to counter the mushroom growth of regional trading blocs, the EC has already brought down its tariff level to a very low level for making its industry internationally more competitive. Yet, the EC is having a plethora of non-tariff barriers (NTBs) in the form of physical, fiscal and technical which cause severe damage to its internal as well as international competitiveness.

Perturbed by rapid change in the international economic scenario characterized by the proliferation of regional trading blocs, the EC statesmen assembled together and discussed the future prospect of the commission. The completion of Single European Market (SEM) was the only way of economic integration through which member countries would make concerted efforts to remove all internal barriers. Finally, in order to give this idea a concrete shape, and to find out the modalities of economic integration, the European Commission in 1985 appointed a Committee led by **Lord Cockfield.** He was asked to identify the factors required for shaping up the Single European Market (hereinafter SEM) and also to prescribe what type of structural changes were needed for the completion of the internal market and to locate the areas where these changes could be carried out.

Lord Cockfield prepared a White Paper portraying the current scenarios of different sectors and the changes that are required for the completion of SEM. The objectives of the committee were consistent with the resolution adopted in principle by the Heads of States in Milan in June 1985. Cockfield had completed his task on 6 June 1986. Initial progress report showed that 27 out of 61 targetted proposals had been accepted by 1986 and 71 proposals were accepted during 1987. The White Paper proposed a time-bound programme for the completion of SEM. In this regard, following suggestions were made[13]:

(i) Removal of non-tariff barriers existing between the member countries in the form of customs, posts, immigration and passport controls during inter-state transactions. Harmonisation of public health standards among the Community members and finally the abolition of transport controls.

(ii) Fixing up a time-schedule for the removal of technical barriers.

(iii) Ensuring smooth and steady flow of capital (both physical and human) among the member countries, and taking appropriate measures to protect industrial and intellectual property rights. Harmonization of indirect taxation (VAT and excise tax) was also the focal point of the reform programme.

Basic Premises of the Cockfield Report

For the completion of SEM, Cockfield proposed following measures that were essential to rejuvenate the European economy on one hand, and to counter the threat of the growing menace of regionalism on the other.

— Removal of physical barriers
— Removal of technical barriers
— Removal of fiscal barriers
— Harmonization of rules and standards
— Approximation of legislation and tax structure
— Introducing Common Exchange Rate Mechanism (ERM)
— Common Economic and Monetary Union

The SEM had three objectives viz.

Firstly: to bring 12 different European countries having wide diversities in socio-economic and culture, on to one platform. The programme envisaged single market and single monetary and political entity comprising the member states.

Secondly : in order to counter the growth of regionalism and to fight with increasing competitiveness from Japan and the USA, it was imperative for the Community to make concerted efforts for cost reduction through the removal of all barriers.

Thirdly : ensuring the maximum flexibility in respect of inter-state movement of man and material, and to exploit economies of scale through changing the scale of operation.

1. Removal of Physical Barriers

Non-tariff barriers in the form of physical controls are mainly of two types, viz. *(a)* control of goods and *(b)* control of individuals.

(a) Control of Goods

Every member state has its own national regulations on border control which restrict free-flow of goods between the member states. The Commission proposal was that all different rules pertaining to internal control were to be harmonized and the border controls (in the form of administration of transit procedures) were to be removed and "single administrative documentation system" would be introduced. The entire gamut of policy framework has the following four areas:

(i) Commercial and Economic Policy

The White Paper had set the time limit for abolition of all types of national protective measures and regional quotas by 1992 except for agriculture due to its special features.

(ii) Health and Environment

Health protection was mainly in the form of veterinary and plant health checks in the border, the extent of which varies from country to country because of different national regulations. The White Paper proposed harmonization of all national rules on health standards for the establishment of SEM (Single European Market). As a precondition of SEM all veterinary controls (on live animals and animal products) and plant health control would have to be limited to the places of departure. As regards, environment, special care was taken to control over transportation and disposal of dangerous and hazardous toxic materials that would emerge after the abolition of internal frontier.

(iii) Transportation

In the area of transportation, the White Paper proposed a common transport policy among the member states for ensuring smooth flow of goods. Until recently, transport operators in the EC were guided by the intra-Community quota system for which every vehicle must have to carry transport authorization certificate. These certificates and books of record sheets were subject to rigorous checks at the frontier. Therefore, after the abolition of frontier control transport quota was likely to be dismantled except some dangerous products on safety grounds.

(iv) Statistics

The harmonization of statistical methods for compilation, storing and documentation of data was an integral part of the SEM.

(b) Control of Individuals

Movement of persons among the member states was controlled by national regulations, which were basically of two types, viz: (i) Police check relating to the identity of the persons, and (ii) Tax checks. As regards the first, the White Paper proposed to make the check at internal frontier for the first, EC nationals more flexible except in case of the tourists and drugs. As part of the move, the Report proposed the introduction of a common passport testifying the position of an individual as a citizen of any member state and also introduction of "self-identification" system. With a view to dismantling checking system by 1992, the EC proposed the following directives :

(i) Approximation of arm legislation which meant that absence of checking must not provide an incentive to buy arms from countries with a liberal legislation.

(ii) Approximation of drug legislation was proposed in 1987 and implemented in 1989.

(iii) Personnel of non-member states will also seem to be the beneficiaries of liberalizing control because after abolition of checking system, people of member states would be able to move from one state to another without any rigorous checking. The White Paper proposed to frame suitable policies for non-community nationals in respect of employment, residence and entry.

(iv) Together with the removal of internal barriers, the White Paper provided a comprehensive package to streamline the community's visa policy for non-community personnel. Besides, the cockfield commission mooted a common extradition policy which was proposed to be adopted in 1990 and 1991.

2. Removal of Technical Barriers

Existence of technical barriers to trade was another major non-tariff barrier applied on the intra-Community movements of goods, services, labour and capital. There was no reason to believe that rules and regulations pertaining to health, quality and protection of human life would necessarily be the same for all countries. What was more important that selling products of one country to the markets of others required a uniform system. Removal of technical barriers would work upon following areas :

—Free movement of goods
—Public procurement
—Free movement for labour and persons
—A common market for the Community members
—Free movement of capital
—Creation of suitable category for industrial cooperation
—Application of Community Law.

Free movement of goods between member states was often restrained by health and sanitary standards, phytosanitary regulations and different national standards. In order to ensure the free movement of goods, the Commission proposed the following measures :

— identifying areas for harmonization or for mutual cooperation.
— legislative harmonization was proposed to be restricted to health and safety requirements; and
— harmonization was proposed to be at par with the European standard rather than multiplicity of national standards.

Public procurement policy was discriminatory between the members. It was normally alleged that a sizeable portion of public procurement/ purchase contract was awarded to the national agencies which was detrimental to the healthy growth of common internal market. In this regard the Commission proposed to make the auction/bid as transparent as possible in respect of timing, quality and speed of publication of tenders. Four major groups were excluded from liberalization process, viz. water, energy, transport and telecommunication.

Regarding free movement of labour and professionals, the Commission was very particular in removing all barriers, it was a proven fact that the standard of education was not the same in all states. In such cases the Commission favoured introduction of "vocational training card" and harmonization of professional qualifications. This measure would enable the nationals of member states to be eligible to get jobs across the Community.

Common Market for Services was the most potential sector, which remained untapped until recently. Regarding traditional services like banking, insurance and transport, the Report favoured opening up of the cross-border market.

Regarding credit institutions, especially banking and insurance services, Commission had emphasized coordinated action in respect of fund allocation to the priority sectors and extending the facility across the border. In security services, the Commission had proposed harmonization of investment norms across the border, harmonization in management and distribution of portfolios and dissemination of information across the borders. In addition to that, the Commission was in favour of establishing a Common European Security market in line with the European Stock Exchange which would facilitate the security transfer on a day to day basis.

Transport Services comprised 7 per cent of the Community's GDP. Recognising the importance of transport services in trade and industry, the Report had suggested the following measures:

— Abolition of quantitative restrictions (quotas) to transport operators (by road) among the members and creating opportunities for non-resident operators.
— Freedom of transport of passengers by road.
— In case of international transport of goods through inland waterway, members were given priority but some facilities were proposed to be given to carriers from non-member countries.
— The same facility was proposed to extend to air cargo also.

New-Technology and Services

All the members of the Community were not equally advanced in high-tech areas. Therefore, the Commission's proposal was that there should be an intra-Community network in disseminating any innovation in areas of audio and visual services, information services, data processing services and computer marketing and distribution services. Regarding audio-visual services the Commission was in favour of setting up a communitywise broadcasting area through which it would transmit all information on trade and commerce and economic activities to all of its members. Common broadcasting services, common banking services and common information services are essential ingredients of a common market.

5. Capital Movements

One of the major ingredients of "Europe 1992" was the free-movement of capital across the border. Henceforth, liberalization of capital market is required for three proposes, viz:

— Free movement of goods, services and persons across the border requires access to efficient financial system.
— Monetary stability through the European Monetary System (EMS) was the essential precondition for the development of the internal market which required greater dynamism of capital market.
— The decompartmentalization of financial market would boost economic development of the Community by promoting optimum allocation of savings of members and non-member states.

6. Creation of Suitable Conditions for Industrial Cooperation

Active cooperation between member states was constrained by excessive legal, fiscal and administrative bottlenecks. The protected measures are given as below:

(i) Creation of Legal Framework Facilitating Corporations

Due to the complex legal framework of the Community, a large number of joint projects were not getting materialized. In order to cope with the situation, it was suggested in the Report to harmonize different national legal systems under the aegis of "European Economic Interest Grouping".

(ii) Intellectual or Industrial Properties

Three main areas in the intellectual properties were, viz. copyrights, trademarks and patents. These were suggested to be made more dynamic consistent with the rapid technological change in areas of computer, software, micro-circuits and biotechnology. The Luxembourg Convention on the Community patents was signed in 1975. The Commission wanted its members to get it ratified and it had prepared a patent protection on biological inventions and legal protection.

(iii) Taxation

In the Community there had been several national laws on taxation which were again characterized by the lack of coordination between different tax authorities. This was due to different tax treatment of the partner companies as well as subsidiaries. Therefore such tax differentiation between parent and subsidiaries taxation on managers and prevention of double taxation were some of the important obstacles of internal markets. In order to remove such multiplicity of taxation, the Commission intended to publish a White Paper on the taxation of categories of the Community and the Community-wise harmonization of tax rules.

7. Application of Community Law

If the necessary infrastructure are not properly built up for the creation of internal market then the entire political and legislative efforts are likely to be endangered. It has increasingly been observed that some members are taking recourse to quantitative restrictions (QRs) as a tool of restraining imports. About 60 per cent of the total complaints (on an average 225 every year) are related to QRs. Due to lack of enfo[illegible]nt mechanism, it only settles around 100 complaints every yea[illegible]

3. Remova[illegible] o[illegible]al Barriers

The EC has been under customs union since 1968, which meant removal of custom tariffs among the member states. But this was not enough because the EC was already protected by exorbitant turnover tax. In 1967, all members unanimously decided that existing turnover tax would be replaced by the VAT and 1 per cent of VAT would be given to the Community for financing its activities through own source. The most urgent reform which is required in the fiscal area is the harmonization of the direct taxes including VAT. In its first move, the Commission identified tobacco, alcoholic drinks and hydrocarbon oil as the products on which excise duties were levied. In case of tobacco, a limited degree of harmonization has already been over, and in alcoholic drinks and hydrocarbon oils little progress has been made so far in spite of clear directive.

(a) Commercial Traffic and Value Added Tax (VAT)

According to 14th VAT Directive the entire accounting procedures on VAT have been shifted from frontiers to the inland tax offices which is expected to be the first step for removing border control on the operation of commercial traffic. Since then now sales and purchase operations across the border have been treated as similar to that of member states.

(b) Individual Traveller

Due to prevalence of differential structure in the member states it is an impossible task to check illegal transactions until harmonization of indirect tax is done. If a traveller buys a product from a country and sells it to another, then there is no mechanism to stop it. Therefore, it is suggested that "travellers' allowance" should be introduced enabling the genuine travellers to buy some dutiable products.

(c) Excises

The variation of excise is not so significant in case of individual travellers, but, certainly it matters in case of goods which are traded like "bonded house" because levies are not charged when the goods are kept in "bonded house' but when it is not routed through such system levies are charged. The excise duty would not be charged until the goods were taken out of "bonds" in the country of destination. If frontier controls are dismantled then excised goods will be routed through a bonded warehouse in a low-rate country, taken out of "bond" there and shipped on for consumption in a high rate country. Thus removal of frontier control will require not only setting up a "clearing house" system of VAT but also approximations of excise duties.

(d) Approximations

Removal of border control and harmonization of tax structure would help to eliminate the variation of tax rates. In case of the USA, the variation is about 5 per cent which could easily be accommodated. It is estimated to be around + or -2.5 per cent in case of the EC. But in case of VAT, the Community would provide sufficient flexibilities. If the standard rate is 16.5 per cent then the actual rate for member states would be at the range of 14 to 19 per cent which was supposed to be imposed by the six of the nine members those who introduced VAT in 1985. In 1982, the average share of EC's VAT was 7.05 per cent of GDP which was 3.63 per cent for excise of all commodities and 3.37 per cent for tobacco products including bear, wine, spirit and mineral products. But weighted average of the EC's VAT and excises was 10.68 per cent of the GDP in 1982.

(e) Value Added Tax

EC's VAT has mainly three interlocking issues, viz.

— the common base or coverage,
— the number of rates, and
— the level of rates particularly the mean or standard rate.

Regarding common base, the Second VAT Directive laid down main principles and the Sixth VAT Directive went a long way to fulfill the necessary details of a common VAT base in the EC. In spite of that, areas of differences were in food, second hand goods, fuel and transport and the treatment of small traders and firms. As regards rates, seven out of nine member states imposed VAT at a reduced rate in addition to the standard rate and three of them imposed higher rates. But regarding level of rates six out of nine states adopted VAT approximations range of 14 per cent to 19.8 per cent for the standard rate (i.e.+ or - 2.5 per cent).

A range of 15 to 20 per cent (a norm of 17.5 per cent + or - 2.5 per cent) was for five members states out of nine.

(ii) Excises

According to Commission's observation, member states had common coverage in excise duties in case of manufactured tobacco, alcoholic beverage and hydrocarbon oils. The rate of taxation varied from 0.28 ECUs per packet of 20 cigarettes (Greece) to 1.96 ECUs (Denmark). The most important feature was that for beer, wine and spirit, the highest rate of taxation was found in Denmark, Ireland and the UK. Excise duties were disproportionately high to the retail price (up to 69 per cent for cigarettes, 52 per cent for petrol) and these were bound to affect the market rate.

As a part of the completion of internal market, the Commission proposed to rationalise VAT and excises. Regarding value added tax, Commission emphasised on common base. They covered subjects like works of art, antiques, used goods and the import of second hand goods by final consumers. Regarding approximations of excise rates, following proposals were made :

— the rate structure whether the common VAT system should be one or two or have more rates, and
— the target rate(s) together with the permitted ranges of variation around them.

CECCHINI REPORT ON THE "COST OF NON-EUROPE"

The entire study was carried out in five countries, viz. Belgium, France, Germany, Italy and the UK. The rationale behind selecting only five countries in the EC was that the value of transactions, carried out by these countries was more than 80 per cent of the total value.

Though the EC has been in the customs union since 1968, yet there exist labyrinthine non-tariff barriers within the Community which restrict free movement of goods and services. Existence of such barriers is a major constraint to the completion of the internal market. In order to estimate the probable cost of these barriers and cost saved after the removal of these identified barriers, the European Commission appointed a committee under the Chairmanship of Mr. P. Cecchini, then Vice-President of the European Commission in 1986[14]. Mr. Paulo Cecchini was the head of a project initiated by the

Commission whose objective was to evaluate the economic impact of completing the internal market by 1992 and was asked to submit final report by 1988.

Other members of the Committee were :

1. External Members :

Sergio Alessandrini, Jean-Michael Charpin, Wolfgang, Gerstenberger, Jacques Pelkmans, Nanfred Wegner, Paul Champsaur, Michael Delean, Peter Homes and Carlo Secchi.

2. Commission of European Communities :

(*i*) Director-General of Economic and Financial Affairs : Michael Emerson, Michael Catinat, Alexis Jacquemin, Michael Anjean, Phillippe Goybet.

(*ii*) Director-General for the Internal Market and Industrial Affairs : Micheal Loy (Coordinator), Michael Ayral, Jean-Francois Marchipont.

The Committee chiefly covered sixteen broad product areas and had shown the tentative cost reduction and change in other macroeconomic variables after the elimination of controls restricting free movement of intra-Community trade. He estimated the "Cost of Non-Europe" in the following areas :

— Border related controls and administrative formalities
— Road haulage sector
— Public sector procurement
— Case study of technical barriers in six industries
— Obstacles to trans-border business activities
— Business services
— Financial services
— Benefits of completing the internal market for telecommunication equipment in the EC
— Automobile industry
— Food staff industry
— Textile and clothing industry
— Pharmaceutical industry, etc.

The quantitative findings of Cecchini Report are shown in Tables 2.1 to 2.4. While estimating economic benefits, the study mentions that total gains will be around 200 bn ECUs, responding to an annual growth of GDP of around 5 per cent. European prices are expected to decline by 6 per cent, and this change will generate 2 to 5 million

TABLE : 2.1 : Estimate of the total economic gains from completing the internal market, according to partial equilibrium estimation method (EUR 7, based on benchmark data for 1985 = 100)

	billion ECUs Variants		*% GDP Variants*	
	A	*B*	*A*	*B*
Stage - 1 :				
Cost of barriers affecting trade only	8	9	0.2	0.3
Stage - 2 :				
Cost of barriers affecting all products	57	71	2.0	2.4
Total direct cost of barriers	65	80	2.2	2.7
Stage - 3 :				
Economies of scale from restructuring and increased production	60	61	2.0	2.1
Stage - 4 :				
Competition effects on X-ineffeciency and monopoly rents	46	46	1.6	1.6
Total market integration effects :				
Variant - I				
(sum of stages 3 & 4 above) (b)	106	107	3.6	3.7
Variant - II				
(alternative measures for stages 3 & 4) (e)	62	62	2.1	2.1
Total of costs of barriers and market integration effects :				
Variant I = (a) + (b)	171	187	5.8	6.4
Variant II = (a) + (c)	127	142	4.3	4.8

Notes : Variants A and B relate to the use of alternative primary source of information introduced in the calculation of stage 1 and 2. Variants I and II relate to different approaches to evaluating competitiveness when the total figures, ranging from 127 to 187 billion ECUs for seven Member States at 1985 prices are scaled to represent the same GDP share for the 12 Member States in 1988 prices, the range becomes 173 to 257 billion ECUs.

Source : Commission of the European Communities, *European Economy*, No. 35, March 1988, (Brussels), spl. issue on *The Economies of 1992*, p. 157.

additional jobs[15].

The quantitative results of the report which have been depicted

TABLE 2.2 : Macroeconomic Consequences of the internal market : Community as a whole in the medium term

	Frontier control	*Public Procurement*	*Financial Services*	*Supply Effects*	*Total Average*	*Total Range*
Relative Change						
As % of GDP	0.4	0.5	1.5	2.1	4.5	(3.2 to 5.7)
Consumer prices	–1.0	–1.4	–1.4	–2.3	– 6.1	(–4.5 to –7.7)
Absolute Change						
Employment (X 1000)	200	350	400	850	1800	(1300 to 2300)
General government borrowing requirement as a % of GDP	0.2	0.3	1.1	0.6	2.2	(1.5 to 3.0)

Source : Commission fo the European Communities *European Economy* No. 35, March 1988, spl. issue on *The Economies of 1992*, (Brussels), p. 159.

Table 2.3 : Potential consequences of the internal market for the Community in the medium/Long term

Micro economic approach				*Welfare gain as = of GDP*	
				4.5 to 6.5%	
Macro economic approach	*GDP as %*	*Prices as %*	*Employment in million*	*Public balance as % point of GDP*	*External balance as % point of GDP*
Without accompanying economic measures (1)	4.5	-6.0	1.75	2.25	1.00
With accompanying economic measures (1)	7.0	-4.5	5.00	0.5	-0.25

(1) Margin of error ± 30%

Source : Commission fo the European Communities *European Economy* No. 35, March 1988, spl. issue on *The Economies of 1992*, (Brussels), p. 167.

in Tables 2.1 to 2.4 are more optimistic. In reality this may not be achievable. But the positive aspects of such estimation is the identification of strengths and weakness of the European industries and to restructure them according to emerging global competition. So far only big industries were expected to enjoy the fruits of EC-92,

TABLE 2.4 : Estimates of costs of barriers based on sectoral studies or working hypothesis

	bn. ECUs.
I. Cost of specific types of barriers	
1. Custom formalities (1.7 to 1.9% of intra-community trade flows)	8 - 9
2. Public procurement	21
Total	29 - 30
II. Cost of barriers in specific industries	
1. Food (0.75 to 1.5% turnover)	0.5 - 1.0
2. Pharmaceuticals (1 to 2% turnover)	0.3 - 0.6
3. Automobiles (5% of turnover)	2.6
4. Textiles and clothing (0.5 to 1% of turnover)	0.7 - 1.3
5. Building materials (1.75 % of turnover)	2.8
6. Telecommunication (equipment) (10 to 20% of turnover)	3.0 - 4.8
Total	9.1 - 13.1
III. Cost of barriers in specific Service sectors	
1. Financial services (10% of turnover)	22.0
2. Business services (3% of turnover)	3.3
3. Road transport (5% of turnover)	5.0
4. Air transport (10% of turnover)	3.0
5. Telecommunication (services)	6.0
Total	38.3

Source : Commission of the European Communities, Cost of Non-Europe, European Commission (Several Volumes, i.e., 1-16), Brussels, 1988.

Notes : The table reveals the result of special studies undertaken by the consultants except the transport case which rely on earlier published sources. Working hypthesis have also been adopted, for the purpose of the partial equilibrium calculation below : For cost of price reduction for agriculture (0 to 5%) and energy (2%). Addition of categories I and II would imply double counting, since some but not all the costs of customs formalities and government procurement are covered under branches in cost-specific barrier to trade.

but the credit for the Report relies on the fact that due to identification of potential areas, small and medium industries will also equip themselves to face the competition rising from the members themselves after the completion of the SEM. The Cecchini Report is certainly not very ambitious but it confirms and crystalizes expectations of the Europeans. The success of results depends on fulfillment of some conditions, viz, (i) all measures proposed by the Commission must be adopted and implemented, and (ii) the national governments of the various member states must pursue orthodox and mutually compatible economic, social and financial policies[16].

It is true that after customs union tariffs, quantitative restrictions on trade have largely reduced in the Community. But in spite of that fact, there have been other barriers which restrict the movements of goods, services, capital and labour.

These can be broadly defined as[17]:

(i) differences in technical regulations between countries which impose extra cost on intra-EC trade.

(ii) delays at frontiers for customs purposes and related administrative burdens for companies and public administrations which impose further costs on trade.

(iii) restrictions in competition for public purchases through excluding bids from other Community suppliers which often result in excessively high cost of purchase.

(iv) restrictions on freedom to engage in certain services transactions, or to become established in certain service activities in other Community countries. This concerns particularly financial and transport services where the cost of market entry barriers also appears to be substantial.

In economic terms, the barriers can be grouped as:

—tariffs
—quantitative restrictions
—cost-increasing barriers
—market entry restrictions
—market distorting subsidies and practices[18].

The estimation of the cost of non-Europe is very approximate in nature in the sense that the success of newly adopted measures, depends on the interaction of several complicated economic and non-economic factors in majority of the cases which may not be . It also depends on better coordination of policies across the members disregarding their differences in political and economic parameters. While estimating the "cost of non-Europe", the CECCHINI Report finds[19]:

(i) the direct costs of frontier formalities and associated administrative costs for the private and public sector may be of the order of 1.8

per cent of the value of goods traded within the Community or around 9 billion ECUs at 1985 prices.

(ii) It is estimated that total cost of identifiable barriers affecting industry in the internal market is about 40 billion ECUs or 3.5 per cent of industrial value added.

(iii) Some studies show that removal of existing barriers would result in cost reduction of 1 to 2 per cent for food and beverages industry, construction materials, pharmaceuticals and textiles and clothing. It is 5 per cent for automobiles.

(iv) Savings would be enormous if the restrictions on market entry are removed from service sector branches. After removing the barriers, the gain in the area of public sector procurement alone could be 20 billion ECUs. For financial services also a range around 20 billion ECU in potential savings has been estimated[20].

(v) Taking note of the present industrial structure with a more rationalized but still less than optimal one, it is estimated that about one-third of European industries could profit from varying cost reductions of between 1 to 7 per cent yielding an aggregate cost-saving of the order of 60 billion ECUs.

(vi) Encouraging competition among member states results in a reduction in X-inefficiency. Such inefficiency can be minimized by proper allocation of resources i.e. human, physical and financial. Weak competition causes X-inefficiency. The cost of X-inefficiency may often be as great as those resulting from unexpected economies of scale. The total effect of moving to a competitive integrated market, with fuller achievement of potential economies of scale and reduction of X-inefficiency may be twice to three times the direct cost of identified barriers in the situation[21].

(vii) After removing all barriers, the estimated gains range starts with around 70 billion ECUs or 2.5 per cent of the GDP[22]. This is rather a conservative estimate of the benefit, but markets become more competitive and integrated than the potential benefit which may be around 125 to 190 billion ECUs i.e. 4.5 to 6.5 per cent of GDP[23].

The gains discussed above need not be short term in nature. In normal cases a) it may take 5 or possibly more years for the larger part of the effects to be realized, and b) in any event it is assumed that micro and macro economic policy would ensure that the resources released as costs are reduced, are effectively re-employed. The effects of internal market programme can be grouped under four major categories, each having a different type of macro economic impact, a) the removal of customs delays and costs, b) the opening of public markets to competition, c) more general supply side effects, reflecting changes in the strategic behaviour of enterprises in a new competitive environment, d) the liberalization and integration of financial markets[24].

Pursuing a relatively passive macroeconomic policy, it is unlikely to achieve perceptible results at least in the short run, though there would be some manifestation in the earlier years. Most of the desired results showing impact of the removal of barriers will start coming from medium-run i.e. after 5 to 6 years of the integration. It is estimated that after this period GDP will grow by 4.5 per cent while the magnitude of price decline would be around -6 per cent. On employment the impact is slightly negative in the initial years, but in the medium term it is expected that about 2 million new jobs (nearly 2 per cent of the initial employment level) may be created. As an aftermath of SEM, budget balance is likely to increase significantly and the current account balance of payment may improve remarkably. Removal of barriers results in improvement of all macroeconomic variables[25].

The above phenomenon is in case of passive macro-economic scenario, but after this phase if we follow active macro economic policies by improving monetary and financial equilibrium,, then certainly one can set growth on a higher trajectory. This is possible by adjusting macro economic variables like inflation, budget or balance of payment deficit . In the medium term if all these macro economic variables are set together and work properly , it is expected that this will yield 2.5 per cent more GDP in addition to 4.5 per cent which means GDP would increase by a spectacular rate of 7 per cent. There is an apprehension that increase in income would lead to higher inflation,. but in our model economic growth this remains well below the projected level due to successful implementation of the internal market programme by making the budget balance and BOP situation remains at a sustainable level[26].

Synthesizing the macro and micro economic policies, we can say all the quantitative estimates presented above are approximate and based on certain assumptions. The estimates have been assembled in an eclectic manner. The estimates have been worked out through various macro and micro economic methodologies to produce desired results. Different approaches converge together and suggest consistent results. It is not a trivial job to calculate the exact magnitude of the potential gain of the competitive integration.

The above estimates are based on the static framework where we have ignored some important categories of dynamic impacts on economic performance. Especially three important dynamic factors are very important in this connection.

First : Role of technological change has been ignored here. Better competitive condition offers more technological innovation that can only be absorbed if there is scale economy. Only a united market can guarantee such conditions.

Second : There is evidence in fast growing high technology industries of dynamic or learning economies of scale, whereby costs decline as the total accumulated production of certain goods and services increases market segmentation highly limiting such benefits and damaging performance of high technology industries.

Third : The business strategies of European enterprises are likely to be affected in the event of a rapid and extensive implementation of the internal market programme, full integration of the internal market will foster the emergence of truly European companies who can face the global challenge of intense competition[27].

Regarding macroeconomic policies, in order to be truly competitive in the international market. *Firstly*, should be the frontiers must be truly open to the extent that economic agents should easily be able to engage in arbitrage between national market to profit from the price differentials across the border. *Secondly*, the basic pillar of the successful competition policy is to do away with the public subsidies. When any cooperation becomes truly international and operates across the border, then its competition policies would be based on its own economic competence without any government support through subsidies. In the short run it may be feasible but in the medium run, competitive policy should be purely judged on the free market criteria. *Thirdly*, the trend of competitiveness relates to the opening up of the external market. At present, price discrimination among different markets is the common practice of a private enterprise. Competition policy should be based on the commercial antirust without creating any burden to the consumers. Commercial dominance is the common practice where the market is regulated by suppliers. Competition policy for the market to be fully integrated, should be guided by the principle that if prices of inputs are cheaper then imports should not be restricted on any grounds[28].

On the macroeconomic front, the main objective of the demand management policy is to follow non-inflationary growth at best in the medium run. It is also conceptually true that successful implementation of the internal market programme will put downward pressure to the cost and prices which leads more production employment and income with price stability. The more competition, markets will be more free and open and prices will be determined by the buyers not sellers. In the buyer market, price is always non-inflationary provided that there is adequate supply in the market[29].

One of the important drawbacks of the CECCHINI Report is that it always gives community-wise averages. It does not take into account the different socio-economic regime of the member states which are not at all equal. This implies even after the implementation of the internal market programme there is every probability that there will be skewed distribution of the benefits among the members. Relatively richer members will be more beneficial than smaller one. Smaller members have already expressed their apprehension of the effect of market integration into their economies. They opine that removal of national frontiers may lead to more mergers and acquisitions and gradually uncompetitive domestic industries will be wiped out. This will aggravate economic problems of weaker members. Business activities will be entirely governed by the profit criteria. Extensive competition generates more profit which attracts more foreign companies to operate whether they are EC-based or not. The most dynamic and competitive business and economies will derive the greatest gain from the 1992 Programme[30].

Another drawback of the CECCHINI Report is that while estimating the costs of non-Europe, it does not take into account the world and European business cycle. The implementation of SEM cannot be successful if we ignore the reality. As a matter of fact, early 1988 exhibited weakening of world as well as European business cycle. As a result, European exchange rates were higher than US dollar and currencies linked to it. Taking advantage of this situation, some international competitors garnered strategic gains in their share of weakening European market. To counter this situation, European industries should have sufficient safeguards which are: *(i)* support of the European business cycle, sufficient to counter its weakening in the short run in favour of accelerated growth thereafter *(ii)* endeavours to assume that international exchange rate adjustment are adequate but not excessive[31].

The study supports following conclusions :

(i) Presently European industries are in a state of segmentation and weak competition in many markets which means it has greater

potentialities of rationalising production and distribution structures leading to improvement in productivity and reduction in costs and prices.

(ii) If the SEM is properly implemented in both Community as well as member states, then certainly it has a very positive impact on their economic performance. Improvement in economic performance includes non-inflationary growth in employment and output, price stability and sound fiscal, monetary and balance of payment position.

(iii) In order to tap maximum benefits from the market integration all important features of the internal market programme would need to be implemented with sufficient speed and conviction.

(iv) In order to achieve higher growth trajectory through internal market integration, more than complete implementation of the White Paper is required. There must be a strong competition policy making the supply potential of the Community economy more flexible. Demand side management policies should be fully consistent with the competition policy so as to ensure the price stability and economic growth[32].

THE SINGLE EUROPEAN ACT(SEA) : REMOVAL OF NTBS AND CREATION OF SINGLE EUROPEAN MARKET (SEM)

All members of the EC have reached a consensus for removing all internal barriers restraining smooth flow of goods, services, capital and human resources between the members. These barriers are erected on the ground of economic health of the individual countries consistent with their national priorities. The existence of internal barriers are quite antagonist to the idea of a common market.

Being worried about such divergent national laws and the plethora of internal barriers the Commission enacted Single European Act (SEA) to deal with the Single European Market[33]. The basic objective of the SEA was to harmonize the national laws and to enforce uniform system throughout the member states. The SEA also emphasized the removal of tariffs and non-tariff barriers. Tariff barriers between the EC members were transparent. The removal of these barriers was an integral part of the overall measures undertaken for the completion of internal market.

The White Paper had fixed up a time table for the removal of barriers in a phased manner. The probable areas of action were as follows[34]:

(i) The removal of non-tariff barriers prevailing in the member states

in the form of custom posts immigration and passport controls, the harmonization of public health standards, the abolition of national transport controls and the approximation of arms and drugs legislation.

(ii) The White Paper has also proposed the removal of all technical barriers to trade between member states and provision for free movement of goods and harmonization of technical standards.

(iii) The Report also envisages the liberalization of capital movement within the territory of the Community, common provision of industrial and intellectual property. Finally it had strongly recommended the harmonization of indirect taxation (VAT and excise duties) and national regulations concerning the completion of internal market.

The White Paper had given a broad outline of the removal of non-tariff barriers. Prior to the setting of the Cockfield Commission, only customs tariffs were considered to be the most effective barriers to the completion of internal market. This was due to the variation of national laws for setting up customs tariff limit. But, afterwards, it was found that apart from tariff barriers, there have been innumerable non-tariff barriers which are more active in distorting the prospect of the Single European Market. Over the years through several tariff reduction measures, tariff rates have been declined to a considerable extent but, on the other hand, due to labyrinthine NTBs, inter-State transaction of goods and services are severely affected.

The Commission had basically proposed two types of reforms tailored for SEM :

(i) the rate structure, i.e. whether the common VAT system has one two or even more rates, and

(ii) the target rates together with the permitted ranges of variation around them.

In the earlier sections of this Chapter, we have discussed in detail about the existing NTBs in the EC, its nature and dimension, and the Commission's step to remove these barriers. It will be meaningless to discuss in detail about them in this section, but we will present the probable timetable for phasing out of the mentioned NTBs as proposed by the Cockfield Report.

Review of the Progress of the Single European Market.

While reviewing the progress of the single market uptil now, we can divide the entire gamut of the operation in six major areas[35] These are :

(i) completing and streamlining the legislative framework of the single market.
(ii) making the single market work.
(iii) confirming the single market as the cornerstone of economic and monetary union.
(iv) securing single market for the citizen.
(v) adapting the single market to technological and other changes, and
(vi) preparing the single market for enlargement.

As regards **legislative framework** for the completion of the single market, all measures are yet to be adopted. An estimation done by Mr. Ciampi, Chairman of the Competitiveness Advisory group shows that due to non-implementation of the European company statute, the loss incurred by the European business is around 30 billion ECUs a year[36]. The incidence of double taxation is still there. Due to differential fiscal regime among the member states, Europeans are yet to get the product at competitive rates. The rejection in March 1995 by the Parliament of the draft directive on the protection of biotechnological inventions means that European industry is still a significant competitive disadvantage.

Control of free movement of people across the border remains to be one of the major irritant factors of the completion of single market. On 14 June 1985, the Commission approved its White Paper on completing the internal market. Among other aspects, White Paper also recommended the elimination of control at the internal border. This recommendation was subsequently incorporated into Article 8a (now Article 7a) of the EC Treaty by the Single European Act.

The basic objective of the single European market was to dismantle all barriers for the movement of goods, services, capital and labour. But the member states have failed to come into a consensus on a common policy permitting free movement of persons across the border. This is due to :

— stubborn attitude of UK, Ireland and Denmark.
— inability to check drug trafficking across the border.

Considering the need for a universal policy in controlling the movement of personnel across the border, the five states signed the Agreement on 14 June 1985 in Luxembourg city of Schengen[37]. The Schengen Agreement came into force from the date of its signature (i.e., 14 June 1985). Actually the Schengen Agreement originated from the Saarbrucken signed between France and Germany on 13 July 1984. The State of Benelux (Belgium, the Netherlands and Luxembourg) were later associated with the initiative. The Schengen Agreement was followed by the signature of its complementary convention on 19 June 1990 when Italy, Greece, Spain and Portugal joined the Agreement. Austria asked for its membership on 6 March 1995. Sweden and Finland do not exclude themselves from joining the Schengen Club in the long run provided that Scandinavian Agreement on passports can be respected[38]. U.K. Denmark and Ireland remained outside of the agreement but this did not pose any problem because the Schengen Agreement was concluded outside the framework of the European Union[39]. Consequently, these Agreements become part of international law and not European law.

The Schengen Agreement does not discriminate between members and non-members once any one enters into the national frontier. It grants common visa which may be one day to three months, then it is decided by the immigration policy of the national governments. Seven member States[40] committed themselves to implementing the Schengen Agreement irreversibly with effect from 26 March 1995.

Though free movement of personnel among the member states is still a controversial one, yet in July 1995, the Commission prescribed three proposals to eliminate restrictions on controls on the clearly stated condition that they would enter into force only when the essential security measures have been implemented. The Council also adopted two regulations relating to the free movement of people. The first one is the introduction of model type of visa (Regulation (EC) No. 1683/95) and second one is the preparation of a list of countries whose nationals must have a visa to enter Community territory (Regulation (EC) No.2317/95).

Competition policy is another major area where much action is yet to be initiated to complete the single market. In the telecommunication sector, 1998 was the date by which full liberalization was to be achieved, while the use of alternative infrastructures for liberalized services would be allowed in two years earlier. Acceleration in the pace of liberalisation in the telcom sector paved the way for setting up the European Information Society in 1995.

Divergency in national legislations is still a deterrent factor for the successful implementation of a single market. Community policy makers have been making considerable efforts to harmonize the national rules. It was a cause for concern that in 1995 itself, 438 proposals for technical legislations at national level were notified to the Commission,. Simultaneously, unification proposals involving the repeal of about 350 instruments were put forward before the Council and Parliament by the end of 1995.

Among the major achievements in 1995 was the proposal by the Commission of the Customs 2000 Action programme to modernize customs administration. The Council responded positively to the Commissioners request. In spite of this, the Council recently agreed to a new notification system for national measures to come into effect in 1997, strengthening the instruments available for tackling illegal restrictions in framework of goods across the frontiers. As a result the number of complaints about such measures increased from 202 in 1994 to 259 in 1995.

Efforts to harmonize national laws and then to enact them into the Community laws had been going on steadily in 1995. During this period the member states had adopted 93.4 per cent of the national measures required to implement the Community's single market legislation. Extent varies among the states. Denmark, Netherlands, Spain and Sweden were substantially above the Community average of 93.4 per cent, while Greece, Germany and Austria were substantially below. Implementation of agreed Community law remained seriously below the desired level in some key areas which was the major cause of concern for the Community in 1995.

As regards technological and other changes, the vision of the Community was very dynamic. The Commission was determined to do away with the regulatory environment for inviting more technological progress. Through several legislative enactments, the Commission makes much progress in protecting intellectual properties. In July 1995, the Council and the European Parliament adopted a directive on the protection of individuals with regard to the processing of personal data and on the free movement of such data. The Council also reached a common position on the proposal for a directive on the legal protection of data bases. In 1995, the Commission produced Green Papers and carried out extensive consultations among the members on ways to protect copyrights and related rights in the information society as well as the protection of pluralism in the media[41].

NOTES

1. The World Bank, *World Development Report*, (Washington D.C. 1987), pp. 140-146.
2. A.B. Shiela, Page, "The Increased Use of Trade Controls by the Industrilised Countries", *Intereconomies*, (Hamburg), May-June, 1980, pp.144-51.
3. A. Deardorff, & R. M. Stern, "*Methods of Measurement of Non-Tariff Barriers to Trade*", (1985), (Geneva), UNCTAD/ST/MD/28, pp. 45-50.
4. William Cilne, & et al, "*Trade Negotiations in the Tokyo Round : A Quantitative Assessment*", (Washington DC), The Brookings Institute, 1980, p. 145.
5. United States International Trade Commission, *The Economic Effects of Significant U.S. Import Restraints : Phase-1 : Manufacturing, USITC, (1989)* Publication No. 222, (Washington DC). p. 19.
6. Sam Laird, and Alexander J. Yeats, "Trends in Non-Tariff Barriers of Developed Countries, 1966-86, in Weltwirteschaftlinches Archives, Band 126, Heft 2, 1990, pp. 299-325.
7. The World Bank, *World Development Report*, (Washington DC, 1987), pp. 146-147.
8. A. Olechowski, & Gary Simpson, "Current Trade Restrictions in the EC, the USA and Japan", *Journal of World Trade and Law*, (Geneva), May/June 1980, pp. 230-231.
9. Chopra, H.S., "Western Europe and United States and Japan; Controversial Debate on their Industrial Competitiveness;" in K.V. Kesavan (ed.), *Contemporary Japanese Politics and Foreign Policy*, (New Delhi : Radiant, 1989), pp. 147-176.
10. *(a)* Robert Long, "Japan Threatens USA more than Europe", *European Affairs*, no. 1/87, p. 53.
    (b) Reve Herrmann, "Europe's Technological Comparision with Japan", *Aussen Politik*, (Hamburg), 16/37, 3/86, p. 267.
    (c) Gene Byllinsky, "The High Tech Race : Who's Ahead ?" *Fortune Special Report*, 13 October 1986, pp. 26-31.
11. IMD Publication, "*World Competitiveness Report*, (Geneva and Lusane: World Economic Forum, 1995), p. 14.
12. The Commission of European Commission, "The White Paper, of the Internal Market", Brussels 1985, (This is Known as the *Cockfiled Report*, 1985).
13. Commission of the European Communities, *The Cockfield Report*, (Brussels, 1986).
14. Commission of the European Communities, *The Costs of Non-Europe* Vol.1, (Brussels, 1987), This Report was prepared by a Committee chaired by Mr. P. Cecchini, Vice-President of the European Commission : The Report is Known after his name i.e., Cecchini Report.

15. Commission of the European Communities : *Research on the Cost of Non-Europe* Basic Findings : Executive Summaries (Vol. 1), (Brussels, 1987), p.1.
16. Willy de Clercq and Leo Verhoef, "*Europe : Back to the Top*" NMB (Bank, Brussels), 1990, p. 40.
17. Commission of the European Communities, Director General for Economies and Trade Affair, in "European Economy", *The Economies of 1992*, No. 35, March 1988, p.17.
18. Commission of the European Communities, *European Economy* Special on the *Economies of 1992*, no. 35, (Brussels), March 1988, p.17.
19. Commission of the European Communities, *The Costs of Non-Europe Basic Studies : Executive Summary*, (Brussels, 1985), Vol.1.
20. Ibid n. 44 p. 3-5.
21. Ibid n. 41 p. 18.
22. European Parliament Working Document, Towards Economic Resources A 2-50/85/B, 31 May 1985.
23. Ibid n. 41 p. 19.
24. Ibid n. 41 p. 19.
25. Ibid n. 41 p. 19.
26. Ibid n. 41 p. 19.
27. Ibid n. 41.
28. Ibid n. 41 p. 20.
29. Ibid n. 41 p. 21.
30. Willy de Clercq and Leo Verhoef, Ibid n. 41 p. 41.
31. Ibid n. p. 21.
32. Commission of the European Communities, Ibid n. 43 p. 21-22.
33. Commission of the European Communities, "Single European Act" in *Official Journal of the European Communities* (Brussels), no.1, 29 June 1987, pp. 573-589.
34. Commission of the European Communities, "*The Cockfield Report*", 1985, The Cockfield Report is known in the White Paper.
35. Commission of the European Communities, *The Single Market in 1995 : Report from the Commission to the Council and the European Parliament*, (Brussels), 2 February 1996, pp.1-9.
36. Ibid n. 60 p. 4.
37. (*a*) The European Commission, "*Background Report : The Schengen Agreements* (Brussels), SEC/95, 9 March 1995, pp.1-5.
    (*b*) David O' Keefee, "*The Schengen Convention : A Suitable Model for European Integration*" in *Year Book of European Law*, Oxford (Clarendon Press, 1992), pp. 573-589.
    (*c*) Commission of the European Communities, "*Free Movement of Press : Proposals for Directives*" Press Release by European Commission, IP (95)/726, (Brussels), 12 July 1995, pp.1-3.
    (*d*) European Commission, "*Information Paper on the Implementation of the Convention Applying the Schengen Agreement* XV/4.3, (Brussels), 16 March 1995, pp.14-22.

(e) Commission of the European Communities, "*Proposal for a Council Directive on the Elimination on Controls on Person Crossing internal frontiers*", COM (95) 347, 95/020/(CNS), (Brussels), 12 July 1995, pp.1-18.

38. Ibid n. 62a p. 1.
39. Ibid n. 62a p. 1.
40. These States are : Belgium, Luxemburg, Netherland, France, Germany, Spain and Portugal.
41. Review of the Progress of the European Market has been discussed in 1995 document of European Community, Cf. Commission of the European Communities, "*The Single Market in 1995 : Reports from the Commission to the Council and the European Parliament*, (Brussels), 2 February 1996, pp.1-9.

Chapter 3

"Fortress Europe?" Non-Tariff Barriers: A Conceptual Study

TOWARDS DEFINITION OF NTBs

Despite considerable amount of research on non-tariff barriers (NTBs) carried out by different institutions as also individuals, there has still been a serious lack of an accepted standard definition by which all NTBs can be covered in a most transparent way. The area covered by NTBs is so vast and wide-ranging that a single definition would not suffice to take into account the entire gamut of its operation. Apart from definitional aspects, there have also been differences in terminology used for this purpose. Sometimes it is called non-tariff "measures", sometimes non-tariff "barriers" and sometimes non-tariff "distortions". GATT and UNCTAD prefer to call all trade distorting measures (apart from tariffs) as "non-tariff measures (NTMs)". The World Bank usually prefers the term it non-tariff barriers (NTBs) which cover all distortions and interventions (including subsidies) of all kinds whether applied to exports, imports and or domestic production[1].

Regardless of the differences in terminology and complexities involved in definition, UNCTAD defines that, "non-tariff barriers (NTBs) encompass all trade policy instruments that restrict free movement of goods and thus raise cost of production"[2]. According to a Olechoswki (1987) "non-tariff barriers are all public regulations and government practices that introduce unequal treatment for domestic and foreign goods of the same or similar production"[3].

In spite of the existence of a plethora of definitions by several researchers, the most and apparently acceptable one is suggested by

Robert E. Baldwin (1970). In defining NTBs, he says that a non-tariff trade distorting policy is "any measure (public or private) that causes internationally traded goods and services, or resources devoted to the production of the goods and services, to be allocated in such a way as to reduce potential real world income."[4] Though there is no straightforward way to measure the "potential real world income" indirectly one can easily say what is the attainable level of income if the resources are allocated in an economically efficient way.

Productive resources are said to be efficiently allocated if they cannot be distributed in such a way that some individuals will be better off and none will suffer. But one (not the only) set of circumstances that would satisfy the condition of a perfectly competitive free-market structure in the world economy[5]. Trade distorting measures shall be evaluated in terms of world income rather than the income level of any particular nation. By imposing restrictions on imports through higher tariffs, a country may restrain imports and thus encourage domestic production and employment. But, on the other hand, this action will reduce the income and thus employment of the exporters. Therefore, if every country is guided by selfish motivation in trade most (if not all) of the countries will be ultimately poorer due to weak foreign trade multiplier[6].

To define NTBs more precisely and accurately, **Ingo Walter (1969)**[7] opines that in the broadest sense "non-tariff barriers to international trade encompass all private and government policies and practices that serve to distort the volume, commodity composition and direction of trade in goods and services". Though it is a weak proposition as mentioned by himself but the definition gives a fair judgment as to what constitutes the trade distortion. Trade restrictive measures increases product differentiation through changes in styles or advertizing, will reduce imports if it is practised by import competing firms. Most of the economists would not clarify such policies as NTBs because they are not assumed to convey any unfair competitive advantage. But in regard to dumping or predatory pricing, everybody would agree that these practices should be classified as NTBs due to their content. Whatever may be the complexities involved in identifying NTBs, Walter suggests that the measures are taken on the basis of their apparent intention.

Peter Lloyd (1974)[8] defines NTBs in a somewhat different way from Ingo Walter. According to Lloyd, "non-tariff barrier is an omnibus term for the set of government policy instruments and practices which operate directly (or sometimes indirectly) to restrain imports or distort exports." It is conventional to exclude only exchange rate changes and other monetary and fiscal measures which affect exports and import competing goods.

WIDE RANGING FORM OF NTBS AND METHODS OF THEIR MEASUREMENT

II (a) Different Forms of NTBs

In a broader sense, any cost escalating measure apart from customs duties will be treated as non-tariff barriers. Therefore from the definition it is evident to us that non-tariff barriers are a plethora of measures (i.e. priced or non-priced) enforced to restrain free flow of goods. Most of these measures are government sanctioned policies and practices which distort free movement of goods and services except some qualifications. Ingo Walter (1972) proposed that NTBs broadly encompasses all private and government policies and practices that distort the volume, commodities composition or direction of the trade in goods and services[9]. GATT has so far identified 800 variants or so of wide ranging NTBs, based mainly on bureaucratic technical regulation,[10] the number of which has been ever increasing. Apart from some well known NTBs (like quota, licensing and procurement policies) there are other labyrinthine NTBs which are more apparent and effective in distorting trade of developing countries in which they have comparative advantage. **Kessing**[11] has made an effort to categories the entire gamut of NTBs. According to **Kessing Schema**, there are three broad categories of NTBs. These are :

First : Quantitative restrictions (both exports and imports)
Second : Subsidies to domestic supplies (both on exports and imports)
Third : Cost imposed on imports.

Under each category, there are several reported NTBs.

1. Quantitative Restriction

(i) Quotas (balance of payment reason, Article XII and XVIII)
(ii) Discretionary Licensing of Imports
(iii) Voluntary Export Restraints (VERs)
(iv) Safeguard Measure (GATT Article XIX)

2. Subsidies to Domestic Supplies

(i) Rebates

(ii) Subsidized Credit
(iii) Resale Arrangements
(iv) Insurance Guarantees
(v) Production subsidy including expenditure on R&D

3. **Cost Imposed on Imported Goods**
(i) Surveillance Schemes
(ii) Custom Valuation Practices
(iii) Advance Deposit Scheme (ADS)
(iv) Health and Safety Requirements
(v) Variable Levies
(vi) Lengthy Paper Work
(vii) Cost imposed on imports by fighting legal skirmishes
(viii) Anti-Dumping Legislation

R.E. Baldwin (1970)[12] has prepared another nomenclature of NTBs which is presented below:

(i) Quantitative restrictions (i.e. quotas and restricted state-trading practices.
(ii) Export Subsidies (i.e. taxes and countervailing duties)
(iii) Discretionary Government and Private Procurement Policies
(iv) Selective Indirect Tax and Border Tax Adjustment
(v) Selective Domestic Subsidies and Aid
(vi) Restrictive Custom Practices
(vii) Anti-Dumping Regulation
(viii) Restrictive administrative and technical regulations. (It includes safety regulations for machinery and vehicles, health regulation concerning foods, plants, pharmaceutical products, trade mark and patent rules).
(ix) Restrictive business practices which includes collusions among products of the different countries for the purpose of sharing market prices.
(x) Control over foreign investment which includes local discrimination against foreign owned firms; home government's control over foreign investment and regulation of international monopolistic action that reduce world income.
(xi) Restrictive immigration policies, control over movement of labour among countries can distort trade just as restriction on capital movement.
(xii) Restrictive monetary controls and discriminatory exchange rate policies which includes the regulation which directs that importers must deposit with the customs authorities for six months, the equivalent of 50 per cent of the value of the imported goods. Such a scheme also exists in Japan and in many LDCs.

UNCTAD (1983)[13] has prepared an inventory of NTBs on the basis of information received from its 108 members. According to UNCTAD Scheme, product specific non-tariff measures (i.e. NTBs are applied on a particular product, irrespective of its origin) are grouped into five broad categories depending on their method of operation : fiscal measure, volume restraining measure, import authorization, measure to control price levels and a miscellaneous group of restrictions. Separate records are also maintained by UNCTAD for measures like state trading, general entry and exit control procedures, or foreign exchange controls that influence the general level of imports. The UNCTAD classification scheme for non-tariff trade control measures of a product specific nature is described below :

1. **Fiscal Measures**

1.1	Import Specific Charges
1.1.1	Tariffs
1.1.1.1	Tariffs with quota
1.1.1.1.1	Ad valorem tariffs with quota
1.1.1.1.2	Specific tariff with quota
1.1.1.1.3	Combined tariff with quota
1.1.1.2	Seasonal quota
1.1.1.2.1	Seasonal ad valorem tariff
1.1.1.2.2	Seasonal specific tariff
1.1.1.2.3	Seasonal combined tariff
1.1.1.3	Ad valorem tariff with specific minimum
1.1.2	Changes applied on the basis of declared value
1.1.2.1	Ad valorem charges
1.1.2.2	Specific charges
1.1.2.3	Combined charges
1.1.3	Charges applied on the basis of declared value
1.1.3.1	Variable import duties
1.1.3.1.1	Variable levies
1.1.3.1.2	Variable components
1.1.3.2	Transaction specific charges
1.1.3.2.1	Countervailing duties
1.1.3.2.2	Anti-dumping duties
1.2	Product specific taxes
1.2.3	Combined taxes

2. **Value Restraining Measures**

2.1	Prohibition
2.1.1	Total Prohibition

2.1.1.1	Prohibition of a general nature
2.1.1.2	Health and safety prohibition
2.1.1.3	Wildlife Prohibition
2.1.1.4	Prohibition (Censorship)
2.1.1.5	Seasonal Prohibition
2.1.2	Conditional Prohibition
2.1.2.1	General conditional prohibition
2.1.2.2	Prohibition on basis or origin
2.1.2.3	Prohibition (except certain purchases)
2.1.2.3.1	State monopoly of imports
2.1.2.3.2	Sole importing agency
2.1.2.4	Prohibition for certain use
2.1.3	Quota
2.1.3.1	General quota
2.1.3.2	Global quota
2.1.3.3	Quota by country
2.1.3.4	Seasonal quota
2.1.3.5	Voluntary export restraints

3. **Import Authorization**

3.1	Non-automatic authorization
3.1.1	Authorization to control entry
3.1.1.1	Discretionary authorization
3.1.1.1.1	General import authorization
3.1.1.1.2	Discretionary licensing
3.1.1.1.3	Automatic licensing
3.1.1.1.4	Declaration with visa
3.1.1.1.5	Select Purchaser authorization
3.1.1.1.6	Import permit required
3.1.1.2	Conditional import authorization
3.1.1.2.1	Export dependent authorization
3.1.1.2.2	Supply dependent authorisation
3.1.1.2.3	Dependent on domestic purchase
3.1.1.2.4	Dependent on foreign financing
3.1.2	Authorization to control standard compliance
3.1.2.1	Health and safety authorization required
3.1.2.2	Technical standard authorization required
3.1.2.3	Censorship authorization required
3.2	Automatic authorization
3.2.1	Licence for surveillance purposes
3.2.2	Liberal licensing

3.2.3 Automatic licensing
3.2.4 Declaration with visa requirement
3.2.5 Intra-community surveillance system

4. **Control of the Price Level**

4.1 Minimum prices
4.1.1 Minimum general import price requirement
4.1.2 Reference import price requirement
4.1.3 Basic impor price requirement
4.2 Trigger price system
4.2.1 Anti-dumping investigation
4.2.2 Countervailing duty investigation
4.3 Price surveillance
4.3.1 Price surveillance system

5. **Other Measures**

5.1 Technical requirements
5.1.1 Health and safety regulations
5.1.2 Technical standard
5.1.3 Marking and packaging requirement
5.2 Measures to assist import competition production
5.2.1 Production subsidies
5.2.1.1 Subsidy to material inputs
5.2.2 Subsidies to labour
5.2.3 Subsidies to capital
5.2.3.1 Investment grants
5.2.3.2 Research & Development grants
5.2.3.3 Product specific accelerated depreciation
5.2.4 Product specific tax concession
5.9 Other important measures
5.9.1 Multifibre Arrangement (MFA)
5.9.1.1 MFA Quota
5.9.1.2 MFA consultation level
5.9.1.3 MFA export control
5.9.2 Additional customs formalities
5.9.3 Import deposits

Survey of the Existing Work

The problems of non-tariff barriers were not addressed properly in the Kennedy Round of multilateral trade negotiations (1963-67) though the NTBs have been existing since early 1960s through the enunciation of EC's Common Agricultural Programme (CAP) under whose banner all agricultural imports into the EC have been subject to the EC's variable levies. Kennedy Round basically dealt with the reduction of tariffs and completely ignored the gravity of NTBs in distorting world trade though they reached some consensus on anti-dumping code. Prior to Kennedy Round negotiations were made on different aspects of NTBs, but they failed to reach definite conclusions[14].

Like the earlier rounds of negotiations, Tokyo round[15] also emphasized reduction of tariffs rather than removal or reduction non-tariff barriers. The entire range of studies that have been conducted during this period basically aim to estimate the effects of tariff reduction on trade flows. All the studies have been subdivided into two groups. One was ex-post analyses based on post-Tokyo round liberalization and second was ex-ante studies, i.e. estimating the effects before liberalization took place. Apart from the above mentioned ones, five other studies are available showing the impact of Tokyo round tariff reductions on the export of developing countries. All the studies that have been done so far are on the basis of post Kennedy round tariffs reductions but formulae and coverages vary among different studies.

Cline's (1985)[16] country coverage included mainly **US, Japan, EEC, Canada** and seven smaller industrial countries along with LDCs. On the other hand **Baldwin's** (1975)[17] study concentrated on **US only,** but included bilateral balances with the nine EC countries and selected other EC countries. **Stone** (1977)[18] dealt with the US, EEC and Japan, whereas **Baldwin** and **Murray** (1977)[19] were concerned with the LDCs exports but they had considered US, EEC and Japan as importing countries. **Stern's** (1976)[20] study was unique in the sense that it was based on the general equilibrium framework with the (18) countries which were considered having closed system. **Cline** (1985)[21] used a (1000) tariff line items but **Baldwin** and **Murray**[22] had covered hundred commodity groups. **Stern** and **Stone** (1976)[23] used broader index categories. All these five studies dealt with the effect of tariff reductions on trade flows of the manufacturing sector based on post-Kennedy round tariff rates.

Ingo Walter (1971)[24] launched a study with a view to estimating the impact of DCs, NTBs on the exports of LDCs. Two conclusions emerged from his study, viz. (i) most of the NTBs were enforced by developed countries on the exports of developing countries, and (ii)

NTBs were imposed on items where LDC's competition was much higher than its developed counterpart. Similar to his predecessors **(Yeats (1979)[25], Cline and Baldwin),** he categorized the entire gamut of NTBs into three groups. The main findings in his studies are as follows :

(i) In 1968, 20.9 per cent of the developed countries' imports from the developing countries was subject to former's NTBs. In respect of coverage ratio, Japan was the highest (58.4 per cent) followed by USA (37.9 per cent), France (23.5 per cent) and U.K. (13.9 per cent) respectively.

(ii) A total of 44.3 per cent of US imports of manufactures and semi-manufactures were covered by NTBs, of which 66.9 per cent coming from developing countries. The corresponding figures in case of UK were 13.9 per cent and 9.6 per cent, in case of Japan, these were 35.6 per cent and 57.7 per cent, for FRG and France the respective figures were 18.0 per cent and 10.6 per cent and 43.8 per cent and 72.7 per cent.

(iii) It was observed from his study that the intensity of application of NTBs appeared to have a positive correlation with the competitive strength (1) of developing countries in respect of manufactures and semi-manufactures. The Spearman rank correlation between the variables was 0.2317 which was statistically significant at the 0.95 per cent to level of confidence.

On the basis of UNCTAD inventory on NTBs, **World Bank** has done a study with the leadership of A. Olechoswki (1986)[26] in order to address:

(a) What is the prevalence of major NTBs to imports of industrialized countries?
(b) Whether this phenomenon has increased in recent times, and
(c) How much imports from developing countries are succeptible to these NTBs enforced by developed market economies?

The World Bank study has shown the coverage and frequency ratios of imports of developed countries exposed to NTBs. It has developed **three indices. First** one is based on the value of each country's own imports of particular commodity (as well as exports), the **second one** is the world trade value of these items, and **third one** is the number of flows of these commodities. The first one is the **own import coverage ratio (Ic)** which measures the sum of the values of a country's import group affected by NTBs over the total value of its imports of that group. The **world coverage ratio (Iw)** for each commodity imported by a country measures the sum of the value of world trade of an import group affected by NTBs of these countries. The **frequency ratio (If)** is the number of country's import flows covered by NTBs and this sum divided by the total number of import flows for that country.

For calculating these three ratios for any importer (i) and type of non-tariff barriers (b), let Nqx =1, if there is a barrier on imports of the commodity q, from exporters x, and = O otherwise. For sets of commodities (Q) and exporters (X) all three indices take the form as follows:

$$I = \frac{\sum_{q \in Q} \sum_{x \in X} W_{qx} N_{qx}}{\sum_{q \in Q} \sum_{x \in X} W_{qx}}$$

The authors define Wqx differently for each ratio.

(i) **Ic** defines **Wqx** as the value of i's actual imports of q from X.

(ii) **Iw** for each of the commodities q imported by i, defines Wqx as the value of world imports of q aggregated across all exporters.

(iii) **If** defines **Wqx** as the presence of a flow of q from x to i, thus **Wqx** = 1 if imports of q from X are subject to NTBs and Q equals to Zero (0) otherwise.

The world bank study has come across four conclusions which are as follows:

Firstly, The extent of NTBs is varied and wide ranging. At least 27 per cent of the total imports of 16 major industrial countries (around $ 230 billion in 1981) was covered by one or more selected NTBs as they applied in 1983 and in case of manufactured goods it was 13 per cent during the same period. France, FRG, Australia, Switzerland, Austria, USA, Netherlands and Benelux are some of the major protectionist countries. NTBs are wide spread on some of the agricultural products, textiles and clothing, mineral fuel and iron and steel.

Secondly, Quantitative restrictions appear to be the single most important NTBs that seem to have more trade distorting effects than price control. QR is 8.6 per cent of all NTBs, of own imports (i.e. 27 per cent in Ic). Though monitoring measures attain the highest percentage (i.e. 14.8 per cent) of all NTBs, followed by quantitative import restriction (8.6 per cent) QR mainly applies on agricultural imports.

Thirdly, In 1983, imports worth of $ 86 billion by developed countries from the developing world were subject to NTBs which was $ 79 billion in case of developed countries.

Fourth The study provides ample evidence that use of NTBs has proliferated in the successive periods. From 1981 to 1983, there had been a net increase of 248 NTBs covering imports of $ 12.8 billion in 1981. Since this increase does not reflect the tightening or reinforcement of existing measures, the growth of NTBs and their effect on international trade should be taken very seriously.

Alexander J Yeats (1979)[27] made a significant contribution in measurement of non-tariff barriers. Using UNCTAD Inventory on NTBs and applying UNCTAD inventory approach, he had shown that 34.7 per cent of India's total exports to the EC, the USA and Japan was covered by NTBs in 1974. Yeat's study was basically meant to see the total exports of developing countries exposed to NTBs enforced by USA, Japan and the EC. Yeats had shown the coverage and frequency ratio of NTBs applied by developed countries on its imports from developing countries.

UNCTAD Inventory Approach[28] is nothing but the index of frequency of application of NTBs and its coverage ratio. One measure derived from the NTB inventories is frequency index showing the per cent of tariff lines in major product groups covered by the non-tariff restraints. Frequency measure (Fj) is defined as :

$$Fj = Nr/Nj \times 100$$

Where 'Nr' is the number of commodities subject to reported NTBs in a given product class, and 'Nj' is the total number of commodities in that class. A second was to assess the important of NTBs in the protectionist profiles of various countries and estimate the proportion of total imports in each commodity group subject to restraints. The NTB coverage measure (Cj) is defined as :

$$Cj = Mr/Mj \times 100$$

Where 'Mr' is the value of imports in each commodity group subject to NTBs and 'Mj' represents the total value of imports in product group j.

The measure suffers from the problem that, any "own trade weighted" index in that product facing very restrictive NTBs, will extend the calculation with zero or low weights. The index is therefore downward biased. Since it fails to account for the most trade restrictive NTBs. An alternative to weighing the coverage of national non-tariff measures by country's own imports would be to employ

OECD trade weights.

The measure is defined as :

$$Oj = Mr.W/Mj.W$$

Where 'MrW' represents the sum of OECD imports to the country which applies its NTBs, while 'MjW' indicates the total OECD imports of commodity. The formula employed in estimating the ad valorem incidence of the NTBs (Bj)

$$Bj = Pdj/Pwj - Nj + Tj - 1.0$$

Where Pdj & Pwj are domestic and international prices for commodities prices, Nj is the nominal tariff, Tj is the estimated ad valorem incidence of various taxes.

In another World Bank Study **Sam Laird and Alexander J. Yeats**[29] (1990) have developed an index to measure the extent of NTBs which is closer to UNCTAD inventory approach. One such measure is a frequency index (Fj) showing the percentage of transactions (i.e. imports of a tariff line product from a given country) covered by pre-selected group of NTBs.

$$Fj = (\Sigma å DiNi / Ni) \times 100$$

Where 'Ni' is the transaction 'i', 'Di' is a dummy variable that takes a value of unit if one or more NTB is applied to this transaction (or zero otherwise) and 'Ni' is the total number of transactions in the product group. Given that matched trade data are also available in which individual countries of origin for shipment are identified. A second index showing the share of total imports subject to NTMS can also be computed. This trade coverage measure (Cj) is defined as:

$$Cj = ((\Sigma Di, t-m \; X \; Vi, t-n) / \Sigma Vi, t-n) \times 100$$

Where Vi, 't-n' represents the value of imports in tariff-line item 'i' in year (t-n), and Di t-m is a dummy variable that takes a value of unity if an NTB is applied to the item in year 'm' and zero otherwise. If 'n' and 'm' are zero, the index is based on current trade values, otherwise it is expressed in base year trade weights. Holding 'n' constant and varying 'm' will measure the effect of changes in protection with constant trade weights. In that analysis they have used current year trade weights (i.e. m=n) given the major structural changes that occured in the developed countries over 1966-86. On the basis of their study they have reached three conclusions, viz.[30]

First, it is revealed from the study that in 1966, NTBs affected 25 per cent of developed countries' imports which increased to 48 per cent in 1986. In value terms, $ 30 billion of OECD countries' imports were affected by NTBs in 1966 ($100 bn in 1986 prices) which was $ 356 billion in 1986. The latter figure corresponds to a trade coverage of $ 205 billion while multilateral trade organizations like GATT and UNCTAD have been endeavouring to remove barriers to trade through the reduction of tariffs. At the same time, protectionism in favour of NTBs greatly expanded and in many cases have offset the benefits of liberalized import duties.

Second, spread of NTBs has been uneven across countries and industrial sectors. Study shows that the EC is the most protectionist country in the world according to coverage ratio which is due to the extension of Common Agricultural Policy (CAP) to new products. On the other hand, United States and Japan have registered same NTB growth (below average). But the most disquieting feature is that recently USA and Japan have introduced variable import levies on their agricultural imports similar to that of the EC and Sweden. Textiles, clothing, foodstuffs and ferrous metals were the four major areas where NTBs applied most extensively during 1966-86.

Third, during the last 20 years (i.e. 1966-86) there have been a proliferation of discriminatory NTBs like VER (particularly in the USA) resulting in a significantly higher share of trade affected by NTBs than suggested by commonly used trade coverage ratios.

Stern (1976)[31] has developed a general equilibrium model for estimating the impact of trade barriers. In his model, he has considered 18 industrial countries as a closed system (no LDCs) with 22 tradable and 7 non-tradable items. The full system incorporates 6000 equations and finally it is reduced to 39 equations. **Stern et al** (1976)[32] assumes a uniform worldwide price for each of tradable commodities according to global mainstream. They have developed a system of 22 equations to determine prices plus 17 equations determining exchange rates among the 18 countries by means of which the world price for each commodity is converted with home currency price. The (Simulation) equations are not given within each country. There is a sub-system of about a dozen equations. In addition, there are several overall balancing equations for each commodity over all countries and for each country over all commodities. The main elements included in the evaluation of this procedure are as follows:

(a) Reliability of the parameters (e.g. elasticities obtained elsewhere, Stern's source is different from Cline.

(b) Evaluation of the model itself.

The general equilibrium nature of the model explains the results that shows concentration occurring in the non-traded good industries —a result that should be taken as a long run effect. An assessment of the model requires the 39 equations which are not given. However, the assumption of the law of one price (worldwide) each commodity embodied in the study has been challenged in host of studies.

IIb2 Some Econometric Methods of Measurement of Non-Tariff Barriers

Non-tariff barriers can be classified into two categories: One is the quantitative restrictions barring any direct cost escalating measure and the second one is the various types of para-tariff measures apart from nominal customs tariffs, which have direct impact on cost escalation. The entire premises of theoretical studies on non-tariff barriers is based on some strong assumptions (1971)[33]. These are :

- *(i)* The analysis is based on deterministic and partial equilibrium basis.
- *(ii)* This is a static analysis of "tariff and subsidies" affecting trade.
- *(iii)* Production at home is perfectly competitive.
- *(iv)* The production structure is vertically integrated
- *(v)* Elasticity of foreign supply curve is highly elastic
- *(vi)* Size of the country is small in affecting international trade.
- *(vii)* Single homogeneous product produced at home and import.
- *(viii)* Exchange rate is given.
- *(ix)* Imports are residuals of the domestic production because price is the same for all cases.
- *(x)* Money income remains constant
- *(xi)* Non-tariffs and tariffs have the same trend i.e. increase in non-tariffs means increase in tariffs and vis-a-vis.

The impact of non-tariff barriers on domestic demand, supply, cost, output as well as foreign demand and supply, the elasticities of demand and supply both in domestic as well as foreign countries, and the redistribution effects are shown in the following figure.

In the figure supply curve of imports is highly elastic i.e. SS′, demand curve for domestic good is DD and supply curve of the domestic import competitive production is HH. Domestic demand for the production is DD which is also the demand curve for imports and domestic production. Initially OA was produced at home and consumption was OB, the rest i.e. AB amount of goods were imported. This was free-trade scenario.

FIGURE

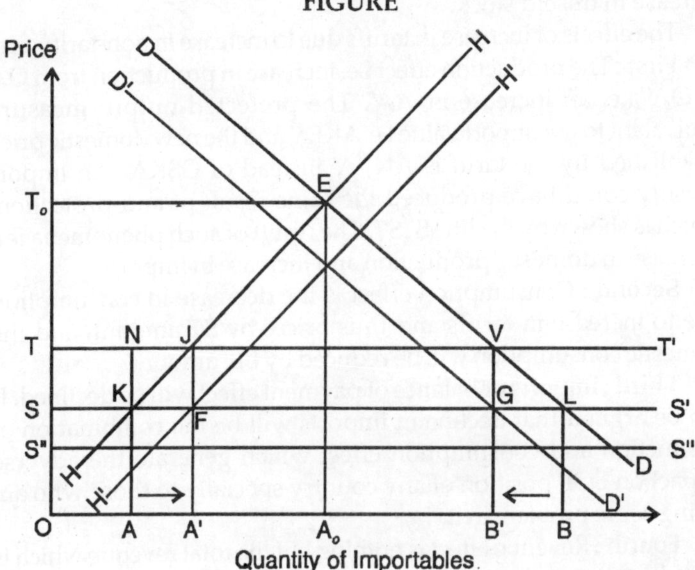

Now NTBs are imposed by ST/OS i.e., at the ad valorem rate not the specific tariff, the implication of which may be different in certain cases. When price of import declines income generation from ad valorem tariffs will be lower than the unit specific tariffs. If tariff is imposed at ST/OS rate, than price of the domestically produced goods increases at the same rate of OT. If tariff is S″T / OS″ then there will be same effects. At first, price of the products will be increased from OS to OT. Second, due to increase in the price of domestically produced goods, the producer will enhance their production from OA to OA′ and consumption will be declined from OB to OB′, due to increase in price. Thirdly; demand for imports will be declined from AA′ to BB′ (in the production effect and consumption effect). Value of imports will be declined by AKFA′ and B′GLB (i.e. production effect AKFA′ and consumption effect B′GLB). As a result of increase in customs tariff, customs revenue will increase by FJVG. Since tariff is higher, it eliminates imports, and a time will appear when tariff will be TO. In that situation production will be OAO and consumption will be OAO also, and then there would not be any import. Therefore, it is simply the rate of tariff which eliminates imports. If the tariff further increases than the equilibrium position, production will be greater than the consumption which leads to increase in unsold stock.

The effects of increase in tariffs due to increase in non-tariffs are:

First : The production effect i.e. increase in production from OA to OA′ i.e. an increase in AA′. The protected output measure equivalent to the import value i.e. AKFA′ and the new domestic price established by the tariff is ANJ′A′ instead of OSKA. An import subsidy could have produced the same result of anti-protection, which is shown by the line S″S″. The result of such phenomena is a decrease in domestic production and increase in imports.

Second : Consumption effect is the decrease in consumption due to increase in tariffs and thus prices by ST amount, and the domestic consumption will be reduced by BB′ amount.

Third : Imports or balance of payment effect will be declined. It can be argued that decline in imports will be the combination of production and consumption effect which generate the adverse impact on BOP position of any country specially to those who are facing acute problem in it.

Fourth : Revenue effect is nothing but the total revenue which is raised by the authority through the increase in tariffs. The only revenue that government can earn is the customs revenue which is equal to tariffs imposed on imported goods.

Fifth : Regarding redistribution effect, of the increase in NTBs/TBs and thus prices, the price of the domestic production will be escalated at the cost of customers. As price rises, domestic producers will increase their supply from OA to OA' by shifting of supply curve from HH to H′H′ i.e. in the downward direction as a result of increase in tariffs. Demand for imports will be shifted to left ward from DD to D′D′ and demand for import will be declined by BB′. Therefore it is clearly seen from the figure that a rise in income due to increase in price due to higher tariffs and non-tariffs, will be enjoyed by the domestic producers. This profit is in excess of normal profit which is regarded as the quota profit that will be enjoyed by the producers. If the producers are in a perfectly competitive situation then it will be shared among them but if they are monopolists, then the entire profit will be enjoyed by the monopolist only. Therefore, the distribution of income due to higher tariff will go in favour of producers against consumers.

Tariff is imposed on imports by ST\OS amount which increases the price from OS to OT. The output has increased from OA to OA′. As a matter of fact, this excess output is subsidized by the consumer on domestic producers, the amount of which is STJF, called as the subsidy equivalent. Since no subsidy is paid by the government the entire amount of which is borne by the consumers. Henceforth, consumers pay in two ways, one is the direct payment to the producers which is called subsidy equivalent, another mode of payment is indirect i.e. in the form of customs revenue which is paid by the customers to the government (i.e. FJVG). Therefore consumers' payment is the combination of STJF (subsidy equivalent) and FJVG (customs revenue) which is equal to STVGT.

Measurement of NTBs can either be specific to particular known NTBs, or it can be generally, designed to capture the net effects of all NTBs together. The study of non-tariff barriers (NTBs) is a vast subject, therefore the methodologies of measurement of NTBs are also of different types suited for particular purpose. Among several methods, two have received wide acceptance among the researchers. One is the general approach which estimates the impact of NTBs through quantity-oriented regression model of trade flows, and other one is the NTB-specific approach which provides an information about the specific NTBs in a particular industry. As these two approaches have considerable amount of merits and demerits, yet they have contributed significantly to the measurement of the impact of NTBs in distorting international trade flow. Therefore, in our present context we will discuss the merits and demerits of both approaches.

On the one hand, under more formal approach, NTB-specific approach provides inputs into a general trade flow regression model, and, on the other hand, in the quantity oriented regression model one can see the change in quantity of exports before/after the enforcement of NTBs. General type of approach has advantages over NTB-specific approach. In spite of that fact it has several disadvantages also :

(i) The direct approach only considers those NTBs that have been identified but is indifferent to a particular type of NTBs that is used by industry.

(ii) Even if the NTBs are included, it is extremely difficult to process the diverse direct information that is available on each in a way that will be comparable across NTBs and then permit them to be added up to obtain a total measure of trade interference.

(iii) In case of presence of more than one NTBs in a given industry, it is understood that presence of one NTBs will reduce the effects of another so that an analysis of each of them separately may lead to an over-statement of their total effects.

Though the direct approach is based on static deterministic and partial equilibrium, yet in evaluating overall levels of protection, general equilibrium effect is bound to matter, such as the effect of barrier for one sector of trade to another and the effect of all together on exchange rates etc. Therefore, in spite of having so many advantages it does not provide a good starting point for a general type analysis. Fortunately, there has emerged a host of studies in general approach which have bypassed such difficulties.

The various general methodologies of measuring the impact of NTBs are classified as follows:

1. Frequency Type of Measurement
2. Price Impact Measures
3. Quantity Impact Measures
4. Elasticity Estimation
5. Estimation of the determinants of variation in elasticity estimates.
6. Estimation of the variation in effect on estimates NTBs over time.
7. Estimates of the binding of NTBs
8. Estimating the risk characteristic of NTBs.
9. Estimating the effects of rent seeking

1. Frequency Type Measures

The information relating to frequency of application of NTBs can only be available from UNCTAD/GATT. The UNCTAD/GATT has been preparing an inventory on NTBs since mid 70's on the basis of complaints of the member countries. With the help of such information it is possible to build up unweighted and trade weighted measures of NTB frequency using the detailed inventory listing of NTBs maintained by UNCTAD/GATT (1974)[34].

a) Survey Evidence

US Tariff Commission (1974)[35] had classified the entire gamut of NTBs into 46 sub-sectors spread among 5 major groups of NTBs. A survey was conducted by US trading firms to elicit information on the experience and complaints they had about particular NTBs. Frequency distributions were then prepared for all NTBs covered and according to each type, country and commodity group.

b) Country / Commodity coverage, unweighted

UNCTAD has been preparing inventory containing information on NTBs enforced by the industrial countries on their imports from developing countries. Based on such data **Ingo Walter** (1972)[36], **Walter and Chung** (1972)[37] and **Yeats (1979)**[38] merged the individual products w h 1-digit and 2-digit SIT commodity groups that were subject to some identifiable NTBs in each major industrialised country. The number of products subject to NTBs was then expressed as a percentage of the total number of products included in each SITC groups.

c) Country/Commodity coverage weighted

Using the same source, the value of imports of each commodity subject to NTBs was aggregated by SITC commodity group and expressed as a percentage of the total value of imports in each SITC group. The weights were based on own country imports and total OECD imports for each SITC group.

2. Price Impact Measures

As already mentioned that NTBs have significant impact on domestic prices, in comparison to some reference (international) prices. Price impact is the basic property of NTBs which one should take into account, and such price comparison can pick up net effect of all NTBs that are present in a market without it being necessary for the investigator to identify what these NTBs are. In the actual world it is impossible to observe the prices before and after the enforcement of NTBs. Instead, actual measures of NTBs have focussed on a comparison of the domestic and foreign prices in the presence of NTBs[39].

Let P' 1 and P1 be the domestic and foreign prices and letting upper-case letters represent the prices themselves as opposed to their logarithms, these price comparisons are normally reported either as price relatives.

$$R = P'_1 / P_1 \times 100$$

as a percentage difference between the prices, comparable to a tariff

$$T = (P'_1 - P_1) / P_1 \times 100$$

which is on the other hand nothing but the "nominal tariff" an "implicit tariff". Implicit protection or "tariff equivalent". But in real world, it is very difficult to do price comparison of the same goods because in most of the cases imported goods are not identical to the domestic goods in respect of different qualities and grades of products. Instead one should employ price of the closest domestic goods as a proxy for P'1 while P1 should be the CIF invoice price of foreign goods facing the NTBs inclusive of tariffs and any special taxes. In some products like steel, cement or some agricultural goods, it is possible to make price comparison. Another problem of price comparison is that it does not include the transport cost inside the country. Domestic wholesale prices are recorded at the nearest consuming centers whereas border prices are normally compiled as ports of entry. In order to avoid such problems let us construct another set of indices on the basis of the following variables :

- Pds : the prices of the domestic substitutes for the imported goods
- Pdi : the prices on the domestic market of the imported goods itself
- Pd : the prices of the goods on the domestic market independently of whose it was produced; thus an index of Pds and Pdi.
- Pi : the invoice price of the imported goods as paid by the domestic importer to the foreign exporter but inclusive of tariffs and transport cost.
- Px : the invoice price received by an exporter of the goods from the domestic country exclusive of transport cost and export tax, if any.

In addition to all these domestic prices there have been also comparable prices for the other countries which is marked with an asterisk (*) or with a country subscript. The "implicit tariff' rate may accordingly be calculated from the formula given above for T, but using Pd and Pi as the relevant price.

$$\mathbf{IT^1 = (Pd - Pi) / Pi \times 100}$$

This is a valid measure of NTBs but it has serious flaw because of its limitation to incorporate information about the apparent substitutability between domestic and foreign goods. In case the invoices of imports are also available, the alternative is made to do with the domestic prices only, but taken from a variety of country.

$$\mathbf{IT^2 = (Pd - Pd)^* / Pd^* \times 100}$$

Here Pd* may be either the domestic price in a particular foreign exporting country where the measure may be of bilateral NTBs or it may be the minimum observable domestic price among all foreign exporters. But if domestic and foreign prices are exactly substitute then it would be the most valid method of measurement otherwise complexities may arise. However, this method of measurement is even subject to error from substitutability. In addition there exists a basic difference between these two measures, IT^2 which includes transport cost while IT^1 does not **(Baldwin 1975)**[40]

3. Quantity Impact Measure

Quantity impact measure is the alternative to price impact measure of an NTBs which mainly shows how the quantum of exports of any country get reduced due to enforcement of NTBs. In a study **Jagar & Lanjouw (1977)**[41] have empirically shown that quantity measure is preferable to price measure in the sense that *cetris peribus*, it will show the movement of quantity of exports due to NTBs which is difficult to cover in the price measure through "tariff equivalence". It would be difficult to find out the relationship between price effect and quantity effects because of elasticities of demand, domestic and foreign supply. Rather, if we know the movement of a particular NTB, then we can build up time-series cross-country and cross-commodity econometric model of the imports that they cover and thus to estimate what would be the impact in absence of such NTBs. But this is NTB specific approach not NTBs as a whole.

But the general type of approach has certain limitations. Before ensuring about the quantum impact of NTBs i.e. to estimate that trade would have been in the absence of NTBs and to compare this with the situation when actually it does occur, one should build up a satisfactory export function model specifying the determinants of trade and for the sake of convenience we should have ***cetris peribus*** assumption and the trading regime would be approximately free. With a view to build up such an econometric model of quantity-impact of non-tariff barriers, **Leamer and Stern (1970)**[42] have built up a single equation export function model where the explanatory variables are country's GNP, resource endowments, utility structure and trade resistance factors which could also be used as indicators of comparative advantage of production and exports as well. The equation stands like this :

$$X = f(Y, R, U, TR)$$

Where X = Quantity of exports
R = Resource endowments
U = Utility structure
TR = Trade resistance
Y = GNP

Existing literature on NTBs shows that ample studies are available showing the quantity impact of NTBs not of a specific nature. All these studies have clearly depicted in **Deardorff's** (1982)[43] analysis. The entire gamut of studies on general type of NTB can be categorized into two broad groups. One is based on Heckescher Ohlin type of analysis and another is ad-hoc study. All econometric analysis on NTBs are based on three different lines of empirical analysis. Some of them follow Heckescher Ohlin (H-O) line of approach in international trade and third one follows the gravity flow analysis.

R.E. Baldwin (1971)[44] has presented his empirical analysis on the basis of single equation export function model where he regressed a country's net trade across commodities with a view to measure the intensity of the various primary factors required for the production of these commodities. A second empirical analysis of H-O type is presented by **Leamer(1974)**[45] who runs separate regression for each commodity across countries where explanatory variables are different factor endowments and trade resistance factor such as distance between the two countries as a proxy to the cost of production.

Finally, a third line of approach is the gravity flow analysis presented by **Tinbergen (1962)**[46]. In the Tinbergen analysis explanatory variables are country size and trade resistance variables such as distance. In the gravity flow analysis of the impact of NTBs, the supply of exports of a country depends on its economic size i.e. GNP, the absorptive capacity for imports is determined by the size of country's market (i.e. GNP of the importing country and the volume of trade will depend on transportation costs which are determined by the distance between two countries. In all the above mentioned econometric analysis, NTBs are treated either as the residuals from the regressions or by using dummy variables.

Saxenhouse (1983)[47] has made an attempt analogous to **Leamer** to determine whether the factors influencing Japan's foreign trade are distinctive in comparison with the other major countries. Following H-O framework he assumes technology and preferences are identical and time-invariant across the countries. His empirical presentation is based on a time-series and cross-section of countries and products covering 109 internationally traded commodities in 1959, 1962, 1964, 1967, 1969, 1971 and 1973 for nine countries (viz. Japan, USA, Canada, France, Germany, Italy, Netherland, UK and South Korea). In his single equation model, explanatory variables include national endowments of directly productive capital stock, labour, educational attainment, petroleum resources, iron ore, resources and cultivable land as well as a measure of distance to approximate the role of transport costs as an impediment to trade. Separate regressions are run for each commodity and includes a set of country-specific dummy variables taken to be time invariant.

The second example of H-O type analysis is the work done by **McCulloch and Hilton (1983)**[48] which is analogous to Baldwin. In their model they have regressed certain bilateral trade flows across commodities on variables which serve to determine bilateral comparative costs. Their model has taken bilateral ratios of exports to imports for 296 industries in explaining US trade with eight major trading partners. They have also followed the H-O framework where they have explained the phenomenon that relative costs between regions are related to factor value shares and relative differences in factor prices for specific commodities (industries). The value shares were calculated from 1970 US census and 1972 input-output ratio for five endowment variables, unskilled labour, skilled labour, capital, land and natural resources. Separate cross-section regression were calculated for the export-import ratios and value shares for the US vis-a-vis Canada, France, West Germany, Italy, Japan, UK, East Asia and South Asia.

In order to find out the extent of non-tariff barriers, the predicted trade ratios were then compared to the actual ratios at the industry level and a large divergence between them was the first hand evidence of the existence of non-tariff barriers. Thus, the residuals from these regressions provide the basis for estimates of NTBs for each commodity and country pair. Using the value of 2.0 to place bounds on the estimated trade ratios, about two-thirds of the actual ratios fell within this range. In about 20 per cent of the cases the export/import ratio was below the range indicating US "under performance" and then "possibility" that NTBs resulted in the US, exporting less and importing more or both in these industries.

Roningen (1978) study is very important in the sense that we can extend this model to include comprehensive NTB frequency and coverage indices as explanatory variables. Such approach could overcome some of the major shortcomings of the IMF restrictive information. The **Roningen**[49] model is the extension of Saxenhouse & McCulloch, where the latter's model reflected the departure from comparative advantage and thus to identify industries and countries in which trade intervention may possibly diminish or augment trade performance. Roningen estimates a cross-section model of bilateral trade flows on an annual basis for 1967-73 for aggregate trade for the 14 major OECD countries. His explanatory variables for the exporting and importing countries include GDP to reflect economic size, area to reflect the potential size of the domestic and foreign sectors, distance to reflect the impediments to trade from cost point of view and dummy variable to reflect preferential trading arrangements and common language. A general index of restrictiveness of each country exchange, payments and trade regime was constructed based on the number of country restriction listed on the IMF Annual Report on export restrictions. Separate indices were also constructed for the three major types of restrictions.

The entire gamut of quantity impact analysis is not immune from flaws. The drawbacks are as follows:

First : If the NTBs are measured as departure of trade from what the included variables can explain; there is a tremendous burden on the model used to explain trade. Indeed, the worse is the model of trade flows the greater will be the estimate of NTBs, thus suggesting a considerable upward bias in their estimation.

Second : It is argued that the theoretical trade models like as H-O are only capable of determining patterns of trade in an average sense and are not adequate to the task of predicting trade exactly in particular industries and countries. Thus a departure of actual trade from what is predicted by a regression model may only reflect this indeterminacy and not the presence of NTBs.

Third : These approaches can only work for comparisons among industries or countries; they cannot tell us for the world as a whole, how far it departs from the free trade. If NTBs restrict trade everywhere that may be "explained" by the constant term in the regression equation and not show up in the residuals of co-efficient of dummy variables.

4. Elasticity Estimation

We have shown in our theoretical analysis that elasticity of import demand curve shifts leftward (i.e. gets reduced) if NTBs are imposed on the importable. The extent of NTBs can be measured from the degree of reduction of import elasticity of demand. The reduction may be both in the aggregate or individual commodities/ sectors using data from several countries and interactive dummy variables in order to determine how these elasticities may differ across countries. This should provide an indication of the extent to which the price responsiveness of import demand is reduced by NTBs in some countries in its coverage since it would include even cultural barriers and other institutional factors that may restrict trade.

5. Variation in Elasticity Estimates

Many studies are available to estimate the import demand elasticities. **Stern, Francis and Schumacher (1976)**[50] and **Goldstein and Khan** (1984)[51] have done a good literature survey on different elasticities (both exports and imports) in international trade. The magnitude of elasticities varies between different countries and industries. It might be feasible to take recourse to regression methods to explain the variations in these estimates in terms of country and industry characteristics. The regression residuals would then provide another estimate of how the price responsiveness departs from what it would otherwise be, presumably again because of the existence generally of NTBs.

6. Effects of NTBs over time

All the theoretical analysis related to non-tariff barriers are based on certain demand and supply conditions. This is based on *cetris peribus* assumption. But incidentally, if such conditions (demand and supply) change due to an indigenous or exogenous factor, keeping the NTBs intact, then the effects of NTBs are expected to be altered. If any one is interested to see these effects over time, it will be worthwhile to repeat any one of the methods mentioned above for seven successive years. The same thing is applicable if the NTBs themselves are to change over time[52].

7. Binding of NTBs

It is equally important to know how restrictions are binding and how they vary over time including their probable impacts on trade flows. With a view to getting answers to such questions one has to calculate either the permitted or potential level of imports and then comparing this with actual imports. The comparisons will be significant in so far as the effects of NTBs will surely depend on whether the they are fully or partially binding or not binding at all[53].

8. Risk characteristics of NTBs

It has increasingly been visualized that since the last decade, developed countries have been taken recourse to increasing amount of administered protection. Trading firms have been confronted with the uncertain NTBs that may appear at any moment of time. As a sequel to that, firms are inclined to do comprehensive insurance coverage to face the uncertainty arising out of unpredictable NTBs. Naturally, cost escalation due to insurance coverage to combat with the uncertain NTBs would be termed as cost due to risk characteristics of NTBs[54].

9. Effects of Rent Seeking

Anne Kruger (1974)[55] has done pioneering work in this area focussing attention on the possible costs in the form of wasted resources that might be incurred in competing for the rents arising from import licensing. Based on the theoretical grounds, she argues that the resources waste would equal to value of rent itself and thus she used estimates of rents as extent of rent seeking. Her calculations suggested that the rents totaled as much as 7.3 per cent of Indian national income in 1964 and 15 per cent of Turkey's GNP in 1968. The Indian estimate was based on the assumption that domestic value of Indian imports was 75 per cent above this value on world market in 1964. This was very much a "conservative estimate" of the government Report, but, in fact, import licenses were worth 100 to 500 per cent of their face value.

Kruger's work has been important in changing the way of thinking as how to estimate the cost of trade barriers. Bhagwati & Srinivasan (1980) have done similar type of theoretical analysis of estimating cost of trade barriers other than quota. Besides Kruger's work of calculating rents that are implicit in various NTBs, hardly any significant work is available to measure directly the rent seeking activities themselves, in order to evaluate the theoretical argument that their value should equal the rents.

Instead, there have been a host of contradictory arguments which state that rents themselves overstates the true cost due to rent seeking. **Bhagwati (1982)**[56] in his argument says that rent seeking inevitably takes place in what is already second best world, and, therefore, even if the resources are used unproductively, could conceivably be beneficial. Bhagwati accepts the assumption that rent seeking equals rent, but shows that it may nonetheless be desirable. **Varian (1982)**[57] has raised a very fundamental question about the validity of assumption that the rent seeking equals the rent. He opines that the supply conditions associated with the rents should take account of free rider problems among the rent seekers, effects on and distortions in related markets, distributional considerations as to who pays and receives the rents and direct transfers to the providers of rents. At least one aspect is clear from the above study that a careful and detailed analysis of specific cases must be carried out in order to determine the extent to which observed quota rents may constitute social costs.

EC-SPECIFIC NTBs

Due to its internal political compulsions, the EC has become one of the most protectionist countries in the world. It has enforced labyrinthine non-transparent barriers to its imports from developing countries with a view to restricting cheaper flow of imports on the ground of market disruption. GATT and UNCTAD have prepared inventory on NTBs identifying the major types enforced by developed contracting parties on its import from rest of the world in general and developing countries in particular. This information is based on the reports of affected parties. The particular allegation of application of NTBs against any contracting party is referred to UNCTAD documents in which the measure has been ratified and which may be referred further details as necessary[58].

The inventory prepared by the UNCTAD contains information on tariff treatment and NTBs applicable to products of interest to developing countries into 11 developed countries' markets. The tables contained in the inventory provide comprehensive information on tariff treatment, trade data and information on NTB on products of interest to developing countries into eleven Developed Market Economies (DMEs). Here, we will mention some of the selected NTBs enforced by European Communities on its imports from developing contracting parties. This is based on the UNCTAD inventory on tariff treatment and non-tariff measures applicable in European Communities to selected products of interest to developing contracting parties applied in 1984. It is assumed that NTBs enforced in 1984 have been applicable thereafter also.

Name of the EC-specific NTBs, corresponding UNCTAD/GATT articles and referees to UNCTAD/GATT documents are shown below[59]:

Name of the NTBs with ***enforcing contracting party***	*GATT Article*	*Reference to* ***GATT documents***
1. State Trading (Spain)	Article XVII	NTM/W/6/R.3
2. Import Levy (EEC)	Article XXIV	AG/FOR/EEC/1
3. Certificates (EEC)	Licensing Procedure	AG/FOR/EEC/1
4. Currency Regulation (EEC)	—	-do-
5. Voluntary Restraint Agreement (EEC)	—	-do-
6. Supplementary Amounts (EEC)	Article XXIV	-do-
7. Non-Automatic Licensing (Spain)	—	NTM/W/6/R.3
8. Licensing (France)	—	-do-
9. Seasonal Restriction (Belgium-Luxm. Denmark, and Ireland)	—	-do-
10. Restriction (France, Greece, Portugal)	—	-do-
11. Quota (Germany, F.R)	—	-do-
12. Restriction (Bel.-Lux., France, Greece, Portugal)	—	-do-
13. Seasonal Restrictions (Denmark)	—	-do-
14. Prohibition for sweet potatoes (EEC)	Article XIX	NTM/W/6/R.3
15. Global Quota (UK)	—	-do-
16. Compensatory Amount (EEC)	Article XIX	AG/FOR/EEC/1
17. Restrictions (BLX, DNK, FRA, FRG, IRL. ITA PRT, GBR)	From non-members	NTM/W/6/R.3
18. Quota (FRA) (EX)	—	NTM/W/6/R.3

Name of the NTBs with enforcing contracting party	*GATT Article*	*Reference to GATT documents*
19. Variable Components (EEC)	Article XIV	AG/FOR/EEC/1
20. Additional duty on sugar (EEC)	Up to 31.12.1992	NTM/W/6/R.3
21. Global Quota (Spain)	—	NTM/W/6/R.3
22. Turnover Tax (ITA)	—	NTM/INV/VEO
23. Government Procurement (Belgium, Denmark, Luxembourg)	USA (Notifying country)	NTM/INV/ I.C.67.11
24. Import Substitution (Ireland)	USA	NTM/INV/ I.D.O.I
25. Issuance of insufficient no. of permits to transport the goods	Czechoslovakia	NTM/INV/I.D.I.
26. Imposition of anti-dumping or Countervailing Duties (EEC)	Korea	NTM/INV/I.A.42
27. Rules of Origin (EEC)	Canada	NTM/INV/II.D.I
28. Customs Formalities (Italy)	Czechoslovakia	NTM/INV/H.G.3
29. Limitation of Entry Point (Italy)	Poland	NTM/INV/II.G.4
30. Technical Visas (France)	U.S.A.	NTM/INV/III.A.3
31. Restrictive Import Licensing (French)	Australia & New Zealand	NTM/INV/ IV.A.36
32. Requirement of prior Import Permit (Greece)	Hungary IV.A.45	NTM/INV/
33. Global Quota (Greece)	Hungary	NTM/INV/ IV.A.47
34. Inappropriate Registration of the utilization	Hungary of Import Quota (Ha)	NTM/INV/ IV.4.5.4.1
35. Case-by-Case Licensing (Italy)	Hungary	NTM/INV/ IV.A.53
36. Compulsory use of French language in transaction and importation	Phillipines	NTM/INV/ IV.KG.1
37. Advance Deposit (Greece)	Hungary	NTM/INV/V.A.2

Name of the NTBs with ***enforcing contracting party***	*GATT Article*	*Reference to* ***GATT documents***
38. Drawback System (Greece)	Hungary	NTM/INV/V.A.3
39. Advance Cost Deposit (Greece)	Japan and USA	NTM/INV/V.4
40. Administrative Duty (Italy)	Brazil	NTM/INV/V.B.II
41. Limit on term of Credit (Greece)	USA	NTM/INV/V.D.4
42. Transmission Tax (Belgium & Luxembourg)	Brazil	NTM/INV/V.E.12
43. Value-Added Tax (Denmark)	USA	NTM/INV/V.E.13
44. Value-added Tax (Germany, F.R.)	Brazil	NTM/INV/V.E.14
45. Luxury Tax, Consumption Tax (Greece)	USA	NTM/INV/V.E.16
46. Anti-Dumping Measures on Consumption Goods Ceramics (EEC)	Czechoslovakia	NTM/INV/II.4.43
47. Import Licensing and Quota on certain textile fibers, textiles and made-up articles (Berlin)	Argentina, Brazil & USA	NTM/INV/IV.A.23
48. Licensing and Quota on Textile and Jewellery (France)	Argentina, Hong Kong, Australia, Japan, Korea, USA and Uruguay	NTM/INV/IV.A.36
49. Licensing and Discriminatory Restrictions (Greece) on Textiles	Canada, Japan Poland, USA	NTM/INV/IV.A.41
50. Licensing, quota, import restriction on textiles (Ireland)	Australia, Hong Kong, Japan & USA	NTM/INV/IV.A.48
51. Discriminatory Import Restriction (Ireland) in certain hosiery and footwear	-do-	-do-

52. Mark of Origin on 300 Industrial Products (UK)	Brazil and Japan	NTM/INV/IV.K.6
53. Turnover Tax on all non-essential items (Netherlands)	Brazil	NTM/INV/V.E.20

FEAR RELATIVE TO "FORTRESS EUROPE"

The EC is now set to remove all internal barriers to trade through the elimination of customs duties and letting free movement of goods, services, capital and labour across the border. The dismantling of customs duties and quantitative restrictions (QRs) to trade among the Common Market countries was accomplished in July 1968, one-and-a-half-years ahead of the original schedule. The irreversible removal of trade barriers contributed to a more than six-fold increase of intra-EC trade in the 12-year period following the ratification of the Treaty of Rome. Imports from the non-member countries increased less than three times, intra-area trade has accounted for one-half of the total imports of the EC countries as against less than one-third at the time of Common Market was created. The share of imports from partner countries increased roughly two-and-a-half times (from 4.8 to 12.4 per cent) between 1958 to 1970 while the share of imports from non-member countries rose by one-third only (from 6.4 per cent to 8.7 per cent)[60].

The economic integration or "Fortress Europe" has some distinct impacts on several aspects of economic activities., viz.

(i) The Effect of "Union" on Employment

One of the most important aspects of the economic union is its influence on employment policy. The main obstacle to effective employment policy in western Europe is the latter's great dependence of foreign trade which would accentuate further due to increase in intra-Community trade as a result of relaxing the barriers. Though achievement of full employment is an important goal of public policy in many European countries, this concept is the main obstacle to economic integration. The only way out of this problem is to frame a concerted employment policy to be monitored by a super national employment authority which is supposed to be the most important goal of the economic union. But this seems to be very difficult to fulfill. By any chance, if this condition fulfills, then it would become easier for West European countries to maintain a stable employment policy without getting into balance of payment problem because it would reduce its dependence on trade with other non-European countries.

(ii) The Effect of Integration on Productivity

The economic integration would certainly enhance the average productivity of labour. The productivity increase is expressed in three ways: viz.

- *(i)* Integration will cause people to change their behaviour and producers to change their methods of production.
- *(ii)* It will cause a reallocation of production and resources among different producers, and
- *(iii)* It will change the volume, nature and direction of investment.

The first two are short-run effects; and the one is a long run effect - long run in the sense that taking more time to come through and requiring more far reaching and thorough-going integration.

(iii) The Effect of Integration on Methods of Production

It is very difficult to measure the economic effect of integration to the method of production. But the most probable effect on productivity of the change in public policy, social and economic institutions and human attitudes, likely to be brought about by close economic, social and intellectual contacts. Though there are glaring contrasts among the different EC countries in respect of tax systems, social services, industrial and commercial practices as well as in the workers' aspirations and work habits, the engineers' imagination and initiative, and the businessman's enterprise, drive and awareness of market opportunities. Fierce competition in the production is the result of economic integration. There will be a large scale production by exploiting the economies of scale. The scale economy is only feasible by changing the method of production from labour intensity to capital intensity.

(iv) The Effect of Integration on the Allocation of Output

A reallocation of output tending to increase international trade and specialization among the Union members is perhaps the main effect that pure theory would attribute to economic union. But in case of the EC, this effect is likely to be neither very great nor very important.

(v) The Effect of Integration on Investment

Though the impact of integration on investment is not prominent, in the short run, in the long run economic integration certainly extended its influence on the volume and pattern of investment. Little is known about the probable effect of economic union on the volume of investment. A common western European market may attract a large inflow of American capital, especially if its establishment discourages the importation of goods from the United States. As to the availability of domestic capital, integration may effect savings either way. By increasing competition and lowering prices, integration might diminish inequalities of income and thus lower the propensity to save, but the effect of this on the volume of savings may be offset if integration is thorough-going enough to increase employment and price stability as well as people's confidence in stability.

Though the EC has been in the customs union since July 1966 and also has made much progress in liberalizing internal economy catering to the successful operation of the Single European Market, (SEM), but even now it continues to erect a labyrinthine of tariff and non-tariff barriers against non-member countries. Unless the EC launches a special programme to dismantle all such anomalies, it will be much more difficult to eliminate various national quotas on imports, especially in sensitive sectors such as cars and textiles, similarly without the renewed efforts to remove the trade-distorting effects of technical regulations and standards, third country exporters would not have the benefit of being able to produce according to one harmonized standard. Local content requirement would be much stricter, even presently the European subsidiaries of third country companies should only be granted an equal right if access to public contract in the EC, atleast 50 per cent of the input value comes from within the company.[61]

"Fortress" Europe

The EC's trade policy is still a hybrid between Community and the national measures. Because at the national level still there has been quantitative restrictions on trade. Most of these residual restrictions were allowed to be retained, for a limited period, under special permission granted under the GATT in 1955, what is referred to as "Hard Core Waiver" (Brian Hinlay 1989)[62]. These quotas are clearly in violation of article XI of the GATT which demands the removal of QRs. As against this, the EC offers MFN facilities to the Developing Countries which means non-discriminatory to a particular country in all Trade Policy Matter[63]. The Community has offered to remove the majority of quota in order to meet the "rollback" obligation as agreed during the Uruguay Round.

The ECs protectionism is characterized by numerous bilateral agreements restraining exports potentiality of developing countries to the EC market. About a quarter of all export restraint arrangements registered by the GATT Secretariat, ranging from voluntary self restraint via orderly marketing arrangements to market. Most of the significant example of this type of protection is MFA agreement under which entire exports of textiles and garment is controlled by a series of national quotas. Internationalization of European Community is unlikely to remove all such protectionist measures. Rather it is feared that negative effects of the SEM will aggravate export prospects of non-member countries and feares have also been expressed that there has been an increase in the average duration of protective measures, and the range of products subjected to protection has broadened. (Spianger 1989)[64]. Moreover, member countries with a relatively high level of protection have been demanding Community-level substitute solutions to replace their own national prospective measures in "sensitive areas". The EC Commission's representatives speak of hard core of a small number of products in respect of which particular economic difficulties in a number of member countries need regulations (for a limited period and on a declining scale) by the Community (H.G. Kvenzer, 1988)[65].

External dimension of SEM programme is not well thought of as internationalisation. There is no exaggerating the fact that internal liberalisation is not extended to trade with third countries which violates GATT's basic principle of non-discrimination. Though the EC has extended MFN status to developing countries but internalization programme is kept outside of its purview (Koopmann & Schareer, 1989)[66]. But inspite of this fact "Fortress Europe" is not necessarily inconsistent with the general agreement because the latter allows for departures from this rule of non-discrimination within the framework of customs union and free-trade areas, under the conditions laid down in Article-XXIV. As the Community is in a customs union, it is useful to look somewhat closer at this provision, to see which disciplines it imposes on a case of regional integration such as internal market programme.

The most important question now arises to all third world country exporters that whether single European market (SEM) is constructing a Fortress-Europe or not[67]. Though completion of internal market opens new era of liberalization among the members as well as non-members, inspite of this fact, there is no gainsaying the fact that in a number of significant areas the EC becomes more and more protectionist, where the EC does not have any comparative advantage. It is true that the Community has not paid much attention to the external dimension of the internal market for a malicious master plan, which the concept of "Fortress Europe" presupposes, but, in number of cases its protectionist measures have deepened[68]. But, in general, the thrust of the programme is to extend liberalization with internally as well as externally. As Pelkman correctly says that one should compare the results of the internal market programme with what the situation would have been in the absence of this programme[69].

STATUTORY SAFEGUARDS AS AN INCENTIVE FOR PROTECTIONISM, ARTICLE 115 OF THE TREATY OF ROME AND SCOPE OF ITS ABROGATION

Article 115 is an important tool of neoprotectionism of the European Community. Apart from tariffs and other transparent barriers, if the members of the Community think to protect their domestic industry, from cheap imports of the developing countries, then under the shield of "import causes material injury to domestic industry", they can evoke safeguard clause. Under the safeguard clause (GATT Article XIX). The EC member states evoke Article 115, through which they put quantitative restrictions on imports from the non-Community members (Chopra, 1990)[70]. This protective tool has been frequently used by the individual member states. Article 115 EEC Treaty enables a member state to block indirect import of goods stemming from countries outside the Community which have first been imported by another member state and thus helps to preserve the existence of national commercial policies as opposed to a uniform community system (Francis Sarre, 1989)[71].

Besides safeguard clause as adopted by the Community in general to put a cap on imports stemming from the non-Community countries, there has been a provision of intra-Community safeguard clause which can block indirect imports from one member state to another. The legal basis of this safeguard mechanism is the Article 115 EEC Treaty. The essence of this treaty is that any good originating outside the Community acquire Community status when brought into free circulations in one of the member states. This means *interalia*, that these are no longer subject to QRs or measures moving equivalent effect within the Community. But this policy is applicable, if the EEC adopts a common commercial policy. In practice, if the member states choose to retain individual quotas for certain goods originating in third countries, then it would be easy just to import those goods via a member state which does not impose similar external restrictions. In such a situation one can evoke Article 115, which basically means pampering national commercial policy measures where trade deflection occurs and when differences in these measures lead to economic difficulties. Under condition laid down in Decision 87/433 of 22 July 1987[72], taken by the Commission implementing Article 115, a member state can apply to the Commission for authorization to introduce either protective measures or intra-Community surveillance measures to monitor the flow of indirect imports. Such measures usually consist of the Community allowing member states not to apply Community treatment to the goods concerned.

This article is basically meant for restricting imports from Eastern European and State trading countries (J. Maslen, 1984)[73]. The rationale behind this is it is presumed that price structure of state trading and Eastern European countries is not market determined. In most of the cases this is administered one, and price structure is often non-transparent. Since pricing is administered, there is enough reason to believe that these economies can sell its products at much less price and its cost actually incurred. Therefore to restrict such type of underpricing, and save domestic industry from imports at price less than cost of production, the Community frequently uses Article 115 under the shield of Safeguard Clause.

In this connection, we can mention to Community regulations which specifically govern trade between EC and state-trading countries: 1) Regulation 1765/82 which contains a list of imports not subject to quantitative restrictions, and ii) Regulation 3420/83[74] which governs the products and liberalized at Community.level. Besides the two above mentioned basic regulations dealing with the state trading countries, there has also been a separate general regulation governing the distribution of imported textiles from outside the Community. The import regime of these goods is governed by Regulation 4136/86. This is a very complex regulation covering the administration of subgroups which have been the deviation from global Community quota agreed upon with the various parties to the Multifibre Arrangements (MFA) under the auspices of GATT.

The application of Article 115 is most prolific in textiles covered under MFA. India has considerable interest in this area because almost entire amount of her exports of textiles and garments to the Community markets has been under stringent quantitative restrictions. This Article empowers European Community as a whole as well as member states to put restrictions on imports of textiles from India. With the help of Article 115, member states also fix quota according to its need, independent of the EC decisions. Apart from textiles, India does not have to worry in other line of exports. This is because Article 115 is specially designed for restricting imports from state trading countries, not the other market economies where prices are determined by market for us. Frequency of application of Art. 115 shows that in most of the times it has been evoked against the state trading countries.

Textiles is the most affected category susceptible to Community Safeguard clause evoked through Article 115 (P. Vogeienzang, 1981[75]). Textile sector is very weak in Europe and that is why it is given excessive protection. For example, in 1987, out of 12 requests granted 10 were concerned with textiles[76]. India has concluded bilateral agreement with the European Community on textiles. EC has fixed textile quota to India annually. But, in fact, the quotas agreed upon in the bilateral agreement, were subsequently divided up among the member states and administered by Community regulations. The fact that the Community itself has assumed competence in this field makes it doubtful whether Article 115 which is designed to protect national commercial policy measure can still be applied. On the other hand the textile products which fall under decisions taken pursuant to Regulations 3420/83 are, in essence, national measures authorized by the Community; therefore, the same uncertainty about their validity does not exist (Timmermans, 1987)[77].

Another major area of concern of Article 115 is the **industrial products**. In industrial products, all the applications for Article 115 involve quotas which have been set pursuant to Regulation 3420/83. As the listed national quotas are mentioned separately for each member state, there can be no doubt that specific Community authorisation as required by the European Court of Justice has been given. However, the Council when setting these quotas must make sure that these quotas will be maintained keeping in mind the objective of single market.

Future of Article 115

Article 115 was specially designed to restrict cheaper imports from the East European countries, not other countries where prices are market determined. The most interesting part is that not all the member states of the European Community have asked for the application of Article 115 with same vigour. Over the years France & Italy have been frequently used Article 115 against the East European states[78]. But the scenario has completely changed. Erstwhile USSR has been disintegrated into CIS and all the socialist economies have been switched over to the capitalist mode of production. Therefore earlier system of administered pricing has now changed to market oriented prices. Therefore justification to evoke Article 115 has come to an end. All Eastern European countries including CIS have introduced capitalist mode of production which means they will allow market force to operate, and they have to compete in the international market in the same way as others. Therefore Article 115 is not redundant and has lost its relevance.

Article 115 may be applied marginally to other third countries for their cheaper exports of textiles to the Community market. According to the Final Act of GATT, all quotas pertaining to textiles are supposed to be over in a ten-year period beginning 1, January, 1995. From 1, January, 2005, textile trade will be quota free and will be integrated with the WTO. Textile trade under WTO regime means, it will be governed by the competitive policy where there will be no barrier barring some exceptional cases. WTO regime promotes price competition rather than state control. State trading system has been completely collapsed. The basic reason for applying Article 115 is no more. East European countries do not have any more state trading system. Even in case of India and other textile exporting countries the basic reason for protection will be over by 2005 when quota system will be completely phased out. Though there is enough provision for enforcing transitional safeguard during transitional period, but it is unlikely that, Article 115 will be used so as a protective measure. The importance of Article 115 as a protective tool is getting evoked and loosing its vigour. Rather other forms of non-tariff barriers are sprouting. These are: social clauses, environmental clauses, echo-labelling, anti-dumping duties etc.

NOTES

1. Nogues, Julio, Andrez Olechowsky and L. Allen Winters, "The Extent of Non-Tariff Barriers in Industrial Countries Imports", in the *World Bank Economic Review* (The World Bank, Washington), Vol.-1, 1986, No. 1, pp. 181-199.
2. UNCTAD (1988a), "*Consideration of the Question of Definition and Methodology Employed in the UNCTAD Data Base on Trade Measures*". (TD/BAC/42/5), (Geneva, UNCTAD).
3. Andrzej, Olechoswki, (1987), "Non-Tariff Barriers of Trade", in J.M. Finger on Andrzej, Olechoswki (eds;), *The Uruguay Round : A Handbook of the Multilateral Trade Negotiations*(The World Bank : Washington). pp.121-6.
4. Baldwin, R.E. "*Non-Tariff Distortions to International Trade*", (Washington, The Brookings Institution) 1970, pp.50.
5. Ibid n. 2. p.51.
6. Ibid n. 2. p.52.
7. *(a)* Walter, Ingo (1969), "Non-Tariff Barriers and the Free Trade Area Option", *Banca Nationale del Lavoro Quarterly Review* (March), pp.16-45.
   (b) Walter, Ingo (1972), "Non-Tariff Protection Among Industrial Countries : Some Preliminary Emperical Evidence", *Economic Internationale* Vol. 55 (May) pp. 335-54
8. Lloyd, Peter (1974), "Strategies for Modifying Non-Tariff Distortions", in Huge Corbell and Robert Jacknson (eds;) *In search of a New World Economic Order* (London, Croon Helm). pp. 199-209
9. Ibid n. 7(b).
10. Hans Joachin Hochstrate and Ralf Zeppennick, "Distortions in World Trade : Recent Development", *Distortions in World Trade* p.10.
11. Kessing, Donald (1967), "Outward Looking Policies and Economic Development", *The Economic Journal*, (Blackwell, Oxford and Cambridge June pp. 235-271.
12. R.E. Baldwin (1970), "*Non-Tariff Distortion in International Trade*", (Washington). The Brooking Institution. (McMillan, London, 1970), pp.11-12.
13. UNCTAD (1983a), "*Non-Tariff Barriers Affecting the Trade of Developing Countries and Transparency in World Trading Conditions*", TD. B-940, (Geneva), UNCTAD, March.
14. *(a)* UNCTAD (1987), "*Problems of Protectionism and Structural Adjustment : Restriction on Trade*", (TD/B/1126/Part-I), *A Report*

by UNCTAD Secretariat, (Geneva), 1987.

(*b*) Balassa, Bela and N.E. Krennin, "Trade Liberalisation under the Kennedy Round : The Static Effects", *The Review of Economics and Statistics*, Vol. 67, (Cambridge Press, 1967), pp. 235-271.

(*c*) Finger, J.M., "Effects of the Kennedy Round Tariff Concessions on the Exports of Developing Countries", *The Economic Journal*, Vol. 67, (Cambridge, 1976), pp. 87-93.

15. Mordechal E. Krennin and Lawarance H. Officer, "Tariff Reduction under the Tokyo Round : A Review of Their Effects on the Trade Flows Employment and Welfare", in *Weltwisstchaftliches Archives* (Hamburg, 1979), pp. 344.

16. (*a*) Cline, William (1985), "Import of Manufacturers from Developing Countries : Performance and Prospects for Market Access", (The Brookings Institution, Washington, 1985).

(*b*) Cline, William (1987), "*The Future of World Trade in Textiles and Apparels*", Institute of International Economies, (McMillan, London), Washington.

(*c*) Cline, W.R., "R Noboru Kawanabe, T.O.M., Kronsjo, and Thomas William (1978) *Trade Negotiations in The Tokyo Round*", *A Quantitative Assessment*, The Brooking Institution, (Washington, 1978).

17. (*a*) Baldwin, R.E., "*Foreign Trade Regime and Economic Development*", (New York National Bureau of Economic Research, 1975).

(*b*) Baldwin, R.E., "*US Tariff Policy : Formation and Effects*" (A Final Report to the office of Foreign Economic Research, Bureau of International Labour Affairs), (Discussion Paper on International Trade, Washington, DC June 1976).

18. Stone, Joe A., "*Price Elasticities and the Effects of Trade Liberalisation for the United States, The EEC and Japan*, (Michigan State University, 1977, Ph. D. Dissertation).

19. Baldwin, Robert, E & Tracy Murray (1977) "MFN Tariff Reduction and Developing Country Benifits Under GSP", *The Economic Journal*, in '87 (March) pp. 30-46.

20. (*a*) Stern, Robert M., (1976), "Evaluating Alternative Tariff Cutting Formulae", *Journal of World Trade and Law* (Geneva), (Jan.-Feb.), pp. 50-64.

(*b*) Stern Robert M., "Evaluating the Consequences of Alternative Policy for Trade Liberalisation in The MTN" *University of Michigan Research Seminar in International Economies, Discussion Paper No. 15*, (Ann Arbor, Michigan), 1977.

21. Ibid n. 16(b).

22. Ibid n. 19

23. Stern, Robert M., & Stone, Joe A., "*Price Elasticity in International Trade*", (London, McMillan Press) 1976.

24. Walter, Ingo (1971), "Non-Tariff Barriers and the Export Performance of Developing Countries", (*American Economic Association Paper and Proceeding* no. 61, May), pp. 195-205.
25. Yeats, Alexander J. (1979), "*Trade Barriers Facing Developing Countries, Commercial Policy Measured and Shipping*", (London, McMillan Press), 1979. pp. 205-220.
26. Nogues, Julis, Adrezej, Olechoswki and L. Allen Winter (1986), "The Extent of Non-Tariff Barriers to Import of Industrial Countries", *The World Bank Economic Review*, (The World Bank, Washington, 1986), pp. 235-271.
27. Ibid n. 25.
28. *(a)* UNCTAD (1983a), "*Non-Tariff Barriers Affecting the Trade of Developing Countries and Transparency in World Trading Conditions : The Controversy of Non-Tariff Barriers* (TD/B/940), Geneva, UNCTAD Publication.
    (b) Laird, Samuel and Alexander J. Yeates, (1986), "*The UNCTAD Trade Policy Simulation Model : A Note on the Methodology, Data and Uses*", UNCTAD Discussion Paper No. 19, (Geneva, UNCTAD). pp. 1-25.
29. *(a)* Sam Laird and Alexander J. Yeates, "Quantitative Methods for Trade-Barriers Analysis, (McMillan, 1990), pp. 20-21.
    (b) Ibid n. 11 p. 116
30. Ibid n. 21 p. 21.
31. Stern, R.M. (1976), "Evaluating Alternative Tariff Cutting Formulae", *Journal of World Trade and Law*, (Geneva), (July-February), pp.50-64.
32. Ibid n. 23.
33. Corden V.M., "*Theory of Protection*", (Oxford University Publication, 1971), pp.5-12.
34. *(a)* Ibid n. 28(a).
    (b) UNCTAD (1974), "*Liberalisation of Non-Tariff Barriers (Inventory of Non-Tariff Barriers)*", Report by the Secretariat, (TD/B/C.2/115/ REV.2), Geneva.
    (c) UNCTAD, "*Reports on Trade, Tariff and Non-Tariff Barriers (Inventory)*", (Several Issues, UNCTAD, Geneva), 1974.
35. US Tariff Commission, "Trade Barriers : An Overview", *TC Publication 665*, (Washington D.C.).
36. Ibid n. 7(b).
39. Deardorff, Allen V. Stern, Robert M. (1985), "*Methods of Measurement of Non-Tariff Barriers*, UNCTAD Working Paper, pp. 1-92
37. Walter and J.W. Chung (1972), "The Pattern of Non-Tariff obstacles to International Market Access, *Weltwirfchaftliches Archieves*. 108 (Hamburg) pp 122-136.
38. Ibid n. 25.
39. Deardorff, Allen V. Stern Robert M. (1985), "*Methods of Measurement*

of Non-Tariff Barriers, UNCTAD Working Paper, pp. 1-92
40. Baldwin, R.E., "*Foreign Trade Regime and Economic Development : The Phillipines*", (New York, National Bureau of Economic Research, 1975), p.99.
41. Jagar, M. and G. J. Lanjouw (1977), "An Alternative Method for Quantifying International Trade Barriers," *Weltwirtschaftliches Archives*, (Hamburg), 113 (Heft 4) pp. 719-40.
42. Leamer, Edward E. and Robert M. Stern, "The Commodity Composition of International Trade in Manufacturers : An Empirical Analysis", *Oxford Economic Paper*, (Oxford, 1974), pp. 350-374.
43. Deardorff, Allen V. (1982), "The General Validity of the Heckscher-Ohlin Theorem", *American Economic Review '72*, (American Economic Association, Nashville), (September), pp. 683-694.
44. Baldwin, Robert E., (1971), "Determinents of the Commodity Structure of U.S. Trade", *American Economic Review '61* (AEA, Nashville), March pp. 126-146.
45. Leamer, Edward E. (1974), "The Commodity Composition of International Trade in Manufacturers : An Empirical Analysis", *Oxford Economic Paper*, (Oxford) pp. 350-374.
46. Tinbergen, Jan. (1962), "*Shaping the World Economy : Suggestion for an International Economic Policy*", (Twentieth Century Fund, Network).
47. Saxenhouse, Gary R. (1983), "A General Equilibrium Model of Trade Structure", in William R. Cline (ed;), *Trade Policy in the 1980s*. (Washington D.C. Institute for International Economics).
48. McCulloch, Rachael and R. Spencer Hilton (1983), "Identifying Non-Tariff Distortion of US Merchandise Trade", *Federal Reserve Bank of New York, Research Paper No. 8310*, (August).
49. Roningen, Vernon O. (1978), "The Effect of Exchange Rate, Payments and Trade Restrictions on the Trade Between OECD Countries 1967-1973", *Review of Economies and Statistics*. (Harvard University, MIT Press, Massachussets) August pp. 471-75.
50. Stern, Robert M. Jonathan Frances and Bruce Schumachar (1976), "*Price Elasticities in International Trade*", (London, McMillan).
51. Goldstein, Morris and Mohsin S. Khan (1984), "Income and Price Effects in Foreign Trade", in Ronald W. Jones and Peter B. Kenen (eds;), *Handbook of International Economic Vol.-II*, (Amsterdum, North Holland).
52. Allen V. Deardorff and Robert M. Stern, "Methods of Measurement of Non-Tariff Barriers", *Institute of Public Policy Discussion Paper No. 203*, (Michigan University Ann Arbor 1984), P. 38.
53. Ibid n. 52. pp.38-39.
54. Ibid n. 52. p. 39.
55. Kruger, Anne (1974), "The Political Economy of the Rent Seeking Society", *American Economic Review*, 64, (AEA, Nashville),

Washington, pp.291-303.

56. Bhagwati, Jagdish (1982), "Directly Unproductive Profit-Seeking (DUP) Activities", *Journal of Political Economy* 90 (October) pp. 988-1002, (University of Chicago Press, Chicago).
57. Varian, Hla R. (1982), "*Analytics of Rent Seeking*".
58. UNCTAD, "*Reports on Trade, Tariff and Non-Tariff Barriers*", (UNCTAD, Geneva), This is UNCTAD Inventory on Tariff and Non-Tariff Barriers. Data Compiled every year for 63 developed and developing countries.
59. The name of the NTBs have been compiled from several UNCTAD publications on NTBs, as well as Tariff and Non-Tariff information of the Non-Tariff Measures (NTM) Division UNCTAD.
60. Ibid n. 59.
61. Robert McDonald, "Lowering the Drawbridge on Fortress Europe", in *Economic Intelligence Unit, European Trends*, (No.1, 1988, P.60), (EIU, London).
62. Brian Hindley, "The Design of Fortress Europe", in *Financial Time*, (London, 6th January, 1989).
63. The main countries affected are Japan, Taiwan, South Korea, and Hong Kong. On the EC's own side, the restriction are concentrated mainly on Italy, France, Greece and the Irish Republic. Cf. George Koopmann : "National Protectionism and Common Trade policy" *Intereconomics*, (Hamburg), May/June 1984, p. 105
64. Dean Spianger, "Building a Fortress Europe in 1992; Some Implications of the Common Internal Market for Hong Kong and other PACRIM Countries", *PRICES Paper no.1*, (Hong Kong and Kiel, 1989), p.13.
65. Cf. Horst G. Kvenzer, "Zwischen Protktionismus & und liberalismus Europaischer Binnenmarnt und Drifflandsbeziehungen, in *Europa-Archiv*. No. 9/1988.p.245.
66. Gorge Koopmann and Hans-Eckart Schareer, "EC Trade Policy Beyond 1992", in *Intereconomics*, (Hamburg) (September/October, 1989), pp. 573-589.
67. For an account of the Fortress Europe debate as it was held from 1988 to 1990 across the Atlantic, see Stphen Woolcock, "Market Access Issue in EC-US Relations; Trading Partners or Trading Blocs" (London, Pinter Publication for the RIIA, 1991), pp. 13-16.
68. "The Community Import Regime for Sensitive Products : Textiles Clothing, Japanese Cars and Bananas", in Piet Eecrhout; *The European Internal Market and International Trade : A Legal Analysis* (Oxford Claridon 1992) pp. 338-373.
69. Ibid no. 68, p. 357.
70. H.S. Chopra, "India and the EC, 1992: New Challenges and Opportunities", *Foreign Trade Review*, (IIFT, New Delhi, Vol. XXV,

No. 3, October/December, 1990), pp.223-231.

71. Francis Sarre, "Article 115 EEC Treaty and Trade with Eastern Europe", *Intereconomics* (Hamburg), September/October, 1999, p. 233.
72. For governing the application, see Commission of the European Communities, "*Official Journal, 1987* (L 23/26, and Commission Decision 87/433), Brussels, 1987 as for the application of the Article 115, see O.J. 1987, L 146/61.
73. J. Maslen, "The European Community's Relation with the State Trading Countries, 1981-83", *Yearbook of European Law*, (Oxford Claredon Press, 1984), pp. 324-345, and see O.J. 1962, L. 195/1 for regulation governing the imports of goods from 11 State Trading Countries except China.71. Francis Sarre, "Article 115 EEC Treaty and Trade with Eastern Europe", *Intereconomics* (Hamburg), September/October, 1999, p. 233.
74. Official Journal 1983, L 346/6 (amended by Regulation 2273/87, O.J. 1987, L 217/1), This regulation also applies to the quantitative restrictions maintained by vis-a-vis China.
75. P. Vogeienzang, "Two aspects of Article 115 EEC Treaty : Its use to Buttress Community-set Sub-Quota, and the Commission Monitoring System", *Common Market Law Review*, 1981, p. 174.
76. Ibid n. 71 pp. 236.
77. C.W.A. Timmermans, "Community Commercial Policy on Textiles : Legal Imbroglio in Protectionism and The European Community", *Deventer*, (Kluwar, 1987), p. 164.
78. lbid n. 71 p. 236.

Chapter 4

EC's Non-Tariff Barriers and their Impacts on Indian Exports

INDO-EC TRADE PATTERN : A TIME SERIES ANALYSIS

1 (a) India's Export Performance to the EC Market

The EC has been India's largest trading partner for more than two decades followed by USA and Japan[1]. The EC's share in India's trade has been growing persistently over the years beginning 1981. In 1980-81, 21.57 per cent of India's total exports were directed towards the European Community, while 21.03 per cent of our total imports came from the EC. Form 21.57 per cent in 1980-81, the share of EC in India's total exports increased to 28.30 per cent in 1992-93, but declined slightly to 26.06 per cent in 1993-94. India's import have also exhibited similar trend. The share of the EC in India's total imports had also jacked up from 21.03 per cent in 1980-81 to 30.18 per cent in 1992-93 and marginally declined to 30.04 per cent in 1993-94[2].

Presently, the EC's contribution to India's trade (both export and imports) is about one-third of the total. Not only the EC's share in India's total trade increased over the years, but the composition of India's exports to the EC has also been diversified significantly. While examining the composition of Indo-EC trade over the years we will discuss this issue in detail. Due to several reasons exports to some member states have been increased disproportionately to others[3].

Let us first see the growth scenario of the EC's **world imports**[4]. In 1981, the EC's total imports were 581 billion the ECUs which increased to 1255 billion ECUs in 1994. The compound growth rate of EC's total imports was 6.09 per cent from 1981 to 1994. The rate varies across from one member state to another. Denmark registered very low growth in imports which was 4.71 per cent during 1981-1994. Growth of imports was the highest in Portugal among all the member states. Portugal (Spain and Portugal became members of the EC in 1986) registered a phenomenal growth of 10.71 per cent during the same period. This was followed by Spain whose imports registered a spectacular growth of 10.68 per cent during the same comparable period. Rate of growth which is mentioned here is expressed in compound terms and formula for calculating the rate is **In Y = a + bt.** Where 'Y' is the imports,'t' is the time, i.e. years, 'a' is the intercept and 'b' is the slope of the equation and 'ln' is the natural log[5]. Almost all member countries have shown higher import growth over the years. In **Table-4.1**, we have shown the EU's (extra) growth of imports from 1992-2002. During this period the EU's import grew at 7.6 per cent rate per annum, which is very high at any standard. Denmark showed the highest import growth of 29 per cent per annum followed by Ireland (14.86 per cent) and Austria (11.89 per cent). For other member states rates of growth of imports vary between 6 and 8 per cent except France and Portugal, whose performance is lacklustre every other member state has shown much higher import growth. Trends of the EU's world imports (extra) from 1992-2002 are shown in **Table 4.1.**[6]

Time series trends of the EU's imports from India (conversely Indian exports to the EU) is shown in **Table-4.2**[7]. Though Euro has been the legal currency in the European Union since January 2000, all the figures given the Eurostat are expressed in terms of European Currency Units (ECUs) i.e. the erstwhile unit of account. Therefore, all the figures in the Indo-EU trade are expressed in terms of ECUs. Apart from showing value of exports, we have also calculated the rate of growth of India's exports to each member state and to the EU as a whole from 1992 to 2002. Since ECUs is a fiat currency, the exchange rate of ECUs is relatively stronger than US dollars. The exchange rates between the EC's ECU, US dollars and Indian rupee are shown in **Table-4.3**[8].

Thus, it is evident from data that our export performance to these two countries (Denmark and Ireland) was extremely lacklustre in spite of having enough potentials[9].

India has so far concluded seven bilateral quota agreements in textiles and garments with the EC, USA, Canada, Norway, Sweden,

TABLE 4.1 : Trend of EU's World Imports (Extra), Value in million ECU's

	1992	*1993*	*1994*	*1995*	*1996*	*1997*	*1998*	*1999*	*2000*	*2001*	*2002*	*Rate of Growth*
France	67866	66622	71622	69774	74319	85665	89062	98274	127469	127717	118217	5.7
Bel-Lux	28685	30872	341292	34263	35635	41020	43563	47710	62361	58028	63750	8.31
Netherlands	46339	42567	53671	52118	57795	69660	73061	86772	115478	112604	109186	8.94
Germany	139167	142828	156611	140521	143503	160446	172418	187667	242987	243002	232189	5.25
Italy	56696	56245	61698	61638	63831	72197	73965	79730	111935	113107	110730	6.92
U.K.	76926	91386	98501	92861	103569	125457	133536	142676	188084	186010	173666	8.48
Ireland	4614	6320	7776	8746	9025	11974	14782	16804	20883	19476	18441	14.86
Denmark	1181	12122	14138	9900	10501	11788	12396	12962	15659	16153	15126	29
Greece	6715	7510	6433	5921	7912	8306	9289	9496	14142	14505	15817	8.94
Portugal	6117	5825	6579	6495	6572	7328	7498	8206	10764	10982	9386	4.37
Spain	29531	25133	27405	27335	29341	34723	35782	39785	56756	56567	56879	6.77
Sweden				15596	16593	18663	18783	20795	28257	24315	23905	6.29
Finland				7884	8596	9937	10080	10435	14210	13306	12800	7.17
Austria				12201	1382315405289		16321	18512	24451	26536	26801	11.89
EU (15)	474536	487428	538628	545253	581015	672568	710538	779825	1033436	1022308	986894	7.59

TABLE 4.2 : Trend of India's Exports to the European Union (Value in Million ECUs)

	1992	*1993*	*1994*	*1995*	*1996*	*1997*	*1998*	*1999*	*2000*	*2001*	*2002*	*Rate of Growth*
France	554	628	747	788	836	957	976	1056	1266	1284	1279	8.72
Bel-Lux	543	709	862	957	1065	1133	1334	1331	1742	1591	1776	12.58
Netherlands	337	410	482	545	611	708	754	760	919	984	1007	11.56
Germany	1245	1592	1748	1833	1976	2002	2046	2021	2292	2358	2354	6.57
Italy	594	697	848	1024	1045	1175	1265	1221	1626	1666	1583	10.3
U.K.	1129	1333	161	1600	1885	2245	2098	2233	2753	2943	2908	9.92
Ireland	23	22	35	59	73	61	68	93	119	131	136	19.45
Denmark	77	90	124	152	150	172	170	173	203	199	213	10.71
Greece	36	43	47	66	90	97	100	94	126	162	189	18.03
Portugal	53	61	68	89	109	127	130	134	170	179	196	13.97
Spain	229	228	258	335	404	457	511	573	748	859	939	15.15
Sweden				152	151	176	169	172	223	232	NA	7.3
Finland				35	43	50	53	53	66	68	NA	11.7
Austria				98	103	95	87	86	97	126	NA	4.27
EU (15)	4819	5813	6834	7734	8540	9455	9771	9999	12351	12784	12984	10.41

* India's exports to the EU means EU's imports from India. Blank spaces means information is not available. Sweden, Finland and Austria became members of EU from 1995

TABLE 4.3 : Exchange Rate of Indian Rupee with ECUs, US$

Year	*Exchange Rate (Rs./ECUs)*	*Exchange Rate (Rs./US$)*
1984	8.87	11.89
1985	9.26	12.24
1986	12.16	12.79
1987	14.14	12.97
1988	16.29	14.48
1989	17.79	16.66
1990	21.99	17.95
1991	27.42	24.52
1992	35.97	24.41
1993	36.55	31.63
1994	37.17	31.40
1995	42.27	33.46
1996*	44.84	35.47
1997	41.29	37.12
1998	45.67	42.08
1999	46.24	43.28
2000	41.51	45.61
2001	42.01	47.53
2002	45.35	48.27

* Exchange rate between Indian Rupees and ECU valid upto 1995. From 1996 onwards these rates are between Rupee and Euro Exchange rates are taken average of the year and the accounting year is financial year instead of calender year eg. 2002 is for the year of 2002-2003.

Source : Commission of the European Union, "Eurostat" for ECU and Euro and for US$ International Monetary Fund, "International Financial Statistics."

Austria and Finland in the beginning of 1971 under the aegis of Multifibre Arrangements (MFA), which expired on 1st January, 1995 when the Final Act of the Uruguay Round became operational. Finland, Sweden and Austria became members of the EU at the same time, naturally since then all bilateral agreements have been dismantled (Rajiv Kumar & Ravi Khanna, 1991)[10]. But the system is relatively more flexible in the case of the EC than United States and other quota countries. The EC is having two types of quantitative restrictions, one is the quota and other is the ceiling. The latter one is more flexible than the former one. If exports exceed the ceiling limit, then until the importing country concludes a new agreement, the old system continues to operate. Though items under quota restrictions are different from the items under ceiling limits, the EC never applies higher tariffs on items exceeding the ceiling limit. This is a significant trade benefit that India has been enjoying in its trade with the EC[11].

Earlier we have mentioned asymmetry in our export performance (i.e. EU's imports from India) to different member states. Against the compound growth of 10.41 per cent of India's total exports to the EU, the rate was highest in the case of Ireland. India's exports to Ireland grew by 19.45 per cent per annum and to Spain it was 19.15 per cent, for Portugal it was 13.97 per cent, to Greece 18.03 per cent during the same period. Compared to smaller countries, India's export performance to the larger member states has been rather somewhat disappointing. If we judge India's export performance by growth rate only, it was below average in the case of Germany (i.e. 6.57 per cent). Rate of growth to France was 8.72 per cent and to UK it was 9.92 per cent respectively during the same period.

Table 4.4 shows that India's share in the EC's total imports has been abnormally low over the years but has been improving later on[12]. In most of the member states, India's share has been stagnating around one per cent (1.0) for the entire period under study. Its share in EC's total imports was 1.02 per cent in 1992, which increased to 1.3 per cent in 2002. It rose to 1.47 per cent in 1996. There may be several reasons as to why Indian share in the EC market has been always at a low level. But the most significant aspect is that it has been increasing since 1981 (Wenston & Cable, 1979)[13]. In spite of having several supply side problems[14], demand side factors are not less important. Factual evidence shows that since mid-seventies the EC has become more protectionist towards India especially in areas of labour intensive goods with less value addition (Yeats, 1979)[15]. The entire gamut of the EC's imports of agricultural goods has been protected by the variable levies under Common Agricultural Programme (CAP) since the sixties (Cline, 1980 & Ian Golden *et al*, 1994)[16]. All imports of textiles and garments have been under stringent quota restrictions since 1961 (Laird & Vassenaar, 1991)[17]. Apart from high tariffs, its market is well-protected by a plethora of non-tariff barriers. Non-transparent barriers hurt more severely than tariff barriers. Higher tariffs can be absorbed through efficient production but non-tariff barriers are difficult to deal with because

TABLE 4.4 : India's Share in EC's Total Imports (Extra)

Countries	*1992*	*1993*	*1994*	*1995*	*1996*	*1997*	*1998*	*1999*	*2000*	*2001*	*2002*
France	0.82	0.94	1.04	1.13	1.12	1.12	1.10	1.07	0.99	1.01	1.08
Bel-Lux	1.89	2.30	0.25	2.79	2.99	2.76	3.06	2.79	2.79	2.74	2.79
Netherlands	0.73	0.96	0.90	1.05	1.06	1.02	1.03	0.88	0.80	0.87	0.92
Germany	0.89	1.11	1.12	1.30	1.38	1.25	1.19	1.08	0.94	0.97	1.01
Italy	1.05	1.24	1.37	1.66	1.64	1.63	1.71	1.53	1.45	1.47	1.43
U.K.	1.47	1.46	0.16	1.72	1.82	1.79	1.57	1.57	1.46	1.58	1.67
Ireland	0.50	0.35	0.45	0.67	0.81	0.51	0.46	0.55	0.57	0.67	0.74
Denmark	6.52	0.74	0.88	1.54	1.43	1.46	1.37	1.33	1.30	1.23	1.41
Greece	0.54	0.57	0.73	1.11	1.14	1.17	1.08	0.99	0.89	1.12	1.19
Portugal	0.87	1.05	1.03	1.37	1.66	1.73	1.73	1.63	1.58	1.63	2.09
Spain	0.78	0.91	0.00	1.23	1.38	1.32	1.43	1.44	1.32	1.52	1.65
Sweden				0.97	0.91	0.94	0.90	0.83	0.79	0.95	NA
Finland				0.44	0.50	0.50	0.53	0.51	0.46	0.51	NA
Austria				.80	0.75	0.00	0.53	0.46	0.40	0.47	NA
EU (15)	1.02	1.19	1.27	1.42	1.47	1.41	1.38	1.28	1.20	1.25	1.30

in most of the cases they are non-transparent. Trade distortionary effects of NTBs are much more prominent than higher tariffs (San Laird, 1995)[18].

Countrywise distribution of share shows that Belgium-Luxembourg tops the list by importing 2.79 per cent of its total imports from India almost every year. **Table-4.4** gives detailed information of India's share in the EC's imports over the years both in average and individual states. Next to Ben-Lux India's share was highest in Portugal where India's contribution was 2.09 per cent of the EU's total imports in 2002. India's share was lowest in the case of Ireland. In 2002, only 0.74 per cent of its total imports came from India. The picture was more or less the same in case of Greece, where India's share was 1.19 per cent of its total imports during the same period. India's share to Portugal's total imports was 2.09 per cent in 2002. Therefore, it is evident that India's shares were relatively less with the smaller countries whereas it was higher in case of larger economies[19]. India's share in Germany's total imports was 1.01 per cent and with France it was 1.08 per cent during the same year. India's share to Italy's total imports was 1.43 per cent and to the Netherlands it was 0.92 per cent respectively during 2002.

From **Table-4.4**, it is also evident that our export performance to some of the EC countries has improved in recent years which is reflected in India's improved share in the markets of these countries. From 1992 to 2002, India's export performance to countries like Belgium, Luxembourg, Germany, Greece, Spain, France, Italy, Netherlands, Portugal and Ireland has improved significantly whereas, on the other hand, it had shown declining trend in case of Denmark only.

1(b) Composition of Indian Exports to the European Community

Since 1986, all products have been codified in Harmonized System (HS) rather than erstwhile CCCN/BTN codes. UNCTAD information on tariff and non-tariff barriers is also available at 8-digit level. While showing the market share of India's exports to the European Union, we have taken commodity groups at 2 digit level[21], and secondly considered three years viz. 1991, 1996 and 2002 and have shown change in India's shares in the EU market.

For analytical purpose, we have again aggregated all groups (based on HS at 2-digit level) into 14 major groups[22]. Here also we have taken three years as mentioned above. The reason being such selection is to compare the relative changes of India's export shares during these periods. Fourteen major groups are as follows:

1. Agriculture and Marine Products
2. Minerals
3. Chemicals
4. Leather and Leather Products
5. Wood, Paper and Board
6. Textiles and Clothing
7. Carpets
8. Umbrellas and Accessories
9. Stone, Ceramics and Glass
10. Gems and Jewellery
11. Engineering and Electronics
12. Sport Goods
13. Arts
14. Miscellaneous[23]

Historical trends of the composition of the India's exports to the European Union show that India has never been a very prominent exporter of hi-tech items. A close look at the composition of her exports reveals that rather she has been exporting primary and labour intensive low value-added manufactured goods. This is the basic feature of India's export pattern to the European Union, in particular western countries in general.[24] Though aggregate trade data reveal that only 10 per cent of the total exports are agriculture and marine products and around 3 percent are primary products composed of minerals, it should not be forgotten that agriculture provides the base of many manufactured goods viz. textiles, tea and coffee.

During 1991, agriculture and marine products was the third largest export group having export share of 13.55 per cent next to textiles and clothing, whose share was 31.88 per cent, followed by leather and leather products having a composite share of 15.04 per cent.

Other important categories in the export basket were gems and jewellery (12.11 per cent) and engineering and electronic items (10.29 per cent). Chemical products had the share of 4.92 per cent and share of mineral export was 4.18 per cent of the total exports. Carpet was anther single largest export item, whose contribution to total export was 4.53 per cent. Shares of other groups were almost non-significant in India's total export basket during 1991.

During 1996, trend remained the same but the relative magnitude of different categories had changed. Share of agriculture and marine products had declined to 11.08 per cent during 1994, increased to 13.44 per cent during 1996. Share of minerals had declined between 1991 and 1996, from 4.18 per cent in 1991 to 3.03 per cent during 1996. Share of chemicals to total exports had increased significantly during these comparable periods from 4.92 per cent to 7.61 per cent. Share of leather and leather products had declined marginally from 15.04 per cent to 13.07 per cent during these periods. Export of textiles and clothing has been showing an upward trend upto 1996 then has started declining. Its share in 1996 increased to 32.02 per cent from 31.88 per cent from 1991 maintaining the upward trend in-between. Other export categories, which have shown significant increase in growth during these periods, are engineering and electronics, whose share increased from 10.29 per cent to 13.96 per cent and wood, paper and paper boards, whose share increased from 0.45 per cent to 0.55 per cent.

At least two product groups whose share have declined significantly during these period are: carpets, gems, and jewellery. Export share of carpet had declined from 4.53 per cent during 1991 to 3.66 per cent during 1996. The rationale behind such declining trend may be attributed to child labour issue. The EU is the strongest votary of child labour issue. Both the EU and USA have been raking up this issue vigorously in all multilateral negotiations under the auspices of WTO. USA was almost on the verge of concluding a multilateral agreement on child labour in the Seattle Ministerial Conference, but it did not materialize simply due to lack of consensus among the developing countries. For quite sometimes, child labour issue in Indian carpet industry becomes very prominent in Germany. As a result, exporters of carpet have to be accredited with RAGMARK and KALEEN from the Indo-German Export Promotion Council in India. Another reason of such sliding trend may be the emergence of new competitors from developing countries like Iran and China[28].

The scenario is completely different during 2002. Share of agriculture and marine products have been declining since 1996 and has declined to 10.01 per cent during 2002. This means India is getting less and less market access in the EU as far as agricultural export is concerned. This is simply because of two reasons. One reason is that the EU agricultural sector is heavily protected by subsidies given in "green box" and "blue box". Historically, the EU has been giving heavy subsidies to protect its farm sector from external competition. The EU puts variable levy under Common

TABLE 4.5 : India's Export Basket to the EU (Percentage Share of Different Product Groups)

	1991	1992	1993	1994	1995	1996	1997	1998	1999	2000	2001	2002
Marine Products	13.55	13.35	12.57	11.08	11.52	13.44	13.23	11.99	11.88	11.78	10.91	10.01
Minerals	4.18	4.08	4.98	3.53	3.28	3.03	2.26	2.11	2.24	2.36	3.03	2.76
Chemicals	4.92	5.7	5.54	6.46	7.22	7.61	8.47	9.06	8.89	9.64	9.56	10.71
Leather & Leather Products	15.04	14.7	15.54	15.08	14.33	13.07	12.79	11.73	11.25	11.19	12.55	11.57
Wood, Paper & Board	0.45	0.48	0.43	0.48	0.49	0.55	0.57	0.56	0.62	0.6	0.62	0.67
Textiles & Clothg.	31.88	33.74	32.24	32.93	34.32	32.02	30.95	30.22	30.3	29.57	29.57	28.25
Carpets	4.53	5.07	5.23	4.13	3.78	3.66	3.64	3.73	3.18	2.65	2.88	2.16
Umbrelas & Acce.	0.02	0.04	0.06	0.75	0.044	0.036	0.052	0.044	0.054	0.058	0.06	0.05
Stone, Ceramics & Glass	0.43	0.52	0.57	0.69	0.86	0.92	1.02	1.1	1.37	1.4	1.53	1.69
Gems & Jewellery	12.11	10.36	11.07	10.33	10.01	9.98	9.99	11.61	11.68	12.24	10.55	12.26
Engineering & Electronics	10.29	10.72	10.27	11.13	12.59	13.96	15.09	16.1	16.28	16.08	16.05	17.14
Sport Goods	0.27	0.32	0.36	0.4	0.43	0.434	0.402	0.45	0.4	0.395	0.384	0.404
Arts	0.08	0.05	0.05	0.03	0.031	0.038	0.068	0.028	0.043	0.022	0.018	0.014
Miscellaneous	0.7	0.87	0.97	1.06	1.08	1.254	1.47	1.63	1.18	2.02	2.3	2.28

Agricultural Programme (CAP), the difference between domestic price and international price. Second reason of getting lower market access in agricultural and marine products in the EU has been the increasing use of standards. Germany is emerging as the most environmental conscious country in the world. EU frequently uses stringent sanitary and phytosanitary standards (SPS) against its import of agricultural items from India. EU is also the votary of using "Precautionary Principle" in all of its imports of agricultural and chemical items. This will have a disastrous impact on India's export of agricultural and mineral products.

Similar to agricultural goods, India's share of minerals has also declined from 4.18 per cent in 1991 to 2.78 per cent during 2002. Share of chemicals has increased tremendously during these comparable periods. Its share was 4.92 per cent during 1991, which skyrocketed to 10.71 per cent during 1996. This shows it is one of the most potential items in Indo-EU trade. Export of engineering and electronic items has shown a significant improvement during this period. Its share was 10.29 per cent in 1991, which phenomenally increased to 17.14 per cent during 2002. Share of leather and leather products has declined from 15.04 per cent to 11.57 per cent during this period.

Most significant aspect of India's export to the EU market has been the gradual declining share of textiles and garments. Nearly one-third of India's exports to the EU market is composed of textiles and garments. And this export pattern has been guided by the quota regime right from the sixties. This was the main constraint of getting better market access to the EU. However, MFA system has been dismantled and will be completely removed from 1 January 2005. EU has started dismantling quota regime from 1 January 1995 since the onset of WTO and has already phased out 51 per cent of the quota items. India could have taken advantage of this quota liberalization. But instead of this, its share has started declining from 1995 and it became lowest in 2002, when its share reduced to 28.25 per cent from 33.74 per cent in 1992. Declining in share may be due to fierce competition arising from other textiles exporting countries like China, Bangladesh, Hong Kong, Pakistan etc. Secondly, most of the quota-free items are not of any interest to India. The phasing out system is highly back loaded. Most sensitive items in India's export basket will be removed from quota only on 1 January 2005 i.e. at the last day of the phase out process. Therefore, India is unlikely to get any benefit from the ongoing quota liberalization, which is also reflected in its share to the EU market. Time series trend in share of India's export to the EU is shown in **Table 4.5.** The values of exports are in ECUs. This is because we have taken the values of EU imports from India instead of India's exports to the European Union.

1(c). Growth of EC's Imports from India: A Sectoral Analysis[30]

At the beginning of this chapter we have analyzed the growth scenario of Indian exports to the EC as a whole and also to its members. Therein we have shown the direction of exports without showing their composition. In such cases problems arise because we cannot identify the potential area of at least HS 2-digit level. Export potentiality of any product is measured in terms of its higher growth (compound), which is absolutely impossible if we consider only total exports[31].

In order to identify some extremely focussed items, one has to judge export performance on the basis of their rate of growth over the years. In this section, we would like to show the compound growth of all items at HS 2-digit level. The market share of major 14 groups has been described in the previous section. Here, we will show the average annual growth rate of all items from 1981 to 1994. Along with the growth of EC's import from India, this table also shows EC's growth of imports from the world as well as from the non-EC countries.

In order to judge the items as potential ones, we have considered the growth parameters rather than market shares. From **Table-4.6,** we have identified items whose rates of growth were more than 10 per cent during 1981-1994. Among 99 broad categories of items at 2-digit level, the items having more then 10 per cent growth in the EC market were fish and crustacean (18.12 per cent), edible fruit and nuts (16.81 per cent), mineral fuels etc. (19.74 per cent), inorganic chemicals (17.83 per cent), pharmaceutical products (12.77 per cent), tanning / dying extract (24.31 per cent), essential oil (13.07 per cent), miscellaneous chemical products (36.0 per cent), plastics (31.71 per cent), leather articles (22.53 per cent), footwear (16.17 per cent), paper (10.24 per cent), silk and waste silk (12.29 per cent), woven garments / AIC (24.42 per cent), stone, cement (16.14 per cent), ceramic products (12.59 per cent), glass and glassware (20.59 per cent), pearls & jewellery (9.61 per cent), articles of iron and steel (61.70 per cent),

TABLE 4.6 : Trends in the EC's Imports Compound Growth Rates 1981-94

CT	*Product Description*	*Imports From World (A)*	*Imports From non-EC (B)*	*Imports From India*
1.	*2.*	*3.*	*4.*	*5.*
Agricultural & Marine PRODUCTS				
1	Live animal	2.61	1.33	-16.76
2	Meat & Edible Meat	4.65	2.34	-27.00
3	Fish & Crustaceans	11.05	11.37	18.12
4	Dairy Products	5.12	1.22	-
5	Prod. of animal origin	4.54	4.00	5.75
6	Live Trees	7.14	8.49	12.95
7	Edible Vegetables	5.33	1.88	3.54
8	Edible fruits and nuts	6.72	4.08	16.81
9	Tea, Coffee etc.	2.14	1.03	3.81
10	Cereals	0.52	-6.17	0.26
11	Malt, Starches etc.	7.31	4.87	1.78
12	Oil seeds etc	2.34	1.83	4.53
13	Lac, Gums etc.	7.08	6.26	3.30
14	Veg. plating material	2.79	2.72	-9.99
15	Animal/Veg. Fats	5.06	2.91	8.43
16	Meats/Fish preparations	5.83	4.66	7.66
17	Sugar, Confectionery	5.89	3.24	7.16
18	Cocoa	5.70	1.89	-3.28
19	Cereal, Flours etc	12.48	11.61	9.64
20	Vegetable, Fruits	7.85	5.17	7.13
21	Misc. Edible prep.	12.72	6.40	14.82
22	Spirits and Vinegar	7.89	3.67	-
23	Waste Food Industries	2.85	1.28	-1.07
24	Tobacco	7.34	6.28	-3.37
MINERALS				
25	Salt, Sulphus etc.	2.87	1.07	18.75
26	Slag, Ores & Ash	0.68	0.21	22.09
27	Mineral Fuels etc.	-3.64	-3.71	19.74
CHEMICALS				
28	Inorganic Chemicals	3.38	2.13	16.83
29	Organic Chemicals	7.70	9.08	9.06
30	Pharmaceutical products	15.31	16.06	12.77

1.	2.	3.	4.	5.
31	Fertilisers	4.60	5.86	-
32	Tanning/dyeing ext.	10.29	10.68	24.31
33	Essential oils	12.84	11.00	13.07
34	Soap etc.	9.92	7.38	11.71
35	Albuminoidal substance	12.81	15.19	16.22
36	Explosives	5.69	7.50	-
37	Photographic goods	6.23	5.83	-7.15
38	Misc. Chem. products	8.27	7.93	36.88
39	Plastics	9.57	11.13	31.71
40	Rubber	7.34	6.62	12.83
LEATHER & LEATHER PRODUCTS				
41	Raw Hides & Skins	7.63	8.35	3.67
42	Leather Articles	8.69	9.85	22.53
43	Artificial Fur etc.	-7.65	-8.80	-6.42
64	Footwear	8.32	10.09	16.17
WOOD, PAPER & BOARD				
44	Wood	5.38	4.88	6.86
45	Cork	7.56	-11.00	-
46	Basketware	3.55	3.12	10.78
47	Pulpwood	3.14	2.05	-
48	Paper	7.70	7.90	10.24
49	Printed Books	7.22	7.43	13.01
TEXTILE & CLOTHING				
50	Silk & Waste Silk	7.60	7.00	12.29
51	Wool, Yarn, Fabric	4.17	9.23	14.40
52	Cotton	9.69	60.22	-
53	Vegetable Fibre	-8.43	-10.86	50.29
54	Man-made Filaments	31.09	37.44	-
55	Man-made Staple Fibre	3.44	-1.00	5.30
56	Wadding, Felt, Non-woven	-3.85	-3.83	4.01
58	Special Woven Fabric	-6.83	-6.90	-16.33
59	Coated Textiles	1.63	1.14	17.62
60	Knitted Fabric	-10.30	-11.77	-2.26
61	Knitted Garment/ACC	6.11	6.21	1.33
62	Woven Garment/ACC	26.30	27.25	24.42
63	Made up textiles	28.70	34.87	-
CARPETS				
57	Carpets	24.19	19.10	16.98
UMBRELLAS & ACCESSORIES				
65	Headgear	10.00	14.03	17.83

1.	2.	3.	4.	5.
66	Umbrellas	9.91	10.59	2.69
67	Feather Articles	12.18	13.42	-
STONE, CERAMICS, GLASS				
68	Stone, Cement	7.16	7.89	16.14
69	Ceramic Product	6.22	6.13	12.59
70	Glass & Glassware	7.91	8.25	20.59
GEMS & JEWELLERY				
71	Pearls, Jewellery	4.08	6.80	9.61
ENGINEERING & ELECTRONICS				
72	Iron & Steel	29.67	18.67	61.70
73	Articles of Iron	-1.57	0.71	18.85
74	Copper & Articles	5.20	4.05	7.92
75	Nickel & Articles	3.34	-2.33	8.37
76	Aluminium & Articles	8.30	10.18	25.73
77	Reserved For Future	-	-	-
78	Lead & Articles	-1.98	-3.53	-
79	Zinc & Articles	6.84	8.63	3.06
80	Tin & Articles	-2.71	-4.51	-
81	Other Base Metals	4.81	5.38	-
82	Tools & Metal Parts	6.35	7.12	9.13
83	Misc. Articles (Base Metal)	7.89	8.14	7.18
84	Nuclear Reactors	9.54	10.32	15.92
85	Electrical Machinery	12.46	13.39	21.18
86	Railways & Tramways	17.20	14.13	-
87	Other Vehicles	9.17	8.35	24.77
88	Aircrafts & Parts	9.03	12.29	44.04
89	Ship, Boats etc.	2.25	4.48	0.75
90	Photographic Apparatus	8.71	8.50	14.00
91	Watch & Clock	6.80	7.57	12.99
92	Musical Instruments	-12.18	-11.70	1.00
93	Arms & Ammunition	4.71	9.60	3.41
MISCELLANEOUS				
94	Furniture etc.	10.26	13.04	25.74
95	Toys, Games etc.	44.99	44.83	21.99
96	Misc. Manu. Articles	25.93	26.27	-
97	Artwork	-3.95	-1.03	-10.44
98	Reserved for special use	7.25	14.12	-
99	Reserved for special use	9.80	9.02	-7.04
	Total	6.09	4.52	12.47

Source : Commission of the European Communities, *Eurostat*, (Several Issues, Brussels).

aluminum and articles (25.75 per cent), nuclear reactors (15.92 per cent), electrical machinery (21.18 per cent), other vehicles (24.77 per cent), aircraft and parts (44.04 per cent), photographic apparatus (14.0 per cent), watch and clock (12.99 per cent), furniture etc. (25.74 per cent) The compound growth of India's exports to the EC was 12.47 per cent during 1981 to 1994.

Out of 99 groups at 2-digit levels, items belonging to 24 groups are of **agricultural and marine products sectors**, of which growth rate more than 10 percent was for 5 groups of items. In the group of **minerals**, there are altogether 3 sub-groups, the growth rate of which was more than 10 per cent in all cases. In **chemicals,** total number of sub-groups were 13, of which export potentiality of 9 groups was higher judged by growth rate more than 10 percent. **Leather and leather products** are divided into 4 sub groups at HS 2-digit level, of which 3 belong to high potential area having growth rate more than 10 per cent. **Wood, paper and books** are put into 6 sub-groups, of which growth rate of more than 10 per cent was for 3.

The group of **textiles and garments** is the most important one in India's export basket[32]. Its potential is quite high in the EC market. . This group is having 14 subgroups, of which growth of export of more than 10 percent is for 5 sub-groups leaving three groups blank due to non-availability of data. Most surprisingly, growth rate of man-made staple fibre was more than 5.3 percent during 1981 to 1994. Export of **carpet** products has also been satisfactory in the EC market because it registered an export growth of 16.98 per cent from 1981 to 1994. The same is true for **umbrella and accessories.** Out of three groups data are available only for two groups, of which one is having rate of growth higher than 10 per cent (i.e.17.83 per cent). **stone, ceramics and glasses** constitute yet another promising group. Growth of export is more than 10 per cent in case of all 3 sub-groups. India is the largest exporter of gems and jewellery in the world next to Belgium, and it is one of the largest importers of diamonds, pearls and different types of gems. Indian export of gems and jewellery grew at 9.61 per cent rate annually in the EC market during 1981 to 1994.

Export of Indian **engineering and electronic** items fares well in the EC market but India's share in that market is extremely low. This group has 22 subgroups in total and all items are basically labour-intensive low value added in nature. If we judge its export performance in terms of growth rates, then out of 22 subgroups,

TABLE 4.7 : Market Shares in the European Community

CT Product Description Share in EC World Imports	Extra EC Share in EC Imports	India's Share in ECs (Extra) Imports	India's Share in EC Extra Imports	Extra EC Share in EC Imports	India's Share in ECs (Extra) Imports	India's Share in EC's Imports	Extra-EU Share in EU Imports	India's Share in EU's (Extra) Imports	India's Share in EU's Total Imports
Product Categories at 2-digit level	*1990*	*1990*	*1990*	*1994*	*1994*	*1994*	*2000*	*2000*	*2000*
1 Live animal	19.94	0.04	0.0080	16.88	0.0037	0.0006	18.33	0.012	0.0023
2 Meat & Edible Meat	16.88	0	0.0004	16.61	0.0066	0.0010	16.11	0.000	0.0000
3 Fish & Crustaceans	57.31	2.09	1.1000	56.85	3.29	1.8800	54.93	2.563	1.4077
4 Dairy Products	7.87	-	-	6.69	0.027	0.0018	6.47	0.338	0.0219
5 Prod. of animal origin	57.60	1.43	0.8200	59.34	1.54	0.9100	54.00	1.674	0.9042
6 Live Trees	13.24	0.58	0.0700	19.69	1.07	0.2100	18.65	1.444	0.2694
7 Edible Vegetables	32.31	0.22	0.0600	30.52	5.32	0.1600	22.52	1.338	0.3014
8 Edible fruit and nuts	50.99	0.88	0.3300	48.14	1.95	0.9400	45.86	2.740	1.2567
9 Tea, Coffee etc.	83.51	3.85	3.2100	80.87	4.89	3.9600	76.77	6.495	4.9867
10 Cereals	17.18	1.86	0.4600	17.51	3.48	0.6100	22.88	5.908	1.3519
11 Malt, Starches etc.	5.79	0.32	0.0190	5.76	0.29	0.0160	4.88	0.625	0.0305
12 Oil seeds etc	62.95	0.68	0.4300	76.59	0.76	0.5800	69.31	1.288	0.8930
13 Lac, Gums etc.	41.66	8.39	-	47.52	9.45	4.4900	47.45	16.480	7.8205
14 Veg. plating material	75.02	2.89	2.1500	78.92	2.79	2.2000	75.44	10.785	8.1365
15 Animal/Veg. Fats	35.12	3.44	1.2600	37.33	2.09	0.7800	33.38	5.681	1.8963
16 Meats/Fish preparations	41.33	0.08	0.0300	44.34	0.23	0.1000	39.44	0.200	0.0789

17 Sugar, Confectionery	37.77	1.94	0.7300	37.4	0.1	0.0400	26.64	1.673	0.4457
18 Cocoa	37.93	0.01	0.0020	34.11	0.04	0.0130	27.74	0.000	0.0001
19 Cereal, Flours etc	8.77	1.07	0.0900	8.81	1.11	0.1000	6.67	0.278	0.0186
20 Vegetable, Fruits	31.24	0.42	0.1300	31.13	0.5	0.1600	29.55	1.331	0.3933
21 Misc. Edible prep.	1.27	0.44	0.0600	11.82	0.9	0.1100	15.83	1.034	0.1636
22 Spirits and Vinegar	8.66	0.06	0.0050	12.35	0.05	0.0060	17.56	0.036	0.0064
23 Waste Food Industries	56.70	2.4	1.3600	56.79	1.84	1.0400	49.80	0.215	0.1073
24 Tobacco	41.43	1.32	0.5400	40.18	1.37	0.5500	29.69	2.671	0.7931
25 Salt, Sulphur etc.	43.49	2.95	1.2800	44.86	5.72	2.5700	43.27	5.945	2.5721
26 Slag, Ores & Ash	77.96	0.77	0.6000	82.08	0.84	0.6700	78.06	0.431	0.3362
27 Mineral Fuels etc.	70.80	0.13	0.0900	72.64	0.09	0.0700	69.51	0.026	0.0179
28 Inorganic Chemicals	34.96	0.29	0.1000	40.01	0.44	0.1800	38.23	0.640	0.2512
29 Organic Chemicals	31.76	0.86	0.2700	34.47	0.17	0.0800	32.84	2.427	0.7970
30 Pharmaceutical products	34.17	0.14	0.0500	35.91	0.1	0.0400	26.40	0.375	0.0991
31 Fertilisers	39.39	0	0.0004	44.58	0.01	0.0050	43.88	0.047	0.0204
32 Tanning/dyeing Ext.	24.98	3.09	0.7600	27.13	4.46	1.2100	23.32	4.914	1.1460
33 Essential oils	19.90	1.48	2.9500	21.72	1.37	0.2900	18.47	1.716	0.3341
34 Soap etc.	14.53	0.1	0.0140	15.43	0.41	0.0600	15.44	0.356	0.0550
35 Albuminoidal substance	17.56	0.12	0.0300	31.88	0.36	0.1100	22.71	0.831	0.1886
36 Explosives	37.18	0.01	0.0040	48.55	0.17	0.0800	60.48	0.352	0.2127
37 Photographic goods	32.58	0.02	0.0070	33.51	0.02	0.0080	30.74	0.045	0.0139
38 Misc. Chem. products	24.29	0.27	0.0600	26.27	0.96	0.2500	26.34	0.729	0.1920
39 Plastics	21.36	0.13	0.0270	24.41	0.29	0.0700	21.74	0.740	0.1609
40 Rubber	29.63	0.17	0.0500	32.39	0.42	0.1300	32.75	0.946	0.3097
41 Raw Hides & Skins	49.35	8.6	4.2500	52.89	6.4	3.2900	49.29	4.831	2,3813
42 Leather Articles	67.01	10.37	6.9400	73.33	14.23	10.4400	69.64	11.739	8.1745

(Contd...)

	1990	*1990*	*1990*	*1994*	*1994*	*1994*	*2000*	*2000*	*2000*
43 Artificial Fur etc.	39.83	0.04	0.0160	47.16	0.57	0.2400	43.63	0.444	0.1938
44 Wood	70.11	0.11	0.0780	73.14	0.16	0.1100	49.35	0.245	0.1208
45 Cork	6.27	0.01	0.0004	7.6	0.009	0.0007	10.81	0.028	0.0030
46 Basketware	80.31	0.47	0.3800	86.51	1.036	0.9000	84.33	1.467	1.2367
47 Pulpwood	77.43	-	0.0000	78.55	0.00004	0.00003	52.95	0.005	0.0028
48 Paper	46.57	0.02	0.0007	47.09	0.028	0.0100	15.63	0.223	0.0349
49 Printed Books	26.63	0.14	0.0360	33.45	0.31	0.1000	28.28	0.509	0.1441
50 Silk & Waste Silk	60.49	8.2	4.9500	60.68	14.49	8.7900	57.74	22.422	12.9476
51 Wool, Yarn, Fabric	45.06	0.1	0.0400	44.39	1.23	5.5000	45.52	1.721	0.7832
52 Cotton	53.30	6.51	3.4500	53.65	7.28	3.9100	48.76	9.844	4.7996
53 Vegetable Fibre	37.57	13.58	5.1000	36.82	17.31	6.3700	38.01	15.883	6.0370
54 Man-made Filaments	27.86	0.82	0.2300	29.57	1.68	0.5000	32.71	3.746	1.2252
55 Man-made Staple Fibre	28.25	4.06	1.1400	34.1	7.2	2.4600	32.62	9.078	2.9609
56 Wadding, Felt, Non-woven	23.28	0.1	0.0200	27.77	0.32	0.0900	25.20	0.807	0.2034
57 Carpets	31.79	17.43	5.5400	42.71	19.24	8.2200	33.23	22.745	7.5579
58 Special Woven Fabric	31.13	2.6	0.8000	38.32	3.43	1.3100	35.19	9.408	3.3104
59 Coated Textiles	22.44	0.18	0.0400	27.75	1.23	0.3400	23.39	1.596	0.3731
60 Knitted Fabric	23.26	0.27	0.0600	34.65	3.54	1.2400	31.46	3.943	1.2404
61 Knitted Garment/ACC	44.06	3.1	1.3100	54.83	3.79	2.0800	57.88	4.297	2.4867
62 Woven Garment/ACC	54.21	5.64	3.0000	64.07	5.56	3.5600	63.40	4.149	2.6304
63 Made up textiles	43.94	7.09	3.1100	56.91	10.83	6.1700	59.30	12.779	7.5778
64 Footwear	35.45	5.49	1.9400	45.35	5.88	2.6700	46.60	5.110	2.3815

65 Headgear	50.14	0.31	0.1500	61.92	1.03	0.6300	61.10	0.508	0.3051
66 Umbrellas	51.46	0.12	0.0500	71.66	0.23	0.1600	71.31	0.125	0.0888
67 Feather Articles	79.70	0.09	0.0700	86	0.2	0.1700	83.83	0.580	0.4862
68 Stone, Cement	17.71	1.75	6.3000	27.04	3.46	0.9300	24.84	6.722	1.6700
69 Ceramic Product	18.64	0.19	0.3000	25.09	0.26	0.0600	29.23	0.516	0.1509
70 Glass & Glassware	21.08	0.1	0.0200	25.8	0.33	0.0800	28.23	1.083	0.3056
71 Pearls, Jewellery	59.77	4.45	26.6000	74.79	3.47	2.6000	74.31	4.230	3.1437
72 Iron & Steel	24.70	0.66	0.1600	28.83	0.57	0.1700	24.35	1.716	0.4179
73 Articles of Iron	25.14	0.45	0.1100	34.32	0.82	0.2800	31.15	1.643	0.5116
74 Copper & Articles	50.41	0.27	0.1400	50.43	0.49	0.2500	42.49	0.469	0.4179
75 Nickel & Articles	72.49	0.12	0.0900	72.4	0.67	0.0500	60.46	0.034	0.0203
76 Aluminium & Articles	36.51	0.05	0.2000	42.2	0.2	0.0900	38.32	0.287	0.1099
77 Reserved For Future	-	-	-	-	-	-	-		
78 Lead & Articles	47.22	0	0.0003	42.4	0.005	0.0020	40.15	0.022	0.0089
79 Zinc & Articles	26.63	0.38	0.1000	32.86	0.049	0.0160	29.45	0.181	0.0532
80 Tin & Articles	67.48	0.01	0.0060	73.57	0.05	0.3900	65.89	0.128	0.0846
81 Other Base Metals	63.60	0	0.0030	67.99	0.03	0.4700	60.69	0.178	0.1080
82 Tools & Metal Parts	40.63	1.5	0.6000	52.9	1.82	0.9600	39.78	1.769	0.7039
83 Misc. Articles (Base Metal)	26.40	3.58	1.0000	30.6	5.14	1.5700	27.05	4.943	1.3372
84 Nuclear Reactors	38.56	0.17	0.0600	44.64	0.26	0.1200	41.30	0.299	0.1234
85 Electrical Machinery	44.65	0.09	0.4100	49.9	0.18	0.0900	48.09	0.269	0.1293
86 Railways & Tramways	31.30	0.07	0.0200	19.32	0.37	0.0070	39.58	0.078	0.0308
87 Other Vehicles	19.41	0.14	0.0300	20.57	0.43	0.0900	19.55	0.455	0.0890
88 Aircrafts & Parts	38.44	0.09	0.0300	42.99	0.29	0.1200	48.18	0.217	0.1046
89 Ship, Boats etc.	54.48	0.01	0.0050	82.31	0.008	0.0070	70.66	0.182	0.1287
90 Photographic Apparatus	46.90	0.28	0.1300	50.38	0.3	0.1600	50.66	0.286	0.1451

(Contd...)

	1990	*1990*	*1990*	*1994*	*1994*	*1994*	*2000*	*2000*	*2000*
91 Watch & Clock	79.22	0.02	0.1400	84.32	0.36	0.3000	83.38	0.122	0.1017
92 Musical Instruments	68.71	0.21	0.0150	75.69	0.32	0.2400	67.12	0.595	0.3992
93 Arms & Ammunition	20.70	0.13	0.0300	45.36	0.17	0.0700	52.03	0.162	0.0845
94 Furniture etc.	23.86	0.28	0.0700	38.43	0.75	0.2900	40.06	1.191	0.4770
95 Toys, Games etc.	57.54	0.34	0.1900	64.42	5.57	0.3100	61.74	0.445	0.2748
96 Misc. Manu. Articles	39.16	0.42	0.1600	44.63	1.2	0.5300	44.77	1.905	0.8528
97 Artwork	65.55	0.09	0.5800	84.66	0.18	0.1500	85.18	0.104	0.0884
98 Reserved for special use	-	-	0.0900	99.94	-	-			
99 Reserved for special use	26.47	0.34	0.4000	33.55	0.15	0.0500	40.22	0.158	0.0636
Total	**40.93**	**0.98**	—	—	—	**0.55**	**40.94**	**1.195**	**0.4892**

Source : Commission of the European Communities, *Eurosat*, (Several Issues), Brussels.

TABLE 4.8 : Frequency Distribution of Indian Market Share in Extra - EC Imports

Indian Share in the Extra - EC Imports (per cent)	*Number of Sub- groups*		
	1981	*1990*	*1994*
upto 1	57	65	57
(57.58)	(65.66)	(57.58)	
1 - 2	9	8	14
(9.09)	(8.08)	(14.40)	
2 - 3	3	5	2
(3.03)	(5.05)	(2.02)	
3 - 4	3	5	7
(3.03)	(5.05)	(7.07)	
4 - 5	2	2	2
(2.02)	(2.02)	(2.02)	
5 - 6	1	2	6
(1.01)	(2.02)	(6.06)	
6 - 7	1	1	1
(1.01)	(1.01)	(1.01)	
7 - 8	2	1	2
(2.02)	(1.01)	(2.02)	
8 - 9	0	3	0
(0.00)	(3.03)	(0.00)	
9 - 10	0	0	1
	(0.00)	(0.0)	(1.00)
10 and above	4	3	5
(4.04)	(3.03)	(5.00)	
Not Available	17	4	-2
(17.17)	(4.04)	(2.02)	
Total	99	99	99

Values in the paranthesis are percentage distribution of the total subgroups.
Sourse : Eurostat (Various issues), European Commission, Brussels.

export growth has been more than 10 per cent in case of 9 groups. We have no information on 5 groups. Finally the **miscellaneous** group includes different types of furniture, toys, artwork and sports goods which do not carry any significant weightage in India's exports to the EC market. Therefore, evaluating export performance in terms of rate of growth, we can certainly come to the conclusion that some agricultural and marine products, export of all mineral items, almost all chemical products, some leather products, almost all items of textiles and clothing and items of stone, ceramics and glasses belong to high potential areas. Rather than diversifying into relatively many unknown areas, India should concentrate on some selected areas where its potential is much high in the Community market[33].

(iv) Share of Indian Exports in the EC market since the 1980s

In this section we will see shares of Indian exports in the Community market since 1981. The details of India's share to the European Community have been shown in **Table-4.7**. The Table deals with 99 major groups at 2-digit level. From **Table-4.7** we have prepared a sub-table showing the **frequency distribution** of India's share in the EC. In **Table 4.4**, we have shown India's share in the EC's import market (i.e. both EC-12 and member states) from 1991 to 2002. Detailed countrywise analysis has also been attempted before. But here, we will show the contribution of different commodity groups (at the 2-digit level) to EC's total imports. While doing this, we mainly concentrate on three periods viz. 1981, 1990, 1994 and 2000.

In this table, we have cited extra-EC share in the EC's total imports, India's share in the extra-EC trade and India's share in the EC's total imports for 1981 and 1990, 1994 and 2000. It is not possible here to mention India's share in extra-EC imports for all commodities because either same commodities are not exported or data are not available. Therefore, we have made another sub-table showing the **frequency distribution** of India's share in extra-EC and imports for all subgroups at HS-2 digit level in 1981, 1990 and 1994. From **Table-4.8**, it is clear that India's share in the extra-EC imports during 1981 ranges between 1 per cent and less than that for 57.58 percent of the total groups of commodities, it varied between 1 and 2 per cent for 9.09 per cent of the commodity groups , 2-3 per cent for 3.03 per cent of the total group of commodities, 3-4 per cent for 3.03 per cent of the total commodity groups exported, and remained 4-5 per cent for 2.02 percent of the total group of commodities. India's share in extra-EC import was equal to or less than 5 per cent for 74.75 per cent of the total group of commodities. Market share is more than 5 per cent only for 8 per cent of the total commodities exported at 2-digit level. No information is available for 17.17 per cent of the total commodities. The above information on India's market share in the extra-EC imports was pertaining to 1981 only.

The structure of India's market share in extra-EC import during 1990 remained almost same with slight change in percentage distribution. In 1990 India's share in the extra-EC imports remained equal to or less than 1 per cent for 66 per cent of her total commodities exported to the EC. Market share of more than 5 per cent was only for 10 per cent of the total commodities exported during 1990.

The trend remained more or less same even in 1994. During this period India's share in extra-EC import remained less than or equal to 1 per cent for 58 per cent of India's total exports to the Community. Finally, India's share in extra-EU imports varied between 5 and 10 per cent for only 14 per cent of the total imports which meant that India had a strong competitive edge in those commodities in the European Union[34].

The above description of market share is only applicable to extra-EC imports, not to its total imports. The major portion of EC's total imports comes from intra-EC trade which is around 55 per cent. Only 45 per cent of EC's total imports emerged from the rest of the world in 1994.

(i) Identification of EU's NTBs Affecting Indian Exports[35]

The European Community became European Union after it ratified the final agreement of the Uruguay Round of multilateral trade negotiations on 15 April 1994 at Marrakesh, Morocco. The basic objective of the trade negotiations was to dismantle all trade barriers both in tariffs and non-tariffs. In order to remove protectionism, the Final Act of GATT has stipulated reduction of tariffs by 38 per cent on all manufactured goods[36]. This is approximately one-third of the total tariffs of the developed countries (WTO, 1994). Developing countries have also made commitments to reduce tariffs on their imports from developed countries. This is for the first time, trade negotiations were based on *quid pro quo* basis i.e. on the basis of reciprocity rather than on MFN basis[37]. In the earlier rounds of multilateral trade negotiations, developing countries were not asked to reduce tariffs in response to tariff cuts of the developed countries. They were MFN countries which meant they would enjoy the benefits of all tariff reductions of the developed countries without reciprocal reductions.

Presently, tariff rates in the developed countries are much less as compared to the developing counterparts. But this does not necessarily mean that developed countries offer better market access than developing ones. Rather markets of the former have been characterized by labyrinthine non-tariff barriers which have more

TABLE 4.9 : Chronology EC's Non-Tariff Barriers to India's Exports

Hs Code Product Description	NTBs 1988	1992	1993	1994
1. Live animal	Variable Levy, 1981 (EC) Qant Rest (NAL and/or Quta) PRT, 1981, 1988 Misc. Rest / Non-Commercial Purpose 1981			
2 Meat & Edible Meat	Variable Levy (EEC), 1981 Qant Rest (NAL and/or Quota) (ESP), 1981 QR (PRT) 1981 Misc Reg/Non Com Pur 1981	Variable Levy (0081)	Variable Levy (0081)	Variable Levy (0081)
3 Fish & Crustaceans	Misce Regilation/Non-Com Pur, (EEC),1981 Ex-Retrospective Surveillance (EEC), 0791 QR (NAL and/or Quota)(PRT),0081 Reference Prices (EEC), 1981 Ex-QR (NAL and/or Quota)(ESP) 0081,1242 Et-QR(NAL and/or Quota) PRT 1981, 1988	Misce Regnl/Non-Commercial Purpose (0081) Reference Prices (0081)	Misc Regnl/Non-Commercial Purpose (0081 & 0191) Reference Prices (0081)	Misc Regnl/Non-Commercial Purpose (0081 & 0191) Reference Prices (0081)
4 Prod. of animal origin	Licence (EEC), 1981 Misce Regln /Non-Com Purs, (EEC), 1981 Surveillance License (ESP), 1981 Ex-Surveillance Licence (FRA) 1981 QRs (NAL and/or Quota)(ESP), 1981 Ex-QRs (NAL and/or Quota)(FRA),1981	Variable Levy (0081) Licence (0081)	Variable Levy (0081) Licence (0081)	Variable Levy (0081) Licence (0081)
5 Live Trees	Surveillance Licence (FSP), 1981 Misc Regnl/Non-Commercial Purpose (0081 & 0191) Misce Reln/ Non Com Pur, 1981	Misce Regnl/Non-Commercial Purpose (0081)	Misce Regnl/Non-Commercial Purpose (0081)	Misce Regnl/Non-Commercial Purpose (0081)

6 Edible Vegetables	Misce Regula / Non Com Purs (EEC), 1981 Misc Regnl/Non-Commercial Purpose (0081) QRs (NAL and/or Quota)(PRT), 1981 Seasonal Tariffs (EEC), 1981	Misce Regnl/Non-Commerial Purpose (0081) Seasonal Tariffs (0081)	Misc Regnl/Non-Commercial Purpose (0081) Seasonal Tarrif (0081)	Misc Regnl/Non-Commercial Purpose (0081) Seasonal Tarrif (0081)
7 Edible fruit and nuts	Licence (EC), 1981 Variable Levis (EC), 1981 Surveillance Licence (ESP), 1981 Ex-Surveillance Licence (FRA), 1981 Surveillance Licence (FRA), 1981 Reference Prices (ESP) 1981	Variable Levy (0081) Liance (0081)	Variable Levy (0081) Licence (0081)	Variable Levy (0081) Licence (0081)
8 Tea, Coffee etc.	Ex-QRs (NAL and/or Quota)(ESP), 1981, 1289 Surveillance Licence (ESP) 1981 QRs (PRT), 1981 QRs (ITA), 1981 QRs (GR), 1981 QRs (FRA), 1981 Seasonal Triffs (EEC), 1981 Reference Price (EEC), 1981 Ex-QRs (FRA), 1981 Licence (EC) Variable Levy (EC), 1981 Ex-Licence (EC) 1981 Ex-Bilateral Quota (EC), 1981 Surveillance Licence (FRA), 1981	Seasonal Tariffs (0081) Reference Price (0081)	Seasonal Tariff (0081) Reference Prices (0081)	Seasonal Tariff (0081) Reference Prices (0081)
9 Cereals	Surveillance Licence (ESP), 1981			
10 Malt, Starches etc.	Variable Levy (EC), 1981 Licence (EEC), 1981	Variable Levy (0189) Liance (0189)	Variable Levy (0189) Licence (0081)	Variable Levy (0189) Licence (0081)

(Contd...)

Hs Code	*Product Description*	*NTBs* *1988*	*1992*	*1993*	*1994*
11	Oil seeds etc.	Variable Levy (EEC), 1981 Licence (EEC), 1981 QRs (ESP), 1981	Variable Levy (0189) Licence (0081)	Variable Levy (0081) Licence (0081)	Variable Levy (0081) Licence (0081)
12	Lac, Gums etc.	QRs (PRT), 1981 QRs (ESP) 1981 Surveillance Licence (FRA), 1981			
13	Veg. plating material	QRs (ESP), 1981, 0889 QRS (FRA) 1981, 0789 Surveillance Licence (FRA), 1981			
14	Animal/Veg. Fats	Misce Regln / Non Com Purs (EC), 1981	Misce Regnl/Non-Commercial Purpose (0081)	Misce Regnl/Non-Commercial Purpose (0081)	Misce Regnl/Non-Commercial Purpose (0081)
15	Meats/Fish preparations	Surveillance Licence (ESP), 1981 Ex-QRs (ESP), 1981, 1290 EX-QRs(PRT), 0386, 1290			
16	Sugar, Confectionery	Misc Regli (EEC), 1981 Ex-Surveillance Licence (FRA), 1981	Misce Regnl/Non-Commercial Purpose (0081)	Misce Regnl/Non-Commercial Purpose (0081)	Misce Regnl/Non-Commercial Purpose (0081)
17	Cocoa	Variable Levy (EEC), 1981 Licence (EEC), 1981 Variable Component (EEC), 1981 Surveillance Licence (ESP), 1981	Variable Levy (0081) Liance (0081)	Variable Levy (0081) Licence (0081)	Variable Levy (0081) Licence (0081)
18	Cereal, Flours etc.				
19	Vegetable, Fruits	Variable Component (EEC), 1981 Surveillance Licence (ESP) PRT, 1981	Variable Component (0081)	Variable Component (0081)	Variable Component (0081)
20	Misc. Edible prep.	Surveillance Licence (ESO) FRA, 1981 Licence (EEC), 1981	Licence (0081) Variable Levy (0081)	Special Taxs (Product Specific) (0088)	Special Taxs (Product Specific) (0088)

	Ref. Prices (EEC), 1981 Ex-QRs (ESP), 1981 Ex-Licence (EEC), 1981 QRs (PRT), 1981 Variable Levy (EC), 1981 QRs (ITA), 1981	Licence (0081)	Variable Levy (0081) Licence (0081)	Variable Levy (0081) Licence (0081)
21 Spirits and Vinegar	Ex-Surveillance Licence (ESP), 1981 Surveillance Licence (FRA), 1981 Misce Regnl (EEC), 1981 Variable Component (EEC), 1981 Variable Levy (EEC), 1981 Licence (EEC), 1981	Variable Component (0081)	Variable Component (00810	Variable Component (00810
22 Waste Food Industries	Licence (EEC), 1981 Ex-QRs (ESP), 1981 Ref Prices (EEC), 1981 Ex-QRs (FRA), 1981 Surveillance Licence (ESP)	Licence (0081)	Licence (0081)	Licence (0081)
23 Tobacco	Variable Levy (EEC), 1981 Licence (EEC), 1981 Surveillance (ITA), 1981 Ex-QRs (DRT), 1981 Surveillance Licence (ESP), 1981	Variable Levy (0081) Licence (0081)	Variable Levy (0081) Licence (0081)	Variable Levy (0081) Licence (0081)
24 Salt, Sulphur etc.				
25 Slag, Ores & Ash				
26 Mineral Fuels etc.				
27 Inorganic Chemicals	QRs (ESP), 1981, 1286 Surveillance Licence (NLD), 1981 QRs (FRA), 1981			
28 Organic Chemicals	Surveillance Licence (ESP DRT), 1981			
29 Pharmaceutical product	Ex-ADDs (EEC)0691	Ex-Antidumping Duties (0691)	Misce Regnl/Non-Commercial Purpose (0081)	Misce Regnl/Non-Commercial Purpose (0081)

(Contd...)

Hs Code	Product Description	1988 NTBs	1992	1993	1994
		Ex-AD Investigation (EEC) 0890 Anti Dumping Duties (0691) Anti Dumping Investigation (0890)	Ex-Anti dumping Investigation (0591) Anti Dumping Investigation (0890)		Anti Dumping Duties (0691)
30	Fertilisers	Surveillance Licence (FRA), 1981			
31	Tanning/dyeing Ext.				
32	Essential oils	Ex-QR (FRA), 1981, 1289			
33	Soap etc.	Ex-Surveillance Licence (FRA), 1981			
34	Albuminoidal substance	Surveillance Licence (ESP< PRT), 1981 Ex-QRs (ESP), 1981			
35	Explosives	Surveillance Licence (ESP PRT), 1981			
36	Photographic goods	QRs (ESP), 1981 & 1990			
37	Misc. Chem. products	Surveillance Licence (ESP), 1981			
38	Plastics	Surveillance Licence (PRT) 1981			
39	Rubber	Ex-QRs (ESP), 1981 Surveillance Licence (ESP PRT), 1981			
40	Raw Hides & Skins	QRs (PRT), 1981, 1988 QR (ESP), 1981 QRs (GRC) 1981 Ex-Surveillance Licence (ESP), 1981 Surveillance Licence (PRT), 1981 Ex-QRs (PRT), 1981, 1988			
41	Leather Articles	Misce Regnln (Non Com Pur (EEC), 1981	Misce Regnl/Non-Commercial Purpose (0081)	Misce Regnl/Non-Commercial Purpose (0081)	Misce Regnl/Non-Commercial Purpose (0081)
42	Artificial Fur etc.	Misce Reglu (EEC), 1981 Ex-QRs (ESP), 1981 & 1291 Surveillance Licence (PRT), 1981	Misce Regnl/Non-Commercial Purpose (0081)	Misce Regnl/Non-Commercial Purpose (0081)	Misce Regnl/Non-Commercial Purpose (0081)

43 Wood	Misce Reglu (EEC), 1981	Misce Regnl/Non-Commercial Purpose (0081)	Misce Regnl/Non-Commercial Purpose (0081)	Misce Regnl/Non-Commercial Purpose (0081)
44 Cork	Surveillance Licence (ESP, ITA), 1981 Misce Reglu (EEC), 1981	Tariff Quota (0088) Misce Regnl/Non-Commercial Purpose (0081)	Tariff Quota (0088) Misce Regnl/Non-Commercial Purpose (0081)	Tariff Quota (0088) Misce Regnl/Non-Commercial Purpose (0081)
45 Basketware				
46 Pulpwood				
47 Paper				
48 Printed Books	Ex-QRs (PRT), 1981 Ex-Surveillance (ESP), 1981 Surveillance (ESP PRT), 1981			
49 Silk &WasteSilk	Surveillance Licence (PRT), 1981 Ex-QRs (FRA), 1981			
50 Wool, Yarn, Fabric	Ex-QRs (ESP), GRE, ITA, 1981			
51 Cotton	Misce Reglu (EEC), 1981 MFA Test Agm (EEC), 1981 QRs (FRA), 1981 Ex-QR (GRE), 1981	Misce Regnl/Non-Commercial Purpose (0081) MFA Restraint Agreement (0081)	Misce Regnl/Non-Commercial Purpose (0081) MFA Restraint Agreement (0081)	Misce Regnl/Non-Commercial Purpose (0081) MFA Restraint Agreement (0081)
52 Vegetable Fibre	MFA Test Agrmt (EC), 1981 QR (GBR), 1981 QR (ESP), 1981 QR (FRA), 1981 Surveillance Licence (PRT) 1981 Ex-QR (GRC) 1981 Ex-QR (IRC) 1981 Ex-Surveillance Licence (ESP), 1991 Anti-Duying Duti (EEC), 0390	MFA Restraint Agreement (0081) Anti-dumping Investigation (0390)	Anti-Dumping Investigation (0390) MFA Restraint Agreement (0390)	Anti Dumping Investigation (0390) MFA Restraint Agreement (0390)
53 Man-made Filaments	Surveillance Licencing (FRA), 1981 QR (ESP), 1981 QR (GBR), 1981, 1989	Tariff Quota (0088)	Tariff Quota (0088)	Tariff Quota (0088)

(Contd...)

Hs Code	Product Description	NTBs 1988	1992	1993	1994
		QR (NCD) 1981, 1989 QR (DNK), 1981, 1989 Ex-QR (BNLX) 1981, 0889			
54	Man-made Staple Fibre	MFA Rest Agrmt (EEC) 1981 Ex-QR (ESP), 1981 Ex-QR (GRC) 1981 Ex-QR (FRA), 1981 Ex-Surveillance Licence (ESP), 1981 Surveillance Licence (ESP FRA), 1981 Anti-Dumping Investigation (EEC), 490	MFA Restraint Agreement (0081) Anti-dumping Investigation (0490)	Anti Dumping Investigation (490) MFA Restraint Agreement (0081)	Anti-Dumping Investigation (490) MFA Restraint Agreement (0081)
55	Wadding, Felt, Non-woven	MFA Rest Agrmt (EEC), 1981 QR ((ESP) 1981 Ex-QR (GRC), 1981 QR (FRA) 1981 Surveillance Licence (PRT), 1981	Anti-Dumping Duties (0792) Anti-Dumping Investigation (1190) MFA Restraint Agreement (0081)	Anti -Dumping Duties (0792) Anti-Dumping Investigation (1190) MFA Restraint Agreement (0081)	Anti -Dumping Duties (0792) Anti-Dumping Investigation (1190) MFA Restraint Agreement (0081)
56	Carpets	MFA Rest Argmt (EEC), 1981 QRs (GBR), 1981, 0889 QRs (ESP) 1981, 0889 Ex-Surveillance Licence (ESP), 1981 Ex-QRs (PRT), 1981 0889 QRs (NLD), 1991, 0889 QRs (ITA), 1981, 0889 Surveillance Licence (IRL) 1981 Ex-QR (FRA), 1981 & 0889 QRs (BLX) 1981, 0889	MFA Restraint Agreement (0081)	MFA Restraint Agreement (0081)	MFA Restraint Agreement (0081)
57	Special Woven Fabric	MFA Rest Agrmt (EEC), 1981 Ex-Surveillance Licence (ESP), 1981 Ex-QRs (ESP) 1981	MFA Restraint Agreement (0081)	MFA Restraint Agreement (0081)	MFA Restraint Agreement (0081)
58	Coated Textiles	MFA Rest Agrmt (EEC), 1981 QRs (ESP), 1981	MFA Restraint Agreement (0081)	MFA Restraint Agreement (0081)	MFA Restraint Agreement (0081)

	Surveillance Licence (PRT IRL), 1981 QRs (FRA), 1981 QRs (GRC) 1981 QRs (GBR), 1981 Ex-QRs (ESP), 1989 Ex-Surveillance Licence (FRA), 1981			
59 Knitted Fabric	MFA Rest Agrmt (EC) 1981 Surveillance Licence (ESP PRT) 1981 Ex-Qrs (GBR) 1981	MFA Restraint Agreement (0081)	MFA Restraint Agreement (0081)	MFA Restraint Agreement (0081)
60 Knitted Garment/ACC	QR (ESP) 1981 Ex-QR (GRC) 1981 MFA Rest Agrmt (EEC) 1981	MFA Restraint Agreement (0081)	MFA Restraint Agreement (0081)	MFA Restraint Agreement (0081)
61 Woven Garment/ACC	MFA Rest Agrmt (EEC) 1981 X-QRs (ESP) 1981 Surveillance Licence (PRT IRL) 1981 X-QRs (GRC) 1981 X-QRs (FRA) 1981 X-QRs (ITA) 1981 X-Surveillance Licence (ESP) 1981	MFA Restraint Agreement (0081)	MFA Restraint Agreement (0081)	MFA Restraint Agreement (0081)
62 Made-up textiles	MFA Rest Agrmt (EEC) 1981 QR (ESP ITA) 1981 Surveillance Licence (IRL PRT) 1981 Ex-QR (GRC) 1981 QRs (FRA GBR) 1981	MFA Restraint Agreement (0081)	MFA Restraint Agreement (0081)	MFA Restraint Agreement (0081)
63 Footwear	MFA Rest (EC) 1981 Ex-QRs (GBR) 1981 Ex-Surveillance Licence (ESP) 1981 Surveillance Licence (PRT IRL GRC) 1981 Ex-QRs (ITA) 1981 QRs (ESP) 1981 QR (FRA) 1981 QRs without limit of Qty (FRA) 1981 1289 QRs (GBR) 1981	MFA Restraint Agreement (0081)	MFA Restraint Agreement (0081)	MFA Restraint Agreement (0081)

(Contd...)

Hs Code	Product Description	NTBs 1988	1992	1993	1994
64	Headgear	Community Surveillance (EEC) 0778 Ex-Surveillance Licence (ESP) 1981 Surveillance Licence (IRL) 1981 Misce Regnl/Non-Com Purs (EEC) 1981	Community Surveillance (0778) Mice Regnl/Non-Commercial Purpose (0081)	Community Surveillance (0778) Misce Regnl/Non-Commercial Purpose (0081)	Community Surveillance (0778) Misce Regnl/Non-Commercial Purpose (0081)
65	Umbrellas				
66	Feather Articles	Misce Reglu/Non-Com Pur (EEC) 1981 QRs (ESP FRA) 1981 Surveillance Licence (FRA) 1981	Misce Regnl/Non-Commercial Purpose (0081)	Community Surveillance (0778)	Misce Regnl/Non-Commercial Purpose (0081)
67	Stone, Cement	Misc Reglu/Non-Com Pur (EEC) 1981	Misce Regnl/Non-Commercial Purpose (0081)	Misce Regnl/Non-Commercial Purpose (0081)	Misce Regnl/Non-Commercial Purpose (0081)
68	Ceramic Product	Surveillance Licence (ESP) 1981			
69	Glass & Glassware	QRs (ESP) 1981 QRs (FRA) 1981			
70	Pearls, Jewellery	Ex-Surveillance Licence (ESP) 1981 Ex-QR (PRT) 1981 0889 Surveillance (PRT) 1981			
71	Iron & Steel	QR (ESP) 1981 1291 Surveillance Licence (FRA PRT) 1981 Misce Reglu/Non-Com Pur (EEC) 1981 Ex-QRs (ESP) 1981, 1291	Misce Regnl/Non-Commercial Purpose (0081)	Misce Regnl/Non-Commercial Purpose (0081)	Misce Regnl/Non-Commercial Purpose (0081)
72	Articles of Iron	Surveillance Licence (ESP FRA) 1981 Basic Import Prices (EEC) 1981 Import Surveillance (EEC) 1986 Community Surveillance (EEC) 0380 QRs (ESP PRT) 1981	Basic Import Prices Community Surveillance (0380)	Basic Import Prices (0380) Community Surveillance (0380)	Basic Import Prices (0380) Community Surveillance (0380)

73 Copper & Articles	QRs (ESP PRT) 1981 Surveillance (PRT FRA ESP) 1981 Import Surveillance (EEC) 1981	Import Surveillance (0086)	Import Surveillance (0086)	Import Surveillance (0086)
74 Nickel & Articles	Surveillance Licence (ESP PRT FRA) 1981			
75 Aluminium & Articles	Surveillance Licence (FRA) 1981			
76 Reserved For Future	Surveillance Licence (PRT) 1981			
77 Lead & Articles				
78 Zinc & Articles				
79 Tin & Articles				
80 Other Base Metals	Surveillance Licence (PRT) 1981			
81 Tools & Metal Parts	Import Surveillance (EEC) 1981			
82 Misc. Articles (Base Metal)	QR (ESP) 1981, 1090 QR (FRA) 1981, 1289			
83 Nuclear Reactors	Surveillance Licence (PRT) 1981 Ex-QRs (ESP) 1981			
84 Electrical Machinery	Quantity Restriction (ESP) (Nal and/or Quota) 1981 Surveillance Licence (PRT ESP), 1981			
85 Railways & Tramways	Surveillance Licence (PRT FRA ESP) 1981 QRs (Nal and/or Quota) (FRA & GRE) 1981 QRs (ESP), 1981 Ex-Surveillance Licence (PRT) 1981 Ex-QRs (PRT ESP) 1981			
86 Other Vehicles				
87 Aircrafts & Parts	QRs (ESP PRT) 1981 Ex-Surveillance Licence (FRA), 1981 Surveillance Licence (PRT IRL FRA), 1981			
88 Ship, Boats etc.				
89 Photographic Apparatus	Surveillance Licence (PRT), 1981 QRs (FRA), 1981			

(Contd...)

Hs Code	Product Description	1988 NTBs	1992	1993	1994
90	Watch & Clock	QRs (ESP FRA) 1981 Surveillance Licence (FRA PRT) 1981 Ex-QRs (FRA SPA ESP), 1981 Ex-Surveillance Licence (FRA), 1981			
91	Musical Instruments Restraint (0383)	QRs (FRA) 1981 Voluntary Export Restraint Misce Regn/Non-Commercial Purps (EEC), 1981	Voluntary Export Restraint (0383)	Voluntary Export Restraint (0383)	Voluntary Export Restraint (0383)
92	Arms & Ammunition	M.sce Renl/Non-Commercial Purps (EEC), 1981	Misce Regnl/Non-Commercial Purpose (0081)	Misce Regnl/Non-Commercial Purpose (0081)	Misce Regnl/Non-Commercial Purpose (0081)
93	Furniture etc.	Misce Regnl/Non-Commercial Purps (EEC) 1981 Ex-QRs (ESP) 1981 QRs (ESP), 1981	Misce Regnl/Non-Commercial Purpose (0081)	Misce Regnl/Non-Commercial Purpose (0081)	Misce Regnl/Non-Commercial Purpose (0081)
94	Toys, Games etc.	Surveillance Licence (PRT), 1981 Ex-Surveillance Licence (FRA), 1981			
95	Misc. Manu. Articles	QRs (ESP PRT FRA GRC) 1981 Misce Regnl/Non-Commercial Purpose (0081) Surveillance Licence (PRT), 1981 Ex-QRs (FRA), 1981	Misce Regnl/Non-Commercial Purpose (0081)	Misce Regnl/Non-Commercial Purpose (0081)	Misce Regnl/Non-Commercial Purpose (0081)
96	Artwork	Regnl/Non-Commercial Purps (EC), 1981 Misce Regnl/Non-Commercial Purpose (0081) Ex-QRs (ESP), 1981 Surveillance Licence ((ESP), 1981	Misce Regnl/Non-Commercial Purpose (0081)	Misce Regnl/Non-Commercial Purpose (0081)	Misce Regnl/Non-Commercial Purpose (0081)
97	Reserved for special use	Misce Regnl/Non-Commercal Purps (EEC), 1981	Misce Regnl/Non-Commercial Purpose (0081)	Misce Regnl/Non-Commercial Purpose (0081)	Misce Regnl/Non-Commercial Purpose (0081)

SOURCE : UNCTAD, *Reports on Trade Tariff and Non-Tariff Barriers*, (For Annual Inventories of NTB's 1988, 1992, 1993 and 1994), UNCTAD, Geneva.

trade distortionary impact[38]. These barriers have been erected clandestinely against their imports from the developing countries. Generally markets of the developing countries are protected by higher tariffs but certainly intensity of non-tariff barriers has been much low barring a few exceptions (Laird & Peats, 1990)[39].

The issue of non-tariff barriers had been discussed in detail in the Uruguay Round negotiations. Finally, at the end of the deliberations all the developed contracting parties have reached a consensus that they would reduce non-tariff barriers[40]. The Final Act of GATT has devised suitable methodologies on how to reduce or eliminate the non-tariff barriers. GATT has proposed the tariffication of the entire gamut of non-tariff barriers under which all NTBs will be converted into tariffs and then these are to be reduced by 36 per cent by developed countries over a period of 6 years and 24 per cent by developing countries over a period of 10 years. The conversion of NTBs into tariffs can only be possible through calculation of tariff equivalents of each product group. This is a grandiose job which requires enormous amount of data on domestic and international prices of different importing countries (Agra Eurpe, 1992)[41]. This is beyond the scope of present analysis.

The EU is having the maximum number of NTBs among all developed countries and obviously it is the most protectionist grouping in the world (Julio Nagues et at, 1986)[42]. The average rate of tariffs in the EU is around 4 percent but in tariff equivalent of non-tariff barriers in agricultural goods of the EU is well over 100 per cent (William Cline, 1980)[43]. While identifying the gravity of NTBs, we have been facing lack of organized data/information on NTBs. It is only Non-Tariff Measures Division of UNCTAD which prepares an inventory on NTBs and updates it annually[44]. On the basis of that inventory we have prepared a list of NTBs enforced on our exports to EU for 1988, 1992 1993 and 1994. 1994 is the latest year for which data are available. The identification and description of NTBs and their date of application as reported by UNCTAD are presented in **Table-4.9** (P. 167).

Let us now cite some of the important NTBs in the EC along with the products subject to such NTBs. We have information for 1988, 1992, 1993 and 1994. Almost all major NTBs in 1988 were present in 1992. In 1992 we have identified 17 major NTBs applied by EU on its imports from India. Apart from EC specific NTBs some NTBs have also been enforced by particular member countries individually. Here, we will analyse the major NTBs and the products covered by them in wider sense.

1. Variable Levy[45]

The variable levy is extensively used by EU on its imports of agricultural goods in order to protect its domestic markets. The extent of variable levy is the difference between domestic price & international price. These (VLs) are special charges imposed on imports of certain goods with the intention of increasing their price in the domestic market. Due to domestic compulsons, the EU keeps international prices artificially high in order to give protection to its uneconomic agricultural sector. One form of such protection is the price differential, but other form of protection to agriculture is the higher amount of subsidy given to the farmers for production as well as for exports. The EC variable Levy had been imposed in 1981 across the countries but to some specific product groups[46].

Indian products subject to the EU's variable levies are : fatty livers of geese or ducks, fresh or chilled fatty/livers of geese or duckseese or ducks, fresh or chilled fatty livers (02073100), Pellets of flour and meal manioc, fresh/dried (0714010), manioc, fresh/dried (0714099), crushed or ground and other spices, of a length/width ratio equal to a greater than 3 (10061098, 10062017) ratio greater than 2 less than 3 (10062096) and of similar products (i.e. HS 10062098, 10063027, 10063065, 10063067, 10063096, 10063098, 10064000, 10070090, 10008200, 11041991), rice, sorghum, millet, cereals, sugar cane, sugar, beet sugar, cane molasses, other food preparation, etc[47].

2. Seasonal Tariffs

This is enforced at a particular time on a particular product in order to check the inflow of cheaper imports. Normally it is enforced on agricultural products with the highest import duties applied during the period of the domestic harvest. It has the same impact as the variable levy. The rationale behind such higher tariffs is to protect the domestic farmers from cheaper inflow of food grains and allow them to sell their products in the markets at higher prices[48].

Indian exports subject to the EU's seasonal tariffs are : different types of grapes (08061015). The grapes attract a nominal tariff rate of 22 percent. Though Indian share in the EU market was extremely low (0.42 percent) but it was very significant from India's point of view because it exported 746,000 tonnes of grapes in 1992 to the Community. Chile is the largest exporter of grapes to the EC market (50 per cent) followed by South Africa (38.4 percent), and USA (27.3 percent). Developing countries jointly exported 56.37 per cent of total EC's imports (272145 thousand tonnes). India's average price per thousand tonnes was $ 1526.00 against its average import price of $ 1549/tonne. South Africa fetched the highest price (i.e. $1664.00) and the lowest was from USA (US$1368.17/tonnes).

3. Anti-Dumping Duties and Anti-Dumping Investigation

Anti-dumping duty is applied on a variety of products of labour intensive manufactured goods like textiles etc. (or product groups) if the exporting country is selling its products at less than domestic prices. If this charge is proved by the investigating authority then the authority will calculate the dumping margin of the dumped product through the generally accepted methodology and hereafter the authority will impose final anti-dumping duties equal to the dumping margin which is the difference between domestic price and the export price of a particular product. There is a provision in the erstwhile anti-dumping Code, that during the pendency period (i.e. when the investigations are carried out the importing country if it wants, can enforce the provisional duties to temporarily check the flow of dumped imports (Tharakan et at, 1994)[49].

Indian exports covered by EU's anti-dumping duties/ investigations in 1992 are some form of acids (2917100) some items of cotton textiles, yarn, polyester yarn, synthetic, staple fibers (only against India and Korea and have been enforced since 1990) of different types, sewing thread of synthetic staple fibres unbleached/bleached single yarn, multiple or cabled yarn, mixed mainly or solely with artificial staple fibres yarn, cotton, etc. If we take the items at 8-digit HS Level, then about 50 items are covered by EC's anti-dumping duties/ investigations since 1990. Although all items are textiles and yarn in which India has comparative advantage in the EC market. In addition to NTBs, these items are also subject to higher tariffs in the EC markets.

4. Multi-Fiber Arrangement (MFA), MFA Restraint Agreement, MFA Quota, Bilateral Quota, MFA Administrative Cogeneration Agreement and QRs (unspecified)[50]

The entire gamut of India's textile exports has been under stringent quantitative restrictions of the developed countries. This was a temporary exemption to GATT principle which had maintained the system for more than last 30 years beginning with Short-Term Arrangement (1962-64) followed by Long-Term Arrangement (1964-72) and MFA's (1973). The MFA started in 1973 and expired in December 1992 after its four terms. But most of our exports of garments and textiles are still under stringent MFA quota, which is supposed to be phased out from 1st January, 2005, as per the agreement reached by contracting parties to GATT related to trade in textiles and garments at Marrakesh on 15 April, 1994[51].

MFA is a bilateral arrangement outside the GATT framework based on mutually exclusive terms. This bilateral process of negotiations is called MFA Restraint Agreement/Bilateral Quota. In 1992, total 439 items of textiles and garments (at HS 8 digit level) were covered by EC's MFA restraint agreement, the frequency and coverage ratios were almost 100 per cent. This NTB has been enforced on 19 developing countries including India since 1981. Tariff rates for these items are exorbitantly high (i.e. three time higher than the average). The details of the nature of NTBs, tariff rates, ratios and competitive position are shown in the **Table-4.9 and 5.13** (i.e. for 1988,1992,1993 and 1994).

5. Licence

Licences applied by the EC are of two types, viz. (i) automatic licenses, (ii) non-automatic licences. Both of them are consistent with the GATT licensing codes. According to NTBs requirements, an approval is a must before any importation, and hence, the it is not automatic. Licensing which is to be used to administer a quota is included in the GATT Data base under that category (i.e. quota) only. Non-automatic licensing has two distinct categories. viz. 1) this is not subject to specific condition. It is used to restrict the volume of imports when quotas have not been fixed in advance or used for unspecified purposes; and ii) non-automatic licensing is a system which requires meeting certain specific conditions i.e. minimum export performance, authorized use of imported goods or purchase of domestic products.

A total of 24 items (at HS 8-digit level) of Indian exports to EC in 1992 were covered by EC's licensing requirements. These items have been spreading over HS-O, 1 and 2 at the UNCTAD inventory on NTBs as reported in 1992. The items covered by EC's licensing requirements are palliates of flour, meals/manioc fresh or dried

(07141010, 01741099), some types of spices, some forms of rice (broken & flaked), grain sorghum, millet, raw cane sugar, white sugar, (cake), cane molasses, some types of vegetable fruits, (prepared/preserved) champagne and sparking wine, some vegetable materials waste and residual used for animal feed etc. The tariff rates of these items are cited in next chapter.

6. Community Surveillances[52]

There is a good deal of controversy in the GATT/UNCTAD about the question whether or not these NTMs have trade restrictive effects. Community surveillance is a tool used by EC to control imports through the issuance of automatic licenses. This surveillance procedure has several forms viz., surveillance license, monitoring, retrospective surveillance and Community surveillance.

Surprisingly 65 items, which India export to the EU are covered by some of these surveillance schemes introduced by the Community as mentioned in the last paragraph of which 49 items are in HS-6, and 16 are in HS-7 category. Items covered by Community surveillance scheme are : footwear of different types and different materials for different uses, parts of footwear, assembles of footwear etc. (HS-6); items are in HS-7 of iron & steel, light engineering goods, items of nickel etc. Community surveillance scheme on footwear was introduced in 1978 and on iron & steel items it has been operational since 1980.

7. Basic Import Prices and Import Surveillance

Import surveillance is a set of measures enforced in different forms for monitoring imports through the issuance of automatic licences. If at any time it is felt that some imports are injurious to domestic industry, then EC with the help of licences restricts the imports of these sensitive items.

Indian exports put under Community surveillance schemes are also covered by import surveillance scheme and basic import prices. Basically exports of some items of iron & steel, nickel and different types of light engineering goods are covered by this schemes. All these items fall under HS-7. At this level 18 items are covered by basic import prices and 8 are covered by import surveillance scheme.

8. Reference Prices

Reference price is another hard-core NTB. This is a special type of levy imposed on imports. With the help of this tool, EC increases the price of imported goods with reference to its domestic goods. The average tariff rates of these items are higher than the average tariffs on all goods. This NTB is normally applied on agricultural imports and its impact is similar to that of EC's variable levy. In 1992, three items of India's exports to EU were subject to reference prices. Cattle fish and squid (excl. live fresh or chilled) other cattle fish and squid (excl.-live fresh or chilled) and finally fresh grapes were subject to reference prices. India's share is quite significant in the EC market at least in first two items. Indian share was 24.3 per cent for the first item and 34.54 per cent for the second item in 1992. Market share for the last item was very small i.e. 0.42 per cent in the EU during the same year. The average rate of duty was 6 per cent for the first two items and 22 percent for the last item.

9. Miscellaneous Regulations/Non-Commercial Purposes

Miscellaneous regulations include many unspecified as well as specified regulations that do not have any price impact at least directly. Almost all regulations are for commercial purposes to save the domestic industry through restraining cheap imports. But some restrictions are imposed purely on non-commercial grounds. Some of these NTBs are health regulations, sanitary regulations, phytosanitary regulations etc. In such cases restrictions are consistent with the national priorities and health objectives. The degree of restrictiveness varies from country to country. The reason behind such restrictiveness is that developed countries are understood to be more health conscious than the developing nations. Food and Drug Administration (FDA) in the USA follows very stringent criteria of issuing certificates. Rather one should call it "grey areas" than purely a barrier because of the objective principles. Miscellaneous regulations pose a serious threat to Indian exporters because exports of 104 items at 8 digit level have been covered by these regulations. 15 items are in HS-0, 2 items are in HS-1, 39 items are in HS-4, 35 items are in HS-6, 11 items are in HS-9. This means some items from almost every group are covered by miscellaneous regulations.

NOTES

1. EC is the amalgam of 12 countries upto 31 December 1994, and became 15 members states thereafter. In the WTO, EC is considered

as a single contracting party, because it is a trading bloc and has already completed integration of internal market, we consider EC as a single trade partner.

2. (a) Ministry of Commerce, Government of India, "Monthly Statistics of Foreign trade of India", (Several Issues;) DGCI & S, Calcutta.
   (b) Ministry of Commerce, Government of India, "Foreign Trade Statistics of India" (Several Issues;) DGCI & S, Calcutta.
3. This may be due to the fact that India has colonial background with UK and has been maintaining a very sound political and economic relation with Germany, France and Italy.
4. Commission of the European Communities, "*Eurostat*" (Several Issues), Brussels.
5. The above equation is called the **trend equation** which is used to measure rate of growth of one variable with respect to time. This is a straight line equation where 'a' and 'b' are constants. This is a standard formula for measuring rate of growth.
6. The value of imports has been expressed in ECUs terms, because it is a notional currency of the EU, therefore, it is against price fluctuations.
7. Ibid n. 4.
8. Ibid n. 4.
9. Ibid n. 4.
10. Rajiv Kumar an Ram Khanna, "India : The Multifibre Arrangement and the Uruguay Round" in *The Uruguay Round, Textile Trade and the Developing Countries : Eliminating the Multifibre Arrangements in the 1990s*, (A World Bank Publication, Washington, Chapter - 8), pp. 182-212.
11. (a) M. Lipton and Peter Tulloch, "India and the Enlarged EEC in *International Affairs*, January 1974, p. 53.
   (b) Vincent Cable and Ann Weston, *South Asia Exports to the EEC : Obstacles and Opportunities,* Overseas Development Institute (London), 1979, pp. 137-167.
12. Ibid n. 12.
13. Anne Weston and Vincent Cable, *South Asian Exports to the EEC : Obstacles and Opportunities*, (Overseas Development Institute, London, 1979) pp. 108-137.
14. Ibid n. 13 pp. 168-172.
15 Alexander J Yeats, "*Trade Barriers Facing Developing Countries, Commercial Policy Measures and Shipping*", London, McMillan Press, 1979, pp. 104-43.
16. (a) Cline, W.R. et al, "*Tokyo Round Negotiations : A Quantitative Assessment*" The Brookings Institute, Washington, 1980, pp. 145-163.
   (b) Ian Goldin, D. Van der Mensbruggle and A. Coredella, "The

Consequences of Common Agricultural Policy Reforms for Developing Countries", European Commission, Director General for Economic and Financial Affairs, *European Economy*, No. 5, 1994, sp. ed. on *The Economies of Common Agricultural Policies*, p. 49-71.

17. Sam Laird and Rene Vassenaar, "Why Should We Worried About Non-Tariff Measures", *Information Commercial Espanola*, Spl. Issue on Non-Tariff Barriers, October 1991, pp. 1-35.
18. Laird Sam, "Quantifying Commercial Policies", *in Applied Trade Policy Modelling : A Handbook*, (Cambridge University Press, 1995), pp.1-45.
19. Though India's share in EC's total imports is relatively higher in case of larger countries compared to smaller ones, but if we measure in terms of growth, it is relatively high in smaller countries rather than larger ones. One plausible explanation may be the base level is very high with the larger countries.
20. This may be due to increase efficiency in Indian Industries. Modernisation in Indian Industry has been started from early eighties coupled with liberalisation in trade policies.
21. UNCTAD, *Inventory of EU Tariff & Non-Tariff Barriers* (Various Issues), UNCTAD, Geneva.
22. This suggestion of groups has been done by Commission itself as HS-2 digit level. Commission of the European Communities, *Eurostat* (Section on EC's imports from India, Several Issues), Brussels.
23. This Classification is done by the European Commission itself for the sake of convenience.
24. Swapan K. Bhattacharya, *Indian Export Performance : A Sectoral Analysis* ICRIER, Working Paper No. 60, ICRIER, New Delhi, 1990.
25. *(a)* Biswajit Dhar and S.K. Mohanty, "Prospectus of Market Access for Developing Countries in the Post-Uruguay Round Agricultural Trade", in B. Bhattacharya and A.K. Sengupta (eds;) *Trade in Agriculture : The Uruguay Round and After*, Indian Institute of Foreign Trade, 1994, pp. 130-151.
    (b) Ashok Prasad, "Impact of GATT on Agricultural Exports : Some Issues", Ibid n. 25 pp. 12-26.
    (c) M. Dattatrevlu, "Uruguay Round : New Opportunities for Boosting Agro-Export" Ibid n. 25 pp. 32-53.
    (d) A.K. Sengupta and R.K. Wadhwa, "Impact of Uruguay Round on Agro-Exports", Ibid n. 25 pp. 53-68.
    (e) K.K. Gupta, "Uruguay Round : Its advantages to Indian Farmers", lbid n. 25 pp. 78-86
    (f) C.C. Mair and A. Bhattacharya, "Marker Access Commitment : Emerging Export Opportunities", lbid n. 25 pp. 111-130.
26. *(a)* Richard Hugues, "The Uruguay Round : New Approach for the

Textiles and Clothing Sector", in K.R. Gupta (ed;) *World Trade Organisation and India,* (Atlantic Publisher, New Delhi, 1996), pp.112-124.

(b) Rajat Acharya, "How Far is the Emerging World Trading System Beneficial for India and other LDC's in Transition", Ibid no. 26(a) pp. 169-173.

27. Swapan K. Bhattacharya, "Transition from MFA to WTO : Prospects for the India's Trade in Textiles and Garments", in K.R. Gupta (ed;) *World Trade* (Atlantic Publisher. New Delhi), 1995. pp. 240-311.

28. (a) Swapan K. Bhattacharya, "GATT, WTO and Social Clauses", *International Industries Annual,* (New Delhi), 1994. pp. 69-77.

(b) Kalyan Raipuria, "Phasing in Social Norms to World Trade System : The Conceptual, Operational and Research Issues". in B. Bhattachrya & Vijaya Katti (ed;) *Emerging Trade Agenda : South Asian and German Perspectives,* (Indian Institute of Foreign Trade. New Delhi; 1995), pp. 185-199.

(c) Hartman Kuchle, "*Social Norms and World Trade*" Ibid n. 28(b) pp.199-207.

29. Ministry of Commerce, Government of India, "*Export-Import Policies,* 1995-1996", Vol-I, New Delhi, 1995.

30. Ibid n. 24.

31. Mission of India to the European Union, "*Commercial Relations between EU and India : An Overview of Principal Trade Trends*", Brussels, February 5, 1995, pp.1-5 and Annextures.

32. (a) Mission of India to the European Union, "*Indo-EC MoU and Market Access for Textiles*", Brussels, February 15, 1995 : Indo-EC/Textiles/ flierl. pp.1-4.

(b) Mission of India to the European Union, "*Indo-EC News Bulletin*" Vol-II, No. 2, February 3, 1995, pp.1-13.

33. Shanti Jagannathan, *EC and India in the 1990's : Towards Corporate Synergy,* (Indus Publishing Comapany, New Delhi, 1993), pp. 265-281.

34. In order to prove Competitiveness of Indian products we have to see the Revealed Comparative Advantage (RCA) index of the products in each category, which is shown in the next chapter, Cf. Bela Balassa, *Trade Liberalisation and Revealed Comparative Advantage : The Manchester School,* (1965), Vol. XXIII, no. 2 pp. 99-123.

35. (a) Sam Laird and Alexander J. Yeates, "Quantitative Trade Barriers Analysis" McMillan, Press Ltd., London, 1991), pp. 17-19.

(b) Ibid n. 15.

(c) Robert E. Baldwin, "Non-tariff Distortions to International Trade", The Brooking, Institute, Washington, 1970, p. 10-12.

(d) Allexander J. Yeats, "Trade Barriers, Facing Developing Countries : Commercial Policies Measures and Shipping" (London,

McMillan Press), 1979. pp. 107-108.

36. World Trade Organisations, "The Final Act of Embodying The Results of the Uruguay Round of Negotiations", 15th April, 1994, WTO, Geneva, pp. 21-41.

37. (*a*) Ministry of Commerce, Government of India, "*Indo-EC Textiles Accord*", 31st December, 1994, New Delhi, (Press Release).

 (*b*) Mission of India to the European Union, "*Indo-EC MOU and Market Access for Textiles*", February 15, 1995, Brussels, pp. 1-3.

38. (*a*) Ibid n.15 pp. 104-143.

 (*b*) Rudlof Adlug, "Non-Tariff Barriers as the Uruguay Round", *Intereconomics*, (January/February 1990), pp.24-27.

 (*c*) Michael Daly, "Pattern and Parvassiveness of Tariffs and Non-Tariff Border Measures in the QUAD" A Paper Presented for the 51 Congress of the International Institute of Public Finance, (June, 1995, Lisbon), pp. 1-13.

39. Sam Laird and J. Yeates, "Trend in Non-Tariff Barriers of Developed Countries", 1966-1986, Weltwirtscahafliches Archives (Band 126, Heft 2), 1990, pp. 299

40. (*a*) World Trade Organisation, "Uruguay Round : The Final Act" Annex IA, (Marakesh, 15 April, 1994), pp. 43-273.

 (*b*) Josling, Tim (1990), i.e.," Of Models and Measures, Some Thoughts on the Uses and Abuses of Policy Indicators", Paper presented at the *International Agricultural Research Consortium*, Sandiego, December.

 (*c*) "Agricultural Protection, Domestic Policy and International Trade" Paper presented at the FAO, UN Rome, 10-29 November 1973.

 (*d*) and Anderson, Kym ,"The Challenge of the Economists of Multilateral Trade Negotiations on Agricultural Production", Food Research Institute, Studies, 1993, (22), No. 3, pp. 275-304.

41. Commission of the European Communities, "EC-Tariff Equivalents for Market Access", in *Agra Europe* (March 20, 1992) Database Schedule Code TABAGRTRA pp. E 12-17.

42. Nogues Julio, Andrez Olechowski and Allen Winter, "The Extent of Non-Tariff Barriers to Industrial Countries Imports, *The World Bank Economic Review* Vol 1, 1986, No. 1., pp. 181-99

43. Cline, William et al, "*Tokyo Round Negotiations : A Quantitative Assessment*", The Brookings Institution, Washington, 1980, pp. 145.

44. UNCTAD, "*Report on Trade, Tariffs and Non-Tariff Restrictions*" (Several Issues and for various countries), UNCTAD, (Geneva).

45. European Commission, Directorate General of Economic and Finance Affairs : European Economy, No. 5, 1994. Spl. Issue on the Economies of Common Agricultural Policies (CAP), (Brussels)

46. (*a*) A. Larsen and J. Hansen, "Agricultural Support and Structure

and Development, Ibid n. 45, pp. 165-179.

(*b*) R.N., Anderson, "Market Standardisation and the Reform of the Common Agricultural Policy, Ibid n. 45, pp. 207-229.

47. UNCTAD, "Inventory on Trade, Tariffs and Non-Tariff Barriers", UNCTAD, Geneva, UNCTAD has NTM Division which updates annual data on tariff and non-tariff barriers and stored in Computer Disk. So far they have coupled information for 63 Countries.

48. Seasonal Tariff is not a regular phenomenon. It is enforced for a particular period of time when supply increases due to seasonal variation. This is applicable to agricultural goods only.

49. (*a*) EU's frequently uses anti-dumping duties to restrict cheaper import from the developing countries. Indian Textiles Exports are subject to EC anti-dumping duties as well as investigation is going on to some items, see Swapan K. Bhattacharya's *Managing Anti-dumping Measures in the WTO Regime : Indian Scenario and International Pratices*", (ASSOCHAM Monograph, Assocham, New Delhi), 1996.

(*b*) Tharakan, P.K.M. Waelbrock, J., "Anti-dumping and Contracting Duty Decision in the EC and the US : An Experiment in Competitive Political Economy", *European Economic Review*, (Brussels), 1994(3), No. 1, pp. 171-194.

(*c*) Schuknecht l. and Stephen J., "EC Trade Protection Law : Produmping or Anti-dumping", *Public Choice*, No.1-2, 1994, pp. 143-156.

50. (*a*) Ibid n. 10.

(*b*) Ram Khanna, "Impact of QRs on Indian Apparel Export Industry", mimeo, (ICRIER, New Delhi, 1987).

(*c*) Ibid n. 27.

51. World Trade Organisation "Agreement on Textiles and Clothing in Uruguay Round : The Final Act (Marakesh 15th April 1994). pp. 85-117.

52. Sam Laird and Allexander J. Yeates "Glossary of Non-Tariff Barriers in *Quantitative Methods for Trade Barriers Analysis* (McMillan Pvt. Ltd. 1990) pp. 245-251.

Chapter 5

EC'S Non-Tariff Barriers and their Impacts on Indian Exports : An Empirical Study

INCIDENCE OF EU'S NON-TARIFF BARRIERS TO INDIAN EXPORTS DURING 1988

The EU's protectionism has been growing over the years instead of receeding. (Doglas, 1994)[1]. Since the inception of the General Agreement on Tariffs and Trade (GATT), there is no denying the fact that EC has reduced tariff levels to a considerable extent, but, on the other hand, in the guise of apparent liberalization they have erected an intricate structure of non-tariff barriers to protect domestic industries from external competition (Low & Yeats, 1994)[2]. Rate of customs tariffs in the developed countries was 60 per cent during late 1930s which has now been reduced to around 3-4 percent on an average (Cassing, 1990)[3]. This reduction tariffs does not ensure operation of free trade; neither does it reduce protectionism; rather the protectionist tendency has been penetrated into other areas as well in the form of several complicated non-tariff barriers (Deardorff & Stern, 1985)[4]. It is estimated that the average rate of tariffs on industrial goods in the developed countries ranges between 10-15 per cent but tariff equivalent of non-tariff barriers in agriculture and some items of textiles is well over 100 per cent (Cline *et. at.*, 1975)[5]. This is true in the case of textiles also[6]. It is very difficult to identify the non-tariff barriers because these measures often lack transparency and are not covered under any trade rules (Papillon, 1994)[7]. In most of the cases, enforcing countries like to treat them as "grey areas" because according to them, these measures are consistent with their national objectives[8]. These measures have frequently been used to safeguard their industry from foreign competition. This poses a very common argument to buttress their protectionist measures.

Macro-economic cost of protection is extremely high which nullifies their gains due to protection. In the case of the erstwhile Federal Republic of Germany, the **Cologne Institute of Economic Policy** put this cost at DM 75 bn. in 1985[9]. The magnitude must be much higher by now. According to another estimation done by **IFO Institute, Munich** (1987)[10], the German Institute of Economic Research in Berlin, and the **Kiel Institute of International Economics,** the removal of protectionism could increase Germany's gross domestic product by 6 per cent or DM 100 bn., and employment by 9 per cent equivalent to 2 million jobs. Another estimate of the cost of protection purporting to show that as a result of the complete liberalization of OECD countries import-trade could lead to a 10 per cent increase in developing countries exports and a 3 per cent growth in their national product[11].

Contrary to the substantial reduction in tariffs, the magnitude of non-tariff barriers had surged tremendously in the eighties, especially after the second oil shock[12]. The GATT bases its calculation on the assumption that around 40 per cent of world trade is affected by non-tariff barriers. The extent of protectionism varies from industry to industry e.g. it was 67.5 per cent of the clothing industry, 64 per cent of the steel industry and around 50 per cent of the agricultural sector in 1987 according to another estimate[13]. Due to higher degree of non-transparency, it is very difficult to identify NTBs, but, on the basis of reports of the contracting parties, UNCTAD has enlisted 800 variants of NTBs based mainly on bureaucratic and administrative regulations[14]. Again between March and September 1987 GATT has recorded 135 "grey area" measures. The forms that NTBs restraints on trade shall assume are extremely varied[15]:

Since the EU is one of the most protectionist groupings in the world with a wide variety of NTBs in its basket, a host of Indian products have been subject to Community NTBs[16]. We do not have data on continuous basis[17]. We have got only discrete information from UNCTAD. On the basis of the this information, we have calculated the **NTB-coverage ratio, frequency ratio, average rate of tariffs and revealed comparative advantage of different HS categories at 2-digit level**. For the sake of our convenience, we have aggregated entire 8-digit level items into 99 major groups at 2-digit level. We have taken only four years viz. 1988, 1992, 1993 and 1994[18].

While studying India's exports subject to Community NTBs in 1988, we find that most of India's textiles exports to EC have been under MFA quota since 1974; before that they were under STA and LTA[19]. The entire gamut of exports of agricultural items has been under the EU's variable levies which are part of Community's Common Agricultural Programme (CAP). Under this programme the EU gives heavy subsidy to its agricultural production as well as exports and puts levy on imports of agricultural goods equivalent to the difference between domestic and international prices (Goldin *et al*, 1993)[20].

From UNCTAD inventory on tariffs and non-tariff barriers, we have identified some major NTBs enforced by the EU in 1988[21]. The **chronology of NTBs** is shown in **Table-4.9**[22]. The table also shows the source of information, year of application and the affected countries. The major NTBs enforced by the EU during 1988 are as follows : Variable levy, miscellaneous regulations/non-commercial purposes, ex-retrospective surveillance ('ex' means partial) reference price, ex-reference prices, licence, variable components, MFA restraint agreement, anti-dumping investigation, Community surveillance, basic import prices, import surveillance, ex-anti dumping investigations[23].

The UNCTAD inventory on tariff and non-tariff barriers contained one peculiar system during 1988. Apart from Community NTBs, the inventory also provided names of national NTBs enforced by a particular country[24]. In our analysis we have considered only EC-specific NTBs and excluded country specific NTBs. **Portugal** enforces quantitative restrictions, ex-quantitative restrictions surveillance licence, and ex-surveillance licence. **France** separately adopts quantitative restrictions (NAL and/or quota), ex-surveillance licence, surveillance licence, ex-quantitative restrictions and quantity restrictions without limit of quantity. **Italy** also enforces quantitative restrictions, surveillance licence and ex-quantitative restrictions. **Ireland's** NTBs are same in nature i.e. ex-quantity restrictions, surveillance licence and quantity restrictions. **Netherlands'** NTBs are quantitative restrictions and ex-QRs, **Great Britain** also enforces QRs on some specific products, **Greece's** NTBs are QRs, ex-QRs and surveillance licence. **Denmark** adopts only one NTB i.e. QRs, otherwise all other NTBs applicable to this country are Community NTBs. **Belgium and Luxembourg** also have QRs and ex-QRs regimes to restrict their imports from the rest of the world. Some of the Indian

TABLE 5.1 : Structure of EU's Tariffs and Non-Tariff Barriers to Indian Exports in 1988

HS Code	Product Description	Total value of exports (000$)	Total value of exports cov by NTBS (000$)	Total no. of items exported	Total no. of items covered by NTBS	NTB Coverage Ratio	Frequency Ratio	Avg. Rate of Tariffs (Wtd)	Avg.Tarriff (WTD) on NTB affected items
1	2	3	4	5	6	7	8	9	10
01	Live Animals	382.00	382.00	2.00	2.00	100.00	100.00	-	-
02	Meat and Edible meat offal	12.00	12.00	3:00	3.00	100.00	100.00	10.00	10
03	Fish and crustacean, molluscs	81841.00	1073.00	58.00	13.00	1.31	22.40	11.73	14.02
04	Fish and crustances, molluscs and other acquantic in vertebrates	16.00	3.00	4.00	2.00	18.75	50.00	22.44	12.67
05	Products of Animal orgin or included	13292.00	3453.00	17.00	7.00	25.98	41.18	0.032	0.11
06	Live trees and other plants,	2440.00	2419.00	12.00	10.00	99.13	83.33	6.66	6.63
07	Edible Vegetables and certain roots and tubers	4073.00	32.00	23.00	6.00	0.78	26.00	12.80	12.06
08	Edible fruits and nuts, peel of citrus fruit or melons	50695.00	28.00	25.00	6.00	0.05	24.00	1.66	9.75
09	Coffee, Tea, mate and Spices	182867.00	-	34.00	-	-	-	2.92	-
10	Cereals	22409.00	22409.00	8.00	8.00	100.00	100.00	NA	NA
11	Products of milling industry matts, starches, innlia, wheat gutton	218.00	188.00	12.00	11.00	86.24	83.33	0.89	1.03
12	Oilseeds and leaguminous	22265.00	-	17.00	-	-	-	0.21	-

(Contd...)

1	2	3	4	5	6	7	8	9	10
13	Lac Jums resins and other veg. saps and extracts	44781.00		13.00	-	-	-	0.08	–
14	Veg. Plaiting materials, veg. products	9514.00	8405.00	6.00	1.00	88.34	-	-	–
15	Animals & Veg. fats and oils and their clearage products, animals or veg. waxes	3111.00	-	25.00	-	-	-	1.27	–
16	Preparations of meat & fish or of crustacean, molluscs	1495.00	56.00	6.00	1.00	3.74	16.67	19.79	20
17	Sugars and sugar confec-tionery	8573.00	8573.00	7.00	7.00	100.00	100.00	0.19	27
18	Coca and Coca Products	-	-	-	-	-	-	-	–
19	Preparations of Cereals, flower, starch or milk, pastry & cooked products	3987.00	3987.00	15.00	15.00	100.00	100.00	11.12	11.2
20	Preparations of Veg., Fruits, nuts or other parts of plants	8454.00	5108.00	35.00	17.00	60.42	48.52	13.42	14.79
21	Misc. edible prepartions	1668.00	583.00	12.00	6	34.95	50.00	12.04	12.8
22	Bererages, spirits and vinegar	226.00	146.00	7.00	2	64.60	28.57	14.16	11.53
23	Residens and waste from the food industries prepared animal fodder	54100.00	1828.00	12.00	4	3.37	33.33	0.0016	0
24	Tobacco and manufactured substitutes	24144.00	-	21.00	-	-	-	8.42	–
25	Salt sulpher, earths, stores, plastering mfgrs, lime and cement	59724.00	-	39	-	–	–	0.03	–

26	Ores, slag and ash	35773.00	-	10	-	–	–	–	–
27	Mineral fuels, minerals oils and products, bituminus substances mineral	5794.00	–	1.00	–	–	–	7.00	–
28	Inorganic chemicals and its compounds	6501.00	–	39.00	–	–	–	6:85	–
29	Organic chemicals and its Compounds	57379.00	–	143.00	–	–	–	7.77	–
30	Pharmaceutical products	3116.00	–	21.00	–	–	–	6.07	–
31	Dyeing, tawning and colouring materials	45237.00	–	29.00	–	–	–	9.80	–
32	Essential oils and resinoids, cosmetics	9630.00	–	32.00	–	–	–	1.87	–
33	Soap and similar preparations	108.00	–	9.00	–	–	–	6.35	–
34	Albuminnidal substances.	947.00	–	5.00	–	–	–	6.06	–
35	Explosive, marches, certain combustables	20.00	–	2.00	–	–	–	6.60	–
36	Photographic or cinematographic items	1026.00	–	16.00	–	-	–	3.94	–
37	Misc. chemical products	2652.00	–	15.00	–	-	–	6.32	–
38	Plastics and articles thereof	10883.00	–	53.00	–	–	–	12.11	–
39	Rubber and Articles thereof	6281.00	–	40.00	–	–	–	4.62	-
40	Raw hides and skins.	266859.00	238442.00	47.00	42.00	89.35	87.23	4.83	5.38
41	Articles of leather.	182921.00	153053.00	39.00	14.00	83.67	35.89	6.74	6.32
42	Furskins and artifical far, mfg. thereof	537.00	479.00	10.00	8.00	89.20	80.00	4.82	4.98
43	Wood and articles of wood	11824.00	7.00	41.00	–	0.05	2.43	5.60	0.00
44	Manufacturing plating material	1181.00	-	8.00	-	-	-	5.80	–

(Contd...)

1	2	3	4	5	6	7	8	9	10
45	Paper and paper board, articles	1509.00	–	40.00	–	–	–	10.93	–
46	Printed books and other products	2654.00	–	14.00	–	–	–	1.16	–
47	Articles of sale	64765.00	–	23.00	–	–	–	6.40	–
48	Wood, fine or coarse animal hair	1228.00	360.00	14.00	7.00	29.31	50.00	1.00	3.12
49	Articles of cotton	250907.00	247980.00	139.00	137.00	98.83	98.56	8.56	8.60
50	Other Veg. textile fibres	49962.00	–	28.00	–	–	–	6.46	–
51	Man-made fibre	8864.00	6881.00	48.00	46.00	77.62	95.83	9.85	9.95
52	Man-made staple fibre	39465.00	37620.00	68.00	60.00	95.32	88.23	9.85	9.66
53	Wadding felt and non-woven; spl. yarn,	782.00	773.00	18.00	16.00	98.85	88.89	7.25	9.19
54	Carpet and other textile floor covering	246084.00	236435.00	36.00	33.00	96.08	91.67	6.29	6.22
55	Special Woven fabrics.	7084.00	6655.00	39.00	36.00	93.94	92.30	5.76	5.71
56	Impregnated, Wated, laminated text, fibres	354.00	223.00	15.00	13.00	62.99	86.67	8.44	8.36
57	Knitted or wocheted fabrics	957.00	906.00	14.00	12.00	94.67	85.71	11.92	12.00
58	Articles of apparels and clothing acc.	132233.00	132044.00	113.00	104.00	99.85	92.03	13.62	14.00
59	Articles of apparels and clothing	530910.00	511400.00	163.00	146.00	96.32	89.57	13.49	14.20
60	Other than man-made text, articles,	75219.00	72295.00	61.00	53.00	96.12	86.88	12.13	13.00
61	Footwear, gaiters and the like such items	171908.00	171725.00	59.00	58.00	99.89	98.30	5.77	5.75
62	Headgear and pents thereof	248.00	-	11.00	-	-	-	5.66	–

63	Umbrella, walking and seat etc.	242.00	90.00	5.00	2.00	37.19	60.00	6.84	4.88
64	Prepared leathers and down with articles,	68.00	29.00	4.00	1.00	42.64	25.00	5.65	55.00
65	Articles of stones plaster, combs, mica	10731.00	_	32.00	_	_	_	2.30	_
66	Ceramic products	831.00	_	21.00	_	_	_	10.22	_
67	Glass and glassware	1537.00	_	28.00	_	_	_	11.92	_
68	Pearls, precious or semi-precious metals	584741.00	33272.00	34.00	3.00	5.69	8.82	0.35	3.50
69	Iron & steel articles	16559.00	14364.00	25.00	14.00	86.74	56.00	6.22	4.69
70	Articles of iron and steel.	11073.00	122.00	84.00	_	1.10	1.19	5.57	10
71	Copper and articles thereof	18018.00	_	23.00	_	_	-	4.32	_
72	Copper and articles thereof	622.00	_	2.00	_	_	-	4.52	_
73	Aluminium and articles thereof	1514.00	_	23.00	-	_	-	7.32	_
74	Zinc and articles thereof	176.00	_	5.00	_	_	-	3.79	_
75	Tin and articles thereof	600.00	_	1.00	_	_	-	7.00	_
76	Other base-metals, cermets, articles	89.00	_	2.00	_	_	-	0.059	7.00
77	Tools and their parts of base metal	270.00	_	8.00	_	_	-	0.70	_
78	Misc. articles of base metal	24055.00	_	86.00	_	_	-	4.71	_
79	Nuclear reactor, boilers, mechanical apparatus parts thereof	44973.00	_	28.00	_	_	_	1.98	_
80	Elect. machinery and equipment thereof	45012.00	_	312.00	_	-	_	3.88	-
81	Rly/Tramway Locomotives, trucks etc.	16739.00	_	241.00	_	_	-	5.92	_

(Contd...)

1	2	3	4	5	6	7	8	9	10
82	Road Vehicles and parts thereof	324.00	-	5.00	-	-	-	4.35	-
83	Aircraft, Spacecraft and parts	18049.00	-	67.00	-	-	-	7.96	-
84	Ship, boat and floating structure	295.00	-	5.00	-	-	-	1.91	-
85	Ship, boat and floating structure	3166.00	-	1.00	-	-	-	0.00	-
86	Clock and matches and their parts	10392.00	7194.00	127.00	84.00	-	66.14	6.89	-
87	Musical instruments,parts and accessories	35.00	7.00	8.00	10.00	35.00	12.50	5.94	7.00
88	Arms and ammunition, parts etc.	993.00	73.00	,20.00	4.00	7.35	20.00	5.77	5.47
89	Furniture, bedding and allied articles,	376.00	324.00	12.00	-	88.83	58.33	4.35	4.23
90	Toys, games and sports requisites etc.	5840.00	-	46.00	-	-	-	5.73	-
91	Misc. manufacturing articles	9061.00	707.00	45.00	3.00	7.59	6.66	4.98	5.60
92	Works of art, collection rise and artiques	3337.00	1788.00	35.00	10.00	53.58	28.57	5.64	5.74
93	Project goods some special uses	1225.00	-	6.00	-	-	-	-	-
	Total	3665032.00	1933933.00	3217.00	1037.00	52.80	32.23	6.11	8.92

Source : UNCTAD, Reports on Trade, Tariffs, Non-Tariff Barriers (Geneva, 1988).

products are covered by these NTBs[25].

Table 5.1 shows the **structure of the EU's tariff and non-tariff barriers to Indian exports during 1988**[26]. It is evident that some items at HS-2 digit level are entirely covered by NTBs. In this table, we have taken two indicators of measuring the degree of restrictiveness i.e.- 1) **NTBs coverage ratio** and 2) **frequency ratio**[27]. NTB coverage ratio shows how much of India's exports are covered by Community NTBs. This is measured by the extent of value of exports covered by NTBs to the value of total exports at any particular period. According to second method (i.e. frequency ratio), how many products of a certain trade flow line (at HS-8 digit levels) of exports are subject to Community NTBs. These two ratios measure the degree of protectionism in the EU market as applicable to Indian products (Laird & Peats, 1990)[28].

The year 1988 was very significant because during this year Uruguay Round negotiations were progressing in full swing. All the tariff reduction packages submitted by the contracting parties to GATT were based on 1986-88 average level. Therefore, from the protectionist point of view the year 1988 had immense importance (WTO, 1994)[29].

Table 5.1 gives detailed description about the extent and coverage of NTBs during 1988. If we segregate Indian exports which have higher potentiality in the EU market in terms of NTB-coverage ratio of more than 50 per cent, then the items are: live animals (100 per cent), meat etc. (100 per cent), live tree and other plants (99.13 per cent), preparation of vegetables, fruits, and nuts (60.42 per cent), beverages spirit (64.6 per cent) raw hides and skins (89.35 per cent), articles of leather (83.67 per cent), cotton (98.83 per cent), man-made filament (77.62 per cent), man-made staple fibre (95.32 per cent), wadding, felt and non-woven (98.85 per cent), carpet and other textile floor coverings (96 per cent), special woven fabrics (93.94 per cent), impregnated, coated cover (62.99 per cent), articles of apparel and clothing accessories (96.32 per cent), other made-up and textile articles (96.12 per cent), items of iron and steel (86.74 per cent), arms and ammunition (88.83 per cent, and miscellaneous manufactured articles (53.58 per cent)[30].

It is evident from **Table 5.1** that almost all items of textiles and garments have been under NTBs[31]. Apart from these, other items like some primary commodities, such as agricultural goods, raw materials like hides and skins and leather are also subject to EC's higher protectionism. Now question arises, whether India is having comparative advantage in exporting these items (Walter, 1971)[32]. Though it is shown here empirically, but on a priori basis we can also say that the items which are very competitive in the EU market are subject to higher tariffs as well as non-tariffs barriers"[33]. Whether Indian items are competitive in the EU market or not that will be revealed through the Revealed Comparative Advantage Index (Balassa, 1965)[34]. This exercise is shown in the next section. Except textiles and garments, India's share in the EU market has been negligible; therefore, there have been no significant NTBs on high-tech manufactured goods emanating therefrom[35].

The complete picture of NTB-coverage ratio and frequency ratio for 1988 are shown in **Table 5.1**. Number of items in 1988 was more because we have covered all items irrespective of any value starting 1000 US dollars. The name of NTBs corresponding to each group (HS 2-digit) is shown in **Table-4.9**. In 1988, India had exported about 3217 items to the Community, of which 1037 items were covered by Community NTBs which meant 32.23 percent of India's total number of items exported were subject to EU's protectionism in the form of NTBs[36]. The NTBs coverage ratio for Indian exports to the European Community was 52.80 percent in 1988 and the corresponding frequency ratio was 32.23 percent during the same year[37].

India's exports to the Community have been facing two types of major barriers. One is of **tariff** and another of **non-tariff** barriers. Majority of non-tariff barriers are in the form of quotas : bilateral or global quotas, applied mainly on textiles and garments. Apart from bilateral quota, several other tools of quantitative restrictions have been existing. These are : ceiling, basket extractor mechanism, safeguard clause (GATT Article XIX), surge mechanism, anti-surge mechanism, cummulative market disruption and quota under Generalized System of Preference (GSP)[38].

In the EU, normally 68 group of items are subject to MFA. Out of these 11 are very much restricted for India. In the case of South Korea restrictive groups were 43, and the number is much higher in the case of Poland, Hungary and other Eastern part of European countries. For India, these 11 groups of items are very restrictive in the EU market[39]. Normally the rate of growth varies from 0.5 per cent to 2 per cent in these categories though it should be of minimum 6 per cent according to GATT prescription (Sharma, 1984)[40]. But applying safeguard clause EU frequently puts stringent quantity

TABLE 5.2 : Major EU NTBs to its Imports from India in 1988

S. No.	Name of the NTBs	Source	Year of Application	Affected countries
		EU (EUROPEAN COUNTRIES)		
01	Variable levy	TARIC	0081	All
02	Misc Regl/Non-Commercial purposes	TARIC/CITIES/ 032	0081	All
03	Ex-Retrospective Surveillance	OJ L151/91	0791	All
04	Reference Prices	TARIC	0081	All
05	Ex-Reference Prices	TARIC	0088	All
06	Licence	TARIC	0081	All
07	Variable Component	TARIC	0081	All
08	Seasonal Tariffs	TARIC	0081	All
09	Ex-Licence	TARIC	0081	All
10	Ex-Bilateral Quota	TARIC/CITIES	0081	All
11	Ex-Variable component	TARIC	0081	All
12	MFA Restraint Agreement	Bilateral	0081	18 Ind. INDIA
13	Anti-Dumping Investigation	OJC 72190	0390	BRA,IND, THA,TUREGY
14	Community Surveillance	REG(EC)288182	0778	All
15	Basic Import Price	OJL 380189	0081	All
16	Import Surveillance	TARIC	0086	All
17	Ex-Anti-Dumping Investigation	OJC 80/90	0390	CAN,OAN, IND, FOR,TUR
		PRT		
01	Quantitative Restrictions (NAL/and/or Quota)	REG.EEC 288/82	0081 0088	All All
02	Ex-Quantiative Restrictions	REG.EEG 288/82	0081 0088	All All
03	Surveillance	OJ L21	0081	All
		ESP		
01	Quantitative Restrictions (NAL/and/or Quota)	REG.EEC 288/82	0081	All
02	Ex-Quantiative Restrictions	REG(EC), 288/82A	0081	All
03	Surveillance Licence	OJ, L21	0081	All
04	Ex-Surveillance Licence	OJ, L21	0081	All
	FRA			
01	Quantitative Restrictions (NAL and/or Quota)	REG.EEC 288/82A	0081	44 Countries
02	Ex-Surveillance Licence	OJ, L21	0081	All
03	Surveillance Licence	OJ, L21	0081	All
04	Ex-Quantiative Restrictions (NAL and/or Quota)	REG(EC), 288/82A	0081	44 Countries
05	Quantity Restrictions without limit & quantity	REG (EC), 288/82	0081	All

S. No.	Name of the NTBs	Source	Year of Application	Affected countries
	ITA			
01	Quantitative Restrictions (NAL and/or Quota)	REG.EEC 288/82A	0081	79 Countries
02	Surveillance Licence	OJ, L21	0081	All
03	Ex-Quantitative Restrictions (NAL and/or Quota)	REG(EC), 288/82A	0081	79 Countries
	IRL			
01	Ex-Quantitative Restrictions (NAL and/or Quota)	REG(EC), 288/82A	0081	79 Countries
02	Surveillance Licence	OJ, L21	0081	All
03	Quantitative Restrictions (NAL and/or Quota)	REG.EEC 288/82A	0081	All
	NLD			
01	Quantitative Restrictions (NAL and/or Quota)	REG.EEC 288/82A	0081	All
02	Ex-Quantitative Restrictions (NAL and/or Quota)	REG(EC), 288/82A	0081	All
	GBR			
01	Quantitative Restrictions (NAL and/or Quota)	REG.EEC 288/82A	0081	All
02	Ex-Quantitative Restrictions (NAL and/or Quota)	REG(EC), 288/82A	0081	All
	GRE			
01	Quantitative Restrictions (NAL and/or Quota)	REG.EEC 288/82A	0081	All
02	Ex-Quantitative Restrictions (NAL and/or Quota)	REG(EC), 288/82A	0081	All
03	Surveillance Licence	OJ, L21	0081	All
	DNK			
01	Ex-Quantitative Restrictions (NAL and/or Quota)	REG(EC), 288/82A	0081	All
	BNLX			
01	Quantitative Restrictions (NAL and/or Quota)	REG.EEC 288/82A	0081	All
02	Ex-Quantitative Restrictions (NAL and/or Quota)	REG(EC), 288/82A	0081	All

Source: UNCTAD: Reports on Trade Tariffs and Non-Tariff Barriers (Geneva, 1988).

limits on imports under the pretext of "injurious to domestic industry".

One **important hypothesis** of this study is that the items whose exports are constrained by NTBs, are also protected by higher tariffs[41]. A priori argument is that if the items are protected by quotas or any other NTBs are also protected by higher tariffs. The simple logic is that higher tariff makes imported products costlier as compared to the price at the domestic market, thereby, causing comparative disadvantage to exporters. Any restrain on imports lowers the elasticity of import demand curve and widens the gap between demand price and supply price. The restriction on imports puts an upward pressure on domestic prices which are to be eventually borne by the consumers[42].

Under the presumption that both tariffs and NTBs have positive correlation, we see from our study for 1988 that NTB-coverage ratio is as high as 52.80 percent and frequency ratio is also 32.23 per cent. The average rate of the EU's tariff as applicable to Indian exports was 6.11 per cent in 1988. This rate covers all items under study i.e. 3217 in total. On the contrary, if one takes only items that were covered by NTBs, then the average rate of tariff for all NTBs affected items was 8.92 per cent i.e. almost 50 per cent higher than the average tariffs on all products[43]. Even in some cases the ratio is as high as 10 to 15 per cent on an average (see **Table 5.1**). This is true in case of some super sensitive items in textiles and garments. Therefore our *a priori* argument holds good that both tariffs and non-tariffs have positive correlation. From UNCTAD inventory on tariff and non-tariff barriers, we have also seen the same phenomenon, i.e. tariff is very high on items which are covered by NTBs[44]. The detailed structure of EU's tariffs and non-tariff barriers to Indian exports during 1988 shown in **Table 5.1.**

NON-TARIFF BARRIERS TO TRADE
The Case of India's Exports in 1992

The intensity of EU's protectionism on India's exports remained more or less the same even in 1992 except with slight change in coverage ratio. Almost all major NTBs were operational even in 1992 barring a few exceptions. India's exports to the EU were subject to 17 major NTBs which are shown in **Table 5.2**[45]. The table shows the names of the NTBs, source of information to authenticate the incidence of NTBs, years of application and the countries affected by such measures. Apart from identified NTBs, there exist a large number of unspecified NTBs which are difficult to identify, as well as its quantitative impact of such NTBs on India's exports.

Major NTBs in the EU market during 1992 were as follows : Variable levy, miscellaneous regulations/non-commercial purposes, ex-reference prices ('ex'-means partial), licence, seasonal tariffs, reference price, variable component, ex-anti-dumping duties, ex-anti-dumping investigations, MFA constraint agreement, anti-dumping duties, anti-dumping investigations Community surveillance, basic import prices and import surveillance[46]. Among these 17 NTBs, all are not equally restrictive, neither frequency of application follow a similar pattern. The entire gamut of India's exports of textiles and garments to the EC has been affected by two major NTBs, viz. MFA restraint agreement and anti-dumping duties. There is a lurking fear among EU importers that the textiles exported by India are underpriced and thus cause material injury to their domestic textile industry. Therefore it should be under the purview of EC's anti dumping duties. Most of the anti dumping measures enforced by EU are provisional and investigations are still going on. But during investigations, they have put provisional anti-dumping duty (Tharakan et al, 1994)[47].

Another major NTB that erodes our export prospects to the EU market is MFA quota. On textiles India has concluded bilateral agreement with the EC and six other developed countries like USA, Canada, Austria, Sweden, Norway and Finland. These agreements restrain India's exports to these countries in spite of having comparative advantage. All agreements relating to textiles are under MFA, a special arrangement made outside the GATT framework. India is a unique case where textiles exports have been subject to anti-dumping duties also enforced since 1991. MFA restraint agreement is applicable to 19 textile exporting countries including India. Apart from India, the other countries affected by EU's anti-dumping duty are Korea, China, Oman, Indonesia and Turkey and more other countries. The frequency of application of anti-dumping duty is much higher in the case of India than other countries.

According to UNCTAD Inventory on Tariff and Non-Tariff Barriers, India had exported about 1605 items to the EU market in 1992 of which 733 items i.e. 39.19 percent were covered by single or multiple NTBs. The reason behind lesser number of export items in 1992 than in 1988 is because of the selection of trade cut-offs[48]. In 1988, we have taken all items exported at any level (i.e. on or above 1000 US dollars) but in 1992, we have considered only those items whose exports were valued at more than 50,000 US dollars. The frequency ratio of EC's variable levy is 2.59 (here frequency ratio calculated as the number of items under particular NTBs to the total number of items affected by NTBs), the same ratio for miscellaneous regulations (non-commercial purpose) was 14.19, for licensing it was 3.27. It was almost insignificant in case of seasonal tariffs, reference prices and variable components where the ratios were less than 1. Highest ratio is certainly in case of items under MFA quota, where the ratio is 59.89 followed by anti-dumping duties (ratio is approximately 8) Community surveillance scheme is also an important NTB in the Community market, the magnitude of which was 8.86 in 1992 followed by basic import prices (2.45) and import surveillance scheme (1.09). The entire picture of frequency of application of EC's NTBs during 1992 is shown in **Table 5.3**)[49].

Now let us see the groups whose NTB-coverage ratios[50] are more than 50. The value of NTB-coverage ratio has been shown in the parenthesis. These groups (at 2-digit HS category) are : meat and edible meat offal (100 percent), live trees and other plants, bulbs, roots and the like, cut flowers and ornaments foliage (100 percent), cereals (100 percent) vegetable planting materials, vegetable products not elsewhere specified or included (80.33 percent), sugar and sugar confectionery (100 per cent) preparations of cereals, flour starch or milk, pastry and cooked products (100 percent) preparation of vegetable, fruits, nuts or other parts of plants (62.23 percent), raw hides and skins (other than fur skins) and leather (97.21 percent), articles of leather, saddling horses and animal gut (85.91), fur skins and artificial fur manufacturing thereof (100 percent), wood and articles of wood (78.18%) wool, fine or coarse animal hair (97.58%), articles of cotton (100 percent), man-made fibre (91.14) man-made staple fiber (99.0 percent), wadding falt and non-woven, special goods, twine cordage, ropes and labels and articles thereof (100 per cent), carpet and other textile floor covering (99.9 percent), special woven fabrics, tufted textiles, fabrics lace, tapestries, trimmings and embroidery (97.0 percent), impregnated coated laminated textiles, fibre, textile articles for industrial use (100 percent), knitted or crocheted fabrics (100 percent), articles of apparels and clothing's accessories, knitted or crocheted (100 percent), articles of apparels and clothing accessories not knitted or crocheted (94.35 percent). Other than man-made fibre textile articles, woven, textile, articles, rug (89.12%), footwear, gaitess and like such items (99.7 percent), umbrellas, walking stick and seat and riding crops and parts thereof (51.12 percent), articles of iron and steel (90.34 percent), furniture, bedding and allied articles, lighting, fittings, non-illuminated articles, prefabricated buildings (75.26 percent).

TABLE 5.3 : Structure of EU's Tariff and Non-Tariff Barriers to Indian Exports in 1992

HS Code	Product Description	Total value of exports (000$)	Total value of exports cov by NTBS (000$)	Total no. of items exported	Total no. of items covered by NTBS	NTB Coverage Ratio items	Frequency Ratio	Value of exports (wtd) by tariffs	Avg. rate of Tariffs on NTB covered
1	2	3	4	5	6	7	8	9	10
01	Live Animals	----	----	----	----	----	----	----	----
02	Meat and Edible meat offal	136.00	136.00	1.00	1.00	100.00	100.00	408.00	3.00
03	Fish and crustaceans, molluscs	187272.00	52655.00	26.00	8.00	28.12	30.76	2376515.00	6.64
04	Fish and crustaceans, molluscs and other acquantic in vertebrates								
05	Products of Animal orgin or in	14787.00	3585.00	9.00	4.00	24.24	44.44	322.00	2.00
06	Live trees and other plants,	5863.00	5863.00	5.00	5.00	100.00	100.00	38034.00	6.49
07	Edible Vegetables and certain roots and tubers	12890.00	2672.00	13.00	2.00	20.73	15.38	355093.80	81.10
08	Edible fruits and nuts, peel of citrus fruit or melons	96223.00	1139.00	8.00	1.00	1.18	12.50	128738.00	3.00
09	Coffee, Tea, mate and Spices	149206.00	----	19.00	----	----	----	241934.7	----
10	Cereals	50269.00	50269.00	12.00	12.00	100.00	100.00	5392753.10	107.24
11	Products of milling industry m starches, innlia, wheat gutton	291.00	108.00	2.00	1.00	37.10	5.00	11148.60	81.20
12	Oilseeds and leaginous	30732.00	----	7.00	----	----	----	8841.0	----
13	Lac Jums resins and other veg. saps and extracts	24106.00	----	9.00	----	----	----	2302.50	----
14	Veg. Plaiting materials, veg.	4697.00	3773.00	3.00	1.00	80.33	33.33	----	----
15	Animals & Veg. fats and oils a clearage products, animals or veg. waxes	45463.00	----	7.00	----	----	----	207091.90	----

16	Preparations of meat & fish or crustaceans, molluscs	4525.00	483.00	3.00	1.00	18.63	33.33	90500.00	20.00
17	Sugars and sugar confectionory	18458.00	18458.00	3.00	3.00	100.00	100.00	369338.00	20.00
18	Coco and Coco Products	----	----	----	----	----	----	----	----
19	Preparations of Cereals, flower milk, pastry & cooked products	3506.00	3506.00	1.00	1.00	100.00	100.00	38566.00	11.00
20	Preparations of Veg., Fruits, other parts of plants	11546.00	7185.00	9.00	4.00	62.23	44.44	231864.00	22.36
21	Misc. edible prepartions	3353.00	825.00	6.00	1.00	24.60	16.67	46280.20	13.00
22	Bererages, spirits and vinegar	306.00	101.00	2.00	1.00	33.00	50.00	6183.70	12.50
23	Residens and waste from the industries, prepared animal fodder	98563.00	302.00	7.00	1.00	0.30	14.28	----	----
24	Tobacco and manufactured subst	113328.00	----	13.00	----	----	----	1458694.00	----
25	Salt sulpher, earths, stores, mfgrs, lime and cement	113328.00	----	26.00	----	----	----	5911.50	----
26	Ores, slaq and ash	56395.00	----	5.00	----	----	----	----	----
27	Mineral fuels, minerals oils a products, bituminus substances mineral	84616.00	----	6.00	----	----	----	118489.00	----
28	Inorganic chemicals and its co	9958.00	----	19.00	----	----	----	83114.10	----
29	Organic Chemicals and its Comp	----	----	----	----	----	----	----	----
30	Pharmaceutical products	12911.00	----	15.00	----	----	----	73657.10	----
31	Dying, tawning and colouring m	----	----	----	----	----	----	----	----
32	Essential oils and resinoids	89740.00	----	17.00	----	----	----	876262.00	----
33	Soap and similar preparations	17945.00	----	13.00	----	----	----	381505.00	----
34	Albuminnidal substances.	413.00	----	3.00	----	----	----	2579.30	----
35	Explosive, marches, certain co	1569.00	----	2.00	----	----	----	14655.60	----
36	Photographic or cinematograph	104.00	----	1.00	----	----	----	104.00	----
37	Misc. chemical products	37.00	----	2.00	----	----	----	206127.80	----
38	Plastics and articles thereof	32865.00	----	11.00	----	----	----	175881.70	----
39	Rubber and Articles thereof	18984.00	----	30.00	----	----	----	68283.10	----

(Contd...)

1	2	3	4	5	6	7	8	9	10
40	Raw hides and skins.	14950.00	----	24.00	----	----	----	68283.10	----
41	Articles of leather.	203450.00	199213.00	24.00	20.00	97.91	83.33	1081630.90	5.42
42	Furskins and artifical fur, mf	450597.00	387118.00	27.00	13.00	85.91	48.15	3039488.40	6.41
43	Wood and articles of wood	143.00	143.00	1.00	1.00	100.00	100.00	856.00	6.00
44	Manufacturing plating material	19427.00	15189.00	19.00	6.00	98.18	31.57	112527.10	6.02
45	Paper and paper board, article	----	----	----	----	----	----	----	----
46	Printed books and other products	1874.00	----	5.00	----	----	----	7353.90	----
47	Articles of sale	----	----	----	----	----	----	----	----
48	Wood, fine or coarse animal hair	2006.00	----	6.00	----	----	----	22401.00	----
49	Articles of cotton	4045.00	----	8.00	----	----	----	6588.10	----
50	Other Veg. textile fibres	66525.00	----	18.00	----	----	----	445145.50	----
51	Man-made fibre	11695.00	11412.00	11.00	10.00	97.58	90.90	85082.40	7.27
52	Man-made staple fibre	307674.00	307674.00	93.00	93.00	100.00	100.00	2493854.60	----
53	Wadding felt and non-woven; sp	51582.00	----	11.00	----	----	----	311221.30	----
54	Carpet and other textile floor	39063.00	35603.00	36.00	35.00	91.14	97.20	389241.00	10.00
55	Special Woven fabrics.	140763.00	139358.00	46.00	44.00	99.00	95.70	1391132.50	9.91
56	Impregnated, Wated, laminated	828.00	828.00	4.00	4.00	100.00	100.00	72.22	8.72
57	Knitted or crocheted fabrics	316632.00	316406.00	26.00	25.00	99.90	96.15	2228440.50	7.00
58	Articles of apparels and cloth	20140.00	19538.00	15.00	14.00	97.00	93.30	126636.10	6.30
59	Articles of apparels and cloth	4405.00	4405.00	7.00	7.00	100.00	100.00	46630.60	10.58
60	Other than man-made text, arti	6055.00	6055.00	9.00	9.00	100.00	100.00	72660.00	12.00
61	Footwear, gaiters and the like	380083.00	380083.00	71.00	71.00	100.00	100.00	5134819.20	13.50
62	Headgear and pents thereof	872073.00	822809.00	133.00	116.00	94.35	87.22	11986480.60	13.90
63	Umbrella, walking stick etc	197868.00	176347.00	32.00	29.00	89.12	90.67	2393671.50	12.54
64	Prepared leathers and down wit	262733.00	261944.00	50.00	49.00	99.70	98.00	1615112.90	6.15
65	Articles of stones plaster, co	2745.00	----	3.00	----	----	----	10158.00	----
66	Ceramic products	223.00	114.00	2.00	1.00	51.12	50.00	1430.60	4.90
67	Glass and glassware	217.00	----	1.00	----	----	----	1670.9	----

68	Pearls, precious or semi----preci	25595.00	----	21.00	----	----	----	51875	----
69	Iron & steel articles	1594.00	----	8.00	----	----	----	13365.5	----
70	Articles of iron and steel.	3255.00	----	8.00	----	----	----	39302.4	----
71	Copper and articles thereof	646704.00	66236.00	20.00	2	10.24	10	343817.6	3.5
72	Copper and articles thereof	61516.00	55578.00	32.00	2	90.34	68.75	373544.4	6.07
73	Aluminimum and articles thereo	41048.00	----	65.00	----	----	----	258270.7	----
74	Zinc and articles thereof	----	----	----	----	----	----	----	----
75	Tin and articles thereof	----	----	----	----	----	----	----	----
76	Other base----metals, cermets, ar	----	----	----	----	----	----	----	----
77	Tools and their parts of base	329.00	2	----	----	----	----	----	----
78	Misc. articles of base metal	49604.00	----	41.00	----	----	----	229937.3	----
79	Nuclear reactor, boilers, mech apparates parts thereof	65106.00	----	17.00	----	----	----	116751.9	----
80	Elect. machinery and equipment	122081.00	----	121.00	----	----	----	543959.5	----
81	Rly/Tramway Locomotives, trucks	114376.00	----	98.00	----	----	----	805299.7	----
82	Road Vehicles and parts thereof	224.00	----	1.00	----	----	----	1008	----
83	Aircraft, Spacecraft and parts	79085.00	----	35.00	----	----	----	752878.2	----
84	Ship, boat and floating struct	12027.00	----	5.00	----	----	----	585	----
85	Ship, boat and floating struct	----	----	----	----	----	----	----	----
86	Clock and matches and their pa	58903.00	----	52.00	----	----	----	182801.10	----
87	Musical instruments,parts and	390.00	----	3.00	----	----	----	2234.00	----
88	Arms and ammunition, parts etc	1842.00	508.00	5.00	1.00	27.58	20.00	10492.20	5.00
89	Furniture bedding and allied a	465.00	350.00	2.00	1.00	75.26	50.00	1729.50	3.20
90	Toys, games and sports requisi	30812.00	----	21.00	----	----	----	167870.10	----
91	Misc. manufacturing articles	18968.00	725.00	18.00	1.00	3.68	5.55	106243.20	5.60
92	Works of art, collection rise	9411.00	3414.00	17.00	7.00	36.27	41.18	83659.50	6.19
93	Project goods some special use twice cordage, reper and labels and articles thereof	3172.00	576.00	5.00	1.00	18.16	20.00	----	----
		6052648.00	3363049.00	1605.00	629.00	55.56	39.19	50101109.32	12.54

The items mentioned above are aggregated at 2-digit level from 8 digit of the original text. UNCTAD provides information at 8-digit level. In 1988, India's total export items were 3217 of which 1037 were ccvered by NTBs i.e. frequency ratio was 32.23 per cent during 1988. According to UNCTAD inventory, India had exported about 1605 items in 1992 of which 733 items were subject to Community NTBs i.e. 39.19 per cent was the frequency ratio in that year. The reason behind drastic reduction of the numbers of items exported to the EC was the increase of trade cut-offs from $1000 in 1988 to $50,000 in 1992.

In the EU markets, the items which are covered by NTBs are also subject to higher customs tariffs[51]. Presently average rate of nominal tariffs in the EU varies from 3-4 percent, in some industrial goods it is even less because a host of manufactured goods to developing countries have been enjoying duty-free treatment under the scheme of Generalized System of Preference (GSP). The EC has extended the facility to India since 1971 (Laird & Sapir, 1986)[52]. Against an average tariff of 3 to 4 per cent, the average rate of tariffs faced by Indian exporters was 6.11 percent in 1988 and 8.28 per cent in 1992. This is because items exported by India are considered to be competitive in the EU market and therefore subject to higher tariffs.

All rates are MFN and unbound which were prevailing prior to the conclusion of the Uruguay Round[53]. In the Final Agreement of GATT concluded at Marrakesh on 15 April 1994, all developed countries have offered reductions of their average tariffs by 38 percent on all industrial goods and the extent is the same for agricultural goods also[54]. Apparently it seems from the tariff structure that the EU is discriminatory to India, because average tariff charged from Indian exporters is 8.28 per cent against Community's average tariff of 3-4 percent. In both cases, the tariffs are weighted tariffs calculated by formula :

$$\hat{t} = \frac{\sum V_1 t_1}{\sum V_i}$$

where 'V' is the value of exports and 't' is the tariff rate and 'å' is sigma notation, '*i*' is the number of items and t is the weighted tariff[55].

India is one of the 23 founder members of GATT. The fundamental principle behind the establishment of GATT is "non-discrimination". Tariffs are product-specific not country-specific unless any special agreement is concluded with some specific countries like trading

TABLE 5.4: Frequency of Application of NTBs Harmonized Codes (EEC) 1992

	0	*1*	*2*	*3*	*4*	*5*	*6*	*7*	*8*	*9*	*Total*
01 Variable Levy	3.00	16.00	-	-	-	-	-	-	-	-	19.00
02 Misc. Regl/Non Commercial purpose	15.00	2.00	-	-	39.00	-	35.00	2.00	-	11.00	104.00
03 Ex-Reference price	-	-	-	-	-	-	-	-	-	-	-
04 Licence	2.00	17.00	5.00	-	-	-	-	-	-	-	24.00
05 Seasonal Tariffs	1.00	-	-	-	-	-	-	-	-	-	1.00
06 Reference Price	3.00	-	-	-	-	-	-	-	-	-	3.00
07 Variable Component	-	1.00	1.00	-	-	-	-	-	-	-	2.00
08 Ex-Adds	-	-	-	-	-	-	-	-	-	-	-
09 Ex-AD Investigation	-	-	-	-	-	-	-	-	-	-	-
10 MFA Restraint Agreement	-	-	-	-	-	224.00	215.00	-	-	-	439.00
11 AD Investigation	-	-	1.00	-	-	40.00	-	-	-	-	41.00
12 Anti-Dumping Duties	-	-	1.00	-	-	8.00	-	-	-	-	9.00
13 Community Surveillance	-	-	-	-	-	-	49.00	16.00	-	-	65.00
14 Basic Import Price	-	-	-	-	-	-	-	-	7.00	-	18.00
15 Import Surveillance	-	-	-	-	-	-	-	-	8.00	-	8.00

Source: UNCTAD, Reports on Trade, Tariffs, Non-Tariff Barriers (Geneva, 1988).

blocs[56]. On the question of market access and tariffs, the EU has special preferential arrangements with ACP and EFTA countries. Under Lome Convention[57], Community tariff is much low in case of the partner countries. Otherwise tariff rates are the same across the commodities irrespective of countries of origin except the countries with whom the EC has preferential arrangements. The average tariff faced by Indian exporters in the Community market is higher compared to EC's average tariffs because of the fact that more than half of Indian exports to the Community are subject to NTBs, therefore, logically attracting higher customs tariffs. This is the reason why Indian products face higher tariffs in the EU markets as compared to EC's average global tariffs[58].

As already stated, tariff rates are much higher in those items which are covered by NTBs than the items which are not restricted by the same. In 1992, against the average (wtd) tariffs of 8.28 percent on all exports, the rate was 12.54 per cent for the items which were covered by NTBs. The tariff rate of NTBs covered item was at least 50 per cent higher than normal goods which were not protected by NTBs. This phenomenon proves our hypothesis that there exists a positive correlation between NTBs and tariffs. The structure of tariff and non-tariff barriers applicable to Indian exports is shown in **Table 5.4.**

INDIAN EXPORTS SUBJECT TO COMMUNITY NON-TARIFF BARRIER DURING 1993-94 : AN EMPIRICAL ANALYSIS

There has been no perceptible change in EU's protectionism during the first half of the 1990s. Rather it follows the same trend as in 1992. In fact the EU's protectionism has been intensified by the introduction of newer forms of NTBs in protecting her imports. The recent example of green label, RAGMARK, and Azo Dice are some of the examples of it[59]. Anti-dumping measure is another form of NTBs which has been frequently used by the EU as well as other developed countries. It is expected that there may be a remarkable change in protectionist tendency when implementation of the provisions of the Final Act of the Uruguay Round of multilateral trade negotiations will be over i.e. 1 January 2005.

Major NTBs affecting India's exports to the European Union are shown in **Table 5.2.** Among listed NTBs in the UNCTAD Report in 1993 and 1994[60] most important are : miscellaneous regulations

TABLE 5.5: Structure of EU's Tariffs and Non-Tariff Barriers to its Imports from India, 1993

HS	Chapter Description	Total Value Exports ('000$)	Total Value of Exports Covered by NTBs ('000$)	Total No. of Items Exports	Total No. of Items Covered by NTBs	NTB Coverage Ratio	Fre-quency	Average of Tarrifs (WTD)	Avg. Rate of Tafiff (WTD) on NTB affected Items
1	2	3	4	5	6	7	8	9	10
1	Live Animals	–	–	–	–	–	–	10.29 (s)	
2	Meat and Edible Meat Offal	–	–	–	–	–	–	13.66 (s)	
3	Fish & Crustacean, Mollusc & o	173800	50070	33	9	28.800	27.27	12.23	6.07
4	Dairy Prod; Bird's Eggs; Natur	76	1	1	1	1.320	100.00	27	–
5	Products of Animal Origin, nes	13000	3418	10	5	26.290	50.00	2.04	0.1
6	Live Tree & Other Plant; Bulb,	6400	6329	8	8	98.890	100.00	8.59	6.93
7	Edible Vegetables and Certain	18500	5652	15	1	30.550	6.66	12.04	–
8	Edible Fruit and Nuts; Peel of	117300	2649	9	1	2.250	11.10	7.12	3
9	Coffee, Tea, Mat and Spices	178900	-	21	-	–	–	3.14	–
10	Cereals	39300	39281	12	12	99.950	100.00	0	0
11	Prod Mill Indust; Malt; Starch	200	168	1	1	84.000	100.00	12.68	–
12	Oil Seed, Oleagin Fruits; Misc	21100	1	11	-	–	–	5.77	–
13	Lac; Gums, Resins & Other Vege	18600	-	8	-	–	–	0.35	–
14	Vegetable Plaiting Materials;	3200	2424	3	1	75.750	33.33	0	0
15	Animal/Veg Fats & Oils & Their	43100	-	11	-	-	-	7.98	–
16	Prep of Meat, Fish or Crustacean	3900	546	5	1	14.000	20.00	19.98	20
17	Sugars and Sugar Confectionery	27400	27408	3	3	100.000	100.00	23	–
18	Cocoa and Cocoa Preparations	100	10	1	-	10.000	0.00	9	–
19	Prep of Cereal, Flour, Starch/	4900	4912	2	2	100.000	100.00	11.86	–
20	Prep of Vegetable, Fruit, Nuts	9700	6272	11	7	64.660	63.63	21.21	20.47

(Contd...)

1	2	3	4	5	6	7	8	9	10
21	Miscellaneous Edible Preparati	4800	795	7	2	16.560	28.57	13.31	15
22	Beverages, Spirits and Vinegar	2200	117	3	1	5.380	33.33	61.86	11.7
23	Residues & Waste from the food	110800	129	10	1	0.120	10.00	15	0
24	Tobacco and Manufactured tobac	47100	–	12	–	–	–	22.64	–
25	Salt; Sulphur; Earth & ston; p	129100	–	29	–	–	–	1.99	–
26	Ores, Slag and Ash	70200	–	6	–	–	–	–	–
27	Mineral Fuels, Oils & Product	143700	–	5	–	–	–	1.55	–
28	Inorganic Chem; Compds of Prec mt	13900	–	29	–	–	–	7.43	–
29	Organic Chemicals	170000	1033	136	2	0.610	1.47	7.69	7.73
30	Pharmaceutical Products	8400	–	19	–	–	–	5.95	–
31	Fertilisers	200	–	2	–	–	–	–	–
32	Tanning/dyeing Extract;	93400	–	15	–	–	–	9.67	–
33	Essential Oils & Resinoids; pe	14200	–	18	–	–	–	4.82	–
34	Soap, Organic Surgace-active a	2200	–	6	–	–	–	6.88	–
35	Albuminoidal Subs; Modified st	2300	–	9	–	–	–	7.02	–
36	Explosive; Pyrotechnic Prod;	100	–	1	–	–	–	6.63	–
37	Photographic or Cinematographi	500	–	3	–	–	–	7.45	–
38	Miscellaneous Chemical Product	20600	–	12	–	–	–	6.17	–
39	Plastics and Articles Thereof	21200	–	39	–	–	–	10.67	–
40	Rubber and Articles Thereof	11900	–	16	–	–	–	3.24	–
41	Raw Hides and Skins (Other tha	164000	156300	29	24	95.300	82.76	5.48	5.49
42	Articles of Leather; Saddlery/	518100	471410	23	12	90.990	52.17	6.71	6.5
43	Furskins and Artificial fur;	300	324	1	1	100.000	100.00	5.65	6
44	Wood and Articles of Wood; woo	19400	14542	29	7	74.950	24.14	5.36	5.78
45	Cork and Articles of Cork	–	–	–	–	–	–	–	
46	Manufactures of Straw, Esparto	2300	–	8	–	–	–	3.78	–
47	Pulp of Wood/of Other Fibrous	0	–	–	–	–	–	–	–
48	Paper & Paperboard; art of pap	2700	–	13	–	–	–	10.92	–
49	Printed Books, Newspapers, pic	5000	–	12	–	–	–	6.38	–
50	Silk	55300	–	18	–	–	–	6.82	–

* Frequency ratio is based on trade cut offs

1	2	3	4	5	6	7	8	9	10
51	Wool, Fine/Coarse Animal Hair	18500	17655	17	15	95.430	88.23	6.86	6.7
52	Cotton	284000	284000	105	105	100.000	100.00	8.68	8.68
53	Other Vegetable Textile Fibres	62300	16	13	-	0.026	-	2.04	-
54	Man-made Filaments	37800	35327	43	40	93.450	93.02	9.55	9.5
55	Man-made Staple Fibres	145300	144895	64	62	99.720	96.87	9.97	9.9
56	Wadding, Felt & Nonwoven; Yarn	1700	1462	9	7	86.000	77.80	10.56	10.5
57	Carpets and Other Textile Floo	360500	346918	29	27	98.000	93.10	7.06	7
58	Special Woven Fab; Turted Tex	17700	16902	32	30	49.000	93.75	6.45	6.4
59	Impregnated, Coated, Cover/lam	7000	6901	9	9	98.580	100.00	10.62	10.62
60	Knitted or Crocheted Fabrics	9400	9299	8	8	98.920	100.00	11.98	11.98
61	Art of Apparel & Clothing Acce	427600	426820	91	85	99.820	93.40	13.5	13.5
62	Art of Apparel & Clothing Acce	925100	888339	149	133	96.020	89.26	13.46	13
63	Other Made up Textile Articles	227700	206462	41	37	90.670	90.24	11.72	11.7
64	Footwear, Gaiters and the like	307700	307331	51	49	99.880	96.07	6.19	6.19
65	Headgear and Parts thereof	2700	6	6	-	0.220	-	5.48	-
66	Umbrellas, Walking-sticks, se	400	109	3	1	27.250	33.33	7.08	4.9
67	Prepr Feathers & Down; arti fi	900	62	4	1	6.890	25.00	6.62	5.5
68	Art of Stone, Plaster, Cement,	31500	–	25	–	–	–	3.69	-
69	Ceramic Products	3600	–	22	–	–	–	7.71	-
70	Glass and Glassware	3900	–	–	–	–	–	9.1	-
71	Natural/cultured Pearls, prec	762000	72512	29	3	9.510	10.34	4.58	-
72	Iron and Steel	51600	41767	30	29	80.940	96.67	5.17	4.9
73	Articles of Iron or Steel	51500	1189	85	6	2.300	7.05	5.76	9.63
74	Copper and Articles thereof	23700	-	12	–	–	–	4.98	-
75	Nickel and Articles thereof	800	-	2	–	–	–	4.65	-
76	Aluminium and Articles thereof	9500	-	16	–	–	–	7.56	-
77	-	–	–	–	–	–	–	-	

(Contd...)

1	2	3	4	5	6	7	8	9	10
78	Lead and Articles Thereof	–	–	–	–	–	–	–	–
79	Zinc and Articles Thereof	300	–	1	–	–	–	7	–
80	Tin and Articles Thereof	100	–	1	–	–	–	5.3	–
81	Other Base Metals; Cermets; ar	500	–	3	–	–	–	4.36	–
82	Tool, Implement, Cutlery, Spoo	48300	–	50	–	–	–	4.85	–
83	Miscellaneous Articles of Base	73300	–	41	–	–	–	4.92	–
84	Nuclear Reactors, Noilers, mch	185600	–	152	–	–	–	3.06	–
85	Electrical Machy Equip jparts	77400	–	133	–	–	–	6.56	–
86	Rails/tramw Locom, Rolling-sto	100	–	1	–	–	–	4.49	–
87	Vehicles o/t Railw/tramw Roll	100300	–	49	–	–	–	10.65	–
88	Aircraft, Spacecraft, and Part	14900	–	6	–	–	–	3.84	–
89	Ships, Boats and Floating stru	–	–	–	–	–	–	–	–
90	Optical, Photo, Cine, Meas, ch	47000	11	88	–	0.230	–	6.63	–
91	Clocks and Watches and Parts t	1000	543	4	3	54.300	75.00	5.2	5.1
92	Musical Instruments; Parts and	2300	529	7	3	23.000	42.85	5.77	5.17
93	Arm's and Ammunition; Parts and	400	398	1	1	99.500	100.00	3.2	3.2
94	Furnitures; Bedding, Matters,	38200	–	28	–	–	–	5.41	–
95	Toys, Games & Sports Requisite	24700	684	26	3	2.760	7.19	6.39	–
96	Miscellaneous Manufactured Art	13400	5122	24	8	38.220	33.33	7.28	4
97	Works of Art, Collectors' Piec	3200	239	6	1	7.460	16.66	–	–
	Total	6718800	3603482	2192		53.620	34.99	8.59	11.14

Source : UNCTAD *reports on trade, tariff and non-tariff barriers* (Geneva, 1993).

TABLE - 5.6 : Structure of EU's Tariff and Not-Tariff Barriers to the Imports from India, 1994

HS	*Chapter Description*	*Total Value Exports ('000$)*	*Total Value of Exports Covered by NTBs ('000$)*	*Total No. of Items Exports*	*Total No. of Items Covered by NTBs*	*NTB Coverage Ratio*	*Fre-quency Ratio*	*Average of Tariffs (WTD)*	*Avg. Rate of Tariff (WTD) on NTB affected Items*
1	2	3	4	5	6	7	8	9	*10*
1	Live Animals	–	–	–	–	–	–	10.29(1)	–
2	Meat and Edible Meat Offal	200	191	1	1	95.500	100	10	10
3	Fish & Crustacean, Mollusc & o	230700	54152	36	10	23.730	27.78	13.31	6.1
4	Dairy Prod; Bird's Eggs; Natur	300	266	1	1	88.670	100	–	–
5	Products of Animal Origin, nes	14200	3293	10	4	23.190	40	2.06	2
6	Live Tree & Other Plant; Bulb,	9300	9125	12	11	98.110	91.67	10.25	10.24
7	Edible Vegetables and Certain	17000	242	16	2	1.420	12.25	13.24	7.67
8	Edible Fruit and Nuts; Peel of	146400	8189	10	1	5.590	10	6.32	3
9	Coffee, Tea, Mat and Spices	260400	–	21	–	–	–	3.61	–
10	Cereals	45800	45798	11	11	99.900	100	1.09	0
11	Prod Mill Indust; Malt; Starch	300	86	2	1	28.670	50	12.92	–
12	Oil Seed, Oleagin Fruits; Misc	31700	1	12	1	0.003	8.33	3.94	–
13	Lac; gums, Resins & Other Vege	31100	–	.8	–	–	–	0	–
14	Vegetable Plaiting Materials;	3500	2591	3	1	74.280	33.33	0	0
15	Animal/Veg Fats & Oils & their	60600	1	13	1	0.002	7.69	8.34	–
16	Prep of Meat, Fish or Crustacean	200	–	1	–	–	–	14.91	–
17	Sugars and Sugar Confectionery	1700	1692	2	2	99.520	100	23	23

s = simple average

frequency ratio does not give good indication of restrictiveness because in case of 1993 & 1994 cutting point is $50,000

1	2	3	4	5	6	7	8	9	10
18	Cocoa and Cocoa Preparations	800	21	1	1	2.620	100	0	–
19	Prep of Cereal, Flour, Starch/	5400	5400	3	3	100.000	100	11.33	8
20	Prep of Vegetable, Fruit, Nuts	12300	8166	9	5	66.390	55.56	20.95	33.63
21	Miscellaneous Edible Preparati	7300	761	6	1	10.420	16.67	16.58	0
22	Beverages, Spirits and Vinegar	200	106	1	1	53.000	100	12.1	11.7
23	Residues & Waste from the Food	108700	1795	9	2	1.650	22.22	0	0
24	Tobacco and Manufactured Tobac	40900	–	12	–	–	–	22.17	–
25	Salt; Sulphur; Earth & Ston; p	159300	–	26	–	–	–	1.54	–
26	Ores, Siag and Ash	57200	–	7	–	–	–	0	–
27	Mineral Fuels, Oils & Product	71800	–	7	–	–	–	0.33	–
28	Inorgn Chem; Compds of prec mt	19900	–	38	–	–	–	6.76	–
29	Organic Chemicals	211800	1499	134	3	0.700	2.23	9.95	7.68
30	Pharmaceutical Products	7900	–	14	–	–	–	6.03	–
31	Fertilisers	200	–	1	–	–	–	–	–
32	Tanning/dyeing Extract; Tannin	118900	–	17	–	–	–	9.75	–
33	Essential Oils & Resinoids; pe	16200	–	19	–	–	–	4.79	–
34	Soap, Organic Surgace-active a	3300	–	5	–	–	–	6.88	–
35	Albuminoidal Subs; Modified st	3000	–	4	–	–	–	6.46	–
36	Explosive; Pyrotechnic Prod;	300	–	1	–	–	–	6.8	–
37	Photographic or Cinematographi	500	–	2	–	–	–	7.7	–
38	Miscellaneous Chemical Product	32000	–	14	–	–	–	6.15	–
39	Plastics and Articles Thereof	29500	–	47	–	–	–	9.9	–
40	Rubber and Articles Thereof	14600	–	29	–	–	–	3.91	–
41	Raw Hides and Skins (Other tha	232900	220491	27	23	94.670	85.18	5.55	5.5
42	Articles of Leather; Saddlery/	611100	535926	28	12	87.690	42.86	6.75	6.54
43	Furskins and Artificial Fur;	2500	1045	3	2	41.080	66.67	5.82	5.84
44	Wood and Articles of Wood; woo	23000	17835	19	7	77.540	36.84	5.23	5.75
45	Cork and Articles of Cork	–	–	–	–	–	–	–	–

46	Manufactures of Straw, Esparto	3100	–	9	–	–	–	3.68	–
47	Pulp of wood/of Other Fibrous	0	–	–	–	–	–	–	–
48	Paper & Paperboard; Art of Pap	4500	–	13	–	–	–	11.08	–
49	Printed Books, Newspapers, Pic	7500	–	10	–	–	–	6.61	–
50	Silk	69700	–	18	–	–	–	6.72	–
51	Wool, Fine/Coarse Animal Hair	30700	30164	20	19	98.250	95	6.44	6.44
52	Cotton	345400	334781	120	120	96.920	100	8.28	8.28
53	Other Vegetable Textile Fibres	85200	152	19	1	0.180	0.11	1.95	4.6
54	Man-made Filaments	42500	40229	47	43	94.660	91.48	10.13	10.2
55	Man-made Staple Fibres	195900	193995	69	64	99.020	92.75	9.87	10
56	Wadding, Felt & Nonwoven; Yarn	2300	2005	11	9	87.170	81.82	9.45	10
57	Carpets and Other Textile floo	339900	322502	28	25	94.880	89.28	7.04	7
58	Special Woven Fab; Turted Tex	19500	18624	26	24	95.500	92.3	6.72	6.7
59	Impregnated, Coated, Cover/lam	8500	8436	11	10	99.240	90.91	9.99	10
60	Knitted or Crocheted Fabrics	24300	24283	14	14	93.000	100	12	12
61	Art of Apparel & Clothing Acce	453800	452753	92	86	99.770	93.97	13.48	13.5
62	Art of Apparel & Clothing Acce	1139100	1108352	151	130	97.300	86.09	13.37	14
63	Other Made up Textile Articles	282600	269785	42	37	95.460	88.09	12.01	12
64	Footwear, Gaiters and the Like	377300	377006	54	53	99.920	98.15	6.32	6.32
65	Headgear and Parts Thereof	4400	-	9	–	–	–	5.99	-
66	Umbrellas, Walking-sticks, se	400	106	3	1	26.500	33.33	7.19	4.9
67	Prepr Feathers & Down; Arti fi	1000	145	2	1	14.500	50	7.11	5.5
68	Art of Stone, Plaster, Cement,	42700	-	23	–	–	–	3.71	-
69	Ceramic Products	4100	-	16	–	–	–	7.25	-
70	Glass and Glassware	7600	-	19	–	–	–	10.72	-
71	Natural/cultured Pearls, prec	849300	101040	27	3	11.890	11.11	4.5	3.52
72	Iron and Steel	31700	28083	23	17	88.580	73.91	3.49	2.24
73	Articles of Iron or Steel	61300	1532	93	4	2.500	4.3	5.55	-
74	Copper and Articles Thereof	32000	-	16	–	–	–	5.01	-
75	Nickel and Articles Thereof	1100	-	2	–	–	–	4.63	-

(Contd...)

1	2	3	4	5	6	7	8	9	10
76	Aluminium and Articles Thereof	15200	-	26	–	–	–	8.24	-
77	-	-	-	-	–	–	–	-	
78	Lead and Articles Thereof	0	–	–	–	–	–	–	–
79	Zinc and Articles Thereof	200	–	1	–	–	–	7.03	–
80	Tin and Articles Thereof	200	–	1	–	–	–	5.03	–
81	Other Base Metals; Cermets; ar	300	1	2	-	0.330	-	6.04	–
82	Tool, Implement, Cutlery, spoo	58900	–	53	–	–	–	5.11	–
83	Miscellaneous Articles of Base	92300	–	24	–	–	–	4.93	–
84	Nuclear Reactors, Boilers, mch	211600	–	171	–	–	–	3.15	–
85	Electrical Machy Equip jparts	97600	–	156	–	–	–	5.9	–
86	Rails/tram Locom, Rolling-sto	300	–	3	–	–	–	4.46	–
87	Vehicles o/t Railw/tramw Roll	95100	–	47	–	–	–	8.67	–
88	Aircraft, Spacecraft, and Parts	41700	–	7	–	–	–	4.9	–
89	Ships, Boats and Floating Stru	1900	–	1	–	–	–	4.9	–
90	Optical, Photo, Cine, Meas, ch	62000	44	89	-	0.070	–	6.95	–
91	Clocks and watches and Parts t	1300	364	5	2	28.000	40	5.34	5.1
92	Musical instruments; Parts and	2400	369	8	2	15.370	25	5.78	5.03
93	Arms and Ammunition; parts and	600	488	3	3	81.330	100	4.21	3.9
94	Furniture; Bedding, Mattresses,	48000	–	28	–	–	–	5.38	–
95	Toys, Games & Sports Requisite	33100	867	25	2	2.610	8	6.31	5.47
96	Miscellaneous Manufactured art	19400	7387	26	7	38.070	26.92	7	4.64
97	Works of Art, Collectors' Piec	2900	225	5	1	7.750	20	–	
	Total	7895600	4242996	2310	785	53.740	33.98	7.76	8.61

Source : UNCTAD *reports on trade, tariff and non-tariff barriers* (Geneva, 1994).

\non-commercial purpose, reference price, variable levy, licence, seasonal tariffs, reference price, special taxes, variable component, anti-dumping duties as well as anti-dumping investigations, tariff quota, MFA restraint agreement, Community surveillance, basic import prices, import surveillance, voluntary export restraint etc. The date of application is also given in the parenthesis. The detailed description of NTBs against each commodity group at HS-2 digit level is shown in **Table 4.9**[61].

The details of the NTB-coverage ratio, frequency ratio, average (weighted) tariffs and average tariffs of all NTB-affected items of 1993 and 1994 are shown in **Table 5.5 and 5.6**[62]**.** Without repeating names of items which have higher potentiality in the EU market we can extend our early conclusion here that some agricultural items, some raw leather and skins, some items of fruits and vegetables and some items of iron and steel are subject to NTBs in the EU market. Following the trend, the entire gamut of India's exports of textiles and garments have also been under EU's bilateral quota. Though in some cases India has not been successful in utilizing the quota, but in most of the super sensitive items India has not only fulfilled the quota but also the growth has been remarkably higher[63].

While analysing the structure and growth of protectionism, our *a priori* hypothesis has proved that the items under higher NTB-coverage ratio are also subject to higher tariffs. In our analysis for 1988 and 1992 this theoretical assumption holds good both conceptually as well as empirically. The average rate of tariffs for all goods was 8.59 per cent in 1993 but it was 16.09 per cent in case of items covered by NTBs which means tariff rate in NTB-affected items is almost double that of average tariff. The same year NTB-coverage ratio was as high as 53.62 per cent which means that more than 50

TABLE 5.7 : Consolidated Figures of the EU's Growing Protectionism on Indian Exports

	Average Rate of Tariffs (wtd)	*Average Rate of Tariffs (wtd) of NTB Affected Items*	*NTB-Coverage Ratio*	*Frequency Ratio*
1988	6.11	8.92	52.80	32.23
1992	8.28	12.54	55.56	39.19
1993	8.59	16.09	53.62	34.99
1994	7.76	8.37	53.74	33.98

** Figures are based on tables 5.1, 5.4, 5.5 and 5.6.

per cent of our exports to the Community are subject to Community NTBs. In our NTB study for four years the coverage ratios remain almost at the same level i.e. a little over 50 per cent., though trade cut-off in 1993 was $1000 US, but the frequency ratio during the same period was as high as 39.99 per cent. In our case, frequency ratio can not be used as a good index of protectionism simply because of variation of trade cut-offs[64].

The same trend continues even during 1994 which is the latest period for which data are available. The year 1994 was the culmination of the Uruguay Round negotiations. But the package finally agreed to in the Final Act, came into force with effect from 1st January 1995[65]. At the WTO forum India expressed its concern about the growing protectionism of the developed countries. On 31 December 1994, India concluded two agreements on textiles and garments with the USA and the EU[66]. The main provisions of the agreement have already been discussed in Chapter I. Though the EU has given commitment in the WTO form that it will reduce tariff by one-third over a period of ten years beginning from 1st January, 1995, it is hardly believable that there will be any perceptive change in the intensity of protectionism until the last date[67].

From UNCTAD inventory on NTBs it is found that average rate of tariffs applicable to India's exports to the EC was 7.76 per cent during 1994 which was 8.37 per cent if we take only items covered by NTBs. Tariff rate on NTB-affected items during 1994 has been much less. One plausible explanation may be that either India switched over from quota items to non-quota items or it has diverted its exports from quota countries to the non-quota countries[68]. NTB-coverage ratio during 1994 was 53.74 per cent and frequency ratio was 33.98 per cent during the same period.

The comparative and consolidated picture of all tariffs and non-tariffs are shown in **Table 5.7**. This table shows the trend of the EU protectionism during 1988, 1992, 1993 and 1994[69].

In our study we intend to prove **two hypothesis** on the EU's growing protectionism as applicable to India's exports.

First : Indian products in the Community market have been subject to higher NTBs as well as higher tariffs.

Second : Higher tariffs and non-tariffs are imposed on those items in which India has comparative advantage.[70]

The degree of comparative advantage is examined in the following section.

REVEALED COMPARATIVE ADVANTAGE OF INDIA'S EXPORTS TO THE EUROPEAN COMMUNITY

Our **second hypothesis** is that the items in which India has comparative advantage in the EU market are protected by higher tariffs as well as non-tariff barriers. This hypothesis seems to be sound on ***a priori basis***. The logical argument is that imports are restricted for those items in which domestic industry is highly incommunicative. In the case of India, the items which are highly restricted in the EC market are textiles, garments, agricultural goods and low value added industrial goods. Most of the items in these categories are labour-intensive in which EU does not have comparative cost advantage. Wage level as well as availability of raw material play a very significant role in determining competitiveness. EU does not have natural advantage of producing cotton at the same time; its per hour wage rate is among the highest in the world. Since human factor is very expensive, production cost is obviously very high. On the other hand, developing countries with natural endowments and low wage cost have been enjoying comparative cost advantage over the EU countries[71]. Besides, in the EU, growth of real wage is much higher than growth in productivity (World Devlopment Report, 1987)[72] which makes entire industry incommunicative. In order to protect its ailing domestic industries, these countries have taken recourse to increasing protectionist measures. The same argument holds good in case of USA also (Balassa, 1965)[73].

Revealed comparative advantage of all groups (Harmonized Codes at 2-digit levels) has been calculated for four years, i.e. 1988, 1992, 1993 and 1994 which is shown in **Table 5.8.** The formula for the calculation of Revealed Comparative Advantage Index is as follows :

Formula to Revealed Comparative Advantages (RCA) Index

$$RCAi = Xij/Wij$$

where, $$Xij = xij \Big/ \sum_{i=1}^{K} xij,$$ and

$$Wij = Xij \Big/ \sum_{i=1}^{P} Wij$$

$$RCAi = Xij \Big/ \sum_{i=1}^{K} xij \Big/ Wij \Big/ \sum_{i=1}^{P} Wij$$

$$= xij \sum_{i=1}^{P} wij \Big/ wij \sum_{i=1}^{K} xij$$

Where $RCAi$ = Revealed Comparative Advantage for community '*i*' (here commodity group at HS-2 digit)

xij = Import of commodity '*i*' from India to country '*j*' (here EU)

wij = Import of commodity '*i*' from world to country '*j*' (here EU)

$\sum_{i=1}^{K} xij$ = Total Indian Export to country '*j*' (i.e. EU)

$\sum_{i=1}^{P} wij$ = Total World Import to country '*j*' (here EU)

$i \in j$

j = 1,2......K1,K2......P

P > K

The value of index greater than unity indicates relatively strong comparative advantage while a lower value would place a country at a relatively disadvantageous position with respect to export of any particular commodity. The complete picture of RCA Index of Indian exports to the EU market for four years is shown in **Table 5.8**[74].

The table shows that RCA index is higher than unity where both NTB-coverage ratio and tariff rates are higher. This proves the hypothesis that NTBs are enforced on those items where India has better competitive strength in the Community market. RCA index is higher in all textile items and some promising agricultural items also. RCA index is around 15 in vegetable textile fibres which means India's competitive position in the EC market is quite strong compared to other suppliers. In vegetables, cereals and animal products the index is greater than a unity[75].

Table 5.9 depicts the relationship between competitiveness of Indian products in the EU market as well as EU's protectionism[76]. Here the extent of protectionism is measured in terms of higher tariff

TABLE 5.8 : Revealed Comparative Advantage of Indian Exports to EU

HS Code	*CHAPTER DESCRIPTION*	*1988*	*1992*	*1993*	*1994*
1	2	*3*	*4*	*5*	*6*
1	LIVE ANIMALS	0.370	–	–	–
2	MEAT AND EDIBLE MEAT OFFAL	0.750	0.097	–	0.22
3	FISH & CRUSTACEAN, MOLLUSC & O	1.720	4.020	3.05	3.84
4	DAIRY PROD; BIRD's EGGS; NATUR	0.005	–	0.03	0.45
5	PRODUCTS OF ANIMAL ORIGIN, NES	1.090	1.320	0.12	0.99
6	LIVE TREE & OTHER PLANT; BULB,	0.570	3.430	0.54	0.75
7	EDIBLE VEGETABLES AND CERTAIN	0.270	0.300	0.58	0.86
8	EDIBLE FRUIT AND NUTS; PEEL OF	0.760	1.360	1.84	2.47
9	COFFEE, TEA, MAT AND SPICES	1.800	2.630	2.78	2.42
10	CEREALS	3.050	6.920	3.89	2.81
11	PROD MILL INDUST; MALT; STARCH	0.590	6.630	0.33	3.46
12	OIL SEED, OLEAGIN FRUITS; MISC	2.000	1.940	0.3	2.02
13	LAC; GUMS, RESINS & OTHER VEGE	10.000	5.500	4.88	1.99
14	VEGETABLE PLANTING MATERIALS;	10.000	9.070	1.9	1.57
15	ANIMAL/VEG FATS & OILS & THEIR	3.600	12.450	7.46	2.49
16	PREP OF MEAT, FISH OR CRUSTACE	0.130	0.410	3.47	0.06
17	SUGARS AND SUGAR CONFECTIONERY	1.150	2.160	3.5	0.18
18	COCOA AND COCOA PREPARATIONS	–	–	0.02	0.02
19	PREP OF CEREAL, FLOUR, STARCH/	1.690	3.860	1.26	1.26
20	PREP OF VEGETABLE, FRUIT, NUTS	0.860	1.720	0.5	1.26
21	MISCELLANEOUS EDIBLE PREPARATI	0.410	0.030	4.41	0.53
22	BEVERAGES, SPIRITS AND VINEGAR	0.080	0.110	2.33	0.02
23	RESIDUES & WASTE FROM THE FOOD	0.660	1.510	1.78	1.34

(Contd...)

1	2	3	4	5	6
24	TOBACCO AND MANUFACTURED TOBAC	0.830	1.280	1.04	0.97
25	SALT; SULPHUR; EARTH & STON; P	3.050	4.330	5.29	5.51
26	ORES, SIAG AND ASH	0.400	0.450	1.16	0.71
27	MINERAL FUELS, OILS & PRODUCT	0.440	0.070	0.15	0.07
28	INORGN CHEM; COMPDS OF PREC MT	0.720	1.170	0.55	0.67
29	ORGANIC CHEMICALS	0.630	0.930	1.18	1.26
30	PHARMACEUTICAL PRODUCTS	0.090	0.160	0.09	0.07
31	FERTILISERS	–	–	1.07	1.88
32	TANNING/DYEING EXTRACT; TANNIN	2.120	2.380	3.23	2.63
33	ESSENTIAL OILS & RESINOIDS; PE	0.680	1.010	0.56	0.61
34	SOAP, ORGANIC SURGACE-ACTIVE A	0.350	0.130	0.36	0.37
35	ALBUMINOIDAL SUBS; MODIFIED ST	0.210	0.290	0.17	0.39
36	EXPLOSIVE; PYROTECHNIC PROD;	0.030	0.190	0.06	0.16
37	PHOTOGRAPHIC OR CINEMATOGRAPHI	0.080	0.050	0.03	0.03
38	MISCELLANEOUS CHEMICAL PRODUCT	0.090	0.230	0.45	0.06
39	PLASTICS AND ARTICLES THEREOF	0.020	0.240	0.16	0.16
40	RUBBER AND ARTICLES THEREOF	0.120	0.210	0.2	0.18
41	RAW HIDES AND SKINS (OTHER THA	4.800	8.120	0.47	3.8
42	ARTICLES OF LEATHER; SADDLERY/	3.140	5.670	7.81	7.63
43	FURSKINS AND ARTIFICIAL FUR;	0.070	0.040	0.77	0.77
44	WOOD AND ARTICLES OF WOOD; WOO	0.160	0.040	0.16	0.25
45	CORK AND ARTICLES OF CORK	–	–	0	–
46	MANUFACTURES OF STRAW, ESPARTO	0.250	0.120	0.44	0.51
47	PULP OF WOOD/OF OTHER FIBROUS	–	–	0	–
48	PAPER & PAPERBOARD; ART OF PAP	0.040	0.270	0.03	0.05
49	PRINTED BOOKS, NEWSPAPERS, PIC	0.090	0.100	1.2	0.17
50	SILK	5.980	4.430	7.55	7.6

51	WOOL, FINE/COARSE ANIMAL HAIR	0.020	1.270	0.66	1.29
52	COTTON	3.040	3.010	4.32	3.69
53	OTHER VEGETABLE TEXTILE FIBRES	15.110	14.650	14.1	10.81
54	MAN-MADE FILAMENTS	0.500	1.250	1.12	0.98
55	MAN-MADE STAPLE FIBRES	1.520	4.480	4.81	4.6
56	WADDING, FELT & NONWOVEN; YARN	0.370	1.310	0.6	0.33
57	CARPETS AND OTHER TEXTILE FLOO	9.560	9.590	11.76	9.66
58	SPECIAL WOVEN FAB; TURTED TEX	0.940	0.290	2.29	1.9
59	IMPREGNATED, COATED, COVER/LAM	0.090	0.640	0.85	0.86
60	KNITTED OR CROCHETED FABRICS	0.490	1.460	12.53	2.56
61	ART OF APPAREL & CLOTHING ACCE	1.200	1.740	2.08	1.95
62	ART OF APPAREL & CLOTHING ACCE	2.910	2.370	2.72	2.86
63	OTHER MADE UP TEXTILE ARTICLES	3.460	5.280	5.96	5.91
64	FOOTWEAR, GAITERS AND THE LIKE	2.950	2.350	3.01	3.1
65	HEADGEAR AND PARTS THEREOF	0.980	0.710	0.4	–
66	UMBRELLAS, WALKING-STICKS,	0.060	0.080	0.1	0.06
67	PREPR FEATHERS & DOWN; ARTI FI	0.020	0.040	0.11	0.1
68	ART OF STONE, PLASTER, CEMENT,	1.450	2.620	1.98	2.55
69	CERAMIC PRODUCTS	0.070	0.160	1.48	15
70	GLASS AND GLASSWARE	0.220	0.600	0.02	0.29
71	NATURAL/CULTURED PEARLS, PREC	3.880	3.800	3.38	4.06
72	IRON AND STEEL	0.750	1.980	1.67	0.72
73	ARTICLES OF IRON OR STEEL	0.240	0.700	0.55	0.55
74	COPPER AND ARTICLES THEREOF	6.500	1.090	0.45	0.04
75	NICKEL AND ARTICLES THEREOF	0.530	1.020	0.57	3.16
76	ALUMINIUM AND ARTICLES THEREOF	0.030	0.180	0.28	0.13
77		–	–	–	–
78	LEAD AND ARTICLES THEREOF	0.450	–	–	–
79	ZINC AND ARTICLES THEREOF	1.480	0.510	0.38	0.15
80	TIN AND ARTICLES THEREOF	0.340	–	0.02	0.03

(Contd...)

1	2	3	4	5	6
81	OTHER BASE METALS; CERMETS; AR	0.230	0.060	0.13	0.03
82	TOOL, IMPLEMENT, CUTLERY, SPOO	0.660	1.270	1.05	10.62
83	MISCELLANEOUS ARTICLES OF BASE	2.850	2.940	2.86	2.8
84	NUCLEAR REACTORS, BOILERS, MCH	0.070	0.130	0.21	0.2
85	ELECTRICAL MACHY EQUIP JPARTS	0.600	0.250	0.1	0.1
86	RAILS/TRAMW LOCOM, ROLLING-STO	0.210	2.050	0.04	0.15
87	VEHICLES O/T RAILW/TRAMW ROLL	1.390	0.420	0.24	0.24
88	AIRCRAFT, SPACECRAFT, AND PART	0.030	0.320	0.26	0.29
89	SHIPS, BOATS AND FLOATING STRU	0.200	–	–	5.1
90	OPTICAL, PHOTO, CINE, MEAS, CH	0.060	0.300	0.17	0.02
91	CLOCKS AND WATCHES AND PARTS T	0.002	0.120	0.02	0.02
92	MUSICAL INSTRUMENTS; PARTS AND	0.100	0.720	0.25	0.38
93	ARMS AND AMMUNITION; PARTS AND	0.350	5.090	2.24	0.47
94	FURNITURE; BEDDING, MATTERESSES, MATTERS	0.110	0.420	0.37	0.13
95	TOYS, GAMES & SPORTS REQUISITE	0.200	0.340	0.22	0.32
96	MISCELLANEOUS MANUFACTURED ART	0.920	1.060	0.69	0.68
97	WORKS OF ART, COLLECTORS' PIEC	0.190	0.070	0.07	0.06
	Avg.	–	–	–	–

Source : Calculated on the basis of tables 5.1, 5.4, 5.5 and 5.6.

and non-tariff coverage ratio. It is shown in **Table 5.8** that in every year the average RCA index is much higher in the NTB-affected items than items not subject to NTBs. During 1988, the average RCA index was 0.786 for items which were not affected by NTBs but this was 2.45 per cent for items affected by NTBs. Another indicator of protectionism is that higher average tariff was 3.69 per cent during 1988 for items not covered by NTBs, but it was almost double (i.e. 6.41 per cent) for items which were exposed to NTBs. The same trend continues for subsequent years also.

During 1992, RCA index was 2.52 for NTB-affected items but it reduced to only 1.53 for non-NTB items. In 1993 too, average RCA index was 2.39 for NTB-affected items but it was only 1.4 in case of non NTB-affected items. During 1994, the latest year for which data are available shows that average RCA index was 6.6 for NTB-affected items which was only 1.28 in case of non-NTB items. During 1992, average rate of tariffs for NTB-affected items was 11.8 per cent but it was only 6.6 per cent for items whose exports were not subject to NTBs. During 1994, though the difference gets reduced but average tariff for NTB-affected items was as high as 8.61 per cent but it was only 6.74 per cent for the items whose exports were not restrained by NTBs. The entire picture of RCA and average tariffs for NTB-affected and NTB-free items is shown in **Table 5.9**[77].

India's competitiveness in the EU market is judged in terms of its RCA index in an ex-post basis not on ex-ante. Therefore this index cannot give any future projection because both ways trade may change in the coming years due to several exogenous factors especially after the implementation of the Uruguay Round agreements. Therefore, this should be taken as an empirical finding rather than as a base for the future projection. But in our study we have proved that so long India keeps on exporting labour intensive goods and goods based on natural resources in which it has comparative advantage, the extent of protectionism will deepen in the future.

TARIFF EQUIVALENTS OF NON-TARIFF BARRIERS ENFORCED BY THE EUROPEAN UNION

The **third hypothesis** of our study is to see the tariff equivalents of NTBs. Conceptually, the items which are subject to NTBs are also having higher tariff equivalents[78]. This is so on the basis of theoretical

TABLE 5.9 : Relationship between Competitiveness of Indian Products and Protectionism in the European Union

Nature of Items	1988 RCA* (avg)	1988 Average Tariffs	1992 RCA (avg)	1992 Average (wtd)	1993 RCA (avg)	1993 Average Tariffs (wtd)	1994 RCA RCA (avg) (wtd)	1994 Average Tariffs
Items subject to NTBs	2.450	6.41	2.52	11.80	2.39	11.14	2.09	8.61
Items without NTBs	0.786	3.69	1.53	4.73	1.40	6.60	1.28	6.74
Total	—	6.11	—	8.28	—	8.59	—	7.76

* RCA = Revealed Comparative Advantage.
** Figures are based on tables 5.1, 5.4, 5.5 and 5.6.

premises that if the prices in the markets are equal, there is no need to put any restriction on imports. But since domestic price is higher than international price, in order to save the domestic industry, the importing country generally adopts two methods. **Firstly**, this price differential is neutralized by putting equal amount of levy which has direct price effect. **Secondly**, importers put restrictions on imports, thus making imports demand curve more inelastic. By this way importers artificially raise the demand prices keeping the supply price at a very low level. The difference between demand and supply price depends on the elasticity of import demand. Therefore, it can be intuitively said that if the protectionism is higher then tariff-equivalents must also be higher. Rather it can be seen from the reverse angle that the extent of protectionism is higher simply because of the existence of higher tariff-equivalents (Hamilton, 1994)[79].

Calculation of tariff equivalents is a very complicated process requires large and detailed data base which is not available in any organized institute in the world. Perhaps this is the reason why researchers used to do a lot of approximation based on many assumptions and adjustments. Apart from economic reason there happens to be a lot of political interference in this area. EU is very sensitive to give domestic price data for textiles and garments to any Indian even to researchers[80]. In spite of our best efforts to get it we are yet to achieve any success in that area. For calculation of tariff equivalents as mentioned in **Tables 5.10, 5.11 and 5.12** we have

TABLE 5.10 : EU'S Basis Tariff Equivalent as proposed in the Uruguay Round

S. No.	Product (avg)	Year (avg)	Price(Ecu/t) Internal (avg)	External (Ecu/t)(avg)	Tariff Equivalents (avg)	Tariff Equivalents (TE=Pd-PF/PFx100)	TES Excluding subsidy (avg) @ 36% as proposed in the Uruguay Round
1.	Common Wheat	1986-88	241	93	148	159.14	101.84
2.	Barley	1986-88	236	85	145	177.64	113.69
3.	Maiz	1986-88	241	96	197	151.04	96.67
4.	Whole milled rice	1986-88	917	235	680	288.93	184.92
5.	Durum Wheat	1986-88	383	152	231	151.97	97.26
6.	Untreated Olive Oil	1986-88	747	809	-62	-77.00	-4.90
7.	Beet Sugar	1986-88	600	176	424	240.90	154.18
8.	White Sugar	1986-88	719	196	524	266.84	170.77
9.	Grape juice concentrated	1986-88	242	92	151	163.04	104.34
10.	Grape juice concentrated (diff. variety)	1986-88	242	78	164	210.25	134.56
11	Grape juice	1986-88	50	16	34	212.50	136.00
12	Pigament carcasses	1986-88	NA	NA	839	—	
13	Frozen bovine carcasses	1986-88	3436	1423	2013	141.46	90.53
14	Skimmed milk powder	1986-88	2170	685	1485	216.79	138.74
15	Whey Powder	1986-88	509	437	109	16.47	10.54
16	Butter	1986-88	3905	943	2962	314.10	201.03
17	Beef carcasses	1986-88	4289	1526	2763	181.06	115.88

(Contd...)

Notes : 1) Price basis : Cereals internal, intervention price +10% + monthly increments; External commonwheat FOB Argentina (Southern wheat, up river), barley FOB St. Lawrence, Maize FOB Argentina (Plata), rice FOB Thailand, durum wheat FOB Duluth (Hard amber), Olive oil levy applied (internal) plus consumption aid (external) = Tariff equivalent: Sugar internal, intervention price + 10% + storage levy; external, raw sugar New York, white sugar Paris, Grape juice concentrated + 1.33 g/cm3 internal, Production refund (PR) in Ecu |h| ; external, cif border EC +50% duty in Ecu |h|; grape juice concentrated - 1.33 g/cm3 internal, Production Refund (PR) in ECu |h|; external, cif,border EC + 28% duty in EC |h| grape juice internal production refund in Ecu |h|;external, cif, border EC + 28% duty in ECu |h|; spipmeat internal, intervention price for fresh carcasses + 10% skimmed milk powder internal, intervention price + 10% external , IDA minimum price whey powder internal 9%, EC market price + 10%; external xxx EC import prices ; butter internal, intervention price + 10%, external IDA minimum price; Beef carcasses internal, intervention price + 10%; external, FOB Argentina. 2) Tariff Equivalents : Pigmènt carcases levy applied. 3) Non -Tariff Measures tariffed : Production Refund for Concentrated and unconcentrated grape juice,Voluntary Restraint Arrangement for Frozen bovine carcasses, variable levy for all other products. 4) GATT binding : All products unbound except for grape juice and grape juice concentrated -1.33 g/cm3, and frozen bovine carcasses.

Sources : Agra Europe, March 20, 1992.
& EC's submission to the GATT.

TABLE 5.11 : EC's Derived Tariff Equivalents

S. No.	Product (Avg)	Component Products (avg)	Years (Avg) (Ecu/t)	Tariff Equivalents of comp. products (avg) (Ecu/t)	Tariff Equivalents of Specific products (avg)	Proportion (f = e/d)
	(a)	(b)	(c)	(d)	(e)	
1.	Rye	Barley	1986-88	145	145	1.00
2.	Oats	Barley	1986-88	145	139	0.96
3.	Husked rice	Wholly milled rice	1986-88	678	468	0.69
4.	Broken rice	Wholly milled rice	1986-88	679	200	0.29
5.	Sorghum	Maize	1986-88	147	147	1.00
6.	Buck Wheat	Barley	1986-88	145	58	0.45
7.	Canary Seed	Barley	1986-88	145	22	0.15
8.	Lactose	Whey powder	1986-88	109	218	2.00
9.	Molasses	Barley	1986-88	145	145	1.00
10.	Gonda	Butter	1986-88	2962	1079	0.36
11.	Gonda	Skimmed milk powder	1986-88	1585	1367	0.86
12.	Blue varied cheese	Butter	1986-88	2962	1135	0.38
13.	Blue varied chesse chedder	Butter	1986-88	2962	1162	0.39
14.	Chedder	Skimmed milk Powder	1986-88	1485	1449	0.97
15.	Emmental	Butter	1986-88	2962	1093	0.37
16.	"	SMP	1986-88	1485	1590	1.07
17.	Parmigiano	Butter	1986-88	2962	959	0.32
18.	"	SMP	1986-88	1485	1982	1.33

(Contd...)

(a)	(b)	(c)	(d)	(e)	
19. Condensed milk sweet	Butter	1986-88	2962	325	0.11
20. "	SMP	1986-88	1489	338	0.23
21. "	White Sugar	1986-88	524	230	0.44
22. Live bovine Animals	Beef carcasses	1986-88	2763	1453	0.53
23. Fresh bovine carcases	Frozen bovine carcasses	1986-88	2013	2677	1.33
24. Whole milk powder	SMP	1986-88	1485	1086	0.73
25. "	Butter	1986-88	2962	952	0.32
26. Condensed milk unsweet	Butter	1986-88	2962	272	0.09
27. "	SMP	1986-88	1485	270	0.18
28. Plumps	Peaches	1986-88	163	128	0.79

Source : Agra Europe, March 20, 1992, London, Database selection code : TABAGRTRA.

TABLE 5.12 : EC's Tariff Equivalent of Fruits

S. No.	Products	Years	Price (ECUs/t) Internal	External	Tariff Equivalents (ECUs/t)	Tariff Equivalents Pd-Pf / Pf*100	Tariff Equivalents ex. subsidy of @36%
1.	Cucumber	1986-88	1351	727	624	140.85	90.14
2.	Artichokes	1986-88	1000	713	286	40.25	25.76
3.	Courgettes	1986-88	730	540	190	35.18	27.52
4.	Oranges	1986-88	372	283	89	31.45	20.13
5.	Small xxxx	1986-88	675	543	132	24.30	15.56
6.	Lemons	1986-88	622	303	320	105.28	67.37
7.	Table grapes	1986-88	—	—	—	120.00	(a) —
8.	Apples	1986-88	627	330	297	90.00	57.60
9.	Apricots	1986-88	1128	843	284	33.80	21.63
10.	Cherries	1986-88	1562	1220	342	28.03	17.93
11.	Peaches	1986-88	916	753	163	21.64	13.85
12.	Tomatoes	1986-88	2236	828	1408	170.64	108.83

Note : (a) Export refund = Price gap

Source : Agra Europe, March 20, 1992. London.

received date from a London based publication, *Agra Europe*, 20th March, 1992, issue[81]. *Agra Europe* managed to get information from EU's submission to the WTO which is confidential and is not accessible to anyone according to the provisions of the agreement between WTO and contracting parties. Therefore, due to several bottlenecks of getting data on domestic prices, we could not do extensive study on tariff-equivalents of all non-tariff barriers applied on India's exports to the EC at 2-digit level. The study presented here is partial and certainly not an extensive one[82].

There have been two major areas where calculations of tariff equivalents are very significant. These are: i) EC's imports of agricultural goods, and ii) imports of textiles and garments. India has relatively better stake in second area, i.e. especially in textiles and garments. In the previous section, we have discussed areas in which India has competitive strength which was divulged from the Revealed Comparative Advantage (RCA) index. Apart from this tool, we can also measure the degree of competitiveness following method devised by **Ingo Walter**[83]. Most recently **Anderson and Neary (1994)**[84] have also developed Trade Restrictive Index (TRI), where they have first developed a well defined theoretical model followed by empirical testing . Uptil now TRI is the most reliable form of the measurement of trade restrictiveness[85].

In spite of all such tools used to measure the trade restrictiveness, there have been severe lack of suitable indices for covering all types of distortions that restrict trade (Anderson, 1993, Anderson & Neary, 1991, 1992 & 1993, and Anderson & Safadi, 1992)[86]. In spite of all practical difficulties, economists and researchers have taken recourse to several ad hoc measures to gauge the restrictiveness of trade. These include **trade-weighted average tariffs, coefficient of variations of tariffs, or the non-tariff barriers coverage ratio**[87]. For items which are under quantitative restrictions (i.e. quotas), the trade weighted average tariff-equivalents of quota are the standard tool. In order to cover the price impact of quota, or the burden borne by the consumers due to distortion of trade one can take the price differential between the distorted price in the domestic market and international prices, and expressing in percentage terms gives an indication of cost of quotas. This price differential is due to quantitative restrictions, known as the tariff equivalents. This is the ideal measure of trade restrictiveness in absence of free trade. The formula, given here below, may indicate tariff-equivalents of NTB items as under :

TABLE 5.13 : EC's Growing Protectionism to Indian Export

HS Code	Chapter Description	1988 Avg Rate of Tariff (wtd)	1988 NTB-Coverage Ratio	1988 Revealed Comparative Advantage (RCA)	1992 Avg. Rate of Tariff (wtd)	1992 NTB-Coverage Ratio	1992 Revealed Comparative Advantage (RCA)	1993 Avg. Rate of Tariff (wtd)	1993 NTB-Coverage Ratio	1993 Revealed Comparative Advantage (RCA)	1994 Avg. Rate of Tariff (wtd)	1994 NTB-Coverage Ratio	1994 Revealed Comparative Advantage (RCA)
1	2	3	4	5	6	7	8	9	10	11	12	13	14
1	Live animals	–	100.000	0.370	–	–	–	10.29(s)	–	–	10.29(s)	–	–
2	Meat and edible meat offal	6.660	100.000	0.750	3.000	100.000	0.097	13.66(s)	–	–	10(s)	95.5	0.22
3	Fish & crustacean, mollusc & o	11.730	1.310	1.720	12.690	28.120	4.020	12.23	28.8	3.05	13.31	23.73	3.84
4	Dairy prod; bird's eggs; natur	22.440	18.750	0.005	–	–	–	27	1.32	0.03	–	88.67	0.45
5	Products of animal origin, nes	0.032	25.980	1.090	0.020	24.240	1.320	2.04	26.29	0.12	2.06	23.19	0.99
6	Live tree & other plant; bulb,	6.660	99.130	0.570	6.490	100.000	3.430	8.59	98.09	0.54	10.25	98.11	0.75
7	Edible vegetables and certain	12.800	0.180	0.270	27.540	20.730	0.300	12.04	30.55	0.58	13.24	1.42	0.86
8	Edible fruit and nuts; peel of	1.660	0.050	0.760	1.340	1.180	1.360	7.12	2.25	1.84	6.32	5.59	2.47
9	Coffee, tea, mat and spices	2.920	1.110	1.800	1.620	–	2.630	3.14	–	2.78	3.61	–	2.42
10	Cereals	–	100.000	3.050	107.270	100.000	6.920	0	99.95	3.89	1.09	99.9	2.81
11	Prod mill indust; malt; starch	0.890	86.240	0.590	38.310	37.100	6.630	12.68	84	0.33	12.92	28.67	3.46
12	Oil seed, oleagin fruits; misc	0.210	–	2.000	0.280	–	1.940	5.77	–	0.3	3.94	0.003	2.02
13	Lac; gums, resins & other vege	0.080	0.080	10.000	0.100	–	5.500	0.35	–	4.88	0	–	1.99
14	Vegetable plaiting materials;	–	88.340	10.000	–	80.330	9.070	0	75.75	1.9	0	74.28	1.57
15	Animal/veg fats & oils & their	1.270	–	3.600	4.550	–	12.450	7.98	–	7.46	8.34	0.002	2.49
16	Prep of meat, fish or crustace	19.790	3.740	0.130	20.000	18.630	0.410	19.98	14	3.47	19.91	–	0.06
17	Sugars and sugar confectionery	0.190	100.000	1.150	20.000	100.000	2.160	23	100	3.5	23	99.52	0.18
18	Cocoa and cocoa preparations	–	–	–	–	–	–	9	10	0.02	9	2.62	0.02
19	Prep of cereal, flour, starch/	11.120	100.000	1.690	11.000	100.000	3.860	11.86	100	1.26	11.33	100	1.26
20	Prep of vegetable, fruit, nuts	13.420	60.420	0.860	20.000	62.230	1.720	21.21	64.66	0.5	20.95	66.39	1.26
21	Miscellaneous edible preparati	12.040	34.950	0.410	13.800	24.600	0.030	13.31	16.56	4.41	16.58	10.42	0.53
22	Beverages, spirits and vinegar	14.160	64.600	0.080	20.200	33.000	0.110	62.73	5.38	2.33	12.1	53	0.02
23	Residues & waste from the food	0.002	3.370	0.660	–	0.300	1.510	15	0.12	1.78	0	1.65	1.34

(Contd...)

1	2	3	4	5	6	7	8	9	10	11	12	13	14
24	Tobacco and manufactured tobaco	8.420	–	0.830	22.410	–	1.280	22.64	–	1.04	22.17	–	0.97
25	Salt; sulphur; earth & ston; p	0.030	–	3.050	0.050	–	4.330	1.99	–	5.29	1.54	–	5.51
26	Ores, siag and ash	–	–	0.400	–	–	0.450	–	–	1.16	0	–	0.71
27	Miniral fuels, oils & product	7.000	–	0.440	1.400	–	0.070	1.55	–	0.15	0.33	–	0.07
28	Inorgn chem; compds of prec mt	6.850	–	0.720	8.340	–	1.170	7.43	–	0.55	6.76	–	0.67
29	Origanic chemicals	7.770	–	0.630	7.850	0.190	0.930	7.69	0.61	1.18	7.95	0.7	1.26
30	Pharmaceutical products	6.070	–	0.090	5.700	–	0.160	5.95	–	0.09	6.03	–	0.07
31	Fertilisers	–	–	–	–	–	–	–	–	1.07	0	–	1.88
32	Tanning/dyeing extract; tannin	9.800	–	2.120	9.760	–	2.380	9.67	–	3.23	9.75	–	2.63
33	Essential oils & resinoids; pe	1.880	–	0.680	2.120	–	1.010	4.82	–	0.56	4.79	–	0.61
34	Soap, organic surgace-active a	6.350	–	0.350	6.240	–	0.130	6.88	–	0.36	6.88	–	0.37
35	Albuminoidal subs; modified st	6.060	–	0.210	9.340	–	0.290	7.02	–	0.17	6.46	–	0.39
36	Explosive; pyrotechnic prod;	6.600	–	0.030	10.000	–	0.190	6.63	–	0.06	6.8	–	0.16
37	Photographic or cinematographi	3.940	–	0.080	–	–	0.050	7.45	–	0.03	7.7	–	0.03
38	Miscellaneous chemical product	6.320	–	0.090	6.300	–	0.230	6.17	–	0.45	6.15	–	0.06
39	Plastics and articles thereof	12.110	–	0.020	9.260	–	0.240	10.67	–	0.16	9.9	–	0.16
40	Rubber and articles thereof	4.620	–	0.120	4.560	–	0.210	3.24	–	0.2	3.91	–	0.18
41	Raw hides and skins	4.830	89.350	4.800	5.320	97.910	8.120	5.48	95.3	0.47	5.55	94.67	3.8
42	Articles of leather; saddlery/	6.740	83.670	3.140	6.740	85.910	5.670	6.71	90.99	7.81	6.75	87.69	7.63
43	Furskins and artificial fur;	4.820	89.200	0.070	6.000	100.000	0.040	5.65	100	0.77	5.82	41.08	0.77
44	Wood and articles of wood; woo	5.600	0.050	0.160	5.800	78.180	0.040	5.36	74.95	0.16	5.23	77.54	0.25
45	Cork and articles of cork	–	–	–	–	–	–	–	–	0	–	–	–
46	Manufactures of straw, esparto	5.800	–	0.250	3.920	–	0.120	3.78	–	0.44	3.68	–	0.51
47	Pulp of wood/of other fibrous	–	–	–	–	–	–	–	–	0	–	–	–
48	Paper & paperboard; art of pap	10.930	–	0.040	11.160	–	0.270	10.92	–	0.03	11.08	–	0.05
49	Printed books, newspapers, pic	1.160	–	0.090	1.620	–	0.100	6.38	–	1.2	6.61	–	0.17
50	Silk	6.400	–	5.980	6.690	–	4.430	6.82	–	7.55	6.72	–	7.6
51	Wool, fine/coarse animal hair	1.000	29.310	0.020	7.270	97.580	1.270	6.68	95.43	0.66	6.44	98.25	1.29
52	Cotton	8.560	98.830	3.040	8.100	100.000	3.010	8.68	100	4.32	8.28	96.92	3.69
53	Other vegetable textile fibres	6.460	–	15.110	6.000	–	14.650	2.04	0.03	14.1	1.45	0.18	10.81
54	Man-made filaments	9.850	77.620	0.500	9.960	91.140	1.250	9.55	93.45	1.12	10.13	94.66	0.98
55	Man-made staple fibres	9.850	95.320	1.520	9.900	99.000	4.480	9.97	99.72	4.81	9.87	99.02	4.6
56	Wadding, felt & nonwoven; yarn	7.250	98.850	0.370	8.720	100.000	1.310	10.56	86	0.6	9.45	87.17	0.33

57	Carpets and other textile floo	6.290	96.08	9.560	7.030	99.900	9.590	7.06	96.98	11.76	7.04	94.88	9.66
58	Special woven fab; turted tex	5.760	93.940	0.940	6.280	97.000	0.290	6.45	95.49	2.29	6.72	95.5	1.9
59	Impregnated, coated, cover/lam	8.440	62.990	0.090	10.580	100.000	0.640	10.62	100	0.85	9.99	99.24	0.86
60	Knitted or crocheted fabrics	11.920	94.670	0.490	12.000	100.000	1.460	11.98	100	12.53	12	99.93	2.56
61	Art of apparel & clothing acce	13.620	99.850	1.200	13.500	100.000	1.740	13.5	99.82	2.08	13.48	99.77	1.95
62	Art of apparel & clothing acce	13.490	96.320	2.910	13.740	94.450	2.370	13.46	96.02	2.72	13.37	97.3	2.86
63	Other made up textile articles	12.130	96.120	3.460	12.090	89.120	5.280	11.72	90.67	5.96	12.01	95.46	5.91
64	Footwear, gaiters and the like	5.770	99.89	2.950	6.140	99.700	2.350	6.19	99.88	3.01	6.32	99.92	3.1
65	Headgear and parts thereof	5.660	–	0.980	3.700	–	0.710	5.98	0.22	0.4	5.99	0.56	–
66	Umbrellas, walking-sticks,	6.840	37.190	0.060	6.410	51.200	0.080	7.08	27.25	0.1	7.19	26.5	0.06
67	Prepr feathers & down; arti fi	5.650	42.640	0.020	7.700	–	0.040	6.62	6.89	0.11	7.11	14.5	0.1
68	Art of stone, plaster, cement,	2.300	–	1.450	2.020	–	2.620	3.69	–	1.98	3.71	–	2.55
69	Ceramic products	10.220	–	0.070	8.380	–	0.160	7.71	–	1.48	7.25	–	15
70	Glass and glassware	11.920	–	0.220	12.070	–	0.600	9.11	–	0.02	10.72	–	0.29
71	Natural/cultured pearls, prec	0.350	5.690	3.880	0.530	10.240	3.800	4.58	9.52	3.38	4.5	11.89	4.06
72	Iron and steel	6.220	86.740	0.750	6.070	90.340	1.980	5.17	80.94	1.67	3.49	88.58	0.72
73	Articles of iron or steel	5.570	1.100	0.240	6.290	–	0.700	5.76	2.29	0.55	5.55	2.5	0.55
74	Copper and articles thereof	4.320	–	6.500	–	–	1.090	4.98	–	0.45	5.01	–	0.04
75	Nickel and articles thereof	4.520	–	0.530	–	–	1.020	4.65	–	0.57	4.63	–	3.16
76	Aluminium and articles thereof	7.320	–	0.030	–	–	0.180	7.56	–	0.28	8.24	–	0.13
77	-	–	–	–	–	–	–	–	–	–	–	–	–
78	Lead and articles thereof	3.790	–	0.450	–	–	–	–	–	–	–	–	–
79	Zinc and articles thereof	7.000	–	1.480	–	–	0.510	7	–	0.38	7.03	–	0.15
80	Tin and articles thereof	0.060	–	0.340	–	–	–	5.3	–	0.02	5.03	–	0.03
81	Other base metals;	0.700	1.850	0.230	–	–	0.060	4.36	–	0.13	6.04	0.33	0.03
82	Tool, implement, cutlery, spoo	4.710	–	0.660	4.630	–	1.270	4.85	–	1.05	5.11	–	10.62
83	Miscellaneous articles of base	1.980	–	2.850	1.790	–	2.940	4.92	–	2.86	4.93	–	2.8
84	Nuclear reactors, boilers, mch	3.870	–	0.070	4.450	–	0.130	3.06	–	0.21	3.15	–	0.2
85	Electrical machy equip and parts	5.920	–	0.600	7.040	–	0.250	6.56	–	0.1	5.9	–	0.1
86	Rails/tramw locom, rolling-sto	4.350	–	0.210	4.500	–	2.050	4.49	–	0.04	4.46	–	0.15
87	Vehicles o/t railw/tramw roll	7.960	–	1.390	9.510	–	0.420	10.65	–	0.24	8.67	–	0.24
88	Aricraft, spacecraft, and part	1.910	–	0.030	0.040	–	0.320	3.84	–	0.26	4.9	–	0.29
89	Ships, boats and floating stru	0.000	–	0.200	–	–	–	–	–	–	4.9	–	5.1
90	Optical, photo, cine, meas, ch	6.890	–	0.060	3.100	–	0.300	6.63	0.23	0.17	6.95	0.07	0.02

(Contd...)

1	2	3	4	5	6	7	8	9	10	11	12	13	14
91	Clocks and watches; parts and t	5.940	35.000	0.002	5.720	–	0.120	5.2	54.3	0.02	5.34	28	0.02
92	Musical instruments; parts and	5.770	7.350	0.100	5.690	27.580	0.720	5.77	23	0.25	5.78	15.37	0.38
93	Arms and ammunition; parts and	4.350	88.830	0.350	3.710	75.260	5.090	3.2	99.5	2.24	4.21	81.33	0.47
94	Furnitures; bedding, mattresses,	5.730	–	0.110	5.440	–	0.420	5.41	–	0.37	5.38	–	0.13
95	Toys, games & sports requisites	4.980	7.590	0.200	5.600	3.820	0.340	6.39	2.76	0.22	6.13	2.61	0.32
96	Miscellaneous manufactured art	5.690	53.580	0.920	8.880	36.270	1.060	7.28	38.22	0.69	7	38.07	0.68
97	Works of art, collectors' pieces	–	–	0.190	–	18.160	0.070	–	7.46	0.07	–	7.75	0.06
	Avg.	6.110	52.800	–	8.280	55.560	–	8.59	53.62	–	7.76	53.74	–

* RCA is in index form and average rate of tariff is in percentage form

$$TE = Pd - Pf / Pf$$

where 'Pd' is the domestic price, and 'Pf' is the international price.

The extent of protectionism can be gauged by the magnitude of tariff equivalents. If the TEs is higher, which means domestic market is highly insulated from the foreign competitors by several non-tariff barriers. The extent of NTBs is determined by the value/ magnitude of tariff equivalents. Keeping this hypothesis in our mind, we have tried to find out the TEs of EC's import of agricultural goods. In practice it is very difficult to get price information of any item in the domestic as well as international market. Even information of this type would not be theoretically sound unless goods are perfect substitutes. In spite of all such practical difficulties, measurement of TEs will be relatively suitable for agricultural goods rather than manufactured ones[88].

In the Uruguay Round of negotiations, EU has given commitment in principle to start "tariffication" programme in agricultural imports to be carried over a period of ten years beginning 1st January, 1995[89]. The EU has submitted complete schedules of TEs of agricultural imports to GATT[90]. These basic figures will form the platform from where percentage reductions would start. These figures form part of the EC's still-confidential submission of data to the GATT. The tariff equivalents (which are shown here) are based on the difference between the EC's own internal price and the international (world) price over the period 1986-88. The average of each price is taken over the 3-year period, and the difference is expressed as the tariff equivalent. In the EC's submission, the internal price for most of the main CAP products is taken as being the relevant EC-intervention price plus 10 per cent, while the external reference price is selected from a range of international market quotations[91]. In the case of dairy products, the external price is taken to be the GATT IDA minimum price-effectively, the lowest possible traded price over the reference period. The basis of different prices in the domestic and international markets are mentioned at the end of the **Table 5.10**[92].

Methodologies of calculating internal as well as international prices of all products are not possible to mention here, but while doing this, basically we have followed the method mentioned above[93]. But in some cases, especially in wheat, the average internal price over the period 1986-88 is given as 241 ECU/t, which is derived from the intervention price plus 10 per cent relevant monthly increments. All EC prices are given in real rather than "agricultural"

ECUs, for each year the relevant price in agricultural ECUs has been multiplied by the switch over coefficient which was in force at the time to give an undistorted price level. During mid-1980s, the world dairy products slumped at a very low level while EC prices were well supported. EC took advantage of it. In EC, there would have been a very limited scope for adjusting tariffs in the case of subsequent currency and price movements but the initial TEs would in any case be subject to percentage reductions over the period 1993-94 to 1998-99. If the Dunkel proposal of a 36 per cent cut in TEs were to be agreed, the tariff on butter would fall to 1895.7 ECUs/t by 1999, while SMP (skim milk products) tariff would fall to 950.4 ECU/t. For common wheat, tariff would fall progressively from an 149 ECU/t to 95.36 ECU/t by 1999[94].

The EU's submission in the Uruguay Round contained two elements, viz. (i) basic tariff-equivalents for market access, and (ii) derived tariff equivalents[95]. The methodology of calculating TEs has already been explained. The products are taken on items-basis without citing any trade classification code. These are the common agricultural items which are exported to EC, from several countries including India. In the EU, the amount of subsidy is equivalent to the price differential which, on the other hand, is tariff equivalent. Reducing subsidy by 36 per cent will help Indian exporters to get better market access in the EC market. In most of the agricultural goods in the European Community, tariff equivalent is well over 100 per cent which is shown in **Tables 5.10, 5.11 and 5.12**[96]. In the WTO, the EU has made commitment that it will tarrify all non-tariff barriers at the end of the transition period i.e. 1st January, 2005, beginning 1st January, 1995. Though their submission is still confidential apparently from their open commitment it is known that they will reduce 36 per cent of their support measures to agricultural items over a period of 10 years beginning 1 January 1995. In **Table 5.10** we have shown hypothetically that even after full implementation of the Final Agreement of the WTO, tariff equivalents of all agricultural goods will be well over 100 per cent , and it will remain so in the future trade regime of the European Community. In spite of best efforts we could not collect data of the EU's domestic prices of textiles and garments. Therefore we could not calculate the tariff equivalents of quotas in the EU market.

This chapter contains major findings of our research. The objective of our study is to see the extent of the EU's growing protectionism applied on Indian exports and its future direction especially after the provisions of The Final Act of the Uruguay Round of negotiation, getting fully implemented. The intensity of EUs protectionism is shown in **Fig. 5.13.** The major conclusions emerged from this chapter are :

(i) More than half of our exports to the EC have been subject to NTBs, and a majority of them are hard core. Frequency ratios are also more than one-third for all year.

(ii) The items which are covered by NTBs are also subject to higher tariffs. The average (weighted) tariffs of NTB-affected items is almost double than average tariff of all items exported by India to the EC.

(iii) The majority of Indian exports to the EC contain textiles and garments, agricultural goods and low value-added manufactured goods. India's Competitiveness of these items is high. Revealed Comparative Advantage of these items is greater than unity. This proves our hypothesis that NTBs are enforced on those items in which we have higher comparative cost advantage.

(iv) Tariff equivalents are much higher on those items which have been covered by non-tariff barriers. Quotient of NTB-coverage as well a frequency ratio is well above average in case of textiles and agricultural items. though we are not able to calculate tariff equivalents of textiles due to non-availability of data. But while doing the same in case of agricultural exports it is well above 100 per cent even after removing subsidies of 36 per cent as agreed upon in the Uruguay Round.

NOTES

1. *(a)* Nogues Julio, Andrzej Olechowski, L. Allen Winter, "The extent of Non-Tariff Barriers to Industrial Countries Imports : *The World Bank Economic Review*, Vol.-1, No.1, (Washington), pp.181-199.

   (b) Irwin, Doglus A., "*The New Protectionism in Industrial Countries : Beyond the Uruguay Round*", International Monitoring Fund-IMF Paper on Policy Analysis and Assessment : PPAA/94/5, (Washington), 1994, p.24.
2. Patrick Low and Alexander J. Yeats, "Non-Tariff measures and developing countries : Has the Uruguay Round levelled the playing fields?", *World Bank Policy Research Working Paper* No. 1353 (Washington, The World Bank), 1994, p.25.
3. James H. Cassing, "Protectionism and Non-Tariff Barriers", *International Economic Perspectives*, (Washington), Vol.-9, No.4, 1990, p.1
4. Allen V. Deardorff and Robert M. Stern, "Methods of measurement

of Non-Tariff Barriers", Institute of Public Policy Studies Discussion Paper No.203, (Michigan, Ann Arbor), 1985, pp.1-2.

5. Cline, W. et al, "*Trade Negotiations in the Tokyo Round : A Quantitative Assessment*", (Washington, The Brooking Institute), 1978, P. 145.
6. United State International Trade Commission, "*The Economic Effects to Significant U.S. Imports Restraints, Phase-1 : Manufacturing*", USITC Publication No.222, (Washington, D.C.), 1989, P. 19
7. Benoit M. Papillon, "Measuring Non-Tariff Barriers to Differentiated Import products", *Contemporary Economic Policy*, 1994 (12), No.3, pp.67-68.
8. Hans Joachim Hochstrate and Ralf Zeppernick, "*Distortion in World Trade : Recent Development*".
9. Forschungsinstiut Fuir Wirtschaftspolitik en den Universital Koln : Die gesamtwirstchaft Kosten den Protektion, Cologne, 1985, Research Project Commissioned by the Federal Minister of Economic Affairs.
10. Ifo-Institul fur Wirstschaftsforschung (ifo) : Munich, Deutsches Institul fur Wirstschaftsforschung (DIW), Berline, HWWA-Institul fur Wirstschaftsforschung-Hamburg, Institut fur Weltwirchaft (Ifw) Kiel, Rheinisch-Westfalisches Institut fur Wirstschaftsforschung (RWF), Essen, Struturberichte 1987, dec in Bundisministers fur Wirstschaft.
11. OECD observer, "High Cost of Protection", No.150 (February-March), 1988, p.5.
12. Sam Laird and Alexender J. Yeats, " Why Should Be Worried About Non-Tariff Measures", *Information Commercial Espanola*, (Sp. Issue on Non-Tariff Barriers), Vol. XXXV, No.2 (June), pp.99-122.
13. Ibid n.8 p.10
14. Ibid n.8 p.10
15. Developed Countries justify their NTBs as consistent with their National Rules. On the other hand developing countries argue that there are discriminatory as well as trade distortionary, 'Grey areas' normally relates to such measures where transparency is minimum, Cf. lbid n.8 p.10.
16. UNCTAD, "*Reports of Trade, Tariff and Non-Tariff Barriers*", (Information is a Annual Phenomenon Complied every year on a discrete basis for 63 developed and developing countries), (UNCTAD, Geneva).
17. So for we have collected information only for four years in 1988, 1992, 1993 and 1994. We tried to get data on a continues basis but we were not successful.
18. UNCTAD data are available as 8 digit commodity classification course. For the sake of our convenience we have aggregated into 2-digit level.
19. Rajiv Kumar and Ram Khanna, "India : The Multifibre Arrangement

and the Uruguay Round (chapter-8)", in Carl B. Hamilton (ed;), *The Uruguay Round, Textile Trade and The Developing Countries : Eliminating Multifibre Arrangements in the 1990s*, A World Bank Publication (Washington), 1990, p.182-212.

20. Ian Goldin, Odin Knudsen and Dominique Van den Mensbrugghe, "*Trade liberalisation : Global Economic Implications*", The World Bank and OECD Study, (The World Bank, Washington), 1993, pp.78-79.
21. Ibid no.2.
22. The information is based upon UNCTAD inventory on tariff and non-tariff barriers. This is compiled for four years. The year of application in the parenthesis which means unless otherwise mentioned NTB remains in operation since the mentioned year.
23. These are some of the NTBs mentioned in the inventory of NTBs, which are most transparent NTBs.
24. UNCTAD inventory for 1988 contains several national NTBs alongwith EC-specific NTBs. In our analysis we have taken only the value of indices reports which is covered by EC-specific NTBs.
25. In some cases India's products are not only restrained by EC-NTBs, but also these were subject to NTBs of the particular member countries. But we have not found such situation since 1992.
26. The tabulation is done on the basis of UNCTAD inventory on Tariff and Non-Tariff Barriers.
27. The Methodologies for calculating NTB-coverage and frequency ratios have shown in chapter-III - NTB Coverage ratio is the ration of total value of exports as covered by NTBs out of total exports and frequency ratio means number of items covered by NTBs out of total number of items exported.
28. Sam Laird and Alexander J. Yeats, "Quantitative Methods of Trade Barrier Analysis", (McMillan, London), 1990, p.21.
29. World Trade Organisation, "*Uruguay Round of Multilateral Trade Negotiation : Legal Instrument Embodying the Results of the Uruguay Round of Multilateral Trade Negotiations*", Vol.-19, (for EC only), 1994, WTO, Geneva.
30. The Trade cut-off in the above analysis is $ 10,000. Higher coverage-ratio does not mean higher weights in our export basket. Except textiles and some agricultural items, weights in total export basket is minimal.
31. *(a)* Swapan K. Bhattachatya, "Transition from MFA to WTO : Prospects for Indian Trade in Textiles and Garments" in K.R. Gupta (ed) *World Trade*, Atlantic Publisher, (New Delhi), 1995, pp. 240-311.
    (b) Ibid n. 19.
32. Ingo Walter, "Non-Tariff Barriers and the Export Performance of Developing Countries", The *American Economic Review*,

(Washington), May, 1971.

33. In our study it is seen that the items in which Indian has better competitive strength in the EU markets are covered by NTBs as well as higher average tariffs.
34. Bela Balassa, "Trade Liberalisation and Revealed Comparative Advantage" *The Manchester School* (1965), Vol. XXXIII, No. 2, pp. 90-123.
35. India does not have any competitive strength in the hi-tech sector. Therefore, most of the technology-intensive goods are either duty-free in the EU market or negligible duty.
36. *(a)* The methodology of calculating frequency ratio has shown in the chapter-3. In our analysis we have taken UNCTAD inventory approach, Cf. Sam Laird and Alexander J. Yeats, "*The UNCTAD Trade Policy Simulation Model : A note on the Methodology, Data and Use*", *UNCTAD Discussion Paper 19*, (Geneva), October 1986.

    (b) Alexander J. Yeats, "Trade Barriers Developing Countries : Measures and Shipping (London, McMillan Press), 1979, p. 116.
37. Ibid n. 27.
38. *(a)* Ibid n. 31(a).

    (b) Ram Khanna, "Impact of QRs on Indian Approach Exporting Industry", *ICRIER mimeo*, (New Delhi), 1987.
39. Indo-German Chamber of Commerce and Industry, "*MFA Quota and Prospects for Textiles Exports*", (New Delhi), 1991, pp. 1-2.
40. O.P. Sharma, "Quota Restrainsts and MFA-II : Some Empirical Evidence on India's Exports to the EEC" *Economic and Political weekly*, Vol. XIX. No. 39, (Bombay), September 29, 1984, p. 1711.
41. This is a corollary, Protectionism has two tools, viz., i) Price Mechanism and ii) Non-Price Mechanism. In order to check cheap imports non-price mechanism is not sufficient, in such case very high tariff will be the effective check. This is the reason why the items covered by NTBs are also subject higher tariffs.
42. Allen V. Deardorff and R.M. Stern, "*Methods of Measurements of Non-Tariff Barriers*", (Geneva, UNCTAD), 1986, pp.1-78.
43. The Calculation is shown in Table 5.1 based on UNCTAD methodologies, Cf. Ibid n. 27-28.
44. Ibid n. 27-28.
45. The names of NTBs are compiled from UNCTAD inventory on tariff and non-tariff barriers. These NTBs are reported to GATT/ UNCTAD by several contracting parties. This is supported by UNCTAD documents which are also cited here.
46. All these NTBs are reported to GATT by constructing parties, see UNCTAD, "*Reports on Trade, Tariff and Non-Tariff Barriers*", (Geneva, UNCTAD), for several years.
47. *(a)* UNCTAD, "Anti-Dumping and Countervailing Duty Practices",

TD/B/1039. (Geneva), 1985.

(b) Funke, Norbert, "Trend in Protectionism : Anti-Dumping and Trade Related Investment Measures", *Intereconomics*, 1994 (29), no.5, (Hamburg), pp.219-224.

(c) Tharakal P. A., M. and Waclbreck, J., "Anti-Dumping and Countervailing Decision in the EC and in the US : An Experiment in Comparative Political Economy", *European Economic Review*, 1994 (3), no.1, pp.171-194.

(d) Swapan K. Bhattacharya, "Managing Anti-dumping Measures in the WTO Regime : Indian Scenario and Indian Practices", ASSOCHAM Monograph, (ASSOCHAM, New Delhi), 1996.

48. Trade Cut-off for 1988 was $ 1000, but it was $ 50000 in 1992. The variation of trade cut-off would not influence our results because there are few items under NTBs where export were less than $ 50000 to EC.
49. Frequency of NTB application is only shown for 1992. There would not be any perceptible change in the frequency of application in the successive periods.
50. The methodology of calculation of NTB-coverage ratio has shown in chapter-3, as well as UNCTAD Simulation model by Laird and Yeats, Ibid n. 36.
51. Swapan K. Bhattacharya, "Rationalisation of Tariff Structure of Indian Consumer Goods Imports", Paper presented as a USAID Seminar on *Policy Implements to Trade and FDI in India*, at Indian Institute of Foreign Trade (New Delhi), 1995, pp.
52. Sam Laird and Andre Sapir, "Tariff preferences", in Andrzej Olechowsky (eds;) : *A Handbook of the Uruguay Round of Multilateral Trade Negotiation*, The World Bank (Washington), 1986, pp.101-109.
53. World Trade Organisation, "Tariff Reduction Schedules", (Submitted by the Contracting Parties to GATT on 15th April 1994, Vol.-1 - XXXI, 1994, WTO, (Geneva).
54. World Trade Organisation, "The Uruguay Round-The Final Act", 1994, WTO, (Geneva).
55. This is the standard methodology of calculating weighted tariffs. In any scientific analysis, it is customary to take weighted average than simple average.
56. There is no minimum tariff average for the member of a trade block. There may be preferential arrangements with few Tariffs. This is evident in case of EC and ACP countries. But apart from any special bilateral arrangements, Tariffs are always MFN i.e., this is producer specific not country specific.
57. Ibid no.2
58. Average tariff faced by Indian exporters to the EC market is high because as much as more than half of our items are covered by EC-

NTBs.

59. Developed countries including EC have given commitment to GATT to dismantle all NTBs over a period of 10 years battening 1st January, 1995. But, on the other hand both US and EC keep on enforcing newer forms of NTBs which are outside the group of GATT/WTO.
60. UNCTAD, "*Reports on Trade, Tariff and Non-Tariff Barriers*", (An UNCTAD inventory of Non-Tariff Barriers), (Trade partner of EU-India), (Geneva , UNCTAD), 1993 and 1994.
61. Original information is available at HS-8 digit level but in our analysis we have aggregated it at HS-2 digit level. In 1993 and 1994 there is no national NTBs, all are EC-Specific NTBs.
62. The methodology of calculating NTBs-Coverage at frequency ratio are shown in Chapter-III as well as Laird and Yeats, "*UNCTAD Trade Policy Simulation Model*", UNCTAD Discussion Paper No.19, 1986, (Geneva, UNCTAD), pp.1-33.
63. *(a)* Ibid n. 19.
    (b) Ibid n. 3(a).
64. This is because of trade cut-off. In 1988 trade cut-off was $ 1000 but in 1992 it was $ 50000, thereafter again it become $ 11000. This is the reason why frequency ratio can not be a very dependable indicator.
65. Our entire study based on pre-Uruguay Round situation. We have not done any comparative-static analysis after the implementation of the Uruguay Round provisions.
66. *(a)* Commission of the European Communities, "*Official Journal of the European Communities*", (Brussels), 31st December, 1994, no.L348/11.
    (b) Mission of India to the European Union, "India-EC MoUs on Market Access for textiles", (Brussels), February 5, 1995, pp.1-2.
67. Swapan K. Bhattacharya, "India's Textile Agreements with USA and EC : Beginning of a New Era Competitiveness" Foreign Trade Bulletin, (IIFT, New Delhi), May-June 1995, pp. 10-13 & 22.
68. Ibid n. 1.
69. Protectionism is measured here in terms of weighted tariffs, NTB-Coverage and frequency ratio.
70. This phenomenon will be proved in the next section with the help of Bela Balassa, RCA Index.
71. NTBs are applied on those items in which developing countries have comparative advantage, see also Ingo Walter, (1971), Ibid n. 32.
72. *World Development Report*, (The World Bank, Washington), 1987.
73. Bela Balassa, "Trade Liberalisation and Revealed Comparative advantage", *The Manchester School*, (1965), Vol.-XXXIII, No. 2, pp.99-123.
74. Shobha Ahuja, "Liberalisation of Trade in Services : The Revealed Comparative Advantage Approach", *Foreign Trade Review* (New

Delhi), 1993, pp.43-58

75. Ibid n. 74 p.47
76. Ibid n. 32.
77. Weighted average tariff is taken as an indicator of trade restrictiveness and also hte covariation of average tariffs. Protectionism will be higher if average tariff is high vice-versa.
78. This is evident in case of EC's agricultural imports. Almost entire impact of agricultural items are subject to community. Levies under the Common Agricultural Programme (CAP). Tariff equivalents of all agricultural goods are more than 100 per cent in the community, see a) "Agra Europe", 20th March, 1992, London, pp. E.12. b) Cline W.R. et al, "Tokyo Round Negotiations : A Quantitative Assessment", The Brookings Institution, (Washington), 1978, p. 145, c) Gary Sampson and Alexander J. Yeats, "An Evaluation of the Common Agricultural Policy as a Barriers Facing Agricultural Exports to the European Community", American Journal of Agricultural Economics, No. 59, February 1977, pp. 99-106.
79. *(a)* Carl Hamilton, "Voluntary Export Restraints on Asia : Tariff Equivalents, Rents and Trade Barriers Formation", *Seminar Paper no.276, Institute for Economic Studies*, (Stockholm), April, 1994, pp.1.31.

    (b) Joseph Pealzman, "The Tariff Equivalents of the Existing Quotas under the Multifibre Arrangements", ...

    (c) Kala Krishna, "The Importance and Extent of Rent Seeking in the Multifibre Arrangements : Evidence from US-Hong Kong Trade in Apparel",..........
80. In Connection with this study, we have tried our best to get EU-Domestic price data on textiles and garments we not at all successful to get it. Again we tried through H.E. Mr. S. Narayanan our Ambassador to GATT to receive these data. But the result is the same. EU is very sensitive to pass on domestic price data to anybody belonging to the textile exporting countries, especially India.
81. EC's submission to the GATT is a confidential document. In the Final Agreement it has agreed to reduce subsidies of an agricultural exports. Prior to that they have to submit tariff-equivalents of agricultural goods under Cf. it is not public document. But Agra, Europe managed to get these data and published some of EC submission in its Vol. in 20th March, 1992.
82. Ibid n. 78. P. E. 11-17.
83. Ibid n. 32.
84. *(a)* Anderson James E. and J. Peter Neary, "Measuring Restrictiveness of Trade Policy", *World Bank Working Paper*, (The World Bank, Washington), 1994, pp. 151-169.

    (b) __________, "The Trade Restrictiveness of the Multifibre

Arrangement" *World Bank Economic Review,* Vol. 8, No.2, (The World Bank, Washington), May 1994, pp. 170-189.

85. Ibid n. 84(a).
86. *(a)* Anderson, James E., "Measuring Trade Restrictiveness in a single CGE Model with Appendix : A Manual for using the TRI Spreadsheet Model", *Boston College, Dept. of Economics,* (Boston, Massachusetts), 1993.
    (b) Anderson, James E. and J. Peter Neary, "The Trade Restrictive Index : An Application to Mexican Agriculture", *PPR WPS No. 874, International Economic Dept.,* (The World Bank, Washington), 1992.
    (c) __________, "A New Approach to Evaluating Trade Policy", *World Bank Working Paper,* (The World Bank, Washington D.C.), 1991.
    (d) __________ and Raed Safadi, "Trade Restrictiveness of the Multifibre Arrangements", *World Bank Ecnomic Review,* Vol. 8, no. 2, May, (The World Bank, Washington), 1992.
87. *(a)* Ibid n. 5.
    (b) Ibid n. 36(b).
88. One Can Compare the difference between domestic and international prices of any good provided that it is pure or clearly substitute. Since agricultural goods are almost substitutes, it is possible to calculate tariff equivalents of their items. Manufactured goods are not pure substitute therefore, it will give the distorted picture.
89. World Trade Organisation, "*Uruguay Round : The Final Act : Agreement on Agriculture*", (GATT, Geneva), 1994, pp. 43-69.
90. Agra, Europe, "March 20, 1992 (London), TAB AGRTRA pp. E-11-17.
91. Ibid n. 90 p. E-13.
92. Calculation based on Agra, Europe, March 20, 1992, (London), pp.E.-11-17.
93. lbid no. 1 p. 90.
94. lbid no. 90 p.E-11
95. lbid no. 90 p.E.-14.
96. As it is evident from data provided by *Agra, Europe,* March 20, 1992, (London).

Chapter 6

India's Growing Economic Constraints: Its Liberalisation and European Industries Hesitant Response

INDIA'S CHRONIC PROBLEM OF DEFICIT BALANCE OF PAYMENT WITH THE EUROPEAN COMMUNITY.

Introduction

The European Union (EU) comprised of 12 member-state up to 31 December 1994. But since 1st January 1995, it became a Union of 15 States with a long queue of aspirants for future membership. Austria, Sweden and Finland became members of the Union on 1 January 1995. Portugal and Spain became members in 1986 and UK, Ireland and Denmark became members in 1973. The shape of the European Community first crystalized with the formation of European Coal and Steel Community in 1951. The Community first started with six members with the objective of forming a customs union but now it has deepened its process of integration extending to cover economic, monetary and political aspect as well (Pelkmans, 1991, Davenport & Page, 1989, Kol, 1989, McAleese, 1991, Langhammer 1990)[1].

India's economic relations with the EU and its member states are based upon historical foundations and mutual trust. EU has been India's single largest and a dependable trading partner for more than two decades. The 15-member union is considered as a single contracting party to the World Trade Organisation (WTO) and that is why it is treated as a single trading partner for the purposes of global trade. The EU is presently the largest economic/

trading bloc in the world. It is also an active champion of multilateral trading system. Membership of the trading bloc does not prevent any country from being an active member of any other multilateral body like GATT/WTO/ITC/IBRD. Though USA, Canada and Mexico have also formed a trading bloc i.e. NAFTA, it is still at a fluid stage and is expected to get concrete shape after 2004, when all the provisions of NAFTA agreement may be implemented.

In respect of trade policies and treatment to be meted out towards developing countries, EU is more flexible than USA (Clark & Simonetta, 1994)[2], but in terms of trade restrictive measures, it is more protectionist than the United States (Doglas, 1994 and McGee, 1993)[3]. As discussed earlier India's main export items to the EU market are agricultural based, leather, raw hides and skins, articles of leather and fur skins (excluding footwear) and textiles and garments, chemicals, spices, light engineering goods and other low value-added manufactured goods. Textiles is the single largest export item to the EU which constitutes about 30 per cent of India's total exports to the Community[4]. All of our exportables are low- value added with higher labour-intensity based on factor abundance and factor intensity.

Due to the odd composition of our exports, the trade balance and terms of trade always go in favour of the EC[5]. India's chronic and excessive dependence on EU for its quality imports of capital goods and machineries, has increased its trade deficit up significantly over the years[6]. EC's share in India's total exports which was 21.57 per cent in 1980-81 increased to 26.06 per cent in 1993-94 and 26.70 per cent in 1994-95. On the other hand, EU's share in India's total imports was 21.03 per cent in 1980-81 but it jacked up to 30.04 per cent in 1993-94 and 24.80 per cent in 1994-95.

As regards India's exports to the EU, the commodity composition has been radically changing since the early eighties[7]. Our exports to the EU had registered a 52 per cent growth in 1993-94 over 1991-92. In the first quarter of 1995, the exports had crossed the Rs.4542 crore mark. The share of textiles and garments in India's total exports to the EU was the highest among all major groups. Its share was 31 per cent in 1994-95 followed by manufactured leather and footwear (14%). In fact, India's footwear and leather products have a major market in Italy, UK, France, Denmark and Germany. Leading markets for India's gems and jewellery exports (11%) are Belgium and UK[8].

Engineering products emerged as one of the fastest growing

items of Indian exports to the EU in 1994[9]. While EU's total engineering imports from Extra-EU source had increased by 20.6 per cent in 1993, those from India increased by 29.5 per cent. UK and Germany are two large markets for our engineering goods. In this category, exports of transport equipments had shown an impressive growth of 75.22 per cent in 1993-94 over the previous year[10].

Although pharmaceuticals form an important item of India's exports to the EU it accounts for only 0.13 per cent of EU's total imports of this category, lagging behind the other developing countries like China, Brazil, Argentina, Hungary, Poland, Israel and South Korea[11]. Measures are needed to be urgently taken to boost exports of pharmaceuticals as they declined alarmingly by 28 per cent in 1993, compared to a compound growth of 32 per cent during 1988-92. In 1993, our export of this product group had declined to France, Germany, Italy and Greece, whereas they increased to Spain, Denmark and Portugal[12].

In the field of agro-products, the EU is being recognized as one of the most protectionist countries grouping in the world (Goldin, 1993, Gulati & Sharma, 1992)[13]. But recently it has imposed an incredible rate of 100 per cent to 300 per cent import tariffs on cereals and rice. With the signing of the Final Agreement of the WTO, the EU has the moral responsibility to bring down its tariff rates. However, Indian Basmati exports to EU have grown steadily over the last few years and even registered over 100 per cent growth in 1993 in quantity terms[14]. It is important to note that Indian Basmati rice is among the highest paid varieties in the EU markets. Marine exports from India already enjoy expanding market potential in UK, Belgium and France. However, they have shown a slight decline in the Irish and Spanish markets. The other potential items in the agricultural trade are processed foods, vegetables and coffee. In addition to existing exports, India can also increase the exports of a wide range of other commodities to the EU markets. These include : fruits viz. mangoes, horticulture products like cut flowers, meat and meat preparations, dyes and intermediates, iron and steel bars, fine chemicals, machine tools, computer software, agro-chemicals, electronic goods and sports goods[15].

The EU's share in India's exports reached the peak level in 1987-88 (i.e. 33.22 per cent). India's chronic trade deficit with the European Community is another dimension of Indo-EU economic relations. Due to the nature of trade between the two, the balance of trade has always

TABLE 6.1a : INDO-EC TRADE

(values in Rs.million)

	1980-81	1982-83	1983-84	1984-85	1985-86	1986-87	1987-88	1988-89	1989-90	1990-91	1991-92	1992-93	1993-94	1994-95
India's Export to the EC	14474.00	14701.00	17556.00	20021.00	19286.00	27357.00	39573.00	49460.00	69060.00	89307.00	118580.00	151960.00	181820.00	220750.00
India's Imports from the EC	26389.00	34218.00	39615.00	42214.00	52337.00	65415.00	74408.00	90220.00	117360.00	127201.00	139740.00	191239.00	219620.00	223390.00
India's Total Exports	67017.00	88034.00	97707.00	117437.00	108946.00	124524.00	157412.00	202950.00	276810.00	325272.00	438280.00	536880.00	697510.00	826740.00
India's Total Imports	125492.00	142927.00	158315.00	171342.00	196577.00	202007.00	223990.00	281940.00	354120.00	431708.00	477970.00	633740.00	731010.00	899710.00
EC's Share in Indian's Export	21.57	16.70	17.97	17.05	17.07	21.97	25.14	24.37	24.95	27.46	27.05	28.30	26.06	26.70
EC's Share in India's Import	21.03	23.94	25.02	24.64	26.62	32.38	33.22	32.00	33.14	29.46	29.24	30.18	30.04	24.80
India's Trade Deficit with the EC	11915.00	19517.00	22059.00	22193.00	33051.00	38058.00	34835.00	40760.00	48300.00	37894.00	21160.00	39279.00	37800.00	2640.00
Total Trade Deficit	58385.00	54893.00	60608.00	53905.00	87631.00	77483.00	66578.00	78990.00	77310.00	106436.00	39690.00	96860.00	33500.00	72970.00
Trade Deficit with The EC As a Per cent of India's Total Trade Deficit	20.41	35.55	36.40	41.17	37.72	49.12	52.32	51.60	62.47	35.60	53.31	40.55	112.84	3.62

Source : *Monthly Statistics of Foreign Trade of India* (Various Issues), DGCI&S, Calcutta.

favoured the EU. India's trade deficit with the Community was Rs.1191 crore in 1980-81 which rose to highest ever deficit of Rs.4860 crore in 1989-90 and then declined to Rs.3700 crore in 1993-94[16]. The rationale behind such decline in trade deficit is the spectacular performance of our export over 92-93 which is shown in **Table 6.1a**.

During the past few years, while imports for the EU have been increasing slowly, India's exports have grown satisfactorily in the same period leading to the narrowing down of our trade deficit. Comparatively better performance in recent years provides the main impulse for the narrowing down of trade deficit with the EU. This satisfactory performance of Indo-EU trade due to the successful implementation of India's New Economic Policy enunciated in July 1991. This was the first ever experience since independence that our total exports increased by 20 per cent in dollar terms and imports increased by only 6.1 per cent during 1993-94[17]. The entire gamut of India's trade with the EU in rupee terms is shown in **Table-6.1a** and in terms of US dollars in the **Table-6.1b**.

Table 6.1b shows trends of India's trade with the EU from 1999 to 2002 in US dollars. Table shows that India's expert to the EU grows at much faster rate than its imports. From 1991-2002, India's export to the EU grew at 8.07 per cent rate in dollar terms, whereas its import grew only by 7.41 per cent. But another important feature of Indo-EU trade has been that rate of growth of India's expert and import to and from the EU is higher than its overall growth rates of exports and imports. India's total exports grew at 10.24 per cent rate during the same period mentioned about, and imports grew by 10.98 per cent. The EU's shares in both India's exports and imports have been coming down over the years. The EU's share in India's total expert in US dollars was 27.06 per cent in 1991, reached a peak of 28.30 per cent in 1992-93, but declined significantly to 21.73 per cent in 2002-2003. This shows that India has been rapidly losing market access to the EU. The sliding tendency becomes very prominent after 1995, since when WTO came into force. The Reasons may be different, but it is apparently clear that India is not able to dent on the EU market in the era of globalisation especially after the onset of WTO. The trend is same in case of India's imports also. Share of the EU in Indian's imports was 29.24 per cent in 1991-92 reached the peak level of 30.18 per cent in the next year i.e. 1992-93, and started declining thereafter and reduced to 20.92 per cent in 2002-03. Therefore, not only the EU's contribution to Indian exports decision over the years, but also its contribution to India's imports follows the same trend. In import front, reduction in market share is much more prominent than its export front. The entire phenomenon is shown in **Table 6.1b.**

As a part of the overall package of economic reforms, Government has liberalized export-import procedures and have adopted several other measures to promote exports[18]. It has also streamlined all dubious and obsolete procedures of EXIM Policy and replaced them by the New Exim Policy, 1992-97.

First and then new EXIM policies every year with more reform measures in the external sector. Every verson of the EXIM policies, which is promulgated every year with a view to integrating India with the ongoing globalization process. Government continues to modify it every year incorporating suggestions from trade and commerce. India's trade deficit with EU as a per centage of total trade deficit was 53.32 per cent in 1991-92 declined to 32.67 per cent in 1995-96 but it again declined to 12.85 per cent during 2002-03. This is evident from the trend of India's balance of trade with the EU. In spite of several trade barriers, the EU market still remains India's ideal trade destination. Indeed, the EU is becoming more and more attracted to Indian goods than earlier because of significant improvement in quality and competitive costs, compared to those of other exporters. Textiles is a concrete example in this regard. Furthermore India's traditional import of capital goods has now been replaced by imports of technology through joint ventures and foreign collaboration agreements in most areas of manufacturing activity. There is also increasing flow of Foreign Direct Investment (FDI) from the EU to India particularly for setting up of joint ventures using state-of-the-art technology. In many cases, FDI in form of financial collaborations is linked with the export obligations. In other words, Indian industries are becoming more and more export oriented than ever before. Imports are now linked with value-addition norms. Input-output norms for the different products have been introduced by the government to encourage more exports[19].

INDIA'S OPTION TOWARDS THE ERSTWHILE SOVIET BLOC IS AT LOW KEY AFTER DISINTREGATION OF THE USSR

A countrywise performance analysis of Indian exports reveals that

TABLE 6.1b : INDO-EU TRADE

(Figures in millions of $)

	1991-92	*1992-93*	*1993-94*	*1994-95*	*1995-96*	*1996-97*	*1997-98*	*1998-99*	*1999-2000*	*2000-01*	*2001-02*	*2002-03*
India's Exports to the EU	4845.9	4935.4	5790.4	7032.5	8721.27	8662.6	9156.94	8944.69	9348.78	10329.83	9841.53	11382.24
India's Imports from the EU	5710.7	6211.1	6994.3	7116.6	10318.26	10633.71	10693.47	10721.39	10989.28	10382.71	10398.43	12547.97
India's Total Exports	17910.9	17436.8	22213.7	26337.7	31842	33498	35049	33211	36760	44147	43708	52370
India's Total Imports	19532.9	20582.6	23280.6	28662.3	36730	39165	41535	42379	49799	50056	51261	61445
EU's Share in India's Exports	27.06	28.30	26.07	26.70	27.39	25.86	26.13	26.93	25.43	23.40	22.52	21.73
EU's Share in India's Imports	29.24	30.18	30.04	24.83	28.09	27.15	25.75	25.30	22.07	20.74	20.29	20.42
India's Trade Deficit with EU	-864.8	-1275.7	-1203.9	-84.1	-1596.99	-1971.11	-1536.53	-1776.7	-1640.5	-52.88	-556.9	-1165.73
India's Total Trade Deficit	-1622	-3145.8	-1066.9	-2324.6	-4888	-5667	-6486	-9168	-13039	-5909	-7553	-9075
EU Deficit as a % of Total Deficit	**53.32**	**40.55**	**112.84**	**3.62**	**32.67**	**34.78**	**23.69**	**19.38**	**12.58**	**0.89**	**7.37**	**12.85**

Source: Monthly Statistics of Foreign Trade of India(Various Issues), DGCI&S, Kolkata

the Soviet Union had been the largest trading partner of India next only to the USA during pre-disintegration period. But the entire scenario had changed on 21 December 1991 when the USSR disintegrated finally into 15 Independent Republics, out of which 11 came together subsequently to form a voluntary community known as Commonwealth of Independent States (CIS) under the Alma Ata Declaration of 21st December, 1991. Georgia and three Baltic States of Lithuania, Latvia and Estonia opted to remain independent countries outside of CIS.

The disintegration of erstwhile Soviet Union and formation of CIS have entirely changed the morphology of India-USSR trade. Prior to the formation of CIS, India had been one of the noteworthy exporters to the formerly Soviet Union. Its share in India's total exports was as high as 16 per cent in 1990-91 while it accounted for 6 per cent of India's global imports during the same year[20].

In the post-Soviet phase, in 1992-93, India's trade with the USSR declined by almost 68 per cent, as compared to 1990-91. However, the year 1993-94 was marked by a turnaround the in Indo-CIS trade. During that year India's bilateral trade was Rs 3664.2 crore which increased to Rs 4998.5 crore in 1994-95 registering an increase of 36 per cent. It is noteworthy that India's imports from CIS have grown at a faster pace compared to exports during 1994-95. This is revealed from the fact that our imports increased by over 88 per cent , while our exports grew only by 11 per cent between 1993-94 and 1994-95. **Table 6.3** shows the trend of Indo-CIS trade[21].

India has been maintaining a consistent trade surplus with the former Soviet bloc countries over the years. Trade surplus reached its peak in 1990-91 when it rose to Rs 2714.5 crore; afterwards, there had been a steep decline. This was simply because of the fact that the former USSR had disintegrated into smaller States and eleven States set up a loose association known as Commonwealth of Independent States (CIS). During the post disintegration era, trade surplus has declined drastically due to increase in imports on one hand, and slow pace of growth of exports on the other. The situation has become so worse that during the period April 1995 to February 1996 India's trade with CIS registered a negative balance of Rs 305 crore, which is the worst of all the preceding years[22].

USSR share in India's total exports was 16.19 per cent in 1990-91; it declined to 2.9 per cent in 1993-94. While USSR share in India's total imports was 5.91 per cent in 1990-91, the CIS share declined to

TABLE 6.2 : INDO-EC TRADE

(value in million ECUs)

	1980	1981	1982	1983	1984	1985	1986	1987	1988	1989	1990	1991	1992	1993	1994	1995
EC's Total Exports to the World	497137.00	571054.00	626652.00	671884.00	776772.00	849936.00	806958.00	829911.00	901903.00	1043288.00	1071429.00	1116451.00	1136437.00	1156944.00	1293635.00	
EC's Total Imports from the World	557746.00	618870.00	672187.00	707694.00	809357.00	874675.00	796005.00	829135.00	919336.00	1073551.00	1127588.00	1199583.00	1207264.00	1125763.00	1254698.00	
EC's Exports to India	2371.00	3473.00	4110.00	3970.00	4800.00	5762.00	5707.00	5679.00	5628.00	7083.00	6000.00	5208.00	5245.00	6291.00	7053.00	
EC's Imports from India	1841.00	1933.00	2761.00	2281.00	2966.00	2986.00	2395.00	2762.00	3238.00	4180.00	4542.00	4734.00	4878.00	5876.00	6913.00	
Intra-EC Exports	276893.00	301542.00	338297.00	366885.00	421709.00	466595.00	461342.00	486836.00	536939.00	625721.00	656502.00	688175.00	696541.00	669878.00	757835.00	
Intra-EC Imports	274558.00	300026.00	336176.00	365257.00	417466.00	466742.00	459706.00	487395.00	533770.00	624488.00	663529.00	702924.00	715997.00	638566.00	714918.00	
India's Share in EC's Total Exports	0.48	0.61	0.66	0.59	0.62	0.68	0.71	0.68	0.62	0.68	0.56	0.47	0.46	0.54	0.55	
India's Share in EC's Total Imports	0.33	0.31	0.41	0.32	0.37	0.34	0.30	0.33	0.35	0.39	0.40	0.39	0.40	0.52	0.55	
Intra-EC's Share in EC's Total Exports	55.70	52.80	53.98	54.61	54.29	54.90	57.17	58.66	59.53	59.98	60.98	61.64	61.29	57.90	58.58	
Intra-EC's Share in EC's Total Imports	49.23	48.48	50.01	51.61	51.58	53.36	57.75	58.78	58.06	58.17	58.84	58.60	59.30	56.72	56.98	

Source : Commission of the European Community, *Eurostat* (Various Issues), Brussels.

1.11 per cent in 1993-94. In 1990-91, the USSR share in India's total trade was 10.33 per cent which the share of CIS declined to 1.98 per cent in 1993-94[23]. A brief picture of Indo-USSR/CIS trade is shown here below :

Table 6.3 : Trend of Indo-CIS Trade

Rs. Crore

Indo-USSR	*Exports*	*Imports*	*Balance*
1989-90	4462.9	2038.2	2424.7
1990-91	5266.2	2551.7	2714.5
1991-92	4042.7	1795.4	2246.8
Indo-CIS			
1992-93	1693.2	744.7	948.5
1993-94	2475.9	1188.3	1287.6
1994-95	2759.2	2239.3	519.9
1995-96 (April'95-Feb'96)	3454.0	3759.0	-305.0

Source : Monthly Statistics of Foreign Trade of India, (Several Issues), DGCI & S, (Calcutta).

From among all the CIS countries, Russian Federation is the largest trading partner, followed by Ukraine, Turkmenistan, Uzbekistan, Kazakhstan etc. Following the collapse of the USSR, each independent State has concluded separate agreement with India in its individual capacity, consistent with its national priorities[24].

India's trade with the CIS has been declining during the post disintegration period. From 10 per cent share in India's total trade, it came down to around 2 per cent in 1993-94. Several reasons may be cited for such lackluster performance of Indo-CIS trade. Political and economic turmoil in the CIS countries shall be one of the most important reasons. Another hurdle to the healthy growth of Indo-CIS trade has been due to the exchange rate problem. The Rouble is highly overvalued against the Indian rupee, this is because its value is artificially determined rather than through free floating exchange rate which is done in case of hard currencies. Rouble is not internationally convertible currency. In the erstwhile USSR, rupee payment system was the major plank of Indo-USSR trade, but after disintegration this system has been substituted by the payment of hard currencies (Sen, 1990, N. Chandra, 1977, Suresh Kumar, 1987, Sen & Vyas 1989)[25].

Problem of Indo-CIS Trade : The Era of Higher Inflation

Indo-USSR trade had entered into a new phase after 21 December 1991, when USSR disintegrated into 15 independent states, whereafter 11 of them together voluntary formed Commonwealth of Independent States (CIS) and three Baltic States declared their independence. In the beginning, Indo-CIS trade received a big jolt when prices of all goods in the newly formed States started rising without limit and thus losing credibility of international communities[26].

On 2 January 1992, more than 80 per cent of all "prices" were freed. Prices shot up by 250 per cent the very next day. Price controls remained on consumer goods, freight transport and energy. The upward trend in inflation accelerated since the onset of liberalization process in prices initiated in January 1992[27]. During 1992, inflation rate increased to 2000 per cent. A presidential decree abolished all special rates for the Rouble from the beginning of July 1992 and introduced a uniform floating exchange rate[28]. The rate which was still around 125 Roubles per US Dollar in May 1992 had fallen to below 400 Roubles per US Dollar by mid-November 1992, and reached 1230 Roubles per US dollar by December 1993 and 5000 Roubles at the end of 1995[29].

1993 began with a hyperinflationary level of 50 per cent though it was brought down in July 1993 to 15 per cent by limiting credit expansion. However, in August inflation index went up nearly 30 per cent. Though the industry continued to face credit contraction, production did not fall drastically. In the first 8 months of 1993, investment was cut by 45 per cent as a part of the budget squeeze out of which nearly half was in fuel and energy sector[30].

In 1994, the government planned to reduce inflation to 5.7 per cent in a month by the end of the year and restriction on price rise to 4.7 times against 10 times in 1993. Ex-post inflation in 1993 was 1500-1800 per cent. This had supposedly come down by 10 per cent monthly in the first month of 1994. While in 1993, the economy was restricted by low-money supply, the first quarter of 1994 had seen an oversupply. The purchasing power of the people had been seriously eroded with nearly 17 per cent of the total population living below the subsistence level. Inflation slowed down in first half of the year to approximately 10 per cent per month compared to over 20 per cent monthly rate and annual average rate of 1000 per cent in 1993. In 1994, annual inflation rate was 500 per cent compared to more than 1000 per cent in the previous year[31].

Indo-CIS Trade : Move Towards Future Direction

The era of Rupee-Rouble exchange rate system has collapsed completely when the erstwhile USSR disintegrated and in its place can CIS. Now the entire trade is conducted through hard-currencies rather than on the basis of erstwhile system of Rupee payment. In the changing scenario, India has been facing the problem of dual payment system because the huge amount of Russian debt is yet to be paid in rupees whereas trade is conducted in hard currencies[32]. Since Russia has now switched over its trade to hard currencies and is now importing goods from other countries for which it has to depend on India. Now Russian market is flooded with foreign consumer goods where Indian presence is almost insignificant[33]. Prior to disintegration, Russia used to import from India in order to utilise the accumulated rupees. The capacity to import from India depended on availability of rupee resources[34].

Now the morphology of erstwhile USSR has changed completely which paves the way for free market economy. Under the changing scenario, exchange rate problem is no more a significant barrier. Trade from both sides is conducted through hard currency. Rupee rouble exchange rate system has therefore no relevance now[35].

As stated earlier, from among all members of CIS, Russian Federation is the largest trading partner of India. In the post disintegration era, India's major export items to the CIS are : Tea, coffee, tobacco, spices, oil meals, caster oils, processed fruits and juice, leather and manufactures, drugs and pharmaceuticals, cosmetics, machinery and instruments, textiles and garments etc. On the other hand, India's major import items are : fertilizers, news-print, paper machinery and mechanical appliances, defence products, orthopaedic appliances, crude and petroleum products, industrial and laboratory furnaces, and ovens[36]. Most of our exports to the CIS are low value added primary commodities based on natural resources, eg., tea, leather, textiles, jute and jute products, the demand for which is relatively inelastic. Therefore prices are much less than those of finished manufactured goods. On other hand India imports high value added items, and most of them are either processed and finished manufactured goods, therefore prices are comparatively higher. Defence items are India's single largest import group from the CIS, as well as erstwhile USSR.

Indo-Russian bilateral trade is presently being carried out at three different levels :

(a) Hard-currency trade in accordance with the Agreement on Trade and Economic Cooperation signed on 4 May 1992. However, problems that cropped up included purchase of hard currency by Russians which is costly and time consuming as the value of Rouble is always volatile.

(b) Debt repayment in accordance with the EXIM Policy, against India's debt repayment to Russia. The amount presently available is Rs 3000 crore annually.

(c) Counter trade and its variants : This mechanism permits trade in all items except items included in the negative list of our EXIM Policy. This aims at overcoming the difficulties of payments and exchange rates[37].

To take into account such development, it was essential to sign a new treaty enabling smooth operation of Indo-Russian economic relations. Amidst such needs, an Indo-Russian Agreement on Trade and Economic Cooperation was signed in New Delhi in May 1992. This friendship and cooperation agreement was further strengthened through the visit of President Boris Yeltsin to India in June 1993, when many bilateral agreements were concluded including the one on Rupee-Rouble exchange rate. There have also been exchange of letters between Ministers on issues relating to trade matters. These Agreements gave necessary impetus towards liberalization of trade from the inter-governmental protocol to the trade conducted in free foreign currency. These agreements also addressed issues relating to debt rescheduling, technical credits, repayments and special accounts. Subsequently, many other agreements/protocols were signed on matters relating to banking arrangements for trade against the repayment of state credit, revolving credit, health and medical research, etc[38].

The bilateral trading relations between these two countries were strengthened further after the recent visit of India's Prime Minister to Moscow. Some of the outcomes are[39] :

— It was decided that Russian importers could avail of 180 days of credit to buy goods from India.

— Russian Government announced various special concessions on goods imported from India under debt repayment system. Rupees available under the scheme were offered to Russian companies at 20 to 25 per cent discount for goods imported from India.

— India has agreed to participate in the modernization of

Novorossisk port on Black Sea.

- — A joint venture banking arrangement has also been finalized with the Russian Rosexion Bank and the State Bank of India.
- — A shipping agreement, agreement on investment protection, and another agreement on civil aviation were also arrived at.
- — It was agreed in the meeting to further explore the possibility of opening up a land route to CIS through Central Asia.

Recently some measures have been taken to boost Indo-Russian trade. These are[40]:

(i) Diversification of commodity basket;
(ii) Opening warehouses;
(iii) ECGC cover;
(iv) Port facilities;
(v) Banking facilities;
(vi) Opening up trade offices;
(vii) Rationalization of import duties;
(viii) Double taxation agreement;
(ix) Issuance of multiple visas;
(x) Certification of goods;
(xi) Insurance coverage;
(xii) Debt repayment route;
(xiii) Barter trading system.

AUGMENTING EXPORTS : INDIA'S DEMARCHE TOWARDS LIBERALIZATION OF ECONOMY SINCE 1982[41]

India's trade policies experienced spurts and dips over the last 40 years beginning 1951. The importance of augmenting exports for economic development was neglected until the beginning of the fourth plan. Trade Policy makers had all along given pivotal importance to import substitution for saving scarce foreign exchange resources. As a result of such a misleading priority, 40 per cent of the total investment was allocated to the development of heavy and core industry during the Second Plan (Bhagwati & Sriniwasa, 1975)[42]. Heavy industry was supposed to play as an engine of economic development, which proved wrong when import substitution industries got excessively pampered at the cost of export promotion. Export promotion efforts were neglected which resulted in balance of payment problem (Martin Wolf, 1980)[43]. Due to large domestic demand and higher profitability in the domestic market, export culture got bogged down in the quagmire of import substitution[44]. Though it is equally true that the concept of export-led-growth was not a very sensible proposition for a big country like India, the importance of exports in economic development remained unknown until 1966 when Indian rupee was for the first time devalued against major currencies for promoting exports. All the export promotion policies during the seventies were transitory in nature. The policy paradigm was basically short-term-in nature and all EXIM policies were announced annually which left no scope for continuation of any stable policy regime for a relatively longer period. Short-term policies are basically ad hoc in nature that serve no long term goal which is the basic requirement of stable and sustainable economic development.

Trade Policy reforms in India actually started since 1976-77 when 55 items of leather machinery were brought under open general licensing[45]. The Advance Licensing Scheme provided duty free-imports for export production was also introduced for the first time. The year 1977-78 was characterized by the inclusion of more items of leather, jute garment manufacturing machinery into their system[46]. In total, 238 bulk drugs, 54 life saving drugs, 40 items of chemicals, plastic raw materials and 34 items of the raw materials/components were brought under OGL. Licensing of capital goods imports was made less stringent by the "global tender" policy which was introduced in 1978 for 13 major industries. The process which was initiated in the late seventies had gathered momentum in the eighties through several new liberalizing measures.

Trade Policy regime during the 1980s was characterized by two opposite forces : gradual relaxation of restrictions imposed on imports, on the one hand, and substantial increase in tariff rates on the other. As an example, with a view to liberalize capital goods imports, the duty rate on general projects was lowered from 65 to 45 per cent in the budget for 1985-86 but this duty rate was raised to 85 per cent during 1987-88 budget[47]. The import weighted average rate of nominal tariffs (basic plus auxiliary rates of customs duty, taking into account quantifiable exemptions) increased from 38 per cent in 1980-81 to 87 per cent in 1989-90[48]. Another important characteristic was the increase in the rate of tariffs on items for which the import licensing status was made less restrictive.

All EXIM policies announced during the seventies and eighties were basically characterized by direct control mechanism through higher import tariffs. The rationale of higher import tariffs was to restrain imports of capital goods as well as consumer goods[49]. Apart from higher import tariffs, most of the consumer goods imports were put under the negative list of imports. This way government has pampered (i) inefficient domestic industry in the name of import substitution and (ii) discouraged the growth of export sector through restraining import of capital goods. This then also resulted in technology obsolescence in the heavy industry sector. Until 1984-85, the government announced its EXIM Policy every year. But according to the recommendations of **the Tandon Committee (1982)**[50]**, the Alexander Committee (1980)**[51] **and the Abid Hussain Committee (1984)**[52] the Government decided to follow the a long-term stable trade policy covering a period of 3 years.

The first ever long-term trade policy was announced in 1985 for a period of 3 years i.e. 1985-88[53]. This was followed by another three year trade policy for the period of 1988-91. However, in January 1990, the Government decided to announce a trade policy on 1 April 1990 thus limiting the scope of the existing trade policy to just 2 years. Sudden shortening of the period of an official policy apart, even the earlier trade policy announcements were changed in small measures almost every week thus weakening the concept of an annual or three year trade policy. Similarly, even the customs tariffs as announced in the Union Budget underwent considerable changes over the years.

The **Abid Hussain Committee Report (1984)** recommended that import substitution and export promotion should get equal importance and, in fact, liberalization of import is an essential prerequisite for augmenting exports. With a view to assigning utmost importance for augmenting exports, major steps were taken in 1978-79 to liberalize imports of capital goods. The global tender policy system for import of capital goods was introduced in respect of 13 industries including fertilizers, power, petrochemicals, sugar and cement. The import policy was also liberalized in respect of intermediate and raw materials which were not manufactured in India. Import of goods that were manufactured in India were restricted but made available to exporters on the basis of a replenishment system linked to past export performance of the exporter. In anticipation that free import of capital goods would lead to upgradation of technology and modernization of industries, government put import of capital goods under Open General Licence (OGL)[54].

However, in spite of all these concerted efforts to boost exports, until recently customs tariff levels in the country continued to be very high compared to other developing countries. The average duty rates in the developed countries are the lowest ones barring a few products[55]. Presently average duty rates in the USA and EU on all imports range between 4-6 per cent. Rates are minimal in case of manufactured imports.

It is naive to say that the eighties was the beginning of liberalization process which got final shape in July 1991. But it is also worth mentioning that though it started in the eighties it was much sporadic and the policy framework was basically characterized by control mechanism of import. Import was relatively liberalized during this period and was permitted on a complementary basis. During entire 1980s, three long-term EXIM Policies were announced by the Government, **first** in 1985, **second** in 1988 and the **third** one in 1990[56]. The basic features of these policies were the liberalization of licensing system, ensuring better access to domestic producers of cheaper capital good, intermediate and raw materials and to help them in upgradation of technology.

In a move to liberalize the trading regime, a number of items were placed under the OGL while 94 new items of industrial machinery were placed under OGL in the import policy of 1984[57]. The 1985 liberalization package permitted 685 items to be imported without restrictions and finally 1986 import policy brought additional 29 items of machine tools under OGL. As on March 1988, 944 items of raw materials, components and consumables were allowed to be imported under OGL and 26 items were decanalized. An Export-Import Pass Book Scheme was also introduced in the 1985-88 Policy and the scheme of Trading Houses and Export Houses was modified to provide more facilities and incentives for exports[58].

In addition to the benefits mentioned above, exporters continued to get various benefits such as Cash Compensatory support (CCS) as compensation for unrelated indirect taxes on inputs of exported products, drawback of excise duties and domestic taxes on exported goods, modified value added tax to avoid cascading effects on inputs, interest concessions on loans to Export Oriented Units (EOUs) and pre-shipment and post shipment credits, supported by Exim Bank of India in the form of suppliers and buyers' credit. Blanket Exchange Permit, International Price Reimbursement Scheme (IPRS) were other benefits under which iron and steel and certain other items were supplied at international prices to the engineering industries. Exemption of export profits from income tax and various infrastructural facilities and fiscal concessions have been extended for establishment of 100% EOUs, EPZs and Technology Parks.

After the expiry of first three year policy in March 1988, the second announcement of new three year policy was made at the end of March 1988[59]. The 1988 policy emphasized the need for export promotion rather than continuous emphasis on import substitution. This policy allowed greater flexibility in regard to replenishment (REP) licenses. Another novel feature of this Exim Policy was the permission to registered exporters for availing the duty exemption facility under which they could import some specific goods for export promotion at international prices without paying any duty. 99 items were added to the list of OGL and export houses and trading houses were given more facilities and incentives. These items which were kept under OGL included and related ,amongst other things , to electronics, silk and tea industries. Five (5) items of machinery were removed from the restricted list. Import of computers of some configurations was permitted under OGL. The total number of items of raw materials, component and consumables allowed for import under OGL was 944 as of March 1988. At the same time 26 items were decanalized[60].

Under this Policy, the scope of export products qualifying for import replenishment was widened. The policy mentioned that all export products except a few listed ones needed to be provided with facility of import liberalization. Whatever may be the perception, this policy tuned to be more liberalized than the earlier one in areas of capital goods and intermediaries. Import of consumer goods was strictly controlled even during this policy regime. Besides, canalized imports were accounted for about 60 per cent of total imports.

The EXIM Policy 1989-91 was terminated one year earlier and was replaced by New Exim Policy 1991-93 effective from 1 April 1990[61]. The main features of this Exim Policy were continuously greater emphasis on export promotion of more value added items, easy accessibility of raw materials and intermediates for export promotion coupled with the continued emphasis on import substitutes. This is for the first time that export of services was also given paramount importance considering the vast potentiality of the international market. This policy also extended support to recognized R&D institutions for building up their scientific and technological capacities to enable Indian products to face international competition. Another main feature of this policy was the simplified import replenishment licenses (REP) scheme with greater flexibility of imports for some specific purposes. Considering export promotion as the focal point, the new trade policy granted Export Trading House status to the exporters on the basis of Net Foreign Exchange Earnings (NFE). This policy introduced the scheme of Star Trading Houses (STH) for exporters and gave them benefits of importing necessary inputs at concessional rates.

INDIA'S STRIDENT MARCH TOWARDS LIBERALIZATION IN THE 1990s

The liberalization process which was initiated in the 1980s received a major boost in July 1991[62], when Government of India declared the New Economic Policy for rejuvenating economic health[63]. Reforms were introduced in industrial policy, policies relating to foreign collaborations and investment, reforms in financial sectors, and also reforms in the field of trade policy. Though liberalization process is generally perceived to have started in 1980, it was lacklustre and casual in promoting exports in a desired way. Prior to 1991, no serious attempt was made to reforming the economy in order to globalize our exports through enhancing competitive strength of our industry .

So far, India had insulated itself from foreign competition on the ground of an infant industry. But due to identity argument, surge in foreign exchange reserves since early 1990s as well as narrowing down of the trade deficit over the years, the argument of "equal treatment of unequals is unfair" (Laird & Sapir, 1987)[64] is no more a valid proposition. The urge to liberalize its economy, was strongly felt in 1991, when the new government assumed office (Desai, 1989)[65].

The main steps for liberalizing trade during the 1990s are as follows: (i) removal of quantitative restrictions on imports and replacement by higher tariffs; also then gradually phasing it out. (2) reduction of average level of nominal tariffs as well as peak tariffs (3) move towards more uniform tariff structure through harmonization of broad areas[66]. All the above measures are expected to reduce the variation of effective rate of protection which leads to more efficient and optimal resource allocation in more socially desirable ways.

India's external sector was first brought under substantial liberalization in July 1991[67]. The main features of the new policies are (i) downward adjustment of the exchange rate, (ii) automatic clearance of import of capital goods in cases where foreign exchange is earned through export earnings (iii) removal of all restrictions on import of capital goods upto Rs. 200 million. (iv) liberalization in imports of technology, (v) strengthening of Advance License Scheme to provide exporters access to duty free imports, (vi) reduction of export subsidy, and (vii) introduction of Exim scrip scheme replacing the earlier system of REP Licenses.

Prior to 1991, India's trade regime was characterized by an extremely complex import licensing system based on 26 lists of commodities that classified all importables; different approval procedures for each list; and 10 different types of licenses applied to over 4,000 of the approximately 5000 codes of the harmonized system of classification used in the Indian Tariff Schedule. There had been export controls over 440 items (agricultural commodities accounting for about half of the restricted items, minerals and metals for another fourth and chemicals for about 10 per cent); and the exchange rate was a crawling peg fixed periodically by the RBI.

But the entire scenario has changed abruptly in recent years. The proportion of imports subject to licensing had declined from 52.6 per cent in 1989-90 to 33.8 per cent in 1992-93 and 30.2 per cent in 1993-94[68]. At the same time, there had been substantial decline in the number of import licenses issued. The number of import licenses came down markedly from 1,16,094 during 1989-90 to 41,000 during 1993-94. As much as 90 per cent of these import licenses were specifically linked with export obligations. Liberalization in licensing raj was coupled with the liberalization in tariff structure. In order to rationalize the nominal tariffs, the successive budgets have reduced maximum tariffs from 400 per cent in 1990-91 to 150 per cent in July 1991, 110 per cent in February 1992, 85 per cent in February 1993, 65 per cent in February 1994 to 50 per cent in 1995 and 40 per cent in 1997-98 budget[69]. Bulk of the import will be subject to 25 per cent rate as per the 1995-96 budget. Duties on capital goods have been reduced to levels ranging between 25 to 35 per cent and it is even much lower in case of certain export obligations. As a result, collection rate reduced from 49 per cent in 1990 to 27 per cent in 1994[70].

Reforms in *external sector* mainly work in following areas[71]:

(i) Trade Reforms

(ii) Tariff Reforms

(iii) Reforms in licensing policies
(i.e. liberalization in non-tariff barriers)

Trade policy reforms are of two types :

1. Export Policy Reforms
2. Import Policy Reforms

Both these reforms are applicable to *(i)* capital goods *(ii)* intermediate goods and *(iii)* consumer goods.

Trade Policy Reforms initiated by Government of India in July 1991, encompass all the areas mentioned above. Major structural reforms were announced 4th July, 1991 and 13th August, 1991. The main features of this reform are as follows :

1. Exim Scrip System : The replenishment licenses were replaced by a new instrument called Exim Scrips which were freely tradable. The basic rate at which Exim Scrip was issued against exports was generally 30 per cent of FOB value. Certain products like gems and jewellery, handicraft, newspaper, journals and periodicals and cinematographic films, feature films etc. were eligible for higher Exim Scrip entitlement.

2. Decanalization : In the case of exports, 16 items had been decanalized. In the case of imports, 6 items were decanalised and placed on OGL while 14 items were decanalised and listed in Appendix 3 where they were available for imports under Exim Scrips. The Government subsequently reduced further the extent of canalization.

3. Reduction of Import Licensing : Supplementary licenses for import of items in Appendix 3, 4 and 9 of the Exim Policy 1991-93 and additional incentives were abolished.

4. Abolition of CCS : With the adjustment in the exchange rate of the rupee and major reforms of trade policy, the scheme of CCS was rendered reluctant. The Government, therefore, abolished the scheme and reduced the pressure of fiscal deficit of the Central Government in the budget for 1991-92.

One of the most significant aspects of the 1990-93 Policy was the provision for flexibility in regard to replenishment (REP) licenses which were freely transferable to exporters. The exporters could also avail of duty exemption for necessary imports under these categories of licenses viz. *(i)* Advance licenses *(ii)* Intermediate licenses and *(iii)* Special Import Licenses and *(iv)* Blanket Advance Licenses. Also there has been a reduction of customs duty on project imports. The import of capital goods was further permitted under the EPCG Scheme upto a maximum of Rs 100 million. at a concessional duty rate of 25 per cent against export commitments of 3 times the CIF value of equipments imported in the first four years of operations. Further 82 capital goods were added to the existing list of capital goods under OGL. The foreign exchange limit for import of raw materials and components was also raised for the purpose of exemption from licensing. Despite this shift, the share of imports which were completely free from any kind of quantity restrictions remained relatively low.

EXPORT POLICY

The main thrust of the 1992-97 Exim Policy has been the priority given for export promotion[72]. All items are declared to be exportables except 3 banned items, 68 restricted items and 8 canalized items. Special import facilities have been granted for hotels, tourism industry and for sports bodies. Export Promotion Capital Goods (EPCG) scheme has been liberalized and is extended to components of capital goods with concessional customs duty of 15 per cent and export obligations of 4 times the CIF value to be fulfilled in 5 years, or with customs duty of 25 per cent and export obligation of 3 times the CIF value to be fulfilled in 4 years time[73].

With a view to encouraging export activities, Government of India has provided special incentives for units set up primarily for manufacturing goods for exports. These units can be set up in Export Processing Zones (EPZs) or can be 100 per cent EOUs. That can be set up anywhere in the country. These EPZs are designated to provide an internationally competitive duty free environment at low cost for export production. Each of the zones provides basic infrastructure like land, standard design factory buildings, roads, power, water-supply, drainage and custom clearance facilities. The scheme for EOUs is complementary to the EPZ schemes. It adopts the same production regime but offers wider locational options with reference to sourcing of raw materials, ports of export, availability of technological skills, existence of an industrial base and the need for a larger area of land for the project[74].

Some Incentives Given to EPZs and EOUs

- 100 per cent foreign equity is welcome in EOUs and EPZs.
- 25 per cent of the production in value terms may be sold in the Domestic Tariff Area (DTA) at concessional duty rates subject to fulfillment of minimum value addition norms.

— A higher DTA access of 35 per cent and 50 per cent is allowed for electronics and agro-industries respectively, again no DTA sales is permissible for rice, jewellery, diamonds, precious and semi-precious stones and gems, motor cars, liquor, silver bullion and some other items.
— The specified value addition norms that need to be achieved by EOUs and EPZs units are expressed in terms of the difference between the FOB value realised and the cost of all inputs, including the value of payments made in foreign exchange for royalty, fees, etc..
— Single window clearance
— No import licence is required
— Import of oil, industrial inputs exempted from custom duty.
— Supplies from the DTA to EOU and EPZ units are regarded as deemed exports and are hence exempt from payment of excise duty, which means high quality inputs are available at lower costs.
— On fulfillment of certain conditions, EPZs and EOUs are exempted from payment of corporate income tax for a block of 5 years in the first 8 years of operation. Export earnings continue to be exempt from tax even after the tax holiday is over.
— Industrial plots and standard design factories are available to EOUs and EPZs units at concessional rate.
— Private bonded warehouses in 7 EPZs can be set up
  (i) import and sale of goods included in the DTA subject to payment of applicable duties at the time of sale.
  (ii) Trading including re-export after repacking/labelling.
  (iii) Re-export after repair, reconditioning or re-engineering.
— EOUs and EPZs are permitted to sub-contract part of this production on a case by case basis.
— Supplies to the DTA under international competitive bidding against payment in foreign exchange to other EOUs and EPZs units and against import licenses are considered towards fulfillment of the export obligation.
— The FOB value of exports of EOUs and EPZs units can be clubbed with that of parent companies located in the DTA for the purpose of obtaining a Trading or Export House status.
— EOUs and EPZ units may export goods through trading and Export Houses or other EOUs and EPZ units[75].

In order to avail of some special benefits, manufactured goods exporters including those with foreign equities can apply for the status of *(i)* Export House, *(ii)* Trading House *(iii)* Star Trading House and *(iv)* Super Star Trading House/Trading House. Special weightages are given to certain categories of exports in calculating the NFE earned and in assessing the export performance of a company in deciding its classification. The criteria for recognition of Export and Trading Houses are as follows :

Criteria for Recognition of Export and Trading Houses

Category	*Avg. FOB value of eligible exports during the the preceding 3 licensing years*	*FOB Value of eligible exports during the preceding the licensing years*	*Avg. NFE earned from eligible exports during the preceding 3 licensing years*	*NFE earned from earned eligible exports during the preceding 3 licensing years*
Export Houses	100 mn.	150 mn.	60 mn.	120 mn.
Trading Houses	500 mn.	750 mn.	300 mn.	600 mn.
Star Trading Houses	2.5 bn.	3 bn.	1.25 bn.	1.5 bn.
Super Star Trading Houses	7.5 bn.	10 bn.	4 bn.	6.0 bn.

Apart from incentives already mentioned, exporters are given other incentives also. Export profits are exempted from income tax in the proportion of export turnover in total turnover. The Export Promotion Capital Goods (EPCG) scheme allows import of capital goods at concessional rates of duty subject to an export obligation. The EPCG scheme also extended to service sector by allowing import of capital equipment at a concessional duty rate by professionals such as architects, consultants and doctors. The scheme also applicable to hotels and restaurants, travel agents and diagnostic centres. Special import licenses for items in the Negative List are available to : (i) deemed exports, (ii) super star, star trading and export houses, (iii) manufacturers with ISO 9000 or BIS 14000 certificate. Higher royalty payments of 8 per cent (net of taxes) are permitted to export sales as compared to 5 per cent on domestic sales. Export commission upto 10 per cent is also permissible.

Special imprest licenses are given to duty free imports of raw material etc. required for the manufacture and supply of product to UN, multilateral or bilateral agencies, EOUs and EPZ units, specified Indian public sector organisations, concessional export credit at the concessional rate. Moreover, EOUs, EPZs and other exporters capable of generating net foreign exchange (NFE) can also raise foreign currency loan for capital goods, raw materials, components, technology payments or even for financing the local rupee cost of the project. In order to make the quality of Indian products acceptable to international communities, Government of India has launched several programmes to increase awareness of ISO 9000 or BIS 14000. The units which are accredited with any of these internationally recognized certificates are eligible for grant of special import licenses for import of items specified in the negative list of imports. Under the simplifying procedures, minimum value addition under the advance customs clearance permit has been reduced from 15 per cent to 10 per cent.

Value Addition Norms for EPZs and EOUs

Value Addition Achieved	*Permissible Sale in the DTA*
Less than 15 %	Nil
15 - 25%	Upto 25 p.c. of production in value terms.
More than 25 %	Upto 35 p.c. of production in value terms.

As stated earlier EPCG Scheme has been extended to service sectors also, and handicapped persons have also been allowed to import freely certain specified items. Besides, procedures have been simplified to facilitate exports including those from EPZs and 100 per cent EOUs. More benefits have also been given to deemed exporters. The requirement of supporting manufacturers to be indicated in the DEEC (Duty Exemption Entitlement Certificate) book has been dispensed with. The duty exemption scheme has been further simplified and input-output norms have now been finalized for 4200 items (as amended in April 1995) from 2200 items on 31 March 1993[76]. The duty free licence holders have also been allowed to source their goods from local manufacturers instead of importing the same with an added advantage of deemed export benefits.

Facility of advance release order has also been extended to special imprest licenses, advance intermediate licenses, transferred advance licenses and sensitive list items in terms of value. The additional 20 per cent flexibility permissible on such items or value-based licensing are now permitted to advance release orders also. Under the simplified policy, second hand capital goods can now be imported by actual users at normal duty without obtaining a licence, provided they have a minimum residual life of 5 years. The condition of maximum 7 years age as well as submission of chartered engineer certificate has been dispensed with. How exceeding value of Rs. 1 crore, certificate has been dispensed with. But in case of machinery of value exceeding Rs. 1 crore , certification of value by reputed international agency has been prescribed. Some components required for the manufacture of finished products in the electronic industry have been taken out of the negative list of imports. Moreover, relaxation has been provided for the import and export of items which are not covered by the negative list of exports or imports, the restriction of value addition etc., which was acting as an irritant has been removed. Foreign exhibition participating in international fairs, and exhibition being held in India have also permitted to sell items of restricted list upto a CIF value of Rs 5 lakh or payment of normal customs duty.

IMPORT POLICY

Trade reforms is an important ingredient of the overall economic reforms. So far our trade policies have been characterized by static export policy on the one hand, and sufficient control in the import regime on the other. The new EXIM Policy of 1992-97 as amended on 1st April, 1995 gave sufficient flexibility to imports in order to augment exports[77]. The New Exim Policy has given adequate incentives for the agricultural and allied sectors as well as the service sector. The new Policy has expanded the scope of Special Import License (SIL) which paves the way for consumer goods imports.

India's import regime has been characterized by stringent quantitative restrictions apart from putting under highest customs tariff brackets. The annual amendments of EXIM policy has progressively pruned the items covered under negative list of imports. Almost entire set of imports of consumer goods is put under negative list which is segmented into three categories. The new policy has substantially liberalized the quantitative restrictions regime as enforced on imports of consumer goods capital goods, raw materials, intermediates, components, consumable etc. can be imported into India without any restrictions except for certain items in the negative list of imports (Bhagwati & Sriniwasan, 1993)[78].

The Negative list of imports contained in Chapter XV is splitted into three categories viz.

- *(i)* Prohibited items which include 3 items, import of which are not allowed.
- *(ii)* Restricted items which include 65 items (according to 1992-97 Exim Policy as amended in April 1995) import of which is allowed

against an import licence or under general scheme notified separately.

(iii) Canalised items which include 7 items as contained in the canalised list, import of which is permissible only through designated agencies viz. MMTC, STC, etc..

Out of these three categories, items under restricted list are still now fairly large though these have been reduced significantly over the years. Nonetheless, even among the restricted items, presently a large number of items are permitted through SIL under the new Exim Policy. The import of these items is possible under certain conditions or against a licence or in accordance with a Public Notice issued in this behalf. Most of the items which are importable without a licence but subject to certain conditions. The remaining restrictions are on grounds of security, health or environment or because some of the goods are reserved for the small scale sector.

Quantitative restrictions enforced on capital goods and intermediates were almost wholly removed. Barring few items, import of capital goods is no longer in the Negative List of Imports. Besides, the import of second hand capital goods by actual users is permitted freely without a licence provided the goods have a residual life of 5 years. Also import of certain capital goods on a re-export basis is allowed without a licence. The actual user stipulation on imports of industrial inputs has been removed. Special import facilities are available for hotels and the tourism industry and for sport organizations. In order to augment exports, import of inputs at Concessional terms is also allowed under the new policy.

The basic ingredient of import policy is the tariff reforms that has been a part of our Exim Policy followed so far. Most of the imports of the consumer goods were under quantitative restrictions (QRs) regime which was characterised by ban on import as well as higher import tariffs. The most distinguished feature of our Exim Policy is that the items which are in the negative list, especially the consumer goods, attract the highest level of customs tariffs apart from countervailing duties, premium, margin and sales tax etc. These customs tariff rates in India were among the highest in the world prior to reforms. The peak rate of customs duty was 400 per cent in the early 1990 which was reduced to 50 per cent during 1995-96 budget[79]. The duties on capital goods have been lowered to a range of 20-40% while the basic import duty on general capital goods is 25 per cent. A duty rate of 20 per cent is levied on equipment for power projects and there is no duty on equipment for fertilizer projects. Under zero duty import of capital goods, there will be two windows to fulfill export obligations viz. (i) FOB basis (ii) NFE basis.

The new Exim Policy has accepted the recommendations of Tax Reforms Committee headed by Dr. Raja Chelliah. As per the recommendations of this Committee, there will be a phased reduction of customs tariffs over the year. Peak tariff is recommended to be stablished at 50 per cent whereas import-weighted average tariff is to be pegged at 25 per cent by the year 1997-98 as against 30 per cent at present. The *ad valorem* import duty rates on industrial inputs would range from 5 per cent to 30 per cent. During 1994-95, the average collection rate was 27 per cent.

The number of standard input/output norms has been vastly expanded from the current level of 3100 items (1994-95) to over 4200 items (as on April 1995). The Handbook of Procedures (Vol. 2) contain norms for them : 4200 items have also been published with the amendment. Import of capital goods, either new or second hand is also permitted under the Export Promotion Capital Goods (EPCGs) Scheme at a concessional customs duty rate of 15 per cent subject to the fulfillment of specified export obligations. EPCG licence holders may fulfill their export obligation by supply of intermediate products but without benefits provided for "deemed exports"[80].

Another important feature of the New Exim Policy is the introduction of a single market-determined exchange rate for the Rupee since 1st March, 1993 with effect from 20th August, 1994. The Rupee is now convertible in the current account which includes both trade and invisible accounts. This market determined exchange rate is applicable to inflow of foreign equity for investment and outflow of the event of disinvestment, payments in respect of repatriation of dividends, fees and royalties for technical know-how agreements and also foreign travels.

Other salient features of the recently (March 1995) amended Exim Policy are as follows :

- Zero duty import of capital goods in cases where the CIF value exceeds Rs 20 crore.
- Allowing the import of mandatory spares upto 5 per cent of the CIF value of the advance licence.
- The system of Advance Customs Clearance Permit (ACCP) has been abolished. Hereafter goods, including second hand capital

goods can be imported for the purpose of jobbing, repairing, servicing, restoring, reconditioning and renovation on execution of a bond/guarantee which will be redeemed on exports.

— Similarly, patterns of drawings, jigs, tools, fixtures, moulds, textiles, computer hardware, software and instruments may also be imported if they are directly related to the export orders. All goods so imported will be re-exported with a value addition if not less than 10 per cent.

— Import of gifts will no longer require a customs clearance permit.

— "Consumer goods" has been redefined to include consumer durables and accessories thereof but excluding components, spares and parts. Hence components, spares and parts of consumer durables are now freely importable. This will not include consumer goods in CKD/SKD condition.

— Special Import Licence (SIL) is a non-discretionary instrument which serves as an incentive to exports. SILs will be available to the following categories of exports :

(i) Export Houses/Trading Houses/Star Trading Houses/Super Star Trading Houses.

(ii) Exporters of telecommunications equipments and electronic goods and services.

(iii) Deemed exporters.

(iv) Manufacturers/processors who have acquired quality certification under ISO 9000 (SERIES) or BIS 14000 (SERIES) or under any other similar internationally recognised certification of quality.

— The list of freely importable goods popularly known as OGL has been expanded. Raw materials, intermediates and capital goods are already freely importable. Besides, 75 items listed in Chapter XV, Part-II are now freely importable. The list has been expanded from 43 to 75 items.

— The list of items importable under the SIL route has also been expanded. The erstwhile list consisted of 42 items. The new list consists of a total of 75 items. Some more items have been identified but these will be added to the list after closely monitoring the level of import, the trade balance and the premium on the SIL.

TARIFF REFORMS[81]

Tariff reform is the most crucial part of trade policy reforms. India has been one of the protectionist countries in the world because a host of consumer items are put under Negative List of the Exim Policy over the years, though the list has been liberalized substantially in recent years. India's trade policy regime has hitherto been characterised by high tariff barrier as well as higher non-tariff barriers (Pursell & Sharma, 1996)[82]. Under New Economic Policy which was initiated in July 1991, Government has been actively contemplating to get rid of this syndrome through liberalization of tariff and non-tariff barriers. With a view to impressing upon the world trading communities about its recent trade reforms, it has pruned the negative list of imports by putting only 3 items under prohibited list, 65 items as negative and 7 items in the canalized list. Even among the restricted items many are importable without a licence but subject to certain conditions or against a licence or in accordance with a Public Notice issued in this behalf. Almost all restrictions are on grounds of security, health or environment or because some of the goods are reserved for small scale sector.

Three issues are important in Tariff Reforms Policy of the Government of India :

(i) The first issue is regarding the question of Advance Licensing Scheme. This is the more important area of trade reform because while about 30 per cent of imports are subject to licensing. As much as 60 per cent of total licensing is accounted for by export-related licensing of which Advance Licensing constitutes the biggest segment. The facility of Advance Licensing is important because of the high tariff structure. Another important area of the scheme is the VABAL (Value Based Advance Licence) which has introduced much higher degree of flexibility. This Policy does not become successful due to malpractices by unscrupulous elements in the form of over-invoicing of export and underinvoicing of imports.

(ii) The second most important issue of the New Exim Policy (March 1995) is that how EPCG scheme can be made much more effective. Under EPCG scheme imports of capital goods are allowed at a concessional rate of 15 per cent. One of the basic objective of the tariff policy should be to keep the project cost at the lowest level order to enhance international competitiveness of the Indian products. When EPCG scheme was introduced the average tariff level for machinery was above 150 per cent as against the current peak rate of 50 per cent. The current average rate for import of capital goods is around 35 per cent. Therefore, the differential has come down drastically. But more importantly, with an exchange rate which has been artificially kept low and is therefore discriminatory to imports, it is logical to modify the EPCG scheme to allow import at zero duty. The loss in revenue which is estimated to be around Rs 4000 crore will be more than offset in terms of second order benefits.

(iii) The third issue of tariff reduction is related to FDI flow in India. There has been a growing demand from foreign project investors to reduce tariff on their capital good imports on the ground that high tariffs will make their project unviable. This argument is true in case of items which have higher export potential. Since it would be in the interest of India to attract as much FDI as possible, tariff reduction on capital goods appears to be a requirement which will be mutually beneficial to Indian and for foreign investors.

Tariff reforms in India do basically include three areas viz.[83] (i) elimination of end-user exemption, with the main exception of imports used in export production, (ii) rationalisation of customs tariffs, and (iii) import policy for consumer goods. The basic objective of the New Exim Policy is to put all consumer goods on a "tariff-cum-OGL import regime" by 1996-97. Measures have already been adopted in the last two EXIM Policy amendments (i.e. April 1993 & 1995) when Government granted large exporters freely marketable licenses for imports of consumer goods. Under current Exim Policy, imports of consumer goods is feasible through SIL route. However, inspite of such liberalization, import regime for consumer goods is still under control because as many as 1350 items are still under import licenses out of 4000 HS positions. In 1994-95 Exim Policy, components, spares and parts of consumer durables are now freely importable. But this will not include consumer goods in CKD/SKD condition.

Tariff reform is the most important ingredient of the trade policy reform. Government is committed to rationalize tariff structure over next 2-3 years. Government aims at stablising peak tariff at 50 per cent level and to reduce the import weighted average tariffs at the level of 25 per cent by 1996-97. Regarding rationalization of tariffs, Government of India broadly accepts the recommendations of the Tax Reform Committee headed by Dr. Raja Chelliah. Tax Reform Committee suggests a maximum tariff rate of 40-50 per cent for consumer goods, except for a few luxury items, 30 per cent of intermediates, 20 per cent for capital goods and 5-10 per cent minimum tariffs.

As a result of tariffs reforms, started in 1993-94 budget, our level is now at levels comparable to those of major Latin American and East Asian countries before they began to liberalize their trading regime in the mid and late 1980s.

India's peak tariff in now 30 per cent with 5 per cent special additional duty (SAD). SAD has been removed on 8 January 2004 by

Finance Minister Mr. Jaswant Singh. Peak tariff is to be reduced at the ASEAN level of 20 per cent by 2004 and to the East Asian level of 12 per cent the 2007. India has removed all quantitative restrictions (QRs) on imports is on 1 April 2001. It has also liberalized customs tariffs on all imported goods from time to time. Though peak tariff is significantly low at 30 per cent as compared to 400 per cent in 1990-91, this rate is amongst the highest in the world. It has to reduce sustantially in the years ahead in order to match with other trading partners.

EC'S INSTITUTIONAL SUPPORT TO HELP INDIA TO IMPROVE QUALITY OF ITS MANUFACTURED GOODS EXPORTS

The EU is India's largest trading partner, accounting for 30 per cent of imports and exports. But, on the other hand, India's share in the EU's trade is barely 1 per cent. Though India has been under chronic balance of payments deficit with the EC, in 1993 trade between the two sides improved dramatically when its exports increased by 20 per cent amounting to 5.9 billion. ECU and imports by 19 per cent amounting to 6.2 billion. ECU. This was particularly important in a situation when extra-EU imports had declined by more than 1 per cent and export growth by 10 per cent. The EU's development aid since its inception in 1976 had crossed 1.6 billion. ECU (Rs 6324.8 crore) From 1976 to 1991, total EU's ODA to India was $ 8386.1 million. ($7168.8 million by EU member states and $1217.3 million. by the Commission). Japan's ODA to India was $2396.1 and USA's ODA was $1084 million. during the same period[84].

First Treaty strengthening Indo-EC economic cooperation was signed in 1973. The Commercial Cooperation Agreement (CCA), 1973, was the consequence of first organized efforts between two countries to work together in promoting economic development of a developing country like India. The CCA was replaced by the Commercial and Economic Cooperation Agreement (CECA) in 1982, when the area and scope of cooperation were broadened. Finally on 20 December 1993, India's former Commerce Minister, Mr. Pranab Mukherjee (on behalf of India) and Mr. Willy Clas, the Belgian Foreign Minister (on behalf of European Union), concluded a new five-year Cooperation Agreement on Partnership and Development (CAP&D) in Brussels[85]. The CAP&D agreement extends the cooperation not only in the traditional areas like trade, industries, energy, telecommunications, customs and banking, but also it turns into new areas of development, i.e. scientific research, intellectual property rights (IPRs), environments, primary health and education, tourism and other social issues[86].

The major areas of cooperation as enshrined in the new agreement (CAP&D) are institutional structures. The basic objective of cooperation in this area is to provide active support enabling India to improve quality of its manufacturing exports through making suitable changes in the institutional set up. Institutional changes required for the improvement of economic environment for trade and investment are described here. On the other hand, these institutional changes are *sine qua non* for improving quality of India's manufactured exports of the Community. The new areas focus on a number of areas as detailed below :

Standard and Quality

Improvement of standards and quality is the most crucial area of joint cooperation. The main focus of the new agreement is on modernization of Indian testing laboratories, the setting up of a National Accreditation Scheme to International norms, and the introduction of education in quality in engineering colleges. Changes in standards and quality include the following aspects:

Modernization of Technology

Rather than conventional forum of aid the EC has now focussed its attention to imparting better education and training.

In the new agreement, emphasis has been placed on the modernization of laboratories in three key areas viz. automotive sector, domestic electrical appliances and processed food. The assistance is provided in the form of transfer of technical knowhow, to provide training with a view to giving them a knowledge of testing procedures and enabling them to operate and maintain installations according to internationally accepted norms.

Harmonization of Standards

Harmonization of standards is an essential part of the institutional changes. Under this scheme so far 142 Indian standards have been harmonized with the EU Standard and EU directions/ regulations.

Quality Testing

In recent years, the EU has directed its trading partners to accept ISO 9000 as the basic standard for exporting into EC markets. The Final Act of the Uruguay Round, also maintained ISO 9000 as the universal standard. So far 60 Indian offices belonging to various governments and private agencies have been given intensive training to become qualified assessors by Batalas, UK. A further batch of 5 Indian officers was trained as lead assessors[87].

Confederation of Indian Industry (CII) has been accredited by the Government of India as the nodal agency for quality training under the Indo-EU programme. Apart from CII, other apex chambers of commerce like FICCI and ASSOCHAM have also introduced quality management programme to teach industry functioning on how to improve quality of Indian products are being their at par with the international standards. There are two separate sets of training, one for certified quality engineers and the other for instructors, which conducted by German organization.

National Accreditation Scheme

Government of India has made a request to the EU to assist her in preparing a National Accreditation Scheme (NAS). Under this scheme, a 5-member European Expert Group recommended a comprehensive NAS. The elements of this scheme are :

- — The National Quality Council (NQC) would be the apex body for operating the scheme in India. It should be an autonomous body which will control five (5) separate boards.
- — A National Accreditation Board (NAB) for the certification of product and quality management system.
- — A National Accreditation Board for the certification of laboratories.
- — A board for the registration of quality related personnel.
- — A national enquiry service of standards and assessment.

Education in Quality

Education in quality is the top most item on the agenda for cooperation in the new Indo-EC treaty on Partnership and Development. Indian products in the international markets are sold at heavy discounts simply because of their low quality. Quality concept is perceived to be unknown to Indian industry. We also do not have infrastructure to provide that. Sensing wide gap in this area, the EU has taken initiative to provide education in quality in engineering and management colleges in India. the EU has advised India to introduce TQM (Total Quality Management) in undergraduate and post graduate course on a pilot basis. For this purpose, IIT, Delhi will be the nodal agency for implementation of the programme[88].

Intellectual Property Rights (IPRs)

Intellectual Property rights is the main area of technological development. All developed countries give effective protection to IPR, which, on the other hand, play a very dominant role in technology development. Unfortunately, this is reportedly absent in India. We do not have much awareness about the protection of IPRs that may be cited as major hurdle in the integration of research output with the production system. Among seven areas of IPRs, India is having excellent legislation except Patents. In beyond to Patents, we follow Indian Patent Act 1972, which provides product patents in all areas of production except, agro-chemicals, drugs and pharmaceuticals, chemicals, where we have process patent system (Rao, 1989)[89]. These are the areas where most rigorous efforts and R&D activities are needed. Due to lack of effective protection of intellectual property rights in these lines of production, no new technology is expected to come in. Old Indian Patent Act is deterrent for any kind of technology development in these areas. Foreign companies having new technology are reluctant to transfer it to India in the apprehension of getting it pirated. On 15 December 1993, India signed Final Act of the Uruguay Round which was ratified by all contracting parties on 15 April 1994 at Marrakesh. As a signatory of the Final Act, India has also signed the agreement on TRIPs (Dhar, 1995)[90].

Considering that much has to be done in this area, the EU and Government of India have agreed to launch an IPR technical cooperation programme. The programme should help in improving trade, investment and the R&D environment in India and promote economic exchanges between two entities. The EU has identified following areas for modernizing and strengthening IPRs[91]:

- Enhancement of user awareness and enforcement of IPRs through training and information.
- Improvement of the structure and operations of the IPR administration and upgradation of the professional skills of its staff.
- Imparting technical assistance, if required, in the preparations of

a modern IPR legislation in India including the necessary implementing regulations.

EC's programme of economic cooperation with India will take into account opportunities and challenges of the Single European Market as the EU moves towards greater economic and political integration. India also moves towards shaping up an open and more liberalized outward oriented economy. In the light of the liberalized regimes in both the entities, it is expected that cooperative attitude between them will sustain due to spirit of partnership and mutual interest beyond the traditional relationship of donor and recipient countries. Indo-EU economic relationship is based on complementarities and will work in three broad areas :

a. Help improveing the economic business environment in India by providing institutional support and facilitating access to Community know-how and technology, taking into account mutual protection of industrial property rights according to the GATT Agreement including the TRIPs.
b. Both the parties will endeavour to facilitate contacts between economic operators and other measures designed to promote commercial and technology exchanges and investments.
c. In order to get better market access both in India as well as in Europe, both sides will help to improve awareness of their market situation.

In the "Strategy for Economic Cooperation and Development", both India and EC have identified some projects and programmes for implementation. The priority areas are[92]:

a. Identifying sectors of industry where the availability of EC know-how and technology may promote industrial cooperation.
b. Encouraging reforms, modernization and diversification of India's production base in developing linkages with the EC business community.
c. Establishing a favourable climate for private investment, including appropriate conditions for the transfer of capital and exchange of information on mutually beneficial opportunities.
d. Encouraging cooperation between EC and Indian financial institutions.
e. Strengthening the role of industrial organisations, like ASSOCHAM, FICCI and CII to promote investment on a reciprocal and complementary basis.

Apart from strategies in general to be followed in improving Indo-

EC economic cooperation, some specific issues are equally important as how to enhance competitiveness of Indian products to the EC market. Indo-EC cooperation document suggests following issues :

i. Providing technical assistance to workshops in India, disseminating information that will benefit Indian industry to identify the challenges and opportunities of the Single European Market (SEM) for trade and economic cooperation.
ii. Providing expertise for access to information on readily available EC technology for the development of key Indian industry sectors.
iii. Providing expertise in norms, standards, quality and certification on a sectoral basis that will enable Indian industry to interact more effectively with the EC business community.
iv. Providing technical assistance to support liberalization and modernisation of selected area of service (e.g. maritime transport & IPRs).
v. Supporting the activities of EC-India institutions interacting with India and EC associations of industry and commerce.
vi. Facilitating provision of trade, industry and investment information, such as customs duties, product regulations, norms and standards, company and tax legislation, financial regulations.
vii. Exchanging information on monetary matters and the macro-economic environment as mutually agreed.

Standards is the most important issue in the bilateral trade. As stated earlier, EC will provide in future market access to those products which qualify under the system of ISO 9000. This is the only acceptable standard to trade with EC. Until recently, India did not have much awareness about standardization of the products. It does not follow any specific international standards. But in future since every developed country is going to enforce rigorous standards, harmonization of standards is also agreed upon in the Final Act of the Uruguay Round. Regarding standards, specific issues for the Joint Commission are :

i. Providing expertise for institutional development to upgrade standards and quality certification organization in India, promoting linkages between institutions and the setting up of a national accreditation scheme for conformity assessment.
ii. Developing training and technical assistance in connection with meteorology standards and certificate and also in connection with quality awareness/promotion programme in selected sectors.
iii. Promoting measures aimed at achieving mutual recognition of systems of quality certification.

TABLE 6.4 : Flow of Foreign Direct Investment From EU to India (Approval)

(Value in Million Rupees)

Countries	*1991*	*1992*	*1993*	*1994*	*1995*	*1996*	*1997*	*1998*	*1999*	*2000*	*2001*	*2002*
Belgium	1	237	60	76	1659	1947	2163	32888	140	791	1621	2861
Denmark	111	252	319	533	12247	729	1067	295	762	263	259	549
France	193	296	1290	897	4203	16717	7134	5136	14486	2021	6798	6229
Germany	418	862	1759	5693	13395	15379	21558	8538	11429	5938	4139	2531
Greece	0	0	0	0	6	0	0	0	14	0	0	0
Ireland	0	0	1656	64	312	64	228	43	64	167	86	7
Italy	178	893	1113	3909	4603	1389	11950	2784	17595	1073	1715	705
Luxembourg	0	0	29	0	531	93	1737	6	65	51	7	2
Netherlands	557	967	3216	2069	9664	10487	8706	4963	6322	45	36936	5524
Portugal	1	12	140	0	1735	0	42	0	7	15	0	3
Spain	3	19	98	20	227	91	593	606	1810	54	2	263
UK	321	1176	627	12992	17259	15254	44907	32008	29630	4104	50031	18091
Sweden					5023	5330	1090	2154	2739	1012	2364	213
Finland					132	540	1187	495	3	0	174	110
Austria					296	828	259	555	327	56	77	177
EU(15)	1785	4718	10310	26255	73290	68849	102621	90471	85394	15591	104209	37265
USA	1858	12315	34619	34881	70544	100559	135698	35620	35752	41950	49215	20511
Japan	527	6102	2574	4009	15143	14883	19064	12828	15947	8275	7353	7408
Total	**4171**	**23136**	**47503**	**65145**	**158976**	**184291**	**257383**	**138919**	**137093**	**65816**	**160777**	**65184**

EUROPEAN INDUSTRIES' HESITANT RESPONSE TO INDIA'S NEW OPENING UP TO THE WEST

India had been following a closed-door economic policy until recently. Almost all crucial sectors of the economy were reserved for the public sector and only a small area was opened to the private sector with substantial controls. The area of production was basically meant for wage-goods and production of consumer durables.

Though the presence of foreign companies in India was felt since early 1980s, their contribution in the consumer sector was marginal to the total industrial activities. Western companies never thought India as an ideal location for investment because of its labyrinthine rules and regulations discouraging foreign investment. Though liberalization started since mid-eighties, by and large in the eighties, India was characterized basically as a restrictive regime. As a result no significant investments flowed in from European industries to India during the preceding decade.

The whole scenario had changed in July 1991 when Government of India promulgated the New Industrial Policy that revolutionized the investment pattern in Indian industry. The New Industrial Policy, a part of the Government's New Economic Policy has brought a sea change in holding pattern and foreign equity participation in India. Under the NEP, Government has divested its control over many loss-making Public Sector Undertakings (PSUs) industry and paved the way for foreign participation in almost all crucial branches of production and exports barring some areas of strategic importance.

If we assess the pattern of FDI (approved) in India since 1981, we can easily visualize the impact of opening up our economy to the foreign companies. **Table 6.4** shows the flow of FDI into India from European Community, Japan and USA as well as the total flow. The compound rate of growth of FDI flow to India by EC was 23.98 per cent during the 1980s which shot up to 144.88 per cent p.a. during the reform period (i.e. 1991-94). In case of USA, compound growth rate was 35.46 per cent during eighties which registered a phenomenal growth of 165.15 per cent per annum during reform period. The trend is the same for Japan. Flow of FDI from Japan to India grew at 25.55 per cent rate (compound) per annum during the 1980s, but it increased to 96.65 per cent during the nineties. The table shows that FDI only gathered momentum in the nineties, after a long spell of stagnation. The lackluster performance of FDI flow in

India during the eighties has been substituted by the impressive growth during nineties.

The picture as depicted in **Table 6.4** is the approval of FDI. But in actual term, flow of FDI into India from European countries is much less compared to other countries. There is no gainsaying the fact that Europeans are the main agents behind our technology development. With the help of several cooperation agreements between India and the European Community, India's industry is now getting better access to EC's improved technology which makes her more competitive in the global market. **Table 6.4** shows the FDI flow to India from the members of the European Union from 1991 to 2002. Among 15 countries of the European Union, major flow of FDI emanating from four countries only. Significant contributors of FDI from EU states to the India are: France Germany, Netherlands and United Kingdom. Even among these four countries, UK is the highest investor in India followed by France, Netherlands and Germany. Due to historical reason UK is the largest investor in India among all the EU members, but its share has declined from Rs 50031 million to Rs 18091 million only. The trend is same for France & Germany. But FDI from Belgium has shown a phenomenal increase from Rs 1.61 million in 1991 to Rs 32885 million in 1998 again dropped down to Rs 2861 million in 2002. FDI flow from Italy, Sweden, Ireland has declined sustaintially over the years.

Despite the fact that the growth of FDI from EC has been quite impressive during the nineties, it is considered as minuscule compared to EC's total FDI flow to the rest of the world. Flow of FDI from EC to India constitutes less than 1 per cent to its total flow. Growth of FDI flow from EC to India has been much higher since early nineties because of the low base during the eighties. **European industry does not respond favourably to India's opening up of the economy**. The reasons behind such low share of the EU's FDI to Asia is general and India in particular are :

- After the collapse of erstwhile USSR and the formation of CIS, the responsibility of European industries to modernize their industrial structures has become more urgent than their activities in the Asian region.
- Unification of Germany was completed in 1990. Among the Community members, Germany was the largest contributor of FDI to India. But after its unification, it has taken the responsibility to reconstruct its ailing economy of its eastern part. Due to its

own obligation, Germany has undertaken massive investment work in the eastern part and obviously less resource is available for India.

- Not only to erstwhile East Germany, but EC has undertaken a massive investment activities in Central Eastern Europe. After the collapse of the socialist system and disintegration of USSR, EC has emerged as a main source of investment in these countries.
- India is still not considered as an ideal place for investment. In a recent study it is revealed that India is most dangerous place for investment next to Bolivia in the world. Another study reveals that India is the second riskiest country for investment in Asia next to Vietnam. Still there exists lot of non-transparencies in India's policy regime for attracting foreign investment. Though bureaucratic wrangles have reduced these days, but it has not removed completely and massive corruption in the administration is one of the major deterrent factors for inviting FDI.
- Presently there does not exist any licensing system and norms on foreign equity have liberalized significantly since early nineties, yet political instability, frequent changes in policies, lack of proper infrastructure i.e. power, communication, etc. are some of the factors prohibiting European industries to respond favourably to India opening up to the West.
- Till today India is considered to be as a restricted economy on its external front. Its import regime is subject to plethora of restrictions.
- Though peak tariffs in India have been reduced from 400 per cent in 1990 to 50 per cent in 1995, and the import-weighted average tariffs have been at the range of 30-35 per cent, but as yet India is one of the most protective countries in the world in respect of tariffs. India's average tariffs are still highest in the world. It is not easy for MNCs to import anything from the parent countries.
- Despite the fact that import regime in India has been substantially liberalized in recent times but still single window clearance system is a dream to the foreign investors in India. Even nearest neighbours like Singapore, Hong Kong take few days to clear a licence, but in India a couple of months and or even a year may be required to come to any conclusion.
- The largest bottleneck to transfer of new technologies from Europe to India is the lack of effective protection of intellectual property rights in India. Indian markets and production systems are characterized with large-scale piracy of foreign products and technologies by changing processes of production and Indian market is flooded with spurious and counterfeit goods. This often discourages western companies to their technologies to India.

India is still not a member of the Paris Convention on Patents. In the ensuing years, the extent of flow of FDI from Western countries will solely depend on the level of protection given to their intellectual property rights.

— In spite of all odds, India's recent drive to opening its economy is appreciated in the West, but it is considered inadequate as compared to some other World regions such as East Asia and South-East Asia. Therefore, it is expected that India's policies should be work more transparent and sustainable which do not succumb to changes in the Government.

NOTES

1. *(a)* Jaques Pelkmans, "External Aspects of EC's Single Market", Paper presented at South Biennial India-EC Colloquium, *India and the EC : Outlook for the Nineties,* (New Delhi), November 11-13, 1991, pp. 1-18.
   (b) M. Davenport and S. Page, "*Regional Trading Agreements : The Impact of the Implementation of the Single European Market on Developing Countries*", *A UNCTAD Report,* (Geneva), October 1989.
   (c) J. Kol, "The EC after 1992 and Developing Countries" *Economisch-Statistische Berichten,* 26th July, 1989.
   (d) D. McAleese, "The EC Internal Market Programme : Implications for External Trade" in N. Wegner (ed;) *Asian and the EC, The Impact of 1992,* (Singapore). 1991.
   (e) R. Langhammer, "Fuelling a New Engine of Growth or Separating Europe from Non-Europe", *Journal of Common Market Studies,* Vol-29.2, 1990.
2. Clark, Don P. and Zarnilli, Simonetta, "Non-Tariff Measures and United States Imports of CEBRA-elgible products", *Journal of Developing Studies,* 1994(31), No. 1. pp. 214-224.
3. *(a)* Irwin, Doglas A, "The New Protectionism in Industrial Countries : Beyond the Uruguay Round", *International Monetory Fund-IMF Paper on Policy an Analysis and Assessment* PPAA/94/5, (Washington), 1994.
   (b) MacGee, Robert N., "An Economic Analysis of Protectionism in the United States with Implications for International Trade in Europe", *The George Washington Journal of International Law and Economics,* 1993(26), No.3, pp. 539-573.
4. *(a)* Ministry of Commerce, Govt. of India, *Annual Report* (1995-96), (New Delhi).
   (b) Ministry of Textiles, Govt. of India, *Annual Report* (1995-96), (New Delhi).

5. (*a*) Monthly Statistics of Foreign Trade of India (Several Issues), DGCI & S, (Calcutta).
   (*b*) Foreign Trade Statistics of India, "DGCI & S, (Calcutta), (Several Issues).
6. see Table No.-5.1.
7. During eighties Indian export item were basically of primary in nature but the competition of the exports has changed during nineties when the exports manufactured goods including some hightech items. Now manufactured goods constitute 80 per cent of our total exports.
8. In gems and jewelleries India's value addition is much less. India imports raw gems and stones from Belgium and after cutting & polishing she again exports it to Belgium and U.K..
9. This is simply because of the fact that India basicaly an exporter of engineering goods to the EU market having higher labour content. This segment India is successful in penetrating into EU market where EC does not have any competitive strength.
10. Engineering Export Promotion Council, *Handbook of Statistics*, 1994-95, (Calcutta).
11. United Nations Organisation, "*Commodity Trade Statistics, Series D*" United Nations, New York, 1994.
12. Ministry of Commerce, Govt. of India, Annual Report, 1993-94, (New Delhi).
13. (*a*) Ian Goldin, Odin Knudsen and Dominique Van der Mensbruggle", *Trade liberalisation : Global Implications*", (The World Bank, Washington), 1993, pp. 78-79.
    (*b*) Ashok Gulati and A.N. Sharma, "Subsidising Agriculture : A Gross Country View", *Economic and Political Weekly*, (Bombay), September 26, 1992, P.A-108.
14. Ministry of Commerce, Govt. of India, *Annual Report*, 1993-94, (New Delhi).
15. Foreign Trade Statistics of India, (Several Issues), DGCICS, (Calcutta).
16. Ministry of Commerce, Govt. of India, *Annual Report*, 1993-94, (New Delhi).
17. Ministry of Commerce, Govt. of India, *Annual Report*, 1993-94, (New Delhi).
18. (*a*) Ministry of Commerce, Govt. of India, "*Export-Import Policy*", 1991-92, 1992-93, 1993-94 and 1995-96, (New Delhi).
    (*b*) Ministry of Industry, Govt. of India, "*New Industrial Policy*", 19th July, 1991, (New Delhi).
19. see Ministry of Commerce, Govt. of India : *Export-Import Policy* (1992-97), (New Delhi).
20. (*a*) Ministry of Commerce, Govt. of India, *Annual Report, 1990-91*,

(New Delhi).

(*b*) *Monthly Statistics of Foreign Trade of India*, DGCI & S, (Calcutta), March 1991.

21. *Review of Trade and Economic Relation with the CIS Countries*, ASSOCHAM Backgrounds, (New Delhi), 12th July, 1995, pp. 1-26.
22. This is simply because of the fact that since the mode of payment is in the hard-currencies, Russia starts buying goods and services from hard-currency countries. After the collapse of USSR, Rupee-Rouble payment system has also collapsed. Therefore, Russia no more depends on India for its surplus resource on the other hand, India imports bulk item like petroleum products from Russia at a relatively better term and conditions. Therefore imports have gone up over the years. Cf. *Foreign Trade Statistics of India*, March 1996, (DGCI & S, Calcutta).
23. "Strengthentning Economic and Trade Relation with Commenwealth of Independent States (CIS)", *ASSOCHAM Background*, (ASSOCHAM, New Delhi), 1993 p. 65.
24. Ibid no. 21 p. 17.
25. (*a*) Pranab K. Sen, "Rupee-Rouble Exchange Rate", *Economic and Political Weekly*, March 24, 1990, (Bombay), pp. 613-618.

    (*b*) N. K. Chandra, "USSR and the third World : Unequal Distribution of Gains", *Economic and Political Weekly*, Annual Number, (Bombay), 1977.

    (*c*) Suresh Kumar, (ed), "*Indo-CMEA Ecnomic Relation*" Ashis Publication and ICRIER, (New Delhi), 1987.

    (*d*) The Economic Times, "*The Overvalued Exchange Rates*", (editorial), March 3, 1970, (Bombay).

    (*e*) Arvind Vyas and Pranab Sen, "*Dimension of Indo-Soviet Trade and Economic Relation*" *mimeo*, ICRIER, (New Delhi), 1989.

    (*f*) Indo-USSR Trade Awaits Era of Consolidation, *The Economic Times*, February 15,1990, (Bombay).

    (*g*) The Dilemma of Rouble Conversion, *Times of India*, September, 1990.
26. Baltic State were Socially and culturally different from the rest of the states of the erstwhile USSR. Therefore, they decided to remain independent while 11 of them decided to form a confederation with common defence and foreign policies.
27. International Monetary Fund, "*Economic Review : Russia Federation*", (IMF, Washington), 1992, pp. 1-36.
28. Federation of Indian Chamber of Commerce as Industry, "Reports on Indo-CIS Joint Business Council" (New Delhi), 1993.
29. Economic Intelligence Unit, "*Country Profile on Russian Federation*", (EIU, London), 1995-96, pp. 1-50, Report No. 80.
30. *Review of Trade and Economic Relation with the CIS Countries*",

ASSOCHAM Backgrouner, (ASSOCHAM, New Delhi), 1995, p.5.
31. Ibid n. 29.
32. Ibid n. 25(a).
33. "A Brief of Indo-Russian Federation Commercial Relations", Backgrounds for the *first meeting of India-Russian Federation JBC Core Group*", (FICCI), (New Delhi), 4th September, 1996, pp. 1-14.
34. Ibid n. 25(a).
35. Ibid n. 30.
36. Ibid n. 28.
37. Ibid n. 29(a).
38. Ibid n. 23.
39. Ibid n. 30.
40. Ibid n. 28.
41. Bishawnath Golder, "Trade Reforms in India", in S.P. Gupta, Garry Parsel and John Nash (eds;), *Trade Policy Reforms*, ICRIER, 1994, pp.122-127.
42. *(a)* Bhagwati J.N. and Sriniwasan, T.N., "*Foreign Trade Regime and Economic Development : India*", (Columbia University Press, New York), NBER, 1975.
   (b) Planning Commission, "*Technical Note to the Second Plan*", New Delhi, 1956.
43. Martin Wolf, *Indian Exports*, The World Bank, Washington, 1980.
44. "Industrial Credit and Investment Corporation of India (ICICI)", *Export Performance of the ICICI Financed Companies*, ICICI, (Several Annual Nos.), Bombay.
45. Ministry of Commerce, Govt. of India, "The Export-Import Policy, (New Delhi), 1976-77.
46. Ministry of Commercial, Govt. of India, "Exim Policy", (New Delhi), 1977-78.
47. Ministry of Commercial, Govt. of India, "*Export-Import Policy*", (New Delhi), 1977-78.
48. See Ministry of Commercial, *Exim Policy*, (1989-90), New Delhi.
49. K.S. Mehra, "Liberalisation in Recent Trade Policy Reforms", in S.P. Gupta (ed;), *Liberalisation : Its Impact on Indian Economic*, (ICRIER, New Delhi), 1993, pp. 147-165.
50. Tandon, Prakash (1982), Chairman, "*Reports of the Committee on Exports Strategy*", 1980, Ministry of Commerce, Government of India, New Delhi.
51. Alexander P.C. Chairman, "*Report of the Committee on Trade Policy and Proceeding*", Ministry of Commerce, Government of India, 1978, New Delhi.
52. Hussain Abid, 1984, Chairman, "Report of the Committee on Import-Export", Ministry of Commerce, Govt. of India, New Delhi.
53. This was done at the recommendations of the Abid Hussain

Committee. It was he who recommended that consistent long-run policy are more helpful to exports rather than annual ones.

54. Ibid n. 49.
55. (a) In USA, duties are paid on 60 per cent of imports only, and 40 per cent are duty free. Duties are almost negligible in high-tech goods.
    (b) US Dept. of Commerce, "*Highlight of US exports and imports trade*", (Washington, D.C.), (several issues).
56. Amit Shovan Roy, "Liberalisation and India's Exports Competitiveness" in S.P. Gupta (ed;), *Liberalisation : Its Impact on Indian Economy*, (McMillan, 1993), pp. 182-187.
57. Satinder Palaha, "Policy for Export Sector Development : A Review", in B. Bhattacharya and Satinder Palaha (eds;) Policy Impediments to Trade and FDI in India, (Wheeler Publication, New Delhi), 1996, pp.23-38.
58. Ibid n. 56.
59. Ministry of Commerce, Govt. of India, "*Export-Import Policy, 1987-88*", March 1988.
60. Centre for Monitoring Indian Economy, "*The Liberalisation Process*", Economic Intelligence Unit, (Bombay), February, 1990, pp.16-18.
61. Ministry of Commerce, Govt. of India, "*Export-Import Policy, 1991-93*", (New Delhi), 1st April, 1990.
62. Ministry of Industry, Govt. of India, "*New Industrial Policy*", July 1991, (New Delhi).
63. This was the first ever attempt of the Govt. of India to introduce reforms in all spheres of economic activities initiated by the reforms in indsustrial policies.
64. Sam Laird and Andre Sapir, *Tariff Preferences*, in *The Uruguay Round: A Handbook of Multilateral Trade Negotiations*, The World Bank, Washington, 1987, P.101.
65. Ashok V. Desai, "The Uruguay Round of Negotiations and India", *Economic and Political Weekly*, Annual No. 1989.
66. Ibid n. 41.
67. Ibid n. 41 P. 123
68. B. Bhattacharya et al, "Liberalisation in the External Sector : India's Experience", in B. Bhattacharya and Satwinder Paleha (ed;). *Policy impliment to Trade and FDI in India*, (Wheeler Publication, New Delhi), 1996.
69. Swapan K. Battacharya, "Rationalisation of Tariff Structure of Indian Consumer Goods Imports", paper presented at the USAID Seminar, Organised by IIFT (New Delhi), June 1995.
70. (a) The World Bank, *India : Country Economic Memorandum, Five Years of Stablisation and Reforms : The Challenges Ahead*, (Washington, DC), 1995.
    (b) Ministry of Finance, Govt. of India, "*Economic Survey, 1995-96*",

(New Delhi).

71. (a) B. Bhattacharya, et al, "*Policy Impediments to Trade and FDI in India*", (Wheeler Publication, New Delhi), 1996, pp.23-38.
    (b) Ministry of Commerce, Govt. of India, "*Export-Import Policies*", (Several Issues), New Delhi.
72. See Ministry of Commerce, Govt. of India, "*Export-Import Policies (for 1992-94 and 1995-97)*", New Delhi.
73. Vijaya Katti, "The Liberalisation of Indian Trade Policy", in Karl Fasbender, Otto G. Mayer and Dilip K. Chatterjee (ed;), *Indian-European Trade Relation*, (Hamburg), 1992, pp.71-93.
74. Vasantha Bharueha, "Policy Liberalisation in India With Special Reference to Trade and Investment", in Karl Fasbender, Otto G. Mayer and Dilip Chatterjee (ed;), *Indian-European Trade Relations* : Prospects of the Liberlisation precess in India and Europe, IIFT, GTZ and HWWA, Publication, (Hamburg), 1992, pp.15-18.
75. Ministry of Commerce, Govt. of India, *Export-Import Policies 1992-97)*, New Delhi.
76. Ministry of Commerce, Govt. of India, *Export-Import Policies (1st April, 1995)*.
77. Ministry of Commerce, Govt. of India, *Export-Import Policies, 1995-96*, New Delhi.
78. Bhagwati, J.N. and Sriniwasan, T.N., "*India's Economic Reforms*", Ministry of Commerce, Govt. of India (New Delhi), 1993.
79. Bhattacharya, Swapan K., "Rationalisation of Tariff Structure of Indian Consumer Goods Imports", *mimeo*, prepared for Indian Institute of Foreign Trade as a part of the USAID Project on *Indo-US Trade Relation and Investment Prospect* : 1995, New Delhi.
80. Ibid n. 27.
81. Ibid n. 79.
82. Garry Pursell and Anil Sharma, *Indian Trade Policies since the 1991-92 Reforms*, (The World Bank, Washington), 13th February, 1996, pp.1-28.
83. Bishawnath Goldar, Ibid n. 41.
84. EC Delegation to India, "Partnership for Cooperation and Development", (Several Annual Nos.), (New Delhi),.
85. Commission of the European Communities, "Cooperation Agreement for Partnership and Development", Brussels, December 1994.
86. Ibid n. 85.
87. Ibid n. 84.
88. Ibid n. 85.
89. (a) Swapan K. Bhattacharya, "Intellectual Property Rights in India : Implications for Indian Industry", *ASSOCHAM Backgrounder*, 9th October, (ASSOCHAM, New Delhi), 1995.

(*b*) C. Niranjan Rao, "Recent Development and International Patent System", Economic and Political Weekly, (Bombay), December 23-30, 1989, pp.2841-2848.

90. Bisawjit Dhar, "TRIPs and TRIMs : Issues of Soverignity and National Globalisation Reconsider", in B. Bhattacharya and Vijaya Katti (eds;), *Emerging Trade Agenda : South Asian and German Perspective*, (Indian Institute of Foreign Trade, New Delhi), 1995, pp.143-176.
91. Ibid n. 85.
92. Commission of the European Community, "*Strategy for Economic Cooperation and Development : Asia Policy*", (Brussels), 1994.

Chapter 7

Non-Tariff Barriers to Indo-EU Trade and the World Trade Organization

The EU has been the largest trading partner of India and it has been growing over the years. It's approach toward India has been much participatory and reconciliatory rather than retaliatory in the international forum. Though the EU is pursuing India to agree for the Millennium Round of negotiations in the WTO, it is also much sympathetic to India's genuine demand of phasing out MFA quota and reduction of industrial tariffs mandated in the Uruguay Round of multilateral trade negotiations. Indo-EU relations have only recently passed through a turbulent phase, particularly in regard to India's import regime under quantitative restrictions. At the intervention of the WTO, India and the EU concluded an agreement at Geneva on 12 November 1997, whereby the former agreed to phase out the QR regime by April 2003. Leon Britton, the EU Commissioner for the Trade Relations, described this agreement as highly satisfactory from the EU point of view, for it also symbolized India's increasing commitment to continue liberalization of its trading regime. Since this is the multilateral commitment of India, it is extended on MFN basis to the other members of the WTO.

This reconciliatory attitude of the EU shows its firm commitment to India's economic development and sympathy to address the genuine issues of India's trade. Not satisfying with the Indo-EU accord on phasing out of the QR regime by 2003, USA took India to the dispute settlement body (DSB) of the WTO and wanted to phase out all QRs by 2001. Unfortunately, India was defeated in the DSB panel and forced to prepone its phase-out programme. As an aftermath outcome to the DSB ruling, India removed all items from the QR-list on 1 April 2001. This is one of the glaring examples how the EU is friendly to India in the international forum.

As it is mentioned earlier the EU is India's largest trading partner. During 1999, the share of the EU in India's total imports were 20.5 per cent, where as the EU's share was 25.8 per cent of India's total exports. Though India's rank in the EU's both exports and imports were 20 in 1999, it has improved significantly over the years. Another important aspect of the Indo-EU trade is that the EU's share in India's trade has started showing positive trend since 1998-99. It's share in India's export was 27.38 in 1995 and it was 28.09 per cent in latter's imports during the same period. The same trend continues upto 1997-98,when share in imports was higher than its share in imports. But the trend has become reverse since 1998-99. During 1998-99, the EU's share in India's exports was 26.91 per cent and it contributed 24.70 per cent of India's imports. This is for the first time since when the EU's share in exports continue to be more than its share in imports.

Fluctuation in shares is due to fluctuation in India's exports and imports over the years. But if we see the trade balance in Indo-EU trade we will notice that it always goes in favour of the EU. In 1995-96, India had balance of trade deficit with the EU at the tune of Rs 5343 crore, which increased in the subsequent years and the magnitude of deficit reached at Rs 7084 crore in 1999-2000. But quantum of both way trade has jumped significantly over the years. While India's exports to the Community was only Rs 29120 crore in 1995-96, but it skyrocketed to Rs 40442 crore in 1999-2000. On the import front also same trend continues. India's imports from the European Union were Rs 34463 crore in 1995-96, which increased to Rs 47526 crore in 1999-2000. Both India's exports to and imports from the fifteen members of the EU and its balance of trade with them are shown in **Table 7.1.**

After a long spell of dull trade between India and the EU, finally we have the silver lining since 2000. While examining the growth performance of Indo-EU trade in terms of Euro, after long three years of dismaying performance India's trade with the EU in 2000 has bounced back. During the same period, the Euro value of EU's import from India increased 23.2 per cent over the previous year and exports to India increased a magic figure of 28.6 per cent. EU's imports from India were worth of 12.3 billion Euro in 2000 over 10 billion Euro in 1999. Similarly exports were 13.3 billion Euro over 10.3 billion Euro in 1999. This means that Indo-EU trade has registered a phenomenal growth of 26 per cent in 2000 over the previous year.

TABLE 7. 1: India's Trade with the European Union

(Value in Rs. Crore)

Country	1995-96 Exports	1995-96 Imports	1995-96 Balance	1996-97 Exports	1996-97 Imports	1996-97 Balance	1997-98 Exports	1997-98 Imports	1997-98 Balance	1998-99 Exports	1998-99 Imports	1998-99 Balance	1999-2000 Exports	1999-2000 Imports	1999-2000 Balance
Austria	303	385	-82	335	497	-162	217	302	-85	330	217	113	325	289	36
Belgium	3748	5693	-1945	3879	7993	-4114	4517	9916	-5399	5458	10598	-5140	5788	15952	-10164
Denmark	488	903	-415	536	659	-123	591	337	-254	797	427	370	915	587	328
Finland	179	571	-392	193	709	-516	216	653	-437	311	754	-443	250	601	-351
France	2499	2812	-313	2542	2727	-185	2823	2965	-142	3544	3056	488	3870	3112	758
Germany	6614	10519	-3905	6720	10050	-3330	7155	9398	-2243	7929	8998	-1069	7508	7980	-472
Greece	330	164	166	332	58	274	347	134	213	412	42	370	390	117	273
Ireland	165	85	80	211	72	139	248	133	115	285	175	110	346	241	105
Italy	3392	3560	-168	3315	3505	-190	144	3425	-3281	4480	4603	-123	4849	3183	1666
Luxembourg	9	5	4	11	18	-7	12	118	-106	16	15	1	23	11	12
Netherlands	2572	1907	665	3026	1754	1272	2987	1655	1332	3285	1966	1319	3836	2041	1795
Portugal	307	18	289	312	30	282	414	58	356	453	48	405	540	42	498
Spain	1298	609	689	1509	748	761	1644	599	1045	2152	890	1262	2373	606	1767
Sweden	490	817	-327	538	139	399	618	1020	-402	633	919	-286	628	1035	-407
U.K.	6726	6415	311	7267	7578	-311	7956	9081	-1125	8028	10793	-2765	8801	11729	-2928
EU	29120	34463	-5343	30726	36537	-5811	29889	39794	-9905	38113	43501	-5388	40442	47526	-7084
Total	106353	122678	-16325	118817	128920	-10103	130101	154176	-24075	141604	176099	-34495	159023	215528	-56505
%of EU to total	27.38052	28.09224	-0.71173	25.85994	28.340832	-2.4809	22.97369	25.81076	-2.83707	26.9152	24.70258	2.212618	25.43154	22.05096	3.380578

Source: Monthly Statistics of Foreign Trade of India (Several Issues), DGCI&S, Kolkata.

What are the forces behind such spectacular performance of Indo- EU after so many years of lackluster trend? The reasons may be several. First, good economic climate in Europe, coupled with the increase in international oil price and the Euro/Dollar exchange rate devaluation has meant that the EU's global imports in 2000 increased substantially, by no less than 30 per cent. Secondly, the Indian Rupee revalued by 10-11 per cent vis-à-vis the Euro in 2000 over the previous year.

Thirdly, the overall performance of Indian exports during 2000 was much better than the last few years. In Dollar value it was almost 20 per cent that of the previous year. Another reason behind such a whopping increase in Indo-EU trade may have something to do with the increased visibility given to India in Europe by the Indo-EU Summit held 1999 at Lisbon and at which the leaders from both sides pledged to increase both way trade and flow of investment.

An important feature of Indo-EU trade is the higher rate of growth. In 1990, EU imports from India were ECU 4.5 billion, which means EU's import from India have increased by more than 2.5 times during the last 10 years. The EU continues to be India's largest trading partner accounting 26 per cent of India's exports and 23 per cent of India's imports in 1999-2000. As compared to EU, US share of India's exports and imports are 22.7 and 7.7 per cent respectively. Shares of Japan in India's exports and imports are 4.5 per cent and 5 per cent respectively. Even with the EU, share of three major members viz. Germany, U.K. and Belgium is accounted for 50 per cent of India's trade with the EU as a whole.

The EU's share in India's imports has declined steadily from 31.2 per cent in 1993-94 to 23 percent in 1999-2000. Following the same trend, imports from the US have declined from 11.8 per cent to 7.7 per cent during the same comparable periods. The share of Japan to India's total imports declined from 6.5 per cent to 5 per cent during the same period. In spite of declining percentage shares of the EU, US and Japan, India's imports have, in fact, become double over the past six years. This is because of the entry of new players: Nigeria ($826.5 million in 1993-94 to $ 2.9 billion in 1999-2000), Switzerland ($505.4 million in 1993-94 to $ 2.6 billion in 1999-2000), Malaysia ($249.2 million in 1993-94 to $ 2 billion in 1999-2000), South Africa ($ 30.3 million to $ 1.8 billion during the same period).[1]

As far as sectoral trade is concerned, EU's major items of imports from India in 1999 were: textiles and clothing (33.4 per cent), gems and jewellery (11.7 per cent), leather and leather goods (11.2 per cent), agricultural products (10.2 per cent), chemical and allied products (7 per cent). Textiles and clothing, gems and jewellery, leather and leather goods together constitute more than 55 per cent of Indian exports. The Indian goods that recorded maximum growth in exports over the period of 1993-94 and 1999-2000 are: machinery and instruments, transport equipment, handicrafts including hand-made carpets, and readymade garments of man-made fibres. The EU's major items of exports to India in 1999 were: engineering goods (35 per cent), gems and jewellery (35.5 per cent), chemicals and minerals (9.2 per cent) and metal and steel (6.2 per cent). On the EU's side engineering goods and gems and jewellery alone accounted for 70 per cent of EU's exports.

VIIa: PROBLEMS AND PROSPECTS OF INDO-EU TRADE

In the new multilateral environment, both India and EU have committed to enhance economic cooperation in a mutually exclusive way. Future prospects of trade of any country depends on how much liberalization one will undertake to globalize its economy. Though trading relations of the countries determined by the multilateral rules under the aegis of WTO, its progress basically depends on the bilateral relations between the trading partners. Both India and EU are committed to implement the accords agreed upon in the Uruguay Round of the multilateral trade negotiations. Every country has to face some difficulties in implementing the accords but inspite of this every country will enjoy gains from trade out of openness. Problems and prospects of Indo-EU trade in the years to come are shown separately.

Problems of India's Trade in the EU[2]

Relatively EU market is much open than India. If we see degree of openness measured in terms of tariff and non-tariff barriers to trade, we will find that high tariff and non-tariff barriers characterize India's market. Tariff is calculated on the basis of average MFN tariff as compiled by UNCTAD for different countries. Non-tariff barriers are calculated based on the methodology developed by UNCTAD for calculating the NTB-coverage ratio. The methodology of calculating NTB-coverage ratio is like this: Coverage ratio is an index form.[3] This shows the share of total imports subject to NTBs. The trade coverage measure (Cj) is defined as:

$$Cj = ((D I, t\text{-}m * Vi, t\text{-}n) / (Vi, t\text{-}n)) * 100 \quad \ldots(1)$$

Where Vi, t-n represents the value of imported item 'i' in year t-n and DI t-m is dummy variable that takes a value of unity if an NTB is applied to the item in year 'm' and zero otherwise. If 'n' and 'm' are zero, the index is based on current trade values; otherwise, it is expressed in the base year trade-weights. Holding 'n' constant and varying 'm' will measure the effects of changes in protection with constant trade weights.

Using the above methodology, UNCTAD calculated NTB-coverage ratio. Both average MFN tariff and NTB-coverage ratio of India and EU are taken from UNCTAD CDROM on TRAINS. At TRAINS information is available at 2-digit level, we have aggregated 99 groups into 12 broad groups. It is found from **Table 7.2** that during 1999 (the latest available period), average tariff on India's imports was 29.63 per cent and during the same period, its NTB-coverage ratio was 34. 52 i.e. NTB-coverage ratio was higher only by 16.5 per cent than average tariff. As compared to India, EU's tariff was as low as only 4.4 per cent, i.e. it was almost insignificant to Indian exporters. But, its NTB-coverage ratio was as high as 23.31, which was 432.19 per cent higher than the average tariff. To Indian market major constraints are high tariff as well as high NTB-coverage ratio. But in the EU market major barrier is the higher NTB-coverage ratio. Sector-wise distribution of average tariff and NTB-coverage ratios of the both countries for 1999 is shown in **Table 7.2.**

Trade between the countries is based on comparative advantage, which is again based on the factor endowments in both the countries. This is a static concept. But it can be extended to the dynamic situation also. If we want to see the pattern of over-time changes of the comparative advantage across the products that can be explained by the concept of the "Revealed Comparative Advantage",[5] which is covered by an index developed by Bela Balassa. This index is used to analyse the *ex post* export performance in different products for a country based on its comparative advantage. This is evaluated by comparing the relative shares across the products and for a product across time. We have used this method to examine India's relative strength in the EU market, i.e. EU's imports from India.

In order to calculate the RCA index, we have to see the relative export share of a product in the EU market. The relative export share for a product (S^k) has been computed by taking the ratio of India's share in EU imports from extra-EU world in that product to its (i.e.

TABLE 7.2: Tariff and Non-Tariff Barriers to Indo-EU TRade, 1999*

		India			*European Union*	
(a)	*(b)*	*(c)*	*(d)* *(c/b)*100*	*(e)*	*(f)*	*(g)* *(f/e)*100*
Product Description	*Tariffs*	*NTB-Cov.ratio*	*% Increase*	*Tariffs*	*NTB-Cov.ratio*	*% increase*
Agricultural and Marine Products	30.5	44.77	45.8	5.64	28.09	398.04
Minerals	17.86	1.67		0.4	19.4	4750
Chemicals	28.79	14.08		4.19	9.78	133.41
Leather and Leather Products	18.65	13.45		2.25	25.82	1047.56
Wood, Paper and Board	19.27	29.17	59.67	1.95	7.55	287.18
Textiles &Clothing	38.12	66.43	74.26	8.36	71.43	754.42
Carpets	38.7	58.1	50.12	8	27.3	241.25
Umbrellas& Accessories	40	57.87	44.67	3.57	4.53	26.89
Stones, Ceramics & Glass	38.06	38.47	1.07	3.47	5.43	56.48
Gems & Jewellery	34	23.1		0.8	3.8	375
Engineering & Electronics	27.15	19.85		2.73	8	193.04
Miscellaneous	34.37	48.23	40.32	2.8	16.2	432.19
Total	**29.63**	**34.52**	**16.5**	**4.48**	**23.31**	**432.19**

India's) share in EU imports from the extra-EU world in that product to its (i.e. India's) share in EU global market. The Relative Export Share Index can be expressed as:

$$S^k = (X^k_i) / (X^k_w) / (X_i) / (X_w) \quad ...(2)$$

where, X^k_i and X^k_w stand for the EU imports from India and from the extra-EU world in the k_{th} commodity and X_i and X_w stand for the total EU imports from India and from the extra-EU world respectively.

The index, which is shown above, is worked out in percentage terms and is called the Relative Export Share Index (RESI). This is calculated based on data at a 2-digt level at HS category. The data are obtained from the *Eurostat*, the official statistical journal of the European Union. First, we have calculated the index at 99 broad categories at 2-digit level and then we have aggregated into 12 major product groups for the sake of our convenience. We have calculated RESI for 5 years i.e. 1991,1995,1996,1999 & 2000. We have done this exercise in order the changes in relative strength of Indian products in the EU market.

In **Table 7.5**, we have shown RESI of Indian products in the EU market for 5 years. First row of the every product group shows the total value of the index of that particular year. Values in the parenthesis are the average of the index, which is also the standard of measurement. A value of above 100 of the RESI, say 150, in the k_{th} product would means that India's share in this product group in the EU market is 50 per cent higher than its share in the EU global imports. The excess value of 100 measures the comparative advantage of that product/group in the importing country. Obviously, the value below 100 implies the comparative disadvantage, which means India is not in a favourable position in the EU market. It shows that at a certain product group, if the RESI is 150 which means India has comparative advantage by a margin of 50 per cent at a particular point of time. Values exceeding and lowering 100 imply growing and declining comparative advantage of that particular product group.

Table 7.3 shows that in product groups viz. agriculture & marine products, minerals, leather and leather products, wood, paper and paper boards , textile & clothing and carpets, stones, ceramics & glass, gems and jewellery, RESI is much more than 100 and the indices have been increasing over the years. This implies that India has better market shares on these commodities in the EU over the years and shares have shown increasing trend. This is very good sign for India because majority of India's export basket contains these items. Table shows that India enjoys better/favourable position in the EU market. On the other hand, RESI in umbrella, engineering goods & electronics and miscellaneous groups are much below 100. This is because of the fact that India does not have a comparative advantage in capital-intensive high-tech goods. Therefore, the export shares are much below 100. While considering the RESI of a particular product, we have taken the average values in the parenthesis rather than total indices of that particular product group.

The above index measures the relative strength of a certain product measured in terms of export share of that product at a particular point of time. This is static analysis does not cover dynamism of trade over a period of time. There needs to be an index covers the dynamic aspect of export performance. In order to construct an index, which takes into account the time dynamics of the export performance, Balassa suggested a method, after considering several options, under the presumption that while past trends in relative shares can be expected to continue, this will take place at a declining

TABLE 7.3 : Relative Export Share Index (RESI)

Product Description	*1991*	*1995*	*1996*	*1999*	*2000*
Agricultural & Marine Products	3452.36	2653.11	3601.31	4786.88	4779.44
	(143.85)	*(110.55)*	*(150.05)*	*(199.45)*	*(199.14)*
Minerals *	519.75	444.47	398.55	460.49	479.98
	(173.25)	*(148.16)*	*(132.85)*	*(153.5)*	*(159.99)*
Chemicals	754.47	740.11	1140.49	1014.45	4425.45
	(58.04)	*(56.93)*	*(87.43)*	*(78.03)*	*(340.42)*
Leather & Leather Products	10653.37	1532.72	1400.06	1306.36	1289.1
	(2663.34)	*(358.18)*	*(350.02)*	*(326.59)*	*(322.28)*
Wood, Paper and Board	1121.11	1140.52	1209.8	1950.91	1833.52
	(201.85)	*(190.09)*	*(201.63)*	*(325.15)*	*(305.59)*
Textiles &Clothing	6468.39	7029.3	7327.61	7693.11	6750.72
	(497.57)	*(540.72)*	*(563.66)*	*(591.78)*	*(519.29)*
Carpets	492.69	435.06	394.31	425.83	384.4
Umbrellas& Accessories	40.7	63.79	49.55	82.99	90.13
	(13.57)	*(21.26)*	*(16.52)*	*(27.66)*	*(30.04)*
Stones, Ceramics & Glass**	236.7	436.8	470.5	630.54	616.95
	(78.9)	*(145.6)*	*(156.83)*	*(210.18)*	*(205.65)*
Gems & Jewellery	411.99	259.99	266.49	340.58	315.14
Engineering & Electronics***	878.16	928.12	992.51	1106.07	1055.83
	(41.82)	*(44.2)*	*(47.26)*	*(52.67)*	*(50.28)*
Miscellaneous	157.86	210.18	1100.53	188.09	279.58
	(31.57)	*(42.04)*	*(220.11)*	*(37.62)*	*(59.92)*

* RESI is much higher in minerals because higher export coverage of salt, sulpher and stone ores, siag and ash and lower export coverage of mineral fuels and petroleum products of mineral fuels and petroleum products.

** RESI is higher in this group over the years because of India's spectacular export performance in ceramic products and articles of stones plaster and cement.

*** Very low value of RESI in this sector implies that India does not have comparative advantage in this sector. This is high-tech sector where India is not at all competitive in the European market.

pace as compared to the past (Balassa 1965 & 1989) . This index is commonly known as Revealed Comparative Advantage (RCA) Index for the k_{th} product. In constructing the RCA index, we taken the average of RESI in the current year and its normalized value. For normalization, the RESI in the current year has been multiplied by the ratio of RES in the current year and RESI in the base year. The index is written as follows:

$$RCA^k = S^k_1 + S^k_1 (S^k_1 / S^k_0) / 2 \qquad ...(3)$$

where 0 represents the base year, 1 is the current year of export of a particular product or product group and S^k is the RESI for k_{th} product.

Alternatively, RCA can be calculated as:

$$RCA_i = X_{ij} / W_{ij}$$

where, $X_{ij} = x_{ij} / x_{ij}$, and

$$W_{ij} = w_{ij} / w_{ij}$$
$$RCA_i = (x_{ij} / x_{ij}) / w_{ij} / w_{ij}$$
$$= x_{ij} \; w_{ij} / w_{ij} \; x_{ij}$$

where, RCA_i = Revealed Comparative Advantage for commodity i.
x_{ij} = import of commodity 'i' from India to country 'j' (here EU)
w_{ij} = import of commodity from world to country 'j' (here EU)
x_{ij} = Total Indian export to country 'j' (here EU)
w_{ij} = Total world import to country 'j' (here EU)

Similar to RESI, the numerical value of the RCA ranges between zero and infinity with 100 as the cut off mark. If the value of RCA crosses 100, shows comparative advantage and below it would be treated as comparative disadvantage. It is a relative judgment because the range of RCA varies between 0 and 100. Therefore, any thing nearer to implies comparative advantage. But in our present case, we have taken 100 as cut-off points to measure the relative efficiency of the k_{th} product in the EU market. Both RESI and RCA measure relative strength of export performance in the EU market. But, in fact, RCA is the better indicator of measuring export performance than RESI. Latter measures comparative advantage of a certain product in the EU market at a certain point of time, while RCA takes into account change in the comparative advantage over a period of time i.e. the changes in the relative shares between the current year and the base year.

There is commonality between RESI and RCA because both these indicators measure competitive strength after taking into account the impact of price and non-price factors. While using RCA index, Balassa has observed that it reflects relative costs as well as differences in non-price factors. However, in many cases, application of this index is restricted to manufactured exports because of the fact that exports of primary products are often subjected to several policy variables viz. subsidies, quotas, standards, and several other forms of non-tariff barriers rather than transparent tariff barriers. As a result of which price of these products hardly reflect competitive prices or comparative advantage. Another major drawback of using RCA is that it is mostly usesd to measure the relative strength of manufactured exports. Moreover, manufactured products formed the major part of trade among industrial countries, which were the focus countries of Balassa's study.

Despite several advantages of RCA index in measuring the comparative advantage of a product to the market of the importing country for its consideration of price and non-price factors, it does not separate their impact and does not tell about the source of policy variables or non-price factors, such as whether it is from the importing or the exporting countries or both. Further, it does not make any projection about the potentiality of the export from ex-post export data.[6]

There is no gainsaying the fact that though more than 80 per cent India's exports consist of manufactured goods at present, it is of low-value added items in which it has comparative cost advantage. Table 4 shows the indices of revealed comparative advantage of 12 product groups. Here again, we have aggregated the 99 product categories into 12 product categories for the sake of our convenience. We have shown the change in the relative shares of these product categories into the EU market with respect to certain base year. We have made comparisons for three years i.e. 1991-95,1996-99 & 1996-2000. Here we have shown the comparative advantage of 1995 with respect to 1991. Competitive strength of Indian products in the EU market during 1999 with respect to 1996, and finally comparative advantage of Indian products during 2000 with respect to 1996. Base year in our comparisons are 1991 and 1996 and current years are 1995,1999 & 2000.

From **Table 7.4** we observe that RCA indices of all product categories except three have increased in 1996-2000 over 1991-1995. RCA indices have declined for three major product categories viz. textiles and clothing, carpets and miscellaneous manufactured goods where indices have declined during the comparable periods. Surprisingly, comparative advantage of India's textiles & clothing exports has been declined from 701.03 in 1995 to 565.04 in 1996-2000 in RCA scale. Similarly RCA index of carpets has also declined from 409.62 in 1991-95 to 1996-2000. Though, these are two India's major export items in the EU market. More than one-third of India's exports to the EU market consist of textiles and clothing and it is not much if we add carpets in the list because Indian carpet has a very niche market in the EU. In two product categories, though RCA indices have increased over the years, but these are the areas where we do not have comparative advantage. These are umbrella and &

accessories where the indices are much below 50 and in engineering and electronics where RCA index was 55.59 during 1991-95 increased to the astronomical figure of 136.03 during 1996-2000.

Similarly, in miscellaneous product category, RCA indices were 54.07 and 45.47 respectively during the comparable periods. In respect of other product groups RCA indices have increased over the years, which prove that India's competitive strength in these categories has increased. However, we cannot make similar conclusions confidently in case of agriculture and other primary

TABLE 7.4: Revealed Comparative Advantage Index (RCA)

Product Description	*1991-95*	*1996-99*	*1996-2000*
Agricultural & Marine Products	2441.4	6505.7	6335.03
	(101.07)	*(271.1)*	*(263.96)*
Minerals *	472.22	506.53	532.93
	(157.41)	*(168.8)*	*(177.64)*
Chemicals	820.33	1139	27212.92
	(63.1)	*(87.62)*	*(2093.3)*
Leather & Leather Products	978.26	1269.8	1241.53
	(244.57)	*(317.44)*	*(310.38)*
Wood, Paper and Board	1204.3	2588	2363.41
	(200.72)	*(414.66)*	*(393.9)*
Textiles &Clothing	9113.5	8145.2	7345.51
	(701.03)	*(626.55)*	*(565.04)*
Carpets	409.62	442.8	379.63
Umbrella & Accessories	82.36	146.79	143.79
	(27.45)	*(48.93)*	*(47.93)*
Stones, Ceramics & Glass**	626.97	754.35	727.79
	(208.99)	*(252.45)*	*(242.6)*
Gems & Jewellery	212.63	387.92	343.91
Engineering & Electronics***	1167.5	1262.9	2856.63
	(55.59)	*(60.14)*	*(136.03)*
Miscellaneous	270.36	126.1	227.33
	(54.07)	*(25.22)*	*(45.47)*

* RCA index is much higher in minerals because higher export coverage of salt, sulpher earth and stone ores, siag and ash and lower export coverage of mineral fuels and petroleum products.

** RCA index in this group is high because India's spectacular export performance in ceramic products and articles of stones plaster and cement.

*** The reason behind why RCA index has been growing high in this category is that India export labour intensive items which is not very competitive in the EU market. Though India has comparative disadvantage in this area but index has been growing over the years.

products for the same reasons mentioned above. However, certainly we can make conclusion from Table 4 that comparative advantage of Indian products in the EU market has been increased over the years, which is measured in terms of RCA index.

The most important barrier India may face in the EU market is environmental related standards. Developed countries in general and EU in particular are insisting WTO to include environmental standards as the WTO agenda and ask all countries to strictly adhere to environmental norms. In the years to come environmental related standard may pose serious threat to Indian exporters India has to think seriously how to comply environmental standards of the West. This is the biggest challenge of India to be encountered in the y ears to come in the EU market.[7]

Effective protection of intellectual property rights may be another grey area to Indian exporters. India is yet to give product patent to drugs and pharmaceutical, agro-chemicals and process food. India has already lost a case in the WTO dispute settlement body. India got to make its acts TRIPS consistent. Unless India does that it may have to face difficulties in above lines of industrial products. Another area of concern is the Biosafety Protocol, which India signed on 13 February 2001 and will come into force from November of this year. Precautionary Principle of the Biosafety Protocol, which has much dangerous implications to Indian exports, will address in future all environmental related disputes[8].

Prospects of Indian trade in the EU Market

Despite all these constraints, India's prospects in the EU market are much higher compared to other developed countries. More than one-third of India's exports to the EU is consist of textiles and clothing. Presently, entire trade in textiles and garments is guided by the quota system. In the Final Act of the Uruguay Round, EU has given commitment to remove all quota system by 31 December 2005. Once this is done, India will be in a better position to capture the EU market. India has better comparative advantage in textiles and garments in the EU market. In most cases, it has fulfilled quota. In the quota free regime, India will be able to extract benefits from the quota free world.

EU is a very lucrative market as far as agricultural exports are concerned. EU is a basically agricultural importing nation. Agriculture is highly protected through different forms of subsidies under "green box", "blue box" and "amber box". In the Final Act of the Uruguay round, EU has agreed to reduce subsidies by 36 per cent over a period of six years. This mean's agricultural products in the EU will be expensive by at least 36 per cent after the reduction subsidies. Presently, subsidy in Indian agriculture is –27 to –30 per cent. Since Indian products are much cheaper compared to EU, India has better prospect in the EU market, subject to how better she will address environmental issues in future.

Problems of EU's trade in Indian market

Though quantitative restrictions from India's import have been removed recently, it is not very clear how EU will get better market access on items, which were earlier covered by QRs. According to Article XVIIIb of WTO, India has increased tariff limit. Especially in agricultural goods tariff level is pretty high. India has put 100 per cent tariff on primary goods, 150 per cent on intermediate goods and 300 per cent on edible oil. All the items covered under QRs are now subject to higher tariffs under Safeguard Clause. Unless tariff is reduced to a rational level, no perceptible increase in EU 's export to Indian market is foreseen.

India has to strengthen its IPR acts. The greatest drawback why India cannot draw much foreign investment and foreign technology is its weak protection in intellectual properties. Unless India gives effective protection to all intellectual properties, EU may hesitate to export state-of –the-art technologies to India.

Another problem, which may crop up in future is the EU's insistence of liberalization of investment market. EU is very much in favour of framing a multilateral investment rule. EU has been continuously trying to pursue all countries the need of free flow of investment across the countries ensuring free competition in the investment regime. India does not like to give national treatment to the EU investors at the pre-establishment stage. It may be the major hurdle whey EU may not be very interest to invest in the Indian market.

Obviously, high tariffs are the major barriers to EU exporters in the Indian market.

EU's prospects in the Indian market

Though average tariff is much higher in Indian market, it is unlikely to sustain in future. It is Indian government's conscious policy to reduced tariff at the level of East Asia which is about 10-12 per cent and then to the level of developed countries at the level of 4-5 per cent in phased manner. In order to achieve this objective, it has reduced peak tariffs from 300 per cent in 1991 to 40 per cent in the current year budget. Its continuous endeavour with the Indian government to liberalize trade further, recently, it has removed quantitative restrictions from all of its imports. EU may take advantage of the liberalized trade regime.

India has a growing middle class population of 200 million, whose increasing demand cannot be ignored by any country. Middle class people want to have more choice in the commodity basket whatever may be the source of origin. This will give enough opportunity to EU exporter to present in the Indian market with variety of goods. India has been gradually opening to globalization, only price and quality will matter in determining the demand[9].

VII b: Non-Tariff Barriers to Trade in the Markets of both EU and India: Some Recent Experiences[10]

India's Exports Subject to NTBs in the European Market

EU is one of the most protectionist countries in the world as far as agricultural is concerned. This is true both in production and in exports. Other two prominent protectionist countries are Japan and the USA. At present, total amount of subsidies given by thesc three countries to its agricultural sector is $ 360 billion. Due to its political compulsion, it has erected a plethora of non-transparent barriers to its imports of agricultural goods from India. All information pertaining to EU's NTBs to India's exports are complied in UNCTAD inventory. Latest information available to us on EU NTBs is for 1999, which we have extracted from TRAINS CD-ROM compiled by UNCTAD. In the earlier chapters, we have mentioned about the NTBs that were valid during the first half of nineties. In the course of time especially since after WTO came into existence on 1 January 1995, many of the erstwhile NTBs have been dismantled over the years. Most significant example is the abolition of MFA quota, though complete abolition of quota will take place only on 31 December 2004. Therefore, many traditional NTBs have been dismantled since 1 January 1995. However, newer forms of NTBs in the form of standards have been emerging in recent years. Growing environmental standards in the EU market have been posing serious threat to Indian exporters. Names of some of the NTBs, which have surfaced at the end of the last century are cited below. UNCTAD has complied the names of these NTBs reported by the exporting countries in the EU market. Name of the NTBs in the EU market are:

— Anti-dumping investigations
— Anti-dumping duties
— Countervailing duties
— Retrospective surveillance
— Prior surveillance
— Prior surveillance to protect human health
— Prior surveillance to protect environment
— Non-automatic licences
— Authorization to protect environment
— Authorization to protect wild life (CITES)
— Authorization to control drug abuse
— Allocated quotas
— Quota to protect human health
— Quota to protect environment (Montreal Protocol)
— Prohibition
— Prohibition for human health protection
— Prohibition on the basis of origin (Embargo)
— Technical requirements(TBT)
— Product characteristics requirements for human health protection
— Product characteristics requirements to ensure human safety
— Labelling requirements
— Labelling requirements to protect human health
— Testing, inspection and quarantine requirements.
— Sanitary and phytosanitary standards (SPS)
— Import levy
— Certificates
— Currency regulation
— Supplementary amounts
— Non-automatic licenses
— Licensing
— Seasonal restrictions
— Quota
— Prohibition for sweet potato
— Global quota
— Compensatory amount
— Restrictions
— Variable component additional duty on sugar
— Turnover tax
— Govt. procurement

— Import substitution
— Insurance of insufficient number of permits to transport the goods
— Rules of origin
— Customs formalities
— Limitation of entry
— Technical visas
— Restrictive import licensing
— Requirement of prior import permit
— Inappropriate registration of the utilization
— Case by case licensing
— Compulsory use of French language in transaction and importation
— Advanced deposit
— Draw back system
— Advance cash deposit
— Administrative duty
— Limit on terms of credit
— Transaction tax
— Value added tax
— Luxury tax
— Licensing and discriminatory restrictions on textiles
— Discriminatory import restrictions on certain hosiery and footwear
— Mark of origin on 300 industrial products
— Turnover tax on all non-essential items.'

Most of the abovementioned NTBs have been there since the late eighties. The difference between the existence of NTBs during nineties and prior to that is that prior to 1993 all NTBs were national level NTBs enforced by individual members of the European Community but after 1 January 1993 European Community became European Union all NTBs became EU-specific. Therefore, all country-specific NTBs have marged together during the era of Single European Market (SEM). Most significant non-tariff barrier in the European market has been the MFA quota. Though all quotas on textiles and clothing will be abolished from 1 January 2005 when Agreement on Textiles and Clothing (ATC), under the auspices of GATT, will come into operation, it is unlikely that stringency of quota regime will be less to the Indian exporters during the transition period. This is evident from the fact that though both EU and USA have already integrated 51 per cent of the quota items with the GATT, most sensitive items will be integrated only on the last date. One should not be very optimistic about the prospect of India's exports of textiles and clothing after the phasing out of MFA. There is apprehension that there may emerge several newer forms of non-tariff barriers. This apprehension is not unfounded. Already, a host of textile items that India exports to the EU market is subject to rigorous antidumping duties, which clearly erode India's export potentiality.

Another significant trend in the composition of NTBs during post-Uruguay Round period has been the emergence of health related NTBs. First 23 NTBs mentioned above have emerged since the mid-nineties after the WTO came into force are related to standards on human, animal and plant health and environmental related. Majority of the post Uruguay Rounds NTBs are on standards, which again shows lack of uniformity among the members of the WTO. Lack of harmonization of standards among the members paves the way for individual country to use these as non-tariff barriers to trade. Sanitary and phytosanitary regulation of WTO permits every country to maintain its own national standards independent of other, these are emerging as the most protectionist measures in the post-Uruguay Round era. These are also called "gray measures" because of its opaque in nature in distorting trade of other countries. Nevertheless, as far as trade distortion is concerned, the efficacy of standards is much more than other traditional NTBs like quota and other para-tariff barriers. Some of the items that are subject to NTBs in the EU market are shown here. These are:

— Live animals
— Meat and edible meat offal
— Fish & crustacean, mollusces
— Dairy products
— Products of animal origin
— Live tree and other plant
— Edible vegetables
— Edible fruits
— Coffee, tea, mat and spices
— Cereals
— Millet, Starch
— Oil seed, oleagin, fruits etc.
— Lac, gums, resins etc.
— Vegetable plaiting materials
— Animal vegetable fats etc.
— Preparation of meat, fish & crustaceans
— Sugar and Sugar confection
— Coca and Coca preparation
— Preparation of vegetable fruits & nuts

— Misc. edible preparation
— Beverages, spirit & vinegar
— Residue and waste from the food
— Organic chemicals
— Raw hides and sureness
— Articles of leather etc.
— Furkins and artificial fur
— Wood and articles of wood
— Wool fine/coarse animal hair
— Cotton
— Other vegetable textile fibre
— Man made filaments
— Wadding felt and no oven yearn
— Carpet and other textile floor
— Special woven fabrics etc.
— Impregnated and coated yarn
— Knitted or crouched fabrics
— Articles of apparel and clothing accessories
— Other made up textile articles
— Manufactured pearls etc.
— Iron and Steel
— Articles of iron and steel
— Zinc and articles thereof
— Optical photo etc.
— Clocks watches and parts
— Musical instruments parts
— Arms and ammunition parts
— Toys, games & sports requisites
— Miscellaneous manufactured articles
— Works of Art, collectors' pieces etc.

Consolidated figures of EU's growing protectionism on India's exports are shown in **Table 7.5 & 7.6.** Here, we see that both the MFN tariff rate and NTB-coverage ratio in India is higher than that of EU[11]. Most important aspect of tariff and non-tariff barriers is that the starting difference between the ratios of NTBs to tariff barriers in these two countries. In India NTB-coverage ratio is 113.51 i.e. NTB-coverage is 13.51 per cent than the average MFN tariffs, whereas the same ratio for the EU is 588.66, which means NTB-coverage ratio in EU is 488.66 per higher than their average tariff of 3.97 per cent. One can draw a conclusion from this behaviour that in India average tariff is much higher as compared to EU average tariffs. On the other hand, EU's NTB-coverage is much higher than its average MFN tariff. EU takes resort to more and more non-tariff barriers, whereas in India both average tariffs and NTB-coverage ratio are much higher than that of EU. In **Table 7.5**, we have shown the distribution of tariffs and NTBs of both countries in major commodity groups. **Table 7.6** shows that products covered by environmental related NTBs in the EU market. This shows India's major export items in the EU market are subject to rigorous environmental standards. The table shows the significant portion of India's major export items are covered by EU's rigorous environmental norms. All these are highly potential items in the EU market, which is constrained by growing environmental standards of the EU.

TABLE 7.5: Tariff and Non-Tariff Barriers to Indo-EU Trade, 1999

Sl. No.	*Product Description*	*Tariffs*	*India NTB-Coverage Ratio*	*European Union Tariffs*	*NTB-Coverage Ratio*
1	Agricultural& Marine Products	30.41	43.51	5.17	27.05
2	Minerals	16.97	1.87	0.23	18.97
3	Chemicals	29.45	14.55	4.18	12.18
4	Leather & Leather Products	23.42	26.35	4.3	31.35
5	Wood, Paper & Board	22.07	24.98	2.1	2.63
6	Textile & Clothing	37.15	62.15	6.1	65.85
7	Carpets	40.9	100	7.9	86.2
8	Umbrella & Accessories	40	60.5	3.1	8.33
9	Stones, Ceramics & Glass	38.3	39.1	3.5	4.73
10	Gems & Jewellery	36.2	31.7	0.6	5.8
11	Engineering & Electronics	26.6	17.74	2.54	8.72
12	Miscellaneous	34.62	41.3	2.1	10.92
	Average	30.33	34.43	3.97	23.37

Source: TRAINS-CDROM, UNCTAD, GENEVA, SPRING 2001.

Table 7.6. Import Restrictions on Environmental Grounds imposed by EU on Indian Products, 1996-97

	Item Specification	*Nature of Restriction*	*% share*
030612	Lobsters, frozen	Environmental standards + SPS	8.23
030613	Shrimps and prawn, frozen	Environmental standards + SPS	17.23
030622	Lobster, not frozen	Environmental standards + SPS	4.95
030623	Shrimps and prawn, not frozen	Environmental standards + SPS	6.68
04	Dairy produce, bird's eggs,	GMO + ban on use of hormone	

	Item Specification	*Nature of Restriction*	*% share*
	natural honey edible products of animal origin	SPS + SRM ban + export subsidy	.38.42
0506	Bones & horn cores, unworked, acid treated	SRM ban	24.30
0701	Potatoes, fresh or chilled	GMO	0.22
07095100	Mushrooms, fresh or chilled	GMO + Preferential quota	76.89
07123001	Mushrooms (incl. Morels)	GMO + Preferential quota	14.07
0890300	Bananas including plantains, fresh or dried	GMO + import restrictions	42.77
08045002	Mangoes, fresh	GMO + pesticide residue	12.08
08045003	Mangoes, sliced, dried	GMO + pesticide residue	41.38
080600	Grapes, fresher dried	GMO + pesticide residue	65.58
090100	Coffee, coffee husks/skins, coffee substitutes	Pesticide residue	44.82
090200	Tea	Pesticide residue	25.77
10060	Rice	GMO + Variable levy	4.51
12	Oilseeds oleaginous fruits, misc., grains, seeds, fruits etc.	SPS measure + Pesticide residue	26.90
16	Preparations of meat, fish or crustaceans, molluscs or other aquatic invertebrates	GMO + ban on use of hormone + SPS + SRM ban + export subsidy	16.08
200811	Ground nuts, prepared/ preserved	Pesticide residue	2.03
2401	Unmanufactured tobacco, tobacco refuse	Pesticide residue	44.70
2402	Cigars, cheroots, cigarillos and cigarettes, of tobacco or tobacco substitutes	Pesticide residue	4.04
2403	Other manufactured tobacco/substitutes	Pesticide residue	1.74
30	Drug pharmaceuticals, find chemicals	SRM ban	25.86
42	Articles of leather, saddlery and harness, travel goods, handbags, other leather goods	Use of azo dyes	65.23
60	Knitted or crocheted fabrics	MFA + use of azo dyes	27.44
61	Articles of apparel and clothing accessories, knitted or crocheted	MFA + use of azo dyes	47.57

	Item Specification	*Nature of Restriction*	*% share*
62	Articles of apparel and clothing accessories, not knitted or crocheted	MFA + use of azo dyes	39.80
63	Other made up textile articles, sets, worn clothing and textile articles, rags	MFA + use of azo dyes	44.83
63051006	Plastic coated jute bags & sacks	Anti-dumping + MFA + azo dyes	68.85
630533	Sacks/bags of polythene/ polypropylene	Anti-dumping + MFA + azo dyes	46.06
630539	Sacks/bags of other man-made materials	Anti-dumping + MFA + azo dyes	64.57
630590	Sacks/bags of other textiles materials	Anti-dumping + MFA + azo dyes	24.08
85	Electrical machinery & equipment & parts	Technical standard	22.10

% share shows the share of the EU in total Indian exports for the particular commodity
Key: GMO: Genetically Modified Organism: SRM: Specified Risk Material (of the mad core disease)
SPS: Sanitary and Phytosanitary; MFA: Multifibre Agreement
Source: Compiled from data in Tables 5A and 6A, Bhattacharya (1999) Non-Tariff Measures on India's Exports. (Original source: India Trades, Centre for Monitoring the Indian Economy, Bombay, and UNCTAD TRAINS databases on CDRom.)

Here, we are mentioning some of the important non-tariff barriers (NTBs) to trade enforced by European Union on its imports from the rest of the world. Many of these NTBs have adverse impact on India's export potentiality to the European Union. Though the gravity of protectionism is not same for all the NTBs, some pose real threat to Indian exporters and are likely to emerge in a big way in the years ahead. We would like to give a brief description of some of the important NTBs in the EU.

Description of Some Important NTBs in the European Union

EU has been emerging as one of the most standard-conscious countries in the world. EU-member states still maintain widely differing standards, testing, and certification procedures for some products. These differences may serve as effective barriers to the free movement of products within the EU. EU's "new approach", which streamlines technical harmonization and the development of standards for certain product groups, based on 'essential' requirements, continues the general movement toward the harminizaion of laws, regulations, standards, testing, and certification procedures within the EU.

Standardization: Standardization is one of the 'grey' areas of Indo-EU trade. It will play a very important role in the years ahead. EU legislation and standardization work in the regulated areas is a matter of great concern to India. Although there has been some progress with respect to the EU's implementation of legislation, a number of problems related to this evolving EU-wide trade legislative environment have caused concern to exporters. These include lags in the development of EU standards, delays in the drafting of harmonized legislation or regulated areas; inconsistent application and interpretation by EU-member states of the legislation that is in place, overlap and inconsistencies among Directives dealing with specific product areas, grey areas between the scope of various Directives, and a frequent tendency to rely on design-based, rather than performance-based standards.

Testing: The EU is implementing a harmonized approach to resting and certification, as well as providing for the mutual recognition within the EU of national laboratories designated by member states to test and certify a substantial number of "regulated" products. The EU encourages mutual recognition agreements between private sector parties for the testing and certification of non-regulated products. One major hurdle that Indian exporters face in this regards is that only "notified bodies" located in Europe are empowered to grant final product approvals of regulated products.

Labelling: In addition to Directive 90/220, in May 1997, the EU adopted the Novel Foods Regulation, which governs food safety assessments and labelling for genetically modified foods. The regulation requires labelling of all new processed foods and food ingredients, including those made from GMOs. Neither the novel food regulation, nor Directive 90/220 makes clear which products processed from GMOs must be labelled.

Protocols to the Europe Agreement on Conformity Assessment (PECAs): In 2001, the EU concluded Protocols to the Europe Agreement on Conformity Assessment and Acceptance of Industrial Products (PECAs) with Hungary and Czech republic. The EU is currently negotiating similar agreements with the number of other countries seeking EU membership. PECAs eliminate the need for further product testing and certification of EU origin products covered by the agreements. Products originating in countries not party to the PECAs, even if the products have been tested and certified to EU requirements, may not benefit from these agreements. During 2001, the United States raised concerns, both bilaterally and in the WTO, that the rule of origin provision in these agreements unjustifiably discriminates against non-EU origin products and is inconsistent with WTO obligation. The European Commission initiated steps in late 2001 to drop the problematic origin provision from existing and future agreements.

Biotechnology: The breakdown in the EU's approval process for products made from modern biotechnology has hindered exports of corn and threatens trade in soya. Food processors and exporters are either reformulating or seeking non-biotech sources, and the prospect of new mandatory traceability and labelling requirements is causing enormous uncertainty in the feed and seed sectors. Problems exist for both approved products and products currently undergoing the approval process. Biotechnology continues to be more of a political than a scientific issue in Europe and prospects for improvement remain dim. Few EU-member states are willing to support a resumption of product approvals under current rules.

Voluntary Eco-Labelling Progrmme: On March 23, 1992, the EU Council of Ministers approved a EU-wide eco-labelling scheme. The scheme is a voluntary programme that permits a manufacturer to obain an ecolabel for a product when its production and life cycle meet general and specific criteria established for that particular product. The programme is intended to encourage consumers to purchase products according to their overall environmental performance. The EU eco-label criteria have been adopted and published for eleven consumer product categories; laundry detergents, light bulbs(single ended and double-ended), paints and varnishes, bed linens and t-shirts, photocopy paper, and refrigerators. The Commission plans to develop criteria for converted paper products (e.g. notepads), woolen and synthetic textiles, personal computers and footwear.

Beef Labelling: Beginning March 31, 1998, labels on beef packaged for consumer sales must be approved by EU and member states, to provide consumers information regarding the products. Although the labelling is voluntary, any claim on labels, such as country of origin or production method, must be verified. These requirements currently do not apply to sales of beef for use in hotels, restaurants or institutions in the EU. A EU-wide compulsory beef labelling system is legislated to take effect on January 1, 2000.Detailed application procedures currently are pending within the European Commission.

Packaging and labelling Requirements: In 1996, the Commission put forward a proposed directive that would establish marking requirements for packaging, to indicate recyclability and/ or reusability. India has expressed two potential concerns with this directive. First to the extent that the EU's new marking requirements. The packaging and marketing distribution operations will become more complicated and costly for Indian firms wishing to sell their products without achieving any concomitant environmental benefit. The second concern is related to Article 4 of the proposed directive, which would prohibit the application of other marks to indicate recyclable or reusable packaging. This requirement is likely to pose a particular problem for glass and plastic containers, as it would require companies to create new molds solely for use in the European market.

Ban on Beef from Cattle Treated with Growth promoting Hormones: For more than 10 years, the EU has banned imports of beef from cattle raised with hormonal growth promoters. The United States launched a formal WTO dispute settlement procedure in May 1996 challenging the EU ban. The WTO rules that the EU's ban is inconsistent with the WTO Agreement on Sanitary and Phytosanitary (SPS) measures because it is imposed without evidence of health risks. During 2001, the United States and the EU intensified negotiations on a possible temporary settlement in this dispute. Discussions are still continuing even in 2003. Although the EU recently published a number of new studies that analyzed the use of hormones in beef production, none of these studies presented any new evidence to support the EU's hormone ban.

Poultry Regulations: The EU continues to prohibit the use of anti-microbial treatments in poultry production to prevent transmission of bacteria such as salmonella. In October, the EU published a study on anti-microbial treatments, which recommends that anti-microbial treatment could be used as part of an overall strategy for pathogen control throughout the production chain. Although its forms of treatment such as tri-sodium phosphate(TSP) and lactic acid were deemed more acceptable , the use of chlorinated water was rejected by the study. Recent audits by the Commission have shown that member states are not complying with the EU ban on the domestic use of chlorinated water.

Transmissible Spongiform Encephalopathies (TSE) Regulations: In July 1997, the European Commission adopted Commission Decision 97/534/EC, commonly known as the Specified Risk Materials (SRM) ban. The goal of the ban was to avoid health risks related to transmissible spongiform encephalopathies (TSEs), such as bovine spongiform encephalopathy (BSE), which is linked to new variant of Creutzfeldt-Jakob disease in humans. The ban prohibited the use of SRMs (defined as the skull, tonsils, ileum and spinal cords of cattle, sheep and goats aged more than one year, and spleens of sheep and goats) in any products sold in the EU. In June 2000, Commission Decision 2000/418/EC was adopted, which repealed Commission Decision 97/534/EC, but set new requirements for handing SRMs. This new measure limited the scope of the ban to food, feed and fertilizer and required slaughterhouses and authorized meat cutting and processing plants in all EU member States to remove the SRM mentioned above, regardless of whether BSE exists in each country. The measure became effective October1,2000 for all EU Members.

Initially, the ban was not applicable to third world countries. However, in March 2001, the EU published the results of their geographical BSE risk (GBR) assessment of third countries exporting food, feed or fertilizer products to the EU. In late May 2001, the European Commission adopted Regulation 999/2001, which is eventually intended to supersede all existing TSE legislation, including 2000/418. Among other things, it establishes criteria to classify the BSE status of members and third countries into one of five classification categories. Certain requirements, including removal of SRMs, would then be applied to a country depending on the classification. In the interim, as a result of transitional measures which were passed in July 2001 only countries recognized as provisionally BSE-free are exempt from the requirement to remove SRMs in order to export to the EU. The EU currently only recognizes New Zealand, Australia, Norway, Chile, Argentina, Paraguay, Nicaragua, Botswana, Namibia and Swaziland as provisionally BSE-free.

Chemicals: The European Commission is planning a massive overhaul of the existing EU policy for chemicals regulation. In its

February 2001 White Paper on a "Strategy for a Future Chemicals Policy", the Commission proposed a new, EU-side system for assessing the risks of existing and new chemical substances called REACH (Registration, Evaluation, and Authorization of Chemicals). Under this new system, chemical companies and downstream users would be responsible for testing chemicals carrying out risk assessments, and making this information available to a central database run by the European Chemicals Bureau. The Commission is currently drafting formal legislative proposals, which are slated to be completed by 2002.

Packaging, Marking and Language Barriers: In some European markets texturized yarn is to be supplied in equal length packages only. This is an unnecessary cost addition for exporters. Germany poses a big problem to Indian exporters of engineering products. This is because, the German technical regulations are very rarely made available in English and most often the Indian exporters have to resort to employing translators on their own. But even then the Germans argue that the translations are not identical meanings of the German specifications, and hence Indian exporters are always apprehensive of falling short of German norms. This obviously hurts the export potential.

Product Approvals: Despite the EU Commission approval in 1996-97 of several agricultural and food products that contain genetically modified organisms (GMOs),the products still face lengthy and highly unpredictable approval processes than are affected by political concerns about consumer opposition in several member states. Approval of products of modern biotechnology for environmental release and commercialization is governed by Directive 90/220. However, this legislation is being revised, a process that may take several years to complete. The approval process remains the subject of internal EU executive and parliamentary debate. In the 1997-98 crop year, four varieties of maize have been caught in the current review processes. These products have been subject to unexplained delays, additional procedural steps added at the completion of the designated process and additional scientific reviews established for political rather than scientific purposes.

Product and Process Methods: Many European SPS measures link up quality of the product with production processes also. Thus, what is under surveillance, is not just the end product but also the processes of production of end-product. In India, where most primary production takes place at very unorganized, small scale units, such primary level quality assurances are hard to give. For example, the EU demands that a record of origin of each mango is maintained in the case of mango pulp export. The justification tendered is that in case a consignment of mango-pulp is found to be harmful, then the farmer whose mangoes were bad can be traced. However, as long as a pulp –processor observes strict quality checks at the entry point of mango pulps coming from various orchards into the processing unit, record or farmers need not be maintained. In this situation, if a pulp-processor-cum-exporter can ensure strict compliance with quality norms in his factory's 'entry-point' than the cumbersome task of maintenance of farmer records need not be carried out. Even the milk products, the EU in their standard for milk and milk products, insists that checks should originate from the level of primary production and has laid down the conditions of maintaining animals, types of feed to be given etc. and monitoring these aspects. Under Indian conditions where the population is large, a dairy holding may have just one or two draught animals and milk from a number of such holdings is pooled together before it is processed. It is not possible to monitor each and every animal.

Agricultural Product Subsidies: The logic of the EU's agricultural policy seems to be that everything that can be produced in Europe should not be allowed to be imported at a price lower than that in the EU. Hence, duties are slapped somewhat arbitrarily on Indian agro-produce. Apart from this, the EU grants export subsidies on a wide range of agricultural products including wheat, wheat flour, beef, diary products, poultry and certain fruits, as well as some manufactured products such as pasta. Payments are nominally based upon the difference between the EU price and the world price, usually calculated as the difference between the internal price and the lowest offered price by competing exporters. The Uruguay Round Agreement requires the EU to reduce export subsidies over six years by 21 per cent in volume and 36 per cent in value from a 1986-90 base period. Under the agreement, the EU is required to cut export subsidies by about $5.7 billion from recent levels. However, in a number of areas including poultry, beef, dairy, rice and olive, the EU appears to be "rolling over unused subsidy from one year to the next.

Apart from these non-tariff barriers, there are many more in the list, which have much adverse impact on Indian exports. We can mention a few other NTBs without mentioning details about then.

On **Government Procurement**, trade barriers are: discrimination in the utility sectors, differential member states practices etc. In 1990, in an effort to open government procurement markets within the EU, the EU adopted a utilities directive covering purchases in the water, transportation, energy, and telecommunications sectors. The directive, which went into effect in January 1993, requires open objective bidding procedures but discriminates against non-EU bids in the absence of an international or bilateral agreement.

On **export subsidies**, effective trade barriers in the EU market are: Government support for airbus, government support for airbus suppliers, government support for aircraft engineers etc. On **intellectual property rights protection,** the EU and its member states support strong protection for intellectual property rights (IPRs) and they regularly join hands with other developed countries in encouraging other countries especially developing countries to adhere to and fully enforce high IPR standards consistent with the TRIPS Agreement of the WTO. However, inspite of the stand taken by the EU as one contracting party to the WTO, there are several member states who are yet to fully implement the TRIPS Agreement in their national legislations. This is precisely the reason why USA has put EU under "priority watch list' under "special 301" for non-compliance of the TRIPS Agreement. The areas where practices of many member states are not consistent with the TRIPS Agreement are: Copyrights, designs, and patents, patenting biotechnology inventions, trademarks and geographical indications. In these areas member countries' practices are different.

On **service barriers,** most important non-tariff barriers are: Television broadcasting directives, barriers in postal services in different member countries, barriers in professional services, barriers in legal services, barriers in accounting and auditing services, inadequate market access in telecommunication services given by member states and specific member state practices, which are also discriminatory etc.

On **investment services,** the barriers are ownership restriction and reciprocity provisions, discriminatory member states' practices. **On electronic commerce**, the barriers are: Data privacy and taxation on electronic commerce etc. **Other important NTBs in the European Union** are: Domestic support programme in canned fruit, restricting affecting US wine exports, Spanish and Portuguese corn tariff rate quotas, market access restrictions for pharmaceuticals, import and distribution of bananas, mutual recognition agreements to subcontract the testing and certification procedures which cause unnecessary delays, cosmetic and animal testing, restrictions on the product designs of electricals and electronic equipments, acceleration of the phase-outs of the ozone depletion substance and greenhouse gases, hush kitted or new engine modified and recertificated aircraft, new aircraft certification, gas connector hose standard, roofing shingles, anchor bolts and discriminatory practices in this regard etc.[12]

Non-Tariff Barriers in the Indian Market

Indian market is not free from non-tariff barriers. In both average tariff and non-tariff barriers coverage ratios are higher in India as compared to the European Union. In order to calculate the average tariffs and NTB-coverage ratio we have used TRAINS-CDROM, where country level data are available at 6-10 digit level at HS categories. Latest version of TRAINS-CD is Spring 2001, where latest data are available to us for 1999 only. TRAINS CDROM is complied by UNCTAD on the basis of information sent by all member countries.

According to TRAINS data set, average tariff in India was 30.33 per cent during 1999, whereas the same for European Union was only 3.97 per cent. Obviously, average tariff level in India will be much lower now because of the fact India has been lowering tariff progressively over the year and its peak tariff has been reduced to 30 per cent during 2002-2003 budget and it will be reduced to the ASEAN level of 20 per cent by 2004. Comparative picture of India's tariff and NTBs vis-à-vis is shown in Table 5. We will discuss this aspect some details in the next section. In this section we intend to see the major NTBs in the Indian market and the description of these NTBs. UNCTAD has identified 24 major NTBs in the Indian market compared to 23 in the EU market. We have also seen that 26 per cent of the total items (at 6-digit HS categories) imported by India are subject any form of NTBs, which means the NTB-frequency ratio in India is 26 per cent. Whereas, 34.43 per cent of India's total world imports are subject to any form of NTB, which means as far as value is concerned, NTB-coverage ratio is more than one-third of its total imports. Major NTBs in the Indian market are:[13]

— Automatic licence

— Automatic licence to protect human health
— Automatic licence to protect plant health
— Automatic licence to ensure human safety
— Automatic licence, n.e.s.
— Non-automatic licence
— Import authorization
— Non-automatic licence to protect human health
— Non-automatic licence to protect animal health
— Non-automatic licence to protect plant health
— Non-automatic licence to protect environment
— Non-automatic licence to protect wildlife
— Non-automatic licence to protect drug abuse
— Non-automatic licence to ensure human safety
— Non-automatic licence to ensure national security
— Non-automatic licence n.e.s.
— Prohibition to protect human health
— Prohibition to protect animal health
— Prohibition to protect environment
— Prohibition for wildlife protection
— Prohibition for drug abuse control
— Prohibition n.e.s.
— State trading administration
— Single channel for imports to protect human health.
— Species protected under the Wild Life Protection Act 1972, are prohibited. Others are restricted
— Restricted or prohibited imports for sociological reasons
— Measures are applied to conserve exhaustible natural resources
— Products other than those registered under the Insecticides Act 1968 are restricted
— Imports of hazardous waste are permitted only for the purpose of processing or reuse.
— Naphtha is permitted without licence provided the importer sells the return stream of naphtha to crude oil refineries or uses it for captive consumption
— Silkworm pupae, other than artemia cysts in dry and inactivated state in air tight tins or in polythene vacuum packs

Gravity of NTBs can be measured in two-ways. One is the NTB-coverage ratio, which is expressed as the ratio of the value of imports covered by NTBs to total value of imports of any particular year. Another method of measurement is the frequency ratio, which is expressed as the total number of items (tariff lines at 10 digit HS-categories) covered by NTBs to the total number of items imported (at the same 10-digit level). Frequency ratio depends on method of measurement of the NTBs rather than coverage ratio. This is simple because of the fact that coverage ratio varies from year to year but frequency ratio more or less remains the same over a period of times unless there is substantial change in the EXIM Policies. If the measure the extent of NTBs in the Indian market is measured in terms of frequency ratio, we will get the following picture during 1998-99. Though the methodology of calculating frequency ratio in Table 5 and here is the same, the composition of items under NTBs is different. In Table 2 we have taken UNCTAD inventory approach but here we have taken three types of NTBs viz. *(a)* prohibited items, *(b)* restricted items and *(c)* canalized items. All the items imported are divided into 21-chapters. The values in the parentheses are frequency ratios. Though the scenario has completely changed now. This is because most of the items under restricted and canalized list are put under open general licence (OGL) since 1 April 2001 because the remaining 715 items were removed from the QR-list. By doing so, government has done away with the quantitative-restrictions regime. According to India's commitment given to the WTO, it has to remove all items from QR-list by 2003. This advances by 2 years the timetable India previously greed with the EU , Japan and other trading countries. But until 1 January 2005, it can maintain higher tariffs on these items under Article XVIIIa on one hand and transitional safeguard on the other. But the figures given below show the indicative value of imports subject to NTBs during 1998-99.[14]

- Live animal, animals products (64.77)
- Vegetable products (61.83)
- Prepared foodstuff, beverages (50.43)
- Textile and textile articles (56.59)
- Footwear, headgear and umbrella (59.80)
- Articles of stone plaster (28.89)
- Natural and cultured pearls (78.94)
- Vehicles, aircraft and vessels (48.61)
- Arms and ammunition parts (100)
- Miscellaneous manufactured articles (40.17)
- Works of art collector's pieces (62.66)
- Pulp of wood or other fibre (25)
- Plastic and articles thereof (19.60)
- Mineral products (17.3)
- Products of the chemical (12.16)
- Raw hides & skins, leather (12.72)
- Wood & articles of wood , wood (11.25)

- — Base metals & articles of base (17.19)
- — Machinery and mechanical appliances (16.48)
- — Optical, photograph, cinematograph (12.5)

Apart from NTBs mentioned above, India is having host of other NTBs, which restrict market access of other countries. One of the major trade distorting measures was quantitative restrictions (QRs) regime on BOP ground, which India has been justifying for last 50 years. But, recently, India has removed all QRs on its imports, which is, neutralized by the higher tariff level to restrict its imports. We will now discuss some of the major NTBs in the Indian market. These are:

Canalization: At present, most of the bulk purchases of India are through canalized agency owned by government. Some commodity imports must be channeled (or 'canalized') through public sector companies, although several "canalized" items have been fully or partially decontrolled recently. Currently, the main "canalized" items are petroleum products, bulk agricultural products (such as grains), and certain pharmaceutical products. Pursuant to the December 29,1999, QR agreement described earlier, India eliminated its "canalization" in the form that existed under the BOP regime on 1 April 2001. India has, however, taken steps to bring its state trading practices into compliance with Article XVII of GATT 1994, as recommended by the BOP panel. The Indian government requires imports of certain products, including petroleum products, bulk agricultural products and certain pharmaceutical products to be canalized through public sector companies.

Fertilizer Subsidy Regime: The Indian government maintains a subsidy regime for diammonium (DAP) fertilizer . Under the current DAP subsidy scheme, the Indian government subsidizes sales of domestically-produced and imported DAP at different levels. On 31 July 2000, India raised the subsidy differential to Rs 3400/MT, the highest ever since he programme's inception in 1992. While recently this differential has been reduced to Rs 2350/MT, this differential is still much too high and hinders export potentiality of other countries.

Registration, Documentation and Custom Procedures: Regarding **machinery** India has a strict import licensing system, which renders the exports of second-hand machinery. Machines older than 10 years are excluded from the general import regime regardless of their actual state, type and their previous and intended users. Indian licensing system demands a so-called product machine life expectation certificate, which cannot in practice be given by the manufacturer or the trader. Therefore, the measure could lead to total abolition of imports. On import of automotive, the government of India announced import rules for used and new vehicles through Notification No.4 of 31 March 2001. According to that notification, all imported vehicles are subject to the following conditions: Right hand steering control, speedometer indicating the speed in KM and photometry of the headlamps to suit "keep left" traffic. The imported second hand or used vehicles shall not be older than 3 years from the date of manufacture. Import of these vehicles is allowed only through the customs port at Mumbai. The second hand of used vehicles imported into India shall have a minimum roadworthiness for a period of 5 years from the date of importation into India with assurance for providing service facilities within the country during the five-year period. For this purpose, the importer has, at the time of importation, to submit a declaration. On agriculture and fisheries the customs procedures are as follows:

1. The customs should check the condition of the hold in which the products were transported in order to see whether it meets the requirements of storage and does not cause deterioration or contamination of the products.
2. Physical/visual appearance of goods in terms of possible damage has to be checked whether the product is swollen or bulging in appearance or contaminated by rodents or insects, presence of filth, dirt etc. has to be checked.
3. The products should meet the labelling requirements under the Prevention of Food Adulteration Rules and the Packaged Commodities Rules.

As PFA rules are very detailed and complex, inspectors are alleged to use regulations to discourage imports. In case of foodstuffs, importers need quick procedures, given the short shelf life of products. The opening of India's trade regime has reduced tariff level, but it has not eased some of the most burdensome aspects of customs procedures. Documentation requirements, including ex-factory bills of sale, are extensive and delays are frequent. There have also been private sector reports of misclassification and incorrect valuation of goods for the purposes of duty assessment, in addition to corruption. The Indian customs service would also benefit from a significant streamlining of its procedures for moving products from the border into the stream of domestic commerce.

Standards, Testing, Labelling and Certification: In this area India has a host of barriers. On 24 November 2000, the Indian government promulgated new regulations dictating that imports of all prepackaged commodities intended for retail sale carry specified declarations prior to clearance through Indian customs. They include: Name and address of the importer, generic or common name of the commodity being imported; net quantity; month and year of packaging' and the maximum retail price at which the commodity will be sold to the consumer (including taxes, freight and transport charges). Industry reports that India imposes difficult and extensive requirements for making of imported fabrics, which are expensive to implement. Also on 24 November 2000, the Indian government promulgated new regulations dictating that imports of 131 commodities (including food preservatives, colour dyes, steel, cement, electrical appliances and dry cell batteries) are subject to compliance with specified Indian quality standards and that exporters/manufacturers will be required to register with, and obtain a certificate from the Bureau of Indian Standards before exporting such goods to India. To receive such certification, exporters/ manufactures must establish a presence, pay an annual fee as well as a percentage of the invoice value of shipments to India, and subject all certified exports to inspection. India has not notified these new requirements to the WTO as required by the WTO agreement on technical barriers to trade (TBT). There have been plethora of new standards, which the Indian government has recently enforced and are treated as NTBs because India has not yet reported these new standards in the TBT of the WTO[15].

Sanitary and Phytosanitary (SPS) Restrictions:[16] India applies a range of SPS measures that have not been demonstrated as based on science and, therefore, do not conform to international standards or the WTO SPS Agreement. India's SPS requirements are restrictive and lack of transparency. For example, many of India's quarantine pests are already present in India, while others do not pose a significant level of risk. These requirements are a major hindrance to agricultural imports to India particularly for wheat and soybeans. The India government has issued a restrictive plant protection rules on soybeans. Indian and American agricultural officials are discussing measures that are more reasonable. Labelling of genetically modified products is not yet an issue in India. India's imports of GM food are negligible . Ferrous gluconate is apparently not permitted as a colour stabilizer in India by virtue of the Prevention of Food Act of 1954, Section 5 (iv) and the Prevention of Food Adulteration Rules of 1955 Rules 60 and 61. The Indian government decided in July 2001 to restrict the import into India of all live stock products.

- meat and products of all kinds including fresh, chilled and frozen meat, tissue of organs of poultry, pig, sheep and goat.
- Egg and egg powder
- Milk and milk products
- Bovine, ovine and caprine embryos, ova or semen and
- Pet food products of animal origin.

Government Procurement: Since India is not a signatory of the Government Procurement Agreement of the WTO, its procurement practices and procedures are neither transparent nor standardized and generally discriminate against foreign suppliers, but are improving during the process of Economic Reforms since 1991. Despite several measures taken to make the government procurement more transparent, local suppliers are favoured in most contrast where their prices and quality are acceptable as of now. Reports persist that government-owned companies cash performance bonds of foreign companies even when there has been no dispute over performance. Another problem area involves the fact that some major government entities routinely use foreign bids to pressure domestic producers to lower their prices, permitting the local bidder to resubmit tenders when a foreign contractor has underbid them. When foreign financing is involved, principal government agencies tend to follow multilateral development bank requirements for international tenders. However, in other purchases, current procurement practices usually result in discrimination against foreign suppliers when goods or services of comparable quality and price are available locally.

The Ministry of Shipping issues on 8 June 2001, a circular opening up dredging for competitive bidding for a three-year period from 2001 to 2004. Another circular issued on 15 February 2002 to all the major port trusts reverses the earlier one stating that Indian companies will be granted the first right of refusal before the contract is awarded to a foreign company. Already in June 2001, the Ministry of Shipping had advised the ports to allow the Dredging Corporation of India (DCI) to match the lowest tender received for port maintenance contracts. DCI is a Government of India enterprise, with the government stake of 98.56 per cent.

Competition Issues: India applies canalized trade through designated government agencies for certain products (agricultural products, petroleum products and urea). Canalization agencies are mostly state trading enterprises but some minor private trading is allowed with a license from the DGFT. Most of the total canalized trade concerns petroleum products. State trading enterprises retain exclusive rights regarding imports and exports. According to India's EXIM policy the state trading enterprises are legally obliged to make their purchase and sales involving imports or exports solely in accordance with commercial considerations (including price, quality, availability, marketability, transportation etc.). They should act in a non-discriminatory manner and afford the enterprises of other countries adequate opportunity to compete for participation in such purchases or sales.

Export Subsidies: India provides several hidden subsidies to exports. Export earnings are exempted from income and trade taxes, and exporters may enjoy a variety of tariff incentives and promotional import licensing schemes, some of which carry export requirements. Export promotion measures include duty exemption or concessional tariffs on raw material and capital inputs, and access to special import licence (SIL) for restricted inputs. Pursuant to the WTO panel report on India's quantitative restrictions, the SIL regime were eliminated on 1 April 2001. These subsidies have caused concern to exporter particular in the agrochemical sector. In addition, no corporate tax is levied on income generated from exports by Indian companies, this enables them to price goods below international competitive levels while maintaining a constant profit margin. Commercial banks also provide export financing on concessional terms. The 2000-2001 budget phased out the tax exemption on export income over five years in equal steps. The 2002-2003 budget proposal proposed a reduction in the income tax deduction for export profits from 100 per cent to 90 per cent .

Intellectual Property Rights: The protection of intellectual property rights in India has traditionally been dependent on other policy considerations. India has not up to date acceded to an important number of multilateral conventions of IPR protection. Indian legislation offers weak protection especially for patents. As a developing country India is permitted to delay the patent ability of pharmaceutical and agro-chemical products until 1January 2005. India's Patent Act 1970 prohibits patents for any invention intended for use or capable of being used as a food, medicine or drug, or relating to substances prepared or produced by chemical processes. Under the existing law, India does not give product patents to drugs & pharmaceuticals, agro-chemicals and processed food, which is the main demand of the drugs and pharmaceutical exporters. India has recently passed Patent Act (Amendment) 2002, where it has granted this facility. Though **Indian Copyright Law 1995,** is at par with the international standard, it has failed piracy of copyrighted materials (particularly popular fiction, works and certain textbooks). Video, record, tape and software piracy are also widespread. Cable piracy continues to be a significant problem with estimates of tens of thousands of illegal systems in operation in India at this time. Copyrighted US products are transmitted over this medium without authorization, often using pirated video cassettes as source materials. This widespread copyright infringement has a significant detrimental effect on all motion pictures market segment–theatrical, home video and TV in India. Regarding **trademarks,** protection of foreign marks in India is still difficult, although enforcement is improving. Guidelines for foreign joint venture have prohibited the use of 'foreign' trademarks on goods produced for the domestic market. The required registration of a trademark license has routinely been reused on such grounds as 'not in the public interest', ' will not promote domestic industry', or for 'balance of payments reasons'. Foreign Exchange Management Act 1999, which became operational from June 2000 restricts the use of trademarks by foreign firms unless they invest in India or supply technology. In an infringement suit, trademark owners must prove they have used their mark to avoid a counterclaim for registration cancellation due to non-use.

On **service barriers,** Indian government entities run many major service industries either partially or entirely. However, both foreign and domestic private firms play a large role in advertising, accounting, car rental, and a wide range of consulting services. There have been a plethora of barriers to Foreign Service providers on insurance services, banking services, security services, motion pictures, legal and accounting services and telecommunication services.

On **investment barriers,** major problem lies on equity restrictions. India still restricts foreign capital participation in certain sectors.

However, since 1991, India has opened up considerably, foreign technology requirements no longer exist and in some cases 100 per cent foreign ownership is allowed. Automatic approval is not granted by the Reserve Banks of India for equity investments of up to 51 per cent in 48 industries covering the bulk of manufacturing activates. The Indian government has also authorized existing foreign companies to increase equity holding to 51 per cent. The government now allows automatic approval by the Reserve Bank of India of equity investment of up to 74 per cent in 8 categories including mining services, storage/warehousing, and transport. In addition, 100 per cent of FDI is automatically approved in a few sectors like electricity generating and transmission, construction/maintenance of roads, venture capital funds, pharmaceuticals and business electronic commerce. Industries have expressed concern with the Indian government's stringent and non-transparent regulation and procedures governing local shareholding. Current price control regulations have undermined incentives to increase equity holdings in India. Some companies report forced renegotiation of contracts in the power sector to accommodate government changes at the State and Central levels. Other barriers in this area include trade related investment measures (TRIMS), anti-competitive policies, tax discrimination, electronic commerce etc..

VIIc: Non-Tariff Barriers to Indo-EU Trade: Issues before the WTO

Non-tariff barrier was a separate negotiating group on negotiations in the Uruguay Round of multilateral trade negotiations. It was one of the most important groups of negotiations in the UR. On NTBs, both India and EU have been trying to remove the existing barriers. According to commitments given in the WTO, EU has to convert all NTBs into tariff though tariff equivalent method and has to reduce it by 36 per cent by 31 December 2004. Major NTBs in the EU market is the agricultural subsidy, growing environmental measures, technical barriers to trade, sanitary and phytosanitary standards, biosafety measures, precautionary principle, health related measures, standards related to product and process methods, labelling and packaging standards, eco-labelling standards etc.

Major NTB in the EU market is the agricultural subsidy, which virtually closes door to India's agricultural exporters. In spite of distinct price preference over all agricultural items produced in the European Union, India is not in a position to export in the said market due to heavy subsidy provided to European farmers in the form of 'green box' and 'blue box'. This procedure has been followed since a long past under the umbrella of Common Agricultural Programme (CAP). EU always put variable levy, which is the difference between the domestic and imported price of all agricultural commodities. This issue is one of the major issues in the agreement on agriculture (AoA). In the last four ministerial Meetings, India has been raising this issues and insisting that the EU to reduce the level of agricultural subsidy in order to ensure free trade in this area. This is obviously one of the main issues in the next Ministerial Meeting at Mexico.

Extracting from many research studies in this regard, we can summarize the main negotiating agenda on agricultural subsidy, which requires special attention in the multilateral negotiations in the auspices of WTO. The issue of agricultural subsidy becomes very prominent since 1 January 1995 when WTO came into force and this became much contentious in the last four ministerial Meetings these issues were raised but remained inconclusive due to the stubborn attitude of the EU. India has been addressing these issues in several multilateral fora along with Cairns Group of countries but yet to achieve any success in this regard. These issues are: (i) Market access, (ii) Domestic support, (iii) Export subsidy and finally, (iv) Food security.[17]

On market access, India's approach should ideally be concentrated on three lines of measures viz. (i) Abolition of tariff quota (TRQ), (ii) Capping of tariff peaks at HS 10 digit level and (iii) Abolition of monopoly status of STEs in imports and exports. Alternatively, it wants TRQ should be doubled in every three years and preference should be given to countries whose per capita income is less than $1000. This means developed countries should extend special and differential treatment (S & Dt) to developing countries in general and India in particular. In the Uruguay Round, developed countries abolished S & Dt, which was a major cause of concern for Indian exporters. On capping tariff peaks, India wants maximum bound tariff of 50 per cent across the products rather than at the HS 2 digit level. It is suggested that average bound tariff on the agriculture can be twice the level of the average bound tariff for industrial commodities, while the peak tariff can be thrice the average of industrial tariffs. This logic would accord special treatment to agriculture vis-à-vis industry, but still permit peak tariffs up to 100 per cent for India (as average of industrial tariffs would be somewhere around 30-35 per cent), and at much lower level for the developed countries. Thus there would be an in-built mechanism for special and differential treatment for developing countries.

Higher domestic support to agriculture is yet another major problem faced by Indian exporters. Extensive domestic supports provided by developed countries to its agricultural sector both in production and in exports in the form of blue and green boxes shrinks India's export potentialities. It artificially lowers domestic prices by covering fixed costs of the farmers. During last four ministerial conferences, India has consistently been asking for (i) merging all the support being shown in different boxes (green, blue & amber) into just one box (AMS) and subjecting to reduction commitments, (ii) Capping of the maximum support (AMS) both aggregate and product specific at 40 per cent of the value of the agricultural produce, (iii) Freedom of countries having negative non-product specific subsidies to the positive product specific subsidies. Apart from these three approaches of the domestic support, India has liberty to seek clarity in the estimation procedures for AMS, especially with regard to treatment of currency depreciation and inflation, new base years and the treatment of reference prices (cif or fob) when a country changes its position from being a net importer to a net exporter.

Export subsidy is another area of reservation for India. Given India's comparative advantage in agriculture in one hand and reduction commitment given by the developed countries to reduce export subsidy by 36 per cent over a period of six years on the other, India should be very aggressive on export front. Taking advantage of India's competitive strength on agriculture, where it provides negative subsidy of 27.24 per cent of total agricultural production, as opposed to the benchmark of 10 per cent, it can join hands with the Cairns Group of countries to put pressure on developed countries to reduce subsidy substantially in order to ensure free trade in agriculture. On export subsidy, the issues are of three types. Specifically, in this area, its approach should be offensive and should ask for: (i) abolition of export subsidy (including subsidy on export credits) within three years, and (ii) abolition of the peace clause at the earliest, certainly not beyond 2003, and finally (iii) streamlining the rules for food aid, especially when it is more than a specified quantity, say, 2 million tonnes in case of grains. This is because, food aid in large quantities, many a times, has the same effect as export subsidy. So there is need to regulate this food aid through some agency of the United Nations.

On food security, India's approach is quite contrary to other developing countries. In several ministerial meetings, India has been insisting for "food security box", as Pakistan with Cuba and many other developing countries have been asking for a "development box". In the era of globalization, India's policy of "touch me not" policy is subject to criticism by many developing countries. At the name of food security, India wants to have self-sufficiency in agriculture, which causes distortions in world trade in agriculture. Distortions in world agriculture emerged primarily as a result of "self-sufficiency" phobia during the post-War years. But now the real issue is that of 'self-reliance' rather than 'self sufficiency'. Therefore, the issue of food security should be placed in terms of the availability of foreign exchange rather than self-sufficiency.

There is one more misconception about the food security. Final Act of the WTO says that countries, which maintain quantitative restrictions on agricultural imports must provide for minimal imports at low customs duties. The minimum threshold is defined as 3 per cent of domestic consumption, rising to 5 per cent of domestic consumption at the end of six years. There has been apprehension among Indian academia that this is also applicable to them. This apprehension is baseless on two counts: First, the market access stipulation only applies to countries that maintain quantitative restrictions that are inconsistent with GATT. As long as India has balance of payment problems, under Article XVIIIb, India's quantitative restrictions are not GATT-inconsistent. Second, assuming that India no longer has balance of payments problems, the minimum market access clause will indeed be relevant. But there is no compulsion that 3-5 per cent of consumption needs must be imported. The requirement is that 3-5 per cent of consumption needs must be opened up to imports. More precisely, 3-5 per cent of consumption cannot be on the negative list, but will have to be on the open general licence (OGL) list, subject to whatever tariff exist. At present, on agriculture India has imposed 100 per cent tariffs on primary products, 150 per cent on process products and 300 per cent on edible oils. Therefore, India can not be protectionist under the name of 'food security'.[18]

On 13 August 2003[19], both USA and EU reached an agreement to lowering the trade-distorting subsidies on agriculture. The Doha

Declaration calls for "substantial reductions in trade-distorting domestic support". All developed countries shall achieve reductions in trade distorting support significantly larger than in the Uruguay Round, that will result in member having the higher trade distorting subsidies making greater efforts. Both USA and EU have pledged to do so under the following conditions:

(i) for direct payment if:
- such payment are based on fixed areas and yields; or
- such payments are made on 85 per cent or less of the base level of production; or
- livestock paymens are made on a fixed number of head.

(ii) support under 1.2.(i) shall not exceed 5 per cent of the total value of agriculture production by the end of the implementation period.

(iii) The sum of allowed support under the AMS, support under 1.2(i) and *de minimis* shall be reduced so that it is significantly less than the sum of *de minimis*, payments under Article 6.5, and the final bound AMS level, in 2004.

Another major concern of Indian exporters in the European market is the growing environmental standards. Germany has been emerging as one of the most environmental conscious countries in the world. Considering the importance of environmental protection in sustainable development EU has been insisting on enforcing on stricter discipline on the environmental management. For last few years EU along with US has been trying to entwine the environmental issues with the trade. This has dangerous implications on India's trade in particular and developing countries in general.

The subject of environment has been under study under the auspices of the Committee of Trade and Environment for quite some time. But the Doha Declaration brings into the negotiating agenda for the first time. India and most other developing countries had been opposed to bringing environment into the negotiating agenda in any form but EU had insisted into it. Fortunately, the negotiating mandate is quite limited and unlikely to damage the interests of the developing countries. It calls for negotiations on (a) the relationship between existing WTO rules and specific trade obligations set out in multilateral environmental agreements (MEAs); (b) procedures for regular information exchange between MEA Secretariats and the relevant WTO Committees, and the criteria for the grating of observer status; and (c) the reduction of tariff and non-tariff barriers to environmental goods and services. With respect to the first subject, the declaration explicitly notes that the negotiations shall not prejudice the WTO rights of any member that is not a party to the MEA in question. This means that trade sanctions by MEA signatories on non-signatories are ruled out.[20]

Single most important NTB in the Indian market is the quantitative restrictions (QRs) on imports. India has been following QRs on imports since the inception of planning on the balance of payment ground. But this argument is valid no more. At present India has sufficient foreign exchange reserve at the tune of $66 billion, which is quite comfortable and capable of meeting more than 80 per cent of our import demand. On 1 April 2001, India has completely removed quantitative restrictions on imports. Inspite of this fact, Indian market is very restrictive to the EU. Though QRs are no more, import is restricted through higher tariffs enforced as transitional safeguard. According to Article XVIIIa, India can enforce higher tariffs as transitional safeguard. This is valid only upto 31 December 2004. Though our peak tariff is now pegged at 30 per cent, which is to be brought down to 20 per cent at the ASEAN level by 2004, tariff rate on primary good is now at 100 per cent, on processed food is 150 per cent and on edible oil is 150 per cent. It varies between 200-300 per cent in the case of wine and spirit. Though effective tariff is much higher if we add countervailing duties and other para tariffs. Therefore, India also has to give better market access to the exporters of the European Union.

Another major concern of European exporters is the ineffective protection of intellectual property rights in India. No foreign company wants to transfer its technology to India because of the lack of patent protection. So far, India has not granted product patent to drugs and pharmaceuticals, processed food and agro-chemicals. It grants only process patent. Recently, India has passed Patent (Amendment)Act 2002, which will become law after a year or so. Under the new act, India will give product patent to drugs and pharmaceuticals, agro-chemicals, and processed food. But according to TRIPS Agreement it will start granting product patent from 1 January 2005. The IPR issue is the major bone of contention between India and the European Union.

Concluding Observations

The European Union is the largest trading partner of India over the years and this trend will remain steady in the years ahead. Also, it is much flexible catering to the needs of India. Though both India and European Union have host of "grey areas" in their respective trade regime, both countries have been trying to remove non-tariff barriers under the aegies of the WTO, which will serve as the best platform to protect the trade interest of both these countries. It is in the interest of both to remove existing non-tariff barriers restricting market access to each other. Both have strong faith on multilateralism and a multilateral institution like WTO to settle all disputes related to trade in an amicable way. WTO is not the 'necessary evil' as some people describe, instead it is 'god sent'. In the WTO regime both the countries are liberalizing their trade regimes through several reform measures and market access commitments. In the new international economic order, WTO is the best guarantor of the interests of both the developed and developing counties.

In spite of the concerted efforts made by the WTO to make world trade free and fair by liberalizing tariff an non-tariff barriers, there has been growing apprehension that non-tariff barriers will emerge as major challenge to the free trade in the years ahead. Growth of Indo-EU trade is much vibrant during the process of economic reforms, it is expected to grow much faster once all the twenty eight Agreements of the Final Act get implemented 1 January 2005. The world is now facing newer forms of NTBs in the form of environmental protection, which are required to be addressed through a multilateral forum like WTO rather than unilateral measures. We also suggest that EU should actively help India by transferring environmental technologies for protecting environment. The Doha Meeting has finally launched the Millennium Round, which is also called the developed round that will take care of all new issues emerging international trade.

NOTES

1. The entire figures of India's trade with EU and other countries and vice-versa is taken from, *Direction of Trade Statistics*, IMF, Washington DC, Annual No. 2001
2. Entire spectrum of India-EU trade in the light of new development of the world trading system under the aegies of World Trade Organization has been discussed in detail in my article published in an edited book from ICWA. Ref. Swapan K. Bhattacharya, "India-EU Trade Relations in the 1990s: Role of the World Trade Organization, in H.S.Chopra (ed.), *India and the European Union: Into the 21st Cen-*

tury, Indian Council for World Affairs, New Delhi, 1998

3. The estimation of both NTB-coverage ratio and frequency ratio are based on UNCTAD Inventory Approach, the method adopted by UNCTAD to find out the extent and gravity of NTBs exported by any country. This method is applicable to the destination of exports i.e. on the importing country, where imports from different countries are subject to NTBs. Ref. Sam Laird and Alexander J. Yeats, *Quantitative Methods of Trade Barrier Analysis*, McMillan, London, 1990.
5. Percentage increase in col. (d) and (g) is expressed as follows: col. d=(col.c/col.b) *100, and col.e = (col. f /col. e) *100. The figures in col. (d) & (g) are expressed in percentage increase from the base figures. This is not simply calculation of percentages.
6. Relative advantage of export of one country to the market of another country is measured by the Balassa's Revealed Comparative Advantage (RCA) Index. The methodology of calculation of RCA index is described in detail in (i) Balassa, B. (1965), Trade Liberalization and 'Revealed Comparative Advantage', *Manchester School of Economics and Social Studies*, vol.33 no. 2, May, pp. 99-123. (ii) Balassa, B. (1989), *Comparative Advantage, Trade Policy and Economic Development*, Harvester Wheatsheaf, New York.
7. Atul Sharma, Gerrit Faber and Pradip Mehta, *Meeting the Challenges of the European Union*, Sage Publication, New Delhi, 1997, p. 119
8. Bhattacharya, S.K. (2000), "Trade-Environment Linkage: A Threat of Green Protectionism", in *Margin*, Vol. 32, No. 3, (April-June 2000), NCAER, New Delhi
9. Bhattacharya, S.K. (2002), *TRIPS, Indian Patent (Amendment) Act and India's Agenda in the Next Ministerial Meeting at Mexico*, Paper presented in a national seminar on "TRIPS-Next Agenda for Developing Countries" organized by the Shymaprasad Institute for Social Service, Hyderabad held at Hyderabad from 11-12 October 2002.
10. The entire spectrum of India's prospects and problems of trade in the EU market and vice-versa has been discussed in detail in Bhattacharya, S.K. (2002), "European Union's Trade with Asia and India," in R.K. Jain (ed.), *The European Union in a Changing World*, Radiant Publishers, New Delhi, 2002 pp. 241-270.
11. The entire spectrum of trade barriers of both India and European Union has been discussed in detail in several annual numbers of *Estimating Trade Barriers Analysis* of the Govt of USA and European Commission
12. Bhattacharya, S.K., (2002), *Non-Tariff Barriers, Indo-EU Trade and the World Trade Organization*, paper presented in an international semi-

nar at Jawaharlal Nehru University on " India, the European Union, and the WTO", 16-17 October 2002

13. Yasika Singh, "India-EU Trade, Tariff and Non-Tariff Barriers", Ragiv Gandhi Institute of Contemporary Studies Working Paper Series, No. 13, 2000, RGCIS, New Delhi
14. UNCTAD CD-ROM on TRAINS, Autumn 2001, UNCTAD, Geneva
15. Mehta, R.K. (1999), *"Tariff and Non-Tariff Barriers of Indian Economy: A Profile"*, Research and Information System for the Non-Aligned and other Developing Countries, 1999, New Delhi
16. Standards related to Sanitary and Phytosanitary(SPS) and technical barriers to trade (TBT) in agriculture and chemicals and its relationship with the Multilateral Environment Agreement (MEAs) have been discussed in detail in Bhattacharya, S.K. (2002), Precautionary Principle under Biosafety Protocol : Needs for a Cautious Approach", *Economic & Political Weekly*, June 22, Mumbai
17. See Bhattacharya, S.K.(2002) in EPW as mentioned in footnote 16 above.
18. Gulati, Ashoke, Back to the Negotiating Table, *The Economic Times*, August 17, September 14, & 29, October 12 and November (Vol. 40, No. 214) 2001
19. Debroy, Bibek (ed.), *The WTO Millennium Round: Towards a Negotiating* Agenda *for India*, Confederation of Indian Industry and Rajiv Gandhi Institute for Contemporary Studies, September 1999, New Delhi.
20. EU-US Joint Text on Agriculture, 13 August 2003.
21. Arvind Panagarya, "India at Doha: Retrospect and Prospect", *Economic and Political Weekly*, January 26, 2002, Mumbai.

Chapter 8

Conclusions

EC's single market has opened new vistas of Indo-EC economic relations. It is now a unified market of 15 member states, aiming at abolition of national boundaries restraining free movement of goods, services, capital and human resources. Harmonization of national rules and regulations should be unique achievement of the single market, with far-reaching impact on the exports of developing countries in general, and India in particular. The foundation of Indo-EC economic cooperation lies in different cooperation agreements signed at different points of time. The first such cooperation agreement, Commercial Cooperation Agreement (CCA), was signed in 1974, followed by Commercial and Economic Cooperation Agreement (CECA) in 1984 and the last one, the Cooperation Agreement on Partnership and Development (CAPD) in 1994.

There is enough reason for optimism that Single European Market (SEM) will pave the way for abrogating Article 115 of the Treaty of Rome[1]. Under the provision of this Treaty exporters can send consignments through single port of entry and prohibit automatic transfer of the surplus consignments to other members countries. Moreover, under the shield of Article 115 each member country enforces its own national laws for restraining imports in order to protect its own industry. Article 115 has legitimized this rights of all member countries (Sarre, 1998)[2].

EC is one of the strongest champions of GATT and has been its active member since its inception in 1947. It is now a bloc of 15 countries. Austria, Finland and Sweden joined it on 1 January 1995. According to "non-discrimination" principle of GATT, if any contracting party extends benefit to any of the member countries, then it automatically applies across the countries without any discrimination[3]. This is the fundamental principle of GATT. But this principle does not hold good in case of trade blocs like the EC[4]. Members have removed all internal barriers but they are equally protective to non-bloc countries. Therefore, it seems that EC may be more protective to non-member countries, than it was earlier[5].

Though Indo-EC economic relations are strengthened and diversified by many co-operation agreements which offer India better market access to the Community, yet the EC is considered to be one of the most protectionist entities having labyrinthine trade barriers especially non-tariff types which have jeopardized the growth of India's export of some super-sensitive items with high labour contents. In the earlier sections, we have discussed how both NTB-coverage and frequency ratios of India's exports to EC have been increasing over the years. Not only is this corroborated by a priori reasoning, but also it is proved from the UNCTAD data on tariffs and non-tariff measures that EC is very protectionist in such areas where India has relatively better competitiveness in the Community market[6].

From UNCTAD Inventory on Tariffs and Non-Tariff Barriers, it is also revealed that the items which are covered under NTBs are also subject to higher average (weighted) tariffs than the items which are not covered by NTBs[7]. We have shown this relationship in the earlier sections. Nevertheless, in order to prove our hypothesis that EC is more protective in areas where India has strong comparative advantage, and also to prove the degree of competitiveness, we have taken recourse to Bela Balassa's Index of Revealed Comparative Advantage (RCA) (Balassa, 1965)[8]. The methodology and results have been discussed earlier in detail. The result shows that NTBs are higher in areas where RCA is substantially high. The study has been done using data upto 1994, (the latest data available for this purpose). This indicates that EC has hardly any inclination to slacken the grip of protectionism even after the completion of internal market. Rather, evidence shows that it has erected newer forms of NTBs which did not exist earlier[9].

The above observation seems to be correct if we see EC's "tariff modulations" programme[10]. In this programme, EC aligned all preferential arrangements given to developing countries under GSP Scheme. EC has stopped extending GSP facility from 1st January, 1999. India is one of the major beneficiaries of EC's GSP scheme which is also a part of Indo-EC economic cooperation agreements.

According to the new GSP scheme, India graduated from the developing countries earmarked for this facility from 1 January 1997. All products under GSP scheme were thrown into open competitive tariff modulation scheme. The new system put 85 per cent of MFN tariff to all very sensitive products. In the tariff modulation scheme, EC divided all products under GSP into four (4) categories viz. (i) very sensitive, (ii) sensitive, (iii) semi-sensitive and (iv) non-sensitive[11].

Very sensitive category includes all items of textiles and garments (falling 50-63 HS codes at 2 digit level) and footwear. India has strong comparative advantages in these areas. The entire gamut of India's textile exports has been under stringent community quota under MFA since 1974. Hereafter, all items of textiles and garments were subject to the highest average tariff i.e. 85 per cent of the MFN rate getting waiver of 15 per cent only. In the other three categories tariff rates were 70 per cent, 35 per cent and zero. Therefore, SEM did not bring any respite for Indian exporters[12].

Community anti-dumping laws is another major area of concern for Indian exporters(Koopmann & Schanner, 1992)[13]. A host of India's exports of textile items have been under community anti-dumping duty. In the GATT regime, anti-dumping duties were enforced unilaterally giving little scope to listen to the arguments of developing countries. Though after the completion of the Uruguay Round negotiations, all rules and regulations pertaining to anti-dumping duty are likely to be harmonized across the contracting parties, but even today, EC practices are much more stringent to non-member countries[14]. They are completely different from GATT codes on anti-dumping duties (1979). There might have been sufficient reasons for the worries of Indian exporters that in the ensuing years, anti-dumping duty will be enforced more rigorously to stop imports from developing countries in general and India in particular. Anti-dumping duty will be used as the most protective barrier and world Bank has expressed its apprehension for its rampant use in future (Martin & Winter, 1995)[15]. It has also predicted that when all present NTBs will be removed after 2004, anti-dumping duty will be the most restrictive trade measure.

EC's single market does not say anything about the liberalization of non-tariff barriers to the third countries (Koopmann & Schanner, 1989)[16]. Many of NTBs are often treated as a "grey area", by the enforcing countries, therefore, no retaliatory measures have been taken so far in the GATT regime. NTBs are the complete violation of GATT principle of free-trade and non-discrimination. But since GATT did not have any effective enforcement mechanism as well as a dispute settlement body, no complaint alleging the violation of GATT's free-trade principles had been reported to GATT (Desai, 1988)[17].

But this scenario has changed with the signing of the Final Act of the Uruguay Round on 15th April, 1994 at Marrakesh, Morrocco. In the Uruguay Round negotiations, non-tariff barriers were given status of a separate group under the chairmanship of Australia. There has been a long pending demand of the developing countries for dismantling non-tariff barriers and replacing them with preferential tariffs. But so far developed countries have turned a Nelson's eye to this demand.

In the discussion, all developed contracting parties have reached a consensus for eliminating all non-tariff barriers to trade and to replace them by tariffs. Most of the NTBs are highly non-transparent in their application and cannot be covered under objective measurement. The developed countries had given commitment to convert all non-tariffs into tariffs under the 'tariffication' programme. After tariffication of all NTBs, the developed countries had to reduce 36 per cent over a period of 6 years and developing countries have to reduce tariffs by 24 per cent over a period of 8 years beginning 1st January, 1995[18].

A significant amount of India's agricultural exports to EC is under NTBs. Due to political compulsions, almost all imports of agricultural goods into EC are subject to variable levies under Common Agricultural Programme (CAP)[19]. Especially, France is the most protectionist in agricultural imports as the developed countries provide enough subsidies to agricultural sector. For full agricultural liberalization measures, the elimination of all intervention from tariff to subsidies could add $ 430 billion to global annual income, of which $ 250 billion would accrue to OECD countries and $ 180 billion to the rest of the World (Goldin, et at, 1993)[20]. In terms of welfare gains, partial agricultural trade liberalization leads to an annual global gain of $ 190 billion (1992 dollars); of this amount $ 120 billion accounted for OECD countries and $ 70 billion for the developing countries[21]. On an average OECD countries have given per head $440 subsidy per annum to the agricultural sector which is very difficult to dismantle immediately. It is estimated by a World

Bank - OECD study that consumers had to pay a staggering $ 350 billion in 1992 for government support in agriculture. Europe headed the list with highest consumer cost of $ 160 billion and in terms of $ 450 per capita. The US ranked second with US $ 91 billion or $ 360 per capita. Japan was third in the queue with US $ 74 billion or $ 600 per capita. Total cost of 24 OECD countries was $ 354 billion, amounting to $ 440 per capita[22].

While calculating the Producers' Subsidy Equivalents (PSEs) it is seen that Japan provides 72.5 per cent subsidy to their agriculture, EC provides 37 per cent and USA gives 26 per cent subsidies to their agricultural producers[23]. Total per capita subsidy in the OECD countries is $ 440 per annum. The Final Agreement on subsidies and countervailing measures has stipulated conversion of all subsidies into one Price Subsidy Equivalents (PSEs) or Average Measured Subsidies (AMS) and has asked developed countries to reduce this by 36 per cent over a period of 6 years and developing countries by 24 per cent over a period of 10 years. Apart from reductions in subsidy in value terms the developed countries have also agreed to reduce subsidy on quantity of exports by 20 per cent.

These proposed measures are understood to have a favourable effects for Indian exporters of agricultural products who have long been deprived of better market access in the EC market. This is due to the fact that EC's agriculture in heavily subsidized under the CAP. Agricultural items were put under abnormally high tariffs and often they put variable levies if there has been reduction in international prices. If EC's agriculture is brought under liberalization network, its prices will shoot up after reduction of subsidies. Since India has comparative advantage in exporting agricultural goods she will find a niche to EC market and will fetch better prices. Thus, reduction of subsidy on EC's agriculture is beneficial to Indian exporters. Though the magnitude of reduction is much less compared to the absolute level of subsidy but it is quite encouraging to Indian agro-exporters to the Community[24].

Major NTB-removal package came from the Agreement on Textiles and Clothing[25]. Quota on textiles has been the single largest NTB in the EU market. Though trade in textiles and garments has been conducted by a separate agreement (i.e. multifibre arrangement or MFA) outside the GATT framework for more than three decades, GATT stipulates minimum 6 per cent growth at each level. Despite this fact, EC allows 0.5 per cent to 2 per cent growth in very sensitive categories[26]. EC is the most protectionist in this area even more rigorous than USA and other five countries with which India concluded bilateral agreements on exports of textiles and clothing[27].

According to the Final Act of GATT, all NTBs (i.e. quotas) imposed on imports of textiles and clothing from 19 developing countries (including India) will be removed by 2005 AD. The 10 years transition period beginning 1st January, 1995 and phases are divided as 3:4:3. This is the major achievement of developing countries in general and India in particular[28]. India's export performance in textiles is consistently better especially in the cotton segment. Quota utilization in most sensitive categories has exceeded 100 per cent since the mid-eighties, but it could not export more due to stringent quota and ceiling arrangements in the EU market. When the quota-regime will be completely dismantled from textile exports, India will be the single largest beneficiary of such programme on many grounds[29].

China is India's major competitor in the EC market on textile products followed by other NICs like Singapore, Hong kong, Taiwan and South Korea. But considering the unique feature of India, she can capture a sizeable portion of the EC market on textiles. India may outspace China in the long run simply because of latter's duel pricing policy, on the one hand, and continuous dumping on the other[30]. After MFA phase-out, South Korea, Taiwan, Hong kong, Singapore and other NICs are expected to specialize in area of high value added products vacating lower-end to India. Due to excessive protection given to domestic industry, EC's textiles sector will not be able to compete with India after the abolition of quota system. All these developments provide a unique opportunity to India to capture the lion's share in the community market[31].

But India should not be too much optimistic about the phasing out programme. Quota is the most transparent NTB enforced on India's textiles exports to EC. But apart from MFA quota, so many other complicated trade barriers have been enforced on EC's imports of textiles from India. First, important barrier is the higher tariff level. Average (wtd) tariff on EC's imports from India ranges between 4-5 per cent but the rate varies between 15-20 per cent in case of its imports of textiles and clothing[32]. This is because all imports of textiles from India are from very sensitive categories. Removal of quotas does not mean reduction of tariffs in equal spirit[33]. Rather nominal tariff will be added by "equivalent-tariffs" which varies between 20-100 per cent ad valorem[34]. Therefore, after the removal of quota tariffs will be the main barrier which EC is unlikely to remove. Second, in the Uruguay Round, developed countries have agreed to reduce the average tariff by 38 per cent on all manufactured goods. Textiles will be covered in this area. But at the same time, they have also said that tariff reductions on textiles would not be more than 12 per cent on average[35]. Even this 12 per cent reduction may not be effective for India because this reduction is an average not across the products. Therefore, there is every possibility that EC may reduce tariffs more than 12 per cent on the items where the base level tariff is already low, without touching the items where the rate is very high due to its importance in the EC market.

Third, MFA quota is not the only NTB on our textile exports to EC. Our export potentialities to EC have been getting eroded due to other labyrinthine NTBs which have same distortionary power. These are Safeguard Clause (Article XIX), basket extractor mechanism, anti-surge mechanism, anti-dumping duties, environmental clause, eco-friendly products, eco-labelling, standardization, social clauses etc. These NTBs will remain in the system even after removal of quotas. These NTBs will erode the benefit of free trade that will emerge after the completely dismantling of the MFA quota[36].

Another challenge to India's exports in the EC is the emergence of new issues in the multilateral trade discussions. So far GATT had been the only multilateral body to frame rules and regulations on world trade with a view to making it as free as possible through the removal of tariff barriers on merchandise trade only. But the Uruguay Round has widened the horizon of issues for negotiations from tariff to non-tariff and from goods to services. World Trade Organisation (WTO) replaces GATT, that looks after all issues that directly or indirectly affect trade. It has extended its horizon from economic to non-economic issues like environment, labour standard and child labour[37]. Recently EC passed stringent laws on environment and eco-labelling. EC has already banned some chemicals used in the textiles industry[38]. This ban will adversely affect India's export prospect in the EC but India has been given some time to adjust its textile industry, and to become more environment conscious and not to use chemicals in its products which are not environment-friendly.

Emergence of social clause is another area which is a matter of great concern for Indian exporters to the EC[39]. Under the GSP scheme, EC has already linked GSP facility with sound record on environment protection, human rights, good labour standards and several other conditions related to labour and employment. On the issue of child labour, Indian carpet industry is already under great pressure, and if EC continues to insist on fair labour standards according to their own definition, all our export efforts will come to a halt because most of our products are labour-intensive and are from unorganized sector.

NOTES

1. Article 115 was framed particularly to counter the growth of exports from the erstwhile socialist countries. Since prices of these countries were administered, therefore, some system of adjustment was needed to match with the freemarket price. But that logic does not seem to exist any more.
2. Francis Sarre, "Article 115 EEC Treaty and Trade with Eastern Europe" Intereconomies, (Hamburg), September-October, 1988, pp.233-240.
3. This system is called Most Favoured Nation (MFN) principle of GATT, Developing Countries are beneficiaries of this clause.
4. Setting up a trade block is permitted by GATT under Article XXIV, Under this clause some countries together can form a trading bloc without affecting basic principles of GATT.
5. It was widely discussed in World Bank seminar held on 26-27th January, 1995 in Washington that once the implementation of the provisions of the Final Act will be over by 31st December, 2004, developed countries will emerge with newer forms of NTBs like anti-dumping measures etc. Therefore intensity of protectionism may not be pruned rather it may be accelerated.
6. The above statement is proved through Revealed Comparative Advantage (RCA) Index. Where the index is more than utility, it means competitiveness is high and vice-versa.
7. UNCTAD, "Inventory on Tariffs and Non-Tariff Barriers", Contains in several data tapes for different countries, (UNCTAD, Geneva).
8. *(a)* Ingo Walter, "Non-Tariff Barriers and the Export Performances of the Developing Countries", *American Economic Association* Papers and Proceedings no. 61 (May) pp. 195-205.

   (b) Bela Balassa, "Trade Liberalisation and Revealed Comparative Advantage", *The Manchester School* (1965), Vol. XXXIII, No. 2, pp. 99-123.
9. Recently EC has introduced some new NTBs as India's exports :

viz., AZO Dice, eco labelling, RAGMARK, Child Labour Issues etc. and also contemplating to link social cause with the trade preferences.

10. Commission of the European Communities, "*Official Journal of the European Communities*", (Brussels), 31st December, 1994, No. L348/ 9-25, this Document is categorisation of goods according to sensitivities as describes in the New GSP Scheme of EU.
11. Swapan K. Bhattacharya and Vijaya Katti, "EU's New GSP Modulation Scheme : No Room for optimism", *Business Line*, (New Delhi), 9th October, 1995.
12. Ibid no. 3.
13. *(a)* Swapan k. Bhattacharya, "Managing Anti-dumping Measures in the WTO Regime", *ASSOCHAM Monograph* (ASSOCHAM, New Delhi), 1996.
    (b) George Koopmann and Hans Eekart Schanner, "EC Trade Policy Beyond 1992" in *Intereconomies*, (Hamburg), Sept.-Oct., 1989, pp. 211-212.
14. Ministry of International Trade & Industry (MITI), "*Unfair Trade Practices in the USA and the EC*", (Tokyo), 1993.
15. Will Martin and L. Allen Winters (eds;), *The Uruguay Round and The Developing Economies*, (Washington, The World Bank), 1995, XIV-XV.
16. George Koopmann and Hans Eckart Schanner, "EC Trade Policy Beyond 1992" in *Intereconomies*, (Hamburg), Vol-26, Sept.-Oct. 1989 pp. 207-208.
17. Ashok V. Desai, "India and the Uruguay Round", *Economic and Political Weekly*, (Bombay), Special Number, November 1988, p. 2374.
18. *(a)* World Trade Organisation, "Agreement on Agriculture" (Annex IA) *in The Uruguay Round : Final Act*, Marrakesh, 15th April, 1994, pp. 43-69, (Geneva).
    (b) Joseph Francis, Brad McDonald and Hasen Nordstorm," Assessng the Uruguay Round" in Will Martin and L. Allen Winter (ed;) *The Uruguay Round and the Developing Economies*. (Washington, The World Bank, 1995) pp. 117-215.
    (c) Thomas Herrel, Will Martin, Koji Yanagishima and Beftina Dimaranan, "Liberalising Manufacturers Trade in a changing World Economy, no. 21(b), Ibid pp. 73-97.
    (d) Richard Blackharst, Alice Enders and Joseph F. Francois, "The Uruguay Round and Market Access : Opportunities and challenges for Developing Countries", Ibid n. pp. 97-117.
19. Commission of the European Communities, *European Economy : Special Volume on Variable Levy under Common Agricultural Programme*, (Brussels), 1994.
20. Ian Goldin, Odin Knudsen and Dominique Van der Mensbrugghe,

"*Trade Liberalisation : Global Economic Implications*", (Washington, The World Bank, 1993), p.17.

21. Ibid no. 20, p. 78
22. Ibid no. 20, p. 79
23. Ashok Gulati and A.N. Sharma, "Subsidising Agriculture : A Cross Country View", *Economic and Political Weekly*, (Bombay), 26th September, 1992, p. 108.
24. India is giving negative subsidy to agriculture to the extent of 2.3 percent. This means Indian products are cheaper as compared to those of other countries. Therefore, India certainly can take advantage of the increase in EC price due to reduction in subsidies cf-Ibid no. 21(a).
25. "Agreements on Textiles" (Annex IA), in *The Uruguay Round : Final Act.* Marrakesh, 15th April, 1994). pp. 85-117.
26. O.P. Sharma, "Quota Restrains and MFA-II : Some Empirical Evidence on India's Exports to the EEC", *Economic and Political weekly*, (Bombay), 20th September, 1984, p.1711.
27. *(a)* Rajiv Kumar and Ram Khanna, "India : The Multifibre Arrangement and the Uruguay Round", (Chapter-8), in Carl B. Hamilton, (ed;) *The Uruguay Round, Textile Trade and the Developing Countries : Eliminating the Multifibre Arrangement in the 1990*", (A World Bank Publication, Washington, 1990), pp. 182-212.
    (b) Ram Khanna, "Impact of QRs on India Apparel Export Industry" *mimeo* (ICRIER, New Delhi, 1987).
28. *(a)* Ibid no. 2. pp. 85-117.
    (b) Swapan K. Bhattacharya, "Transition from MFA to WTO : Prospects for Indian Exports of Textiles and Garments" in K.R. Gupta ed., *World Trade (Atlantic Publishing, 1995)*, pp. 210-312.
    (c) "Implication of the Uruguay Round of Negotiations on Small and Medium Enterprises (SMEs) : The Case of the Indian Textiles Industry" Paper presented at a seminar in Delhi organised by Entrepreneurship Development Institute (EDT), Ahemdabad, 1994.
29. Ibid no. 7.
30. Ibid no. 7.
31. Ibid no. 7.
32. Swapan K. Bhattacharya, "India's Textiles Agreements with USA and EU : Beginning of a New Era of Competitiveness" *Foreign Trade Bulletin* (New Delhi), May-June 1995, pp.
33. Swapan K. Bhattacharya, "India's Textiles Agreements with USA and EU : Beginning of a New Era of Competitiveness" *Foreign Trade Bulletin* (New Delhi IIFT), May-June 1995, p. 10-13,22
34. United States International Trade Commission, "*The Economic Effects of Significant US Import Restraints; Phase-I : Manufacturing*"

(USITC Publication No. 222, Washington, D.C.) 1989, p. 19.

35. WTO, "*The Uruguay Round : Tariff Reduction Schedule* (Vol-XIX), (World Trade Organisation, 1994).
36. Ibid no. 7. p. 288.
37. *(a)* Kym Anderson, "The Entwining of Trade Policy with Environmental and Labour Standards" in Will Martin and L. Allen Winter, (ed;). *The Uruguay Round and the Developing Economies*, (Washington, The World Bank, 1994), pp.435-456.
    (b) Rohini Aensman, "Minimum Labour Standards and Trade Agreements : An Overview of the Debate", *Economic and Political Weekly*, 20-27th April, 1996, pp. 1030-1034.
    (c) Hartmut Kuchie, "Social Norms and World Trade" in B. Bhattacharya and Vijaya Katti (eds;) *Emerging Trade Agenda : South Asian and German Perspectives*, (New Delhi, Indian Institute of Foreign Trade, 1995), pp.199-207.
38. Ibid no. 7.
39. *(a)* Swapan K. Bhattacharya, "GATT, WTO and Social Clauses : A Challenge for Developing Countries", *International Industries Annual*, (New Delhi, 1994), pp. 69-77.
    (b) Kalyan Raipuria, "Phasing in Social Norms in World Trade : The Conceptual Operational and Research Issues", in B. Bhattacharya and Vijaya Katti ed., *Emerging Trade Agenda : South Asian and German Perspectives* (New Delhi, Indian Institute of Foreign Trade, New Delhi, 1995), pp. 185-199.

Bibliography

PRIMARY SOURCES

EC Documents

Commission of the European Communities, *Commercial Cooperation Agreement*, (Brussels, 1973).

Commission of the European Communities, *Cooperation Agreement on Partnership and Development*, (Brussels), December 1994.

Commission of the European Communities, "*Official Journal of the European Communities*." (Brussels), Dec. 1994.

Commission of the European Communities, "*Eurostat*" (Several Issues), Brussels.

Commission of the European Communities, "US, Japanese and Community Competitiveness Development", *European Economy*, (Brussels), No. 4. 1994.

Commission of the European Communities, " Community competitiveness in high technology", in *European Economy*, (Brussels), 1994.

Commission of the European Communities, "European Competitiveness in The Triad Macro Economic and Structural Aspects", in *European Economy*, (Brussels), No. 2, 1993.

Commission of the European Communities, "US, Japanese and Community Competitiveness Development", *in European Economy*, (Brussels), Spl. Studies No. 4, 1993, pp. 159-178.

Commission of the European Communities, "Community Competitiveness in High Technology", *European Economy*, (Brussels, 1993). pp. 71-82.

Commission of the European Commission, "*The White Paper, of the Internal Market*", Brussels 1985.

Commission of the European Communities, *The Cockfield Report*, (Brussels, 1986).

Commission of the European Communities, *The Costs of Non-Europe* Vol.I-XVI, (Brussels, 1987).

Commission of the European Communities : *Research on the Cost of Non-Europe* Basic Findings : Executive Summaries (Vol. 1), (Brussels, 1987).

Commission of the European Communities, Director General for Economies and Trade Affairs, in "European Economy", *The Economies of 1992*, No. 35, March 1988.

Commission of the European Communities, "Single European Act" in *Official Journal of the European Communities* (Brussels), no.1, 29 June 1987, pp. 573-589.

Commission of the European Communities, *The Single Market in 1995 : Report from the Commission to the Council and the European Parliament*, (Brussels), 2 February 1996, pp.1-9.

Commission of the European Communities, "*Free Movement of Press : Proposals for Directives* Press Release by European Commission, IP (95)/726, (Brussels), 12 July 1995.

Commission of the European Communities, "*Proposal for a Council Directive on the Elimination on Controls on Person Crossing internal frontiers*", COM (95) 347, 95/020/(CNS), (Brussels), 12 July 1995, pp.1-18.

Commission of the European Communities, "*Economic and Monetary Union*" (Brussels), 21 August 1990 SEC (90) 1659, pp.1-36.

Commission of the European Communities, *On the Establishment of European Monitory System (EMS) and Related Matters : Basic facts*, (Brussels), 5 December 1978, pp.58-90.

Commission of the European Communities, "A Reference Scenario for the Move to the Single Currency" in *Green Paper on the Practical Arrangements for the Introduction of the Single Currency*, (Brussels), 31st May, 1995, COM (95), 333.

Commission of the European Communities, "Attainment of Economic and Monetary Union (Chapter-II)", in J.V. Louis, *From EMS to Monetary Union*, European Commission Document Series, 1990.

Commission of the European Communities, "One Market, One Money : An Evaluation of the Potential Benefits and Costs of Forming an Economic and Monetary Union, "*European Economy*, (Special Issue on EMU) no. 44, October 1990.

Commission of the European Communities, "*Official Journal of the European Communities*", (Brussels), 31st December, 1994, No. L348/9-25.

Commission of the European Communities, *European Economy : Special Volume on Variable Levy under Common Agricultural Programme*, (Brussels), 1994.

Commission of the European Communities, "Strategy for Economic Co-operation and Development : Asia Policy", (Brussels), 1994. In Jaques Pelkmans, "*External Aspects of EC's Single Market*", Paper presented at Second Biennial India-EC Colloquium, *India and the EC : Outlook for the Nineties*, (New Delhi), November, 1991.

David O' Keefee, "The Schengen Convention : A Suitable Model for European Integration in *Year Book of European Law*, Oxford (Clarendon Press, 1992).

European Commission, Directorate General of Economic and Finance Affairs, *European Economy*, No. 5, 1994. Spl. Issue on the Economies of Common Agricultural Policies (CAP), (Brussels)

European Parliament Working Document, *Towards Economic Resources* A 2-50/85/B, 31 May 1985.

European Commission, "*Information Paper on the Implementation of the Convention Applying the Schengen Agreement* XV/4.3, (Brussels), 16 March 1995, pp.14-22.

Commission of the European Communities, "Joint Declaration of Intent, on Development of Trade Relations with Ceylon, India, Malaysia, Pakistan and Singapore in Documents concerning the Accession of The European Communities" *Official Journal of the European Communities*, (Brussels), 27 March 1972.

The European Commission, "*Background Report : The Schengen Agreements* (Brussels), SEC/95, 9 March 1995, pp.1-5.

GATT/WTO DOCUMENTS

Annual Report (Several Issues) (Geneva)

"Agreements on Textiles" (Annex IA), in *The Uruguay Round : Final Act*. Marrakesh, 15th April, 1994). pp. 85-117.

An Analyses of the Proposed Uruguay Round Agreement, with Particular Emphasis on Aspects of Interest to Developing Countries (MTN. TNC/W/122) (MTN. GNG/W/30) (Geneva, GATT 29, November 1993)

Basic Documentation for Tariff Study, (Geneva, GATT, June 1966)

Council Overview of Developments in the International Trading System, Report by the Director General (GATT Document C/RM/OV/Rev.

Development in the Trading System, (GATT, C/W 1948 April 1993 to September 1984), Geneva

Final Act : Embodying the Results of the Uruguay Round of Multilateral Trade Negotiations (Marrakesh GATT, 15 April 1994)

General Agreement or Tariffs and Trade, *Basic Instruments and Selected Documents* (BISD, 205/48)

International Trade (Several Issues) (Geneva).

Import Measures, Variable Levies and other Special charges (Geneva, GATT, 1971)

Prospects for International Trade, Press Communicate (September 1, Geneva, 1986)

Report of the Groups on Quantitative Restrictions and other Non-Tariff Measures, (L/5713, Geneva, 1984)

Reply to the Questions of Licensing USA (GATT, L/5131, Geneva, 1985)

Textile and Clothing on the World Economy (Background Studies Geneva, 1984)

Trade Policy Review Mechanism : European Union (GATT, Geneva, 1995)
Trade Policy for a Better Future (Geneva 1985)
WTO, "*The Uruguay Round : Tariff Reduction Schedule* (Vol-XXXI), (World Trade Organisation, 1994).

GOVERNMENT OF INDIA

Ministry of Commerce, Alexender P.C., "*Report of the Committee on Trade Policy and Proceeding*", Govt.of India, 1980.
Central Statistical Organisation, *Basic Statistics Relating to Indian Economy* (Annual Nos.) (New Delhi).
Engineering Export Promotion Council, *Handbook of Statistics*, 1994-95, (Calcutta).
Ministry of Commerce, Govt. of India "*Annual Reports, 1973-74*", (New Delhi).
Ministry of Commerce, Government of India, "*Monthly Statistics of Foreign Trade of India*", (Several Issues;) DGCI & S, Calcutta.
Ministry of Commerce, Government of India, *Foreign Trade Statistics of India*, "DGCI & S, (Calcutta), (Several Issues).
Ministry of Commerce, Government of India, "*Indo-EC Textiles Accord*", 31st December, 1994, New Delhi, (Press Release).
Ministry of Commerce, Govt. of India, *Annual Report*, 1977-78, (New Delhi).
Ministry of Commerce, Govt. of India, *Annual Report*, 1993-94, (New Delhi).
Ministry of Commerce, Govt. of India, *Annual Report*, 1995-96, (New Delhi).
Ministry of Commerce, Govt. of India, "*Export-Import Policy*", 1991-92, 1992-93, 1993-94 and 1995-96, (New Delhi).
Ministry of Commerce, Govt. of India : *Export-Import Policy* (1992-97), (New Delhi).
Ministry of Commerce, Govt. of India, *Annual Report, 1990-91*, (New Delhi).
Ministry of Commerce, Govt. of India, "*The Export-Import Policy*", (New Delhi), 1976-77.
Ministry of Commerce, Govt. of India, "Exim Policy", (New Delhi), 1977-78.
Ministry of Commerce, Govt. of India, "*Export-Import Policy*", (New Delhi), 1977-78.
Ministry of Commerce, *Exim Policy*, (1989-90), New Delhi.
Ministry of Commerce, Govt. of India, "*Export-Import Policy* : (New Delhi) *1987-88*", March 1988.
Ministry of Commerce, Govt. of India, "*Export-Import Policy, 1991-93*", (New Delhi), 1st April, 1990.
Ministry of Commerce, Govt. of India, "*Export-Import Policies (for 1992-94 and 1995-97)*", New Delhi.
Ministry of Commerce, Govt. of India, *Export-Import Policies, (New Delhi) (1st April, 1995).*
Ministry of Commerce, Govt. of India, *Export-Import Policies, 1995-96*, New Delhi.

Ministry of Commerce, Govt. of India, "*Report of the Committee on Import-Export*", Abid Hussain Commission Committee Report, 1984, New Delhi.

Ministry of Commerce, Government of India, Tandon, Prakash (1982), Chairman, "*Reports of the Committee on Exports Strategy*", 1980, New Delhi.

Ministry of Commerce, Government of India, *Indian Trade Agreement with other Countries* (Several Documents), (New Delhi).

Ministry of Finance, Govt. of India, "Economic Survey (Various Issues) (New Delhi).

Ministry of Finance, *Indian Economic Reforms*, by Bhagwati, J.N. and Srinivasan T.N, 1993 (New Delhi).

Ministry of Finance, Govt. of India, "*Economic Survey, 1995-96*", (New Delhi).

Ministry of Industry, Govt. of India, "*New Industrial Policy*", 19th July, 1991, (New Delhi).

Ministry of Textiles, *Annual Reports* (Various Issues) (New Delhi).

Ministry of Textiles, Govt. of India, *Annual Report*, 1995-96, (New Delhi).

Mission of India to the European Union, "*Indo-EC MOU and Market Access for Textiles*", February 15, 1995, Brussels.

Mission of India to the European Union, "*Commercial Relations between EU and India : An Overview of Principal Trade Trends*", Brussels, February 5, 1995.

Mission of India to the European Union, "*Indo-EC News Bulletin*" Vol-II, No. 2, February 3, 1995.

Mission of India to the European Union, "EU's New GSP Scheme : A Guide", February 1, 1995, (Brussels).

Planning Commission, *Technical Notes to Five year Plan* (Several Issues of Technical Notes related to different Five Year Plans), (New Delhi).

Reserve Bank of India, *Annual Reports of Currency and Finances*, (Various issues), (Bombay)

Reserve Bank of India, *Monthly Bulletin*, (Several Issues) (Bombay).

Secretariat of Industrial Approval, *Monthly Bulletin* (Various Issues) (New Delhi).

The World Bank, *India : Country Economic Memorandum, Five Years of Stablisation and Reforms : The Challenges Ahead*, (Washington, DC), 1996.

OECD DOCUMENTS

OECD observer, "*High Cost of Protection*", No.150 (February-March), 1988, p.5.

OECD, "*The Concept and Measurement of Producer Subsidies Equivalents*" Joint Working Paper of the Committee for Agriculture and the Trade Committee, October 1986.

——*Agricultural Trade with Developing Countries*, Monograph, (Paris), 1984.

Peter J. Glinsman, Thomas Pugle and Ingo Walter, *Mixed Blessing for the*

Third World in Codes on Non-Tariff Barriers, UNCTAD Report Series, (UNCTAD, Geneva).

UNCTAD DOCUMENTS

Andrezej Olechowsky and Alexander Yeats, *The Influence of Non-Tariff Barriers on Export from Socialist Countries of Eastern Europe* (UNCTAD, Discussion Paper No. 6, August 1982).

A Users Manual to TRAINS (Trade Analysis And Information System), (UNCTAD, Geneva DMS/1, 1993).

Alexander J. Yeats, *The Influence of Trade Commercial Barriers on the Industrial Processing of Natural Resources* (UNCTAD, Discussion Paper No. 25, October 1982).

Andrezej Olechowsky and Gary Sampson, *Current Trade Restrictions in the EEC, United States and Japan,* (UNCTAD Discussion Paper No. 34, April 1983).

An overview of Tariff Reduction Formula for the Group of 77 (UNCTAD, Geneva, 1976)

Allen, R.L. and Ingo Walter. "*An Analysis of the Impact of Non-Tariff Measures Imposed by Developed Market Economy Countries on Representative Products of Export Interest to Developing Counties* (UNCTAD Secretariat Working Paper. 1970)

Bela Balassa, *The Structure of Protection in the Industrial Countries and its Effects on the Exports of Processed Goods from Developing Countries.* (UNCTAD Documents TD/B/C.2/36, 25 March 1968)

Changing Pattern of Trade in World Industry : An Empirical Study on Revealed Comparative Advantages (New York, United Nations, 1982).

Consideration of the Question of Definition and Methodology Employed in the UNCTAD Data Base on Trade Measures (TD/BAC/42/5, Geneva, UNCTAD, 1988).

Craig, R. McPhee, "*Evaluation of the Trade Effects of the Generalised System of Preferences*". TD/B/C.5/87, UNCTAD, Geneva, Jan. 19, 1984.

Deardorff A. and R.M. Stern, *Methods of Measurements of Non-Tariff Barriers & Trade.* (UNCTAD/ST/MD/29), 1985.

Gary Sampson, *Contemporary Restrictions and Export of Developing Countries* (UNCTAD Discussion Paper No. 36, August 1983).

Inventory of Non-Tariff Barriers Including Quantitative Restrictions Applied in Developed Market Economy Countries, (TD/B/C-2/115 Geneva, March 1973).

Karsenty, Guy and Sam Laird (1986), "*The Generalised System of Preferences : A Quantitative Assessment of the Direct Trade Effects and Policy options*", UNCTAD Discussion Paper 18, Geneva.

Liberalisation of Tariff and Non-Tariff Barriers. (Geneva, December 1969)

Liberalisation of Non-Tariff Barriers (Geneva, UNCTAD, 1973)

LIberalisation of Non-Tariff Barriers (Report of the UNCTAD Secretariat, TD/B/C.2/1125

Liberalisation of Tariffs and Non-Tariff Barriers.(TD/B/C.2/; TD/B/C.2/R.1, Geneva

Liberalisation of Non-Tariff Barriers (TD/B/C-2/R3, UNCTAD Secretariat Report, Geneva, December 30, 1970.

Liberalisation of Tariff and Non-Tariff Barriers (UNCTAD Documents TD/B/C-2/R-2 : TD/B/C-2/R-3, Geneva, 1970).

M. Davenport and S. Page, "*Regional Trading Agreements : The Impact of the Implementation of the Single European Market on Developing Countries*", *A UNCTAD Report*, (Geneva), October 1989.

Non-Tariff Barriers Affecting The Trade of Developing Countries and Transparency in World Trading Conditions : The Controversy of Non-Tariff Barriers (TD/B/C2/115/Rev.1, 1974).

Non-Tariff Measures Facing Developing Countries Exports of Primary Commodities, An UNCTAD Report).

Prebish, Raul, "*Towards a New Trade Policy for Development : Condensation of Report*" *UN Review*, 11 April 1964, pp. 11-14, UNCTAD (Geneva).

Problems of Protection and Structural Adjustments in the World Economy Part-I. Restrictions to Trade and Structural Adjustments, (TD/B/1039, Geneva).

Protectionism and Standard Adjustment in the World Economy Part-I : Analysis of Major Issues and Policy Requirements (TD/B/981, Geneva).

Protection, Trade Relation and Standard Adjustment (TD/274,1 Belgrade)

Protectionism and Structural Adjustments : Anti-dumping and Countervailing Duty Practices (TD/B/979/ Corr./UNCTAD, Geneva, 1984).

Protectionism and Structural Adjustments in Agriculture (TD/B/399, Geneva, UNCTAD, February 1983).

Problem of Protectionism and Structural Adjustment (TO/B/1282, Geneva, 22 January 1995).

Problems of Protectionism and Structural Adjustments : Restraints on Trade (TD/B/1126, Part-I, Report by UNCTAD Secretariat, Geneva,1987

Restrictive Business Practices. (TF/B/C.2/ 104/Rev.1)

R. Erzan, S. Laird and A. Yeats, *On the Potential for Expanding South-South Trade through the Extension of Mutual Preferences Among Developing Countries* (UNCTAD, Discussion Paper No. 16, June 1986).

R. Erzan, H. Kuwahara, S. Marchese and R. Vossenar, *The Profile of Protection in Developing Countries* (UNCTAD Discussion Paper No. 21, February 1988).

Reports on Trade, Tariff and Non-Tariff Barriers (Annual Inventories of Tariff and Non-Tariff Barriers of India's Trade with the EC) (UNCTAD, Geneva).

Selected Issues on Restrictions to Trade, (UNCTAD/ITP/24, Geneva, 12 March 1990).

Sam Laird and Alexander J. Yeats, *UNCTAD Trade Policy Simulation Model : A Note on the Methodology Data and Uses* (UNCTAD, Geneva, October 1986).

The Kennedy Round Estimated Effects of Tariff Barriers (1968)

The Performance of Developing Countries Exports of Manufacturing to the Developed Market Economy Countries. (TD/B/C.2/91, 22 December 1969).

United Nations Organisation, "*Commodity Trade Statistics, Series D*" United Nations, New York, 1994.

UNCTAD, *Market Disruption; the New Protectionism and Developing Countries: A Notes on Empirical Evidence from the US*, (An UNCTAD working paper 1983).

United Nations Organisation, "*Yearbook of International Trade Statistics* (Several Issues, Part-II), (UNO, New York).

UNO, *Yearbook & Commodity Trade Statistics, Series-D*, (Various Issues : New York).

UNCTAD, "*Non-Tariff Barriers Affecting the Trade of Developing Countries and Transparency in the World Trading Conditions* (TD/B/940), (Genava, UNCTAD) February 1983.

UNCTAD (1968), "*The Kennedy Round Estimated Effects on Tariff Barriers*", (TD/6/Rev.1), (New York), United Nations.

UNCTAD, *Inventory of EU Tariff & Non-Tariff Barriers* (Various Issues), UNCTAD, Geneva.

UNCTAD, "Anti-Dumping and Countervailing Duty Practices", TD/B/ 1039. (Geneva), 1985.

UNCTAD (1983a), "*Non-Tariff Barriers Affecting the Trade of Developing Countries and Transparency in World Trading Conditions*", TD. B-940, (Geneva), UNCTAD, March.

UNCTAD (1987), "*Problems of Protectionism and Structural Adjustment : Restriction on Trade*", (TD/B/1126/Part-I), *A Report by UNCTAD Secretariat*, (Geneva), 1987.

UNCTAD (1974), "*Liberalisation of Non-Tariff Barriers (Inventory of Non-Tariff Barriers)*", Report by the Secretariat, (TD/B/C.2/115/REV.2), Geneva.

US Documents

US Trade Representative Office *Foreign Trade Barriers* (Washington D.C.) Government Printing Office, 1980.

US Tariff Commission, "Trade Barriers : An Overview", *TC Publication 665*, (Washington D.C.).

US Dept. of Commerce, "*Highlight of US exports and imports trade*", (Washington, D.C.), (several issues).

US Tariff Commission, Part-I *Tariff Barriers* and Part-II *Non-Tariff Barriers*, 1974.

US Government, Department of Commerce, *Highlights of US Exports and Imports Trade* (Several Issues).

United States International Trade Commission, *The Economic Effects of Sig-*

nificant U.S. Import Restraints : Phase-1 : Manufacturing, USITC, (1989) Publication No. 222, (Washington DC).

WORLD BANK DOCUMENTS/BACKGROUND PAPERS

Anderson James E. and J. Peter Neary, "Measuring Restrictiveness of Trade Policy", *World Bank Working Paper*, (The World Bank, Washington), 1994.

__________, "The Trade Restrictiveness of the Multifibre Arrangement" *World Bank Economic Review*, Vol. 8, No.2, (The World Bank, Washington), May 1994.

Andrzej, Olechowski, (1987), "Non-Tariff Barriers of Trade", in J.M. Finger on Andrzej, Olechowski (eds;), *The Uruguay Round : A Handbook of the Multilateral Trade Negotiations*.(The World Bank : Washington).

Bela Balassa, "Industrial Protection in the Developed Countries", *World Economy* 7, No.2, June 1984.

Bela Balassa and C. Michalopoulos, *Liberalising World Trade* (Development Policy Issues Series Response VPERS & Washington D.C. World Bank Office of the Vice-President, 1985).

Bela Balassa, *Export Incentive and Export Performance in Developing Countries : A Comparative Analysis* (World Bank Working Paper No. 248, Washington D.C. January 1977).

Bucci, Gabriella, *The Effects of Abolishing Major Non-Tariff Barriers on Inter-OECD Trade.*

Frank Isaiah, *Trade Policy Issues for the Developing Countries in the 1980s* (World Bank Staff Working paper 478, Washington, 1981)

Garry Pursell and Anil Sharma, *Indian Trade Policies since the 1991-92 Reforms*, (The World Bank, Washington), 13th February, 1996.

Hamilton, Carl, *Effects of Non-Tariff Barriers to Trade on Prices, Employment and Imports : The Case of the Swedish Textile and Clothing Industry* (World Bank Staff Working Paper 750, Washington D.C. 1980).

Ian Goldin, Odin Knudsen and Dominique Van der Mensbruggle", *Trade liberalisation : Global Implications*", (The World Bank, Washington), 1993.

International Monetary Fund, "*Economic Review : Russia Federation*", (IMF, Washington), 1992.

Iqbal, Zuber, "Protection and Incentive in Turkish Manufacturing : An Evaluation of Policies and Their Impact in 1981", *World Bank Staff Working Paper* 1984.

Johnson, D. Gale, *Import Restriction : Tariff and Non-Tariff Barriers.*

Kalantzopoulos, Orsalia, "*The Effects on World Trade of a Decrease in Post Tokyo Round Tariff and Major Non-Tariff Barriers.*

Kym Anderson, *Growth of Agricultural Restrictions in East Asia*, (Food Policy 8, 1983).

Nogues J, A. Olechowski and L.A. Winters, *The Extent of Non-Tariff Barriers to Imports of Industrial Countries*, (World Bank Staff Working Paper 789, Washington D.C. 1986).

Sam Laird and Andre Sapir, "*Tariff Preferences" in The Uruguay Round : A Handbook of the Multilateral Trade Negotiations", The World Bank*, (Washington, 1987).

The World Bank, *India : Country Economic Memorandum, Five Years of Stablisation and Reforms : The Challenges Ahead*, (Washington, DC), 1996.

The World Bank, "*World Development Report*", (Washington), 1987.

________, "Protection and Incentive in Turkish Manufacturing : An Evaluation of Policies and Their Impact in 1981" *World Bank Staff Working Paper* 1984.

Verreydt, E. and J. Waclbroeck, *European Community Protection Against Manufactured Imports from Developing Countries : A Case Study in the Political Economy of Protection* (World Bank Staff Working Paper 432, Washington, 1980).

Zieta, J. and J. Waclbroeck, *The Cost of Protection to Developing Countries : An Analysis of the Selected Agricultural Products* (World Bank Staff Working Slaps 769, Washington D.C. 1986).

SECONDARY SOURCES

BOOKS

Alexander J Yeats, "*Trade Barriers Facing Developing Countries, Commercial Policy Measures and Shipping*", London, McMillan Press, 1979, pp. 104-43.

Anderson, Kym and R. Tyrs, *European Community's Grain and Meat Policies and U.S. Retaliation : Effects on International Prices, Trade and Welfare* (Canbra, Australian National University 1983

Anne Weston and Vincent Cable, *South Asia Exports to the EEC; Obstacles and Opportunities*. (London, Overseas Development Institute, 1979), pp.159-161.

Anthony Seaperlanda (ed), *Prospects for Eliminating Non-Tariff Barriers* (Publications of the J.F. Kennedy Institute, for International Studies.7, 1973).

Anthony Scaperlanda (ed;), *Prospects for Eliminating Non-Tariff Barriers*, (Publication of the J.F. Kennedy Institute, Institutes for International Studies 7,) 1973.

Arvind Vyas and Pranab Sen, "*Dimension of Indo-Soviet Trade and Economic Relation" mimeo*, ICRIER, (New Delhi), 1989.

Australian Bureau of Agricultural Economics, *Agricultural Policies in The European Community* (Canbra : Australian Government Publishing Service) 1985.

Australian Industries Assistance Commission, *Report or Textiles, Clothing and Footwear* (Canbra, Industries Association Commission 1982

Balassa, Bela and C. Michaclopolous (1985), *Liberalising World Trade*, Development Policy Issues Series Report VPERS 4. (Washington D.C.), Office of the President, Economics and Research The World Bank).

__________, "*Export Incentives and Export Performance in Developing Countries : A Comparative Analysis* World Bank Working Paper (The World Bank, Washington), No. 248.

__________, "*Liberalising World Trade* (Development Policy Issues Services Report VPERS 4. (Washington D.C.), Office of The President, Economics and Research, The World Bank.

__________, and associates, "*The Structure of Protection in Developing Countries* (Baltimore, John Hopkins University Press) 1971.

Baldwin, R.E. *US Tariff Policy : Formation and Effects; A Final Report of the office of the Foreign Economic Research* (Bureau of International Labour Affairs, Paper on International Trade, Washington D.C. 1976.

__________, "*Non - Tariff Distortion to International Trade*, The Brookings Institution, Washington D.C. 1970.

__________, "*Foreign Trade Regime and Economic Development*", (New York National Bureau of Economic Research, 1975).

__________, and Kruger, A.O., *The Structure and Evaluation of Recent Trade Policy Changes* (Illinois University of Chicago Press), 1984.

__________, and Kruger, A.O. (1984), *The Structure and Evaluation of Recent US Trade Policy Changes* (Illinois University of Chicago Press), and Tracy Murray, "MFN Reduction and Developing Country Trade Benefits under the GSP". *Economic Journal*, Vol. 87, March 1977.

__________, and Richardson (1973), *Government Purchasing Policies Other NTBS and the International Monetary Crisis*, Fourth Pacific Trade and Development Congress Ottawa.

Bhagwati J.N., "On the Equivalent of Tariff and Quota" in R.E. Baldwin et al, *Trade Growth and Balance of Payments.*

Bhagwati, J.N. and Srinivasan T.N. *Foreign Trade Regimes and Economics Development : India* (New York, National Bureau of Economic Research). 1975.

Boryce, Patricia and Hayden LIewellyn, *World Trade Distortions* : A Study in Modern Trade Policies (Melborne, A I.D.A. Research Centre), 1982.

Brian Hindlay, *Britain's Position on Non-Tariff Protection :* (Thames Essay Series No. 40., Trade Policy Research Centre, London).

Bormaun, A. (1985), "*The Significance of the EEC's Generalised System of Preferences*", (Hamburg-Verlag), *W. Archives.*

Brown, Drusilla (1986), "*Trade Preferences of Developing Countries : A Survey of Result*" Discussion Paper 190. University of Michigan Research Seminar in International Economics, Ann Arbor.

Buckwell, A.E., D. Harvey, K. Thomson and K. Parton, *The Costs of The Common Agricultural Polices* (London, Croom Helm) 1982.

Cline, William (1985), "Import of Manufacturers from Developing Countries : Performance and prospects for Market Access", (The Brookings Institution, Washington, 1985).

Cline, William (1987), "*The Future of World Trade in Textiles and Apparels*", Institute of International Economies, (McMillan, London), Washington.

Cline, William, *The Future of World Trade in Textiles and Apparel* (Washington, Institutes of International Economics) 1987

_________, *Imports of Manufactures from Developing Countries : Performance and Prospects for Market Access*, (Washington D.C. the Brooking Institute), (1985)

_________, *'Reciprocity' : A New Approach to World Trade Policy* (Washington D.C. Institute of International Economies), (1982).

Cline, William et al, "*Tokyo Round Negotiations : A Quantitative Assessment*", The Brookings Institution, Washington, 1980.

Clements, Kenneth and Lary A. Sasted (1984) - *How Protection Taxes Exports?* (Thames Essay Series No. 39).

Commission of the European Communities, "EC-Tariff Equivalents for Market Access", in *Agra Europe* (March 20, 1992) Database Schedule Code TABAGRTRA.

Commonwealth Secretariat , *Protection Threat to International order* (London, Commonwealth Secretariat,) 1982.

Corden V.M., "*Theory of Protection*", (Oxford University Publication, 1971).

Curzon G. Neo, and Curzon, V., *Hidden Barriers to International Trade* (London, Trade Policy Research Centre, 1970).

Deardorff Allen and Robert M. Stern, *The Miichigan Model of World Production and Trade : Theory and Applications* (Cambridge, Mass MIT Press) 1986.

Deardorff A.V. and N. Greene, "*The Implications of Alternative Trade Strategies for the United States* (Paper No. 78, 1977).

Donald Kessing and Martin Wolf , *Textiles Quotas Against Developing Countries*, Thames Essay No. 23. Trade Policy Research Centre London, 1980.

Federation of Indian Chamber of Commerce as Industry, "Reports on Indo-CIS Joint Business Council" (New Delhi), 1993.

Federation of Indian Chamber of Commerce as Industry, "A Brief of Indo-Russian Federation Commercial Relations", Backgrounds for the *first meeting of India-Russian Federation JBC Core Group*", (FICCI), (New Delhi), 4th September, 1996, pp. 1-14.

Gerald Curzon and V. Curzon, *Hidden Barriers to International Trade*, Trade Policy Research Centre, (London), 1970.

_________, Global Assault on Non-Tariff Barriers, Trade Policy Research Centre, London, 1972.

Goldstin, Morris and Mohsin S. Khan (1984), "Income and Price Effects in Foreign Trade", in Ronald W. Jones and Peter B. *Kenen* (eds;), *Handbook of International Economic Vol.-II*, (Amsterdum, North Holland).

Greenway, David and Brian Hindlay, *What Britain Pays the Voluntary Exports Restraints* (Thames Essay No. 43, London, Trade Policy Research Centre) 1985.

Greenway, David, *Trade Policy and the New Protectionism*, New York, (St. Martin Press), 1983.

Hans Kramer, *Non-Tariff Barriers to Trade in FRG* (Paper presented at the meeting of *International Research Programme on NTBs*, in Surrey, England January 1977)

Houghes H. and J. Waeibrcek, *Can Developing Country's Exports Keep Growing in the 1980s*, (June 1981).

Hufbauer, G.C., D.T. Berliner., and K.A. Elliot, *Trade Protection in the US : 31 Case Studies*. (Washington D.C.) Institute of International Economics, 1986.

Ian Goldin, D. Van der Mensbrughe and A. Coredella, "The Consequences of Common Agricultural Policy Reforms for Developing Countries", European Commission, Director General for Economic and Financial Affairs, *European Economy*, No. 5, 1994, sp. ed. on *The Economies of Common Agricultural Policies*, p. 49-71.

Ian Goldin, Odin Knudsen and Dominique Van den Mensbrugghe, "*Trade liberalisation : Global Economic Implications*", The World Bank and OECD Study, (The World Bank, Washington), 1993.

IMD Publication, "*World Competitiveness Report*, (Geneva and Lusane : World Economic Forum, 1995).

Indian Institute of Foreign Trade, *Growing Protectionism in Developed Countries: Implications for India*, (IIFT, New Delhi).

_________, *Implications of Non-Tariff Barriers to India's Exports in EEC Counties and Japan*, (IIFT, New Delhi).

_________, *Non-Tariff Measures in USA, Australia, Canada NewZealand, Denmark and Ireland*, (IIFT, New Delhi).

_________, *Non-Tariff Barriers to International Trade*. (IIFT, New Delhi).

Indo-German Chamber of Commerce and Industry, "*MFA Quota and Prospects for Textiles Exports*", (New Delhi), 1991.

International Chambers of Commerce, *Non-Tariff Obstacles to Trade*. (Paris), ICC, 1969.

Industrial Credit and Investment Corporation of India (ICICI), *Export Performance of the ICICI Financed Companies*, ICICI, (Several Annual Nos.), Bombay.

Irwin, Doglus A., "*The New Protectionism in Industrial Countries : Beyond the Uruguay Round*", IMF Paper on Policy Analysis and Assessment : PPAA/94/5, (Washington), 1994, p.24.

J.E. Meade *The Theory of Custom Union* (Amstardam, North-Holland 1955).

Jones, C.D., *Visible Imports Subjects to Restraints*. Government Economic Services, Working Paper 62, Her Majesty's Stationary Office, (London), 1993.

Joseph Pealzman, "The Tariff Equivalents of the Existing Quotas under the Multifibre Arrangements", ...

Martin Wolf, *India's Exports* (The World Bank., 1985)

——Hans Glisenan, Joseph Pelzman and Dean Spinanger, *Cost of Protecting Jobs in Textile and Clothing*, Trade Policy Research Centre (London), 1984.

Ministry of International Trade & Industry (MITI), "*Unfair Trade Practices in the USA and the EC*", (Tokyo), 1993.

Moorkre, M.E. and D.G. Tarr, *Staff Report on Effects of Restrictions on United States Imports : Five Case Studies and Theory*, Federal Trade Commission Staff Report, US Government Printing Office, 1980.

Nayyer, Deepak, *Indian Exports and Export Policies in the 1960s* (Cambridge University Press, 1976).

Pestieu C. and Henry J., *Non-Tariff Barriers as a Problem in International Development* Private Planning Association of Canada, 1972.

Planning Commission, "*Technical Note to the Second Plan*", New Delhi, 1956.

Ram Khanna, "Impact of QRs on Indian Apparel Export Industry", mimeo, (ICRIER, New Delhi, 1987).

Review of Trade and Economic Relations with the CIS Countries", *ASSOCHAM Backgrounder*, (ASSOCHAM, New Delhi), 1995.

R. Langhammer and Andre Sapir (1987), "*Economic Impact of Generalised Tariff Preference*", for the Trade Policy Research Centre, (London, Gower).

Robert E. Baldwin, "Non-tariff Distortions to International Trade", The Brookings, Institute, Washington, 1970.

R. Vernon, *The Technology Factor in International Trade*", (New York : National Bureau of Economic Research, 1970).

Sam Laird and Alexander J. Yeats, "Quantitative Methods of Trade Barrier Analysis", (McMillan, London), 1990.

Saxenhouse, G. *Calculations of the ad valorem Equivalent of Japanese NTBs for Various Years*, 1986, unpublished.

Stanley D. Metzger, *Negotiations on Non-Tariff Barriers*, The Brookings Institute, Washington, 1973.

Stone, Joe A., "*Price Elasticities and the Effects of Trade Liberalisation for the United States, The EEC and Japan*, (Michigan State University, 1977, Ph. D. Dissertation).

Stern, Robert M., & Stone, Joe A., "*Price Elasticity in International Trade*", (London, McMillan Press) 1976.

Stern, Robert M. Jonathan Frances and Bruce Schumachar (1976), "*Price Elasticities in International Trade*", (London, McMillan).

"Strengthentning Economic and Trade Relations with Commenwealth of

Independent States (CIS)", *ASSOCHAM Background*, (ASSOCHAM, New Delhi), 1993.

Suresh Kumar, (ed), "*Indo-CMEA Economic Relation*" Ashis Publication and ICRIER, (New Delhi), 1987.

Swapan K. Bhattacharya, *Indian Export Performance : A Sectoral Analysis* ICRIER, Working Paper No. 60, ICRIER, New Delhi, 1990.

Swapan K. Bhattacharya, "Intellectual Property Rights in India : Implications for Indian Industry", *ASSOCHAM Backgrounder*, 9th October, (ASSOCHAM, New Delhi), 1995.

Swapan k. Bhattacharya, "Managing Anti-dumping Measures in the WTO Regime", *ASSOCHAM Monograph* (ASSOCHAM, New Delhi), 1996.

"The Community Import Regime for Sensitive Products : Textiles Clothing, Japanese Cars and Bananas", in Piet Eecrhout; *The European Internal Market and International Trade : A Legal Analysis* (Oxford Claridon 1992) pp. 338-373.

Tinbergen, Jan. (1962), "*Shaping the World Economy : Suggestion for an International Economic Policy*", (Twentieth Century Fund, Network).

Vergese, S.K., *Export Assistance Policy and Export Performance of India's Export in the Seventies*, Centre for Policy Research, (New Delhi) January 1978.

Vincent Cable and Ann Weston, *South Asia Exports to the EEC : Obstacles and Opportunities*, Overseas Development Institute (London), 1979.

Whalley, John and Randall Wingle, *Are Developed Country Multilateral Tariff Reductions Beneficial?*, Centre for the Study on International Economics, paper 8216c. (London), Ontario, University of Western Ontario., 1982.

Willy de Clercq and Leo Verhoef, "*Europe : Back to the Top*" NMB Bank, (Brussels), 1990.

Will Martin and L. Allen Winters (eds;), *The Uruguay Round and The Developing Economies*, (Washington, The World Bank), 1995, XIV-XV.

World Trade Organisation, "*Submission of Tariff Reduction Schedule by the EC*", Vol. 19, WTO, (Geneva), 1994.

World Trade Organisations, "*The Final Act of Embodying The Results of the Multilateral Trade Negotiations*", 15th April, 1994, WTO, Geneva.

World Trade Organisation, "Tariff Reduction Schedules", (Submitted by the Contracting Parties to GATT on 15th April 1994, Vol.-1 - XXXI, 1994, WTO, (Geneva).

Articles

A.B. Shiela, Page, "The Increased Use of Trade Controls by the Industrilised Countries", *Intereconomies*, (Hamburg), May-June, 1980, pp.144-51.

A. Olechowski, & Gary Simpson, "Current Trade Restrictions in the EC, the USA and Japan", *Journal of World Trade and Law*, (Geneva), May/June 1980.

A. Collyns C. and S. Dunaway, "The Cost of Trade Restraints The Case of Japanese Automobile Exports to the United States", *International Monetary Fund Staff papers* 34 (1987).

A.K. Sengupta and R.K. Wadhwa, "Impact of Uruguay Round on Agro-Exports", in B. Bhattacharya and A.K. Sengupta (eds;) *Trade in Agriculture : The Uruguay Round and After,* Indian Institute of Foreign Trade, 1994.

A. Larsen and J. Hansen, "Agricultural Support and Structure and Development, in European Commission", Directorate General of Economic and Finance Affairs *European Economy,* No. 5, 1994. Spl. Issue on the Economies of Common Agricultural Policies (CAP),

Allen Winter, "Negotiating the Abolition of Non-Tariff Barriers" *Oxford Economic Papers* 39 (1987.)

Allen V. Deardorff and Robert M. Stern, "Methods of Measurement of Non-Tariff Barriers", *Institute of Public Policy Studies Discussion Paper No.203,* (Michigan, Ann Arbor), 1985, pp.1-2.

Amit Shovan Roy, "Liberalisation and India's Exports Competitiveness" in S.P. Gupta (ed;), *Liberalisation : Its Impact on Indian Economy,* (McMillan, 1993).

Anderson J., "Relative Ineffciencies of Quotas : The Cheese Case. "*American Economic Review*", Vol. 75, 1985, Pp. 178-90.

Anderson, Kym ,"*The Challenge of the Economists of Multilateral Trade Negotiations on Agricultural Production*", Food Research Institute, Studies, 1993, (22), No. 3. (Brussels).

Anderson James E. and J. Petre Neary, "The Trade Restrictiveness of the Multifibre Arrangement" *World Bank Economic Review,* Vol. 8, No.2, (The World Bank, Washington), May 1994, pp. 170-189.

Anderson, James E., "Measuring Trade Restrictiveness in a Single CGE Model with Appendix : A Manual for using the TRI Spreadsheet Model", *Boston College, Dept. of Economics,* (Boston, Massachusetts), 1993.

Anderson, James E. and J. Peter Neary, "The Trade Restrictive Index : An Application to Mexican Agriculture", *PPR WPS No. 874, International Economic Dept.,* (The World Bank, Washington), 1992.

__________, "A New Approach to Evaluating Trade Policy", *World Bank Working Paper,* (The World Bank, Washington D.C.), 1991.

__________ and Raed Safadi, "Trade Restrictiveness of the Multifibre Arrangements", *World Bank Economic Review,* Vol. 8, no. 2, May, (The World Bank, Washington), 1992.

Armigton, P. "A Theory of Demand for Products Distinguished by Place of Production" *IMF Staff Papers* Vol. 16 (Washington, IMF) 1969.

Ashok V. Desai, "India and the Uruguay Round", *Economic and Political Weekly,* (Bombay), Special Number, November 1988.

Ashok Gulati and A.N. Sharma, "Subsidising Agriculture : A Cross Country View", *Economic and Political Weekly*, (Bombay), 26th September, 1992.

Axel Neu and Hans H. Glisenan. "Quantitative Aspects of Non-Tariff Distortions of Trade in the FRG," *Weltwirstschftliches Archives*.

_________, "Towards New Agreement of International Trade Liberalisation : Method and Example Non-Tariff Barriers", *Weltwirstschftliches Archives*, April 1971.

Ashok Prasad, "Impact of GATT on Agricultural Exports : Some Issues", in B. Bhattacharya and A.K. Sengupta (eds;) *Trade in Agriculture : The Uruguay Round and After*, Indian Institute of Foreign Trade, 1994.

Bela Balassa, "Trade Liberalisation and Revealed Comparative Advantage" *The Manchester School* (1965), Vol. No. 2, pp. 90-123.

Balassa Bela and Balassa C., "Industrial Protection in the Developed Countries", *World Economy* 7, No. 2, June, 1984.)

Bela Balasa, "Trade Creation and Trade Diversion in the European Market", *The Economic Journal*, (Blackwell, Cambridge), March 1987, pp. 1-17.

_________, "Tariff Protection in Industrial Countries : An Evaluation", *Journal of Political Economy* (Chicago University Press, Chicago), December 1965. pp. 573-589.

_________, "*Export, Policy Choices and Economic Growth in Developing Countries after 1973 Oil Shock*" Discussion Paper Number 48 (Washington) World Bank Development Research Department 1983.

_________, and M.F. Krennin, "Trade Liberalisation under the Kennedy Round : The Static Effects" *The Review of Economics and Statistics* Vol 49, (Cambridge, Manchester), 1967.

Balassa, B and Mirdechai E Krennin , "Trade liberalisation under the Kennedy Round The Static Effects", *The Review of Economies and Statistics*, vol. 49, (Cambridge, Manachuttes), 1967.

Baldwin, Robert E., (1971), "Determinents of the Commodity Structure of U.S. Trade", *American Economic Review '61* (AEA, Nashville), March pp. 126-146.

Baldwin, R.E., "Trade Policies in Developed Countries" in R.W. Jones and Peter B, Keen (eds;) *Handbook of International Economics* Chapter 12, Vol.1.

_________, "Trade and Employment Effects in the United States of Multilateral Tariff Reductions" *American Economic Review*, Vol.66, May 1976.

_________, and Richardson, " *Government Purchasing Policies, other NTBs and the International Monetary Crises*", (Fourth Pacific Trade and Development Conference, Ottawa), 1973

_________, and Tracy Murray "MFN Reduction and Developing Country Trade Benefits under the GSP", *The Economic Journal* (Cambridge) Vol. 87, March 1977.

Benoit M. Papillon, "Measuring Non-Tariff Barriers to Differentiated Import products", *Contemporary Economic Policy,* 1994 (12), No.3, pp.67-68.

Beseler, J.F., "EEC Protection Against Dumping and Subsidies from Third Countries" *Common Market Law Review,* Vol.6, No. 6, July 1969.

Bhagwati, J.N. "On The Equivalence of Tariff and Quota" in R.E. Baldwin et al (eds;) *Trade Growth and Balance of Payment.*

__________, "A Note on The Equivalence of Tariff and Quota", *American Economic Review,* March 1968.

__________, "VER and *quid pro quo* : Foreign Investment and VIEs. Political Economic Theoritic Analysis" *International Economics Journal* Vol.1, 1987

__________, "Direct Unproductive Profit Seeking Activities (DUP)" *Journal of Political Economy,* 1982, Vol. 90, No. 51.

__________, "Economic Costs of Trade Restrictions" in J. Michael Finger and Anrdrzej Olechowski (ed,) *The Uruguay Round : A Handbook on the Multilateral Trade Negotiations* (Washington, World Bank.) PP. 29-36, 1987.

__________, "Revenue Seeking : A Generalisation of the Theory of Tariffs" *Journal of Political Economy,* 1980, Vol. 88, No. 6.

B. Bhattacharya et al, "Liberalisation in the External Sector : India's Experience", in B. Bhattacharya and Satwinder Paleha (ed;). *Policy Impediment to Trade and FDI in India,* (Wheeler Publication, New Delhi), 1996.

Bhattacharya, Swapan K., "Rationalisation of Tariff Structure of Indian Consumer Goods Imports", *mimeo,* prepared for Indian Institute of Foreign Trade as a part of the USAID Project on *Indo-US Trade Relation and Investment Prospect* : 1995, New Delhi.

Bisawjit Dhar, "TRIPs and TRIMs : Issues of Soverignity and National Globalisation Reconsider", in B. Bhattacharya and Vijaya Katti (eds;), *Emerging Trade Agenda : South Asian and German Perspective,* (Indian Institute of Foreign Trade, New Delhi), 1995, pp.143-176.

Biswajit Dhar and S.K. Mohanty, "Prospects of Market Access for Developing Countries in the Post Uruguay Round Agricultural Trade", in B. Bhattacharya and A.K. Sengupta (eds;) *Trade in Agriculture : The Uruguay Round and After,* Indian Institute of Foreign Trade, 1994, pp. 130-151.

Brian Hindley, "The Design of Fortress Europe", in *Financial Times,* (London, 6th January, 1989).

Brown K. Drusilla, "Trade and Welfare Effects of the European Scheme of the Generalized System of Preferences", *Economic Development and Cultural Change,* (Chicago Press, Chicago), 1986.

Brown F. and J. Whalley, "General Equilibrium Evaluation of Tariff Cutting Proposal in the Tokyo Round and Comparison to More Extensive

Liberalisation of World Trade" *Economic Journal* No. 90, 1980.

Bufiniaux J. and J. Waelbreek, "The Impact of the CAP on Developing Countries : A General Equilibrium Analysis" in C. Stevens and J. Verloren Van Themat (eds;) *Pressure Groups, Policies and Developments* (London, Hodder & Stoughton). 1985.

Cassing, James H., "Protectionism and Non-Tariff Barriers" Portfolio on *International Economic Perspective*, Vol. 9, No. 4

Cable, Vincent, "Textiles and Clothing" in J. Michael Finger and Andrezej Olechowski (ed), *The Uruguay Round : A Handbook on the Multilateral Trade Negotiations* (Washington, D.C. World Bank) 1987.

Carl Hamilton - "A New Approach to the Estimation of the Effects of Non-Tariff Barriers to Trade : An Application to the Swedish Textiles and Clothing Industry" *W. Archieves*, June 1981.

Carl Hamilton, "Voluntary Export Restraints on Asia : Tariff Equivalents, Rents and Trade Barriers Formation", *Seminar Paper no.276, Institute for Economic Studies*, (Stockholm), April, 1994.

Christopher C. Lange, "Tariff Preferences and Separable Utility", *American Economic Review*, May 1971.)

Chopra, H.S., "Western Europe and United States and Japan; Controversial Debate on their Industrial Competitiveness;" in K.V. Kesavan (ed.), *Contemporary Japanese Politics and Foreign Policy*, (New Delhi : Radiant, 1989), pp. 147-176.

Chopra, H.S. and Lall, K.B., "The EEC and India" in K.B. Lall, Wolfgang, Ernst and H.S. Chopra (ed;) *India and the EEC*, (New Delhi, Allied, 1984).

Clark, Don P. and Zarnilli, Simonetta, "Non-Tariff Measures and United States Imports of CEBRA-elgible products", *Journal of Developing Studies*, 1994(31), No. 1. pp. 214-224.

C. Niranjan Rao, "Recent Development and International Patent System", *Economic and Political Weekly*, (Bombay), December 23-30, 1989, pp.2841-2848.

Consumers for World Trade (1984), How much do Consumers pay for US Trade Barriers? (*CWT Information* paper Washington DC)

Curzon G., Neo, "Protectionism, MFA and the European Community", The World Economy, Vol. 4, No. 3,

D. McAleese, "The EC Internal Market Programme : Implications for External Trade" in N. Wegner (ed;) *Asian and the EC, The Impact of 1992*, (Singapore). 1991.

David O' Keefee, "The Schengen Convention : A Suitable Model for European Integration in *Year Book of European Law*, Oxford (Clarendon Press, 1992), pp. 573-589.

Deardorff, Allen V. (1982), "The General Validity of the Heckscher-Ohlin Theorem", *American Economic Review '72*, (American Economic Association, Nashville), (September), pp. 683-694.

Deardorff, Allen, V. - The General Validity of the Heckescher-Ohlin Theorem, *The American Economic Review*. Vol. 72, No. 4.

Deardorff, A.V. & Stern, R.M., "The economic effects of the complete elimination of post Tokyo Round tariffs" in W.R. Cline (ed;) *Trade policy in the 1980s* (Washington), Institute of International Economies, 1983.

________, and R.M. Stern and F. Baum, "A multi-country simulation of the employment and exchange rate effects of post Kennedy Round tariff negotiations" (University of Michigan *Research Seminar on International Economics*, Discussion Paper No. 68, (Ann Arbor), March 1976).

De melo J.A. (1978), "Estimating the Cost of Protection : A General Equilibrium Approach", *Quarterly Journal of Economics*.

________, and K. Dravil (1977), "Modelling the Effects of Protection in a Dynamic Framework", *Journal of International Economics*, 4.

De Rosa, D.A., "Trade and Protection in the Asian Developing Region" *Asian Development Review* 5, 1986)

Dean Spianger, "Building a Fortress Europe in 1992; Some Implications of the Common Internal Market for Hong Kong and other PACRIM Countries", *PRICES Paper no.1*, (Hong Kong and Kiel, 1989), p.13.

Elzman, J., "Economic 'Cost of Tariff and Quotas on Textile and Apparel Products into the United States", Paper presented for a Conference on *Crisis in Industries and the Safeguard Provisions of the GATT*, Sponsored by the Trade Policy Research Centre, (London), 1981.

Evans, H.D., "Effects of Protection in a General Equilibrium Framework", *Review of Economics and Statistics*, 1971.

Finger, J.M., "Effects of the Kennedy Round Tariff Concessions on the Exports of Developing Countries", *The Economic Journal*, Vol. 67, (Cambridge, 1976), pp. 87-93.

Finger J. Michael and Andrezej Olechowski "Trade Barriers Who Does What to Whom" Paper Presented on the Conference on *Free Trade in World Economy : Towards an Opening of Markets*, Kiel, Germany, 23-26 June 1986.

Finger, J .M., "The Industry Country Incidence of Less Than Fair Value Cases in US Import Trade", *Quarterly Review of Economics and Business, 1981.*

Franklyn D. Holzman, "Comparisons of Different Forms of Trade Barriers" *Review of Economics and Statistics* No. 51, May 1969, pp. 159-65

Francis Sarre, "Article 115 EEC Treaty and Trade with Eastern Europe" Intereconomies, (Hamburg), September-October, 1988, pp.233-240.

Gary P. Sampson, "Contemporary Protection and Exports of Developing Countries" *World Development*, Vol. 89. 1980.

Gary p. Sampson and Richard Snape , "Effects of the EEC's Variable Import Levies", *Journal of Political Economics* Vol. 88, No. 51, 1980.

George Koopmann and Hans Eekart Schanner, "EC Trade Policy Beyond 1992" in *Intereconomies*, (Hamburg), Sept.-Oct., 1989, pp. 573-589.

Gene Byllinsky, "The High Tech Race : Who's Ahead ?" *Fortune Special Report*, 13 October 1986.

Gerald Curzon, "Neo-Protectionism, MFA and the European Community", *The World Economy*, Vol. 4, No. 3, September 1981.

Ghosh, Ambica, "Tariff and Non-Tariff Protection Through a Social Accounting Matrix - A Case Study in African Economy", *Indian Economic Review*, no. 2, Vol. 22, 1987.

Goldstin, Morris and Mohsin S. Khan (1984), "Income and Price Effects in Foreign Trade", in Ronald W. Jones and Peter B. *Kenen* (eds;), *Handbook of International Economic Vol.-II*, (Amsterdum, North Holland).

Grain ,Waiek, J, de Melo and Shujiro Urata, "A General Equilibrium Estimation of the Effects of Reduction in Tariffs and Quantitative Restrictions in Turkey in 1978", in T.N. Srinivasan and John Whaelley (eds), *General Equilibrium and Policy Modelling*, (Cambridge, Massachussetts, MIT Press) 1980.

Grubel H.G., H.G. Johnson and Chris R. Martins, "Trade Protection : Concepts, Their Role in Evaluating Trade Policies in LDCs", *Journal of Development Studies* 23 January 1987.

Gulbrundsen, O. and A. Lindbein, "Swedish Agricultural Policy in an International Perspectives", *Skandinaviska Banker Quarterly Review*, 1966.

H.S. Chopra, "India and the EC, 1992: New Challenges and Opportunities", *Foreign Trade Review*, (IIFT, New Delhi, Vol. XXV, No. 3, October/December, 1990).

Hamilton, C., "Swedish Trade Restrictions on Textiles and Clothing", (*Skandinaviska Enskilda Banker Quarterly Review*,1984.

Hans Glisenan & Axel Neu, "Towards New Agreements on International Trade Liberalisation and Methods and Examples of Non-Tariff Trade Barriers", *W. Archieves*, 107, April 1971, pp. 235-271.

Hans Joachin Hochstrate and Ralf Zeppennick, "Distortions in World Trade : Recent Development", *Distortions in World Trade*.

Hartman Kuchle, "Social Norms and World Trade" in B. Bhattachrya & Vijaya Katti (ed;) *Emerging Trade Agenda : South Asian and German Perspectives*, Indian Institute of Foreign Trade, (New Delhi), 1995, pp.199-207.

Hiekok, S., "The Consumer Cost of US Trade Restraints", *Federal Reserve Bank of New York, Quarterly Review* 10, 1985.

Houghes H. and A.O. Kruger, "Effects of Protection in Developed Countries on Developing Countries' Exports of Manufactures", Paper presented at NBER Conference on the *Structure and Evaluation of Recent US Trade Policies*, (Cambridge, Massachusetts), December 1982.

Ho Dac Tuong and Alexander Yeats, "On Factor Proportions as Guide to the Future Composition of Developing Country's Export", *Journal of Developing Economics*, 1980, Vol. 7.

Hufbauer, G.C., "The Impact of National Characteristics and Technology on the Commodity Composition of Trade in Manufactured Goods", in Vernon R, "*The Technology Factor in International Trade*, (New York, NEBR, 1970).

Ian Goldin, D. Van der Mensbruggle and A. Coredella, "The Consequences of Common Agricultural Policy Reforms for Developing Countries", European Commission, Director General for Economic and Financial Affairs, *European Economy*, No. 5, 1994, sp. ed. on *The Economies of Common Agricultural Policies*, pp. 49-71.

Indo-USSR Trade Awaits Era of Consolidation, *The Economic Times*, February 15,1990, (Bombay).

Ingo Walter, "Non-Tariff Barriers and the Free-Trade Area Option". *Banca Nationale del lavoro Quarterly Review* 22, March 1969

Ingo Walter and Jae Chung, "The Patters of Non-Tariff Obstacles to Internal Market Access", *W. Archieves*, 1098. March 1972.

Ingo Walter, "On the Equivalance of Tariff and Quota : A Comment", *Kyklos* 25, 1971.

Ingo Walter, "Non-Tariff Barriers and the Export Performance of Developing Countries", The *American Economic Review*, (Washington), May, 1971.

Iqbal, Zuber, "Trade Effects in the Generalised System of Preference" *IMF Occasional Paper*, 1975.

Irwin, Doglas A, "The New Protectionism in Industrial Countries : Beyond the Uruguay Round", *-IMF Paper on Policy an Analysis and Assessment* PPAA/94/5, (Washington), 1994.

Israd, Peter, "How Far Can We Push the Law of One Price?", *The American Economic Review*, vol. 67, 1977.

Jagar, M. and G. J. Lanjouw (1977), "An Alternative Method for Quantifying International Trade Barriers," *Weltwirtschaftliches Archives*, (Hamburg), 113 (Heft 4) pp. 719-40.

James H. Cassing, "Protectionism and Non-Tariff Barriers", *International Economic Perspectives*, (Washington), Vol.-9, No.4, 1990.

Jaques Pelkmans, "External Aspects of EC's Single Market", Paper presented at South Biennial India-EC Colloquium, *India and the EC : Outlook for the Nineties*, (New Delhi), November 11-13, 1991, pp. 1-18.

J.F. Baseler, "EEC Protection Against Dumping and Subsidies from Third Countries", *Common Market Law Review*, Vol. 6, no. July 1970.

J. Vanek (1963), "Variable Factor Proportions and Inter-Industry Flows in the Theory of International Trade". *Quarterly Journal of Economies*, (Harvard University, MIM Press, Massachussetts), 77, Feb. 1963, pp. 29-42.

J. Maslen, "The European Community's Relation with the State Trading Countries, 1981-83", *Yearbook of European Law*, (Oxford Claredon press, 1984), pp. 324-345, and see O.J. 1962, L. 195/1 for regulation governing the imports of goods from 11 State Trading Countries except China.

J. Kol, "The EC after 1992 and Developing Countries" *Economisch-Statistische Berichten*, 26th July, 1989.

John H. Jackson, "Perspective on the Jurisprudence of International Trade", *American Economic Review* Vol. 74, 1984.

Joseph Francois, Brad McDonald and Hasen Nordstorm," Assessng the Uruguay Round" in Will Martin and L. Allen Winter (ed;) *The Uruguay Round and the Developing Economies*. (Washington, The World Bank, 1995) pp. 117-215.

K.G. Ramanathan, "Indo-EC Trade under CCA" - in K.B. Lall, Wolfgang Ernst and H.S. Chopra (eds;) "*India and the EEC*", (New Delhi, 1984).

Kala Krishna, "The Importance and Extent of Rent Seeking in the Multifibre Arrangements : Evidence from US-Hong Kong Trade in Apparel",..........

K.K. Gupta, "Uruguay Round : Its advantages to Indian Farmers", in B. Bhattachrya & Vijaya Katti (ed;) *Emerging Trade Agenda : South Asian and German Perspectives*, (Indian Institute of Foreign Trade. New Delhi, 1995).

Kalyan Raipuria, "Phasing in Social Norms to World Trade System : The Conceptual, operational and Research Issues". in B. Bhattachrya & Vijaya Katti (ed;) *Emerging Trade Agenda : South Asian and German Perspectives*, (Indian Institute of Foreign Trade. New Delhi; 1995), pp. 185-199.

K.S. Mehra, "Liberalisation in Recent Trade Policy Reforms", in S.P. Gupta (ed;), *Liberalisation : Its Impact on Indian Economic*, (ICRIER, New Delhi), 1993.

Kessing, Donald (1967), "Outward Looking Policies and Economic Development", *The Economic Journal*, (Blackwell, Oxford and Cambridge June pp. 235-271.

Kruger, Anne (1974), "The Political Economy of the Rent Seeking Society", *American Economic Review*, 64, (AEA, Nashville), Washington, pp.291-303.

Kirmani, N., L. Molajoni and T. Mayer, *Effects of Increased Market Access of Export of Developing Countries*, IMF Staff Papers 1984.

Krennin, M.E. "Effects of Tariff Changes on the Prices and Volume of Imports", *American Economic Review, (Nashville)*, vol. 51, 1961.

________, *Trade Relation of the EEC: An Empirical Investigation*, Preager Special Studies on International Economics and Development, (New York), 1974.

________, and Lawrance H. Officer, "Tariff Reduction Under the Tokyo Round : A Review of Their Effects on Trade Flows, Employment and Welfare", *W. Archieves*, 1979.

Krause, Lawrance, B., "United States Imports and the Tariff", *American Economic Review*, Vol. 49.

Kym Anderson, "The Entwining of Trade Policy with Environmental and Labour Standards" in Will Martin and L. Allen Winter, (ed;). *The Uruguay Round and the Developing Economies*, (Washington, The World Bank, 1994), pp.435-456.

Laird Sam, "Quantifying Commercial Policies", *in Applied Trade Policy Modelling : A Handbook*, (Cambridge University Press, 1995), pp.1-45.

Lam, N.V., "Export Instability Expansion and Market Concentration", *Journal of Development Studies* 7, 1980.

Lage, G.M., A Linear Programming Analysis of Tariff Protection *Western Economic Journal*, Vol. 53. 1970.

Langhammer, R.L., "The Importance of National Barriers to Trade Among Developing Countries" *World Development* 11, 1983.

Lary Wipf, "Tariff and Non-Tariff Distortions and Effective Protection in US Agriculture", *American Journal of Agricultural Economics*, 53, August 1971.

Leamer, Edward E. and Robert M. Stern, "The Commodity Composition of International Trade in Manufacturers : An Empirical Analysis", *Oxford Economic Paper*, (Oxford, 1974), pp. 350-374.

Lowinger, Thomas C., "Discrimination in Government Procurement of Foreign Goods in the USA and Eastern Europe", *The Southern Economic Journal, Vol.* 42, 1975/76.

Lloyd, Peter (1974), "Strategies for Modifying Non-Tariff Distortions", in Huge Corbell and Robert Jacknson (eds;) *In search of a New World Economic Order* (London, Croon Helm). pp. 199-209

MacGee, Robert N., "An Economic Analysis of Protectionism in the United States with Implications for International Trade in Europe", *The George Washington Journal of International Law and Economics*, 1993(26), No.3, pp. 539-573.

McCulloch, Rachael and R. Spencer Hilton (1983), "Identifying Non-Tariff Distortions of US Merchandise Trade", *Federal Reserve Bank of New York, Research Paper No. 8310*, (August).

Martin Wolf, "Textile Pact : The Outlook", *New York Times*, January 12, 1982.

M. E. Krennin, "Trade Creation and Trade in Customs Union, A Graphical Presentation", *Kyklos*, Fase 4, 1963, pp. 660-661.

__________, "On the Dynamic Effects of a Customs Union", *Journal of Political Economy*, (Chicago University, Press, Chicago), April 1, 1964, pp. 193-195.

__________, "Israel and the EEC" *The Quarterly Journal of Economies*, (Harvard University, MIT Press, Massachussetts), May 1968.

__________, "Effects of the EEC in Imports of Manufacturers", *The Economic Journal*, (Blackwell, Cambridge), September, 1972.

M. Dattatrevlu, "Uruguay Round : New Opportunities for Boosting Agro-Export" Ibid n. 25 pp. 32-53.

M. Lage and Baldwin, R.E. "Trade and Employment Effects in the United States of Multilateral Tariff Reduction", *American Economic Review*, 1976.

M. Lipton and Peter Tulloch, "India and the Enlarged EEC in *International Affairs*, January 1974.

Mission of India to the European Union, "*EU's New GSP Scheme : A Guide*", (Brussels), 1 February, 1995, pp. 1-8.

Michael Daly, "*Pattern and Peravassiveness of Tariffs and Non-Tariff Border Measures in the QUAD*" A Paper Presented for the 51 Congress of the International Institute of Public Finance, (June, 1995, Lisbon), pp. 1-13.

Mordechal E. Krennin and Lawarance H. Officer, "Tariff Reduction under the Tokyo Round : A Review of Their Effects on the Trade Flows Employment and Welfare", in *Weltwisstchaftliches Archives* (Hamburg, 1979).

Munger, Michael, "The Cost of Protectionism : Estimation of the Hidden Trade Restraints" Working Paper 80. *St. Louis Modelling Centre for the Study of American Business*, (Washington D.C.) Washington University, 1984.

Nayer, Deepak, "An Analysis of the Stagnation of Indian Cotton Textile Exports During the Sixties" *Bulletin of Economics and Statistics*, University of Oxford, February 1973.

N. K. Chandra, "USSR and the third World : Unequal Distribution of Gains", *Economic and Political Weekly*, Annual Number, (Bombay), 1977.

Nogues Julio, Andrez Olechowski and Allen Winter, "The Extent of Non-Tariff Barriers to Industrial Countries Imports, *The World Bank Economic Review* Vol 1, 1986, No. 1., pp. 181-99

O.P. Sharma, "Textile Quotas During MFA-II" Economic and *Political Weekly*, (Bombay), September 29, 1984, pp. 1711-1716.

O.P. Sharma and V.L. Kelkar, "Trends and Determinents of India's Exports" *Foreign Trade Review*, (IIFT, New Delhi), December 1976.

Officer, Lowrance and Jules H. Hertubise, "Price Effects of the Kennedy Round on Canadian Trade" *The Review of Economics and Statistics*, Vol. 51, (Cambridge, Masssachussetts), 1969.

Olechowsky, A. and G. Simpson, "Current Trade Restrictions in the EEC : the Use of Japan" *Journal of World Trade Law*, May/June, 1980.

Patrick Low and Alexander J. Yeats, "Non-Tariff measures and developing countries : Has the Uruguay Round levelled the playing fields?", *World Bank Policy Research Working Paper* No. 1353 (Washington, The World Bank), 1994.

P. Staelin, "The Cost and Composition of Indian Exports", *Journal of Development Economies, Vol.* 1, No. 2 September 1974.

P. Vogeienzang, "Two aspects of Article 115 EEC Treaty : Its use to Buttress Community-set Sub-Quota, and the Commission Monitoring System", *Common Market Law Review*, 1981.

Peter Lloyd, *Non-Tariff Distortions of Australian Trade* (Canbera), Australian National University Press, 1973.

Peter Dreyer, H. *NTDs and Beyond, European Community,* No. 131, February 1970.

Pranab K. Sen, "Rupee-Rouble Exchange Rate", *Economic and Political Weekly,* March 24, 1990, (Bombay), pp. 613-618.

Rajiv Kumar and Ram Khanna, "India : The Multifibre Arrangement and the Uruguay Round (chapter-8)", in Carl B. Hamilton (ed;), *The Uruguay Round, Textile Trade and The Developing Countries : Eliminating Multifibre Arrangements in the 1990s*, A World Bank Publication (Washington), 1990, p.182-212.

Reve Herrmann, "Europe's Technological Comparison with Japan", *Aussen Politik*, (Hamburg), 16/37, 3/86.

Richard E. Baldwin, "On the Micro Economics of the European Monetary Union", *European Economy*, Brussels, part 1, Economic Integration, Efficiency and Growth, 1995, pp.21-35.

Richard Lipsey, "The Theory of Customs Union : A General Survey" *Economic Journal* 70, 1960, (Blackwell, Cambridge), pp 496-513.

Richardson and Baldwin, R.E., *Government Purchasing Policies other NTBs and the International Monetary Crisis*, Fourth Pacific Trade and Development Conferences, Ottawa, 1973.

Roningen V. and Yeats, A.J., "Non-Tariff Distortions in International Trade : Some Preliminary Emperical Evidence", *W. Archieves* 112, 1976.

Roy, E.J., "The Determinents of Tariff and Non-Tariff Reductions in the United States", *Journal of Political Economy*, February, 1981.

Robert, E. Baldwin and T. Murray (1977), "MFN Tariff Reductions and Developing Country Trade Benefits under the GSP", *The Economic Journal*, (Blackwell, Cambridge), (March 87), pp. 30-46

Robert Long, "Japan Threatens USA more than Europe", *European Affairs*, no. 1/87, p. 53.

Robert McDonald, "Lowering the Drawbridge on Fortress Europe", in *Economic Intelligence Unit, European Trends*, (No.1, 1988, P.60), (EIU, London).

Rohini Aensman, "Minimum Labour Standards and Trade Agreements : An Overview of the Debate", *Economic and Political weekly*, 20-27th April, 1996, pp. 1030-1034.

Roningen, Vernon O. (1978), "The Effect of Exchange Rate, Payments and Trade Restrictions on the Trade Between OECD Countries 1967-1973", *Review of Economies and Statistics.* (Harward University, MIT Press, Massachussetts) August pp. 471-75.

Ruffin, R., "Tariff, Intermediate Goods and Domestic Protection *The American Economic Review*, June 1969.

RudlofAdlug, "Non-Tariff Barriers as the Uruguay Round", *Intereconomics*, (January/February 1990), pp.24-27.

R. Langhammer, "Fuelling a New Engine of Growth or Separating Europe from Non-Europe", *Journal of Common Market Studies*, Vol-29.2, 1990.

Satinder Palaha, "Policy for Export Sector Development : A Review", in B. Bhattacharya and Satinder Palaha (eds;) *Policy Impediments to Trade and FDI in India*, (Wheeler Publication, New Delhi), 1996.

Sam Laird and Andre Sapir, "Tariff preferences", in Andrzej Olechowsky (eds;) : *A Handbook of the Uruguay Round of Multilateral Trade Negotiations*, The World Bank (Washington), 1986, pp.101-109.

Saxenhouse, Gary R. (1983), "A General Equilibrium Model of Trade Structure", in William R. Cline (ed;), *Trade Policy in the 1980s*. (Washington D.C. Institute for International Economics).

Sam Laird, and Alexander J. Yeats, "Trends in Non-Tariff Barriers of Developed Countries, 1966-86, in *Weltwirteschaftlinches Archives*, Band 126, Heft 2, 1990, pp. 299-325.

Sam Laird and Rene Vassenaar, "Why Should We Worried About Non-Tariff Measures", *Information Commercial Espanola*, Spl. Issue on Non-Tariff Barriers, October 1991, pp. 1-35.

Sam Laird and Allexander J. Yeates "Glossary of Non-Tariff Barriers in *Quantitative Methods for Trade Barriers Analysis* (McMillan Pvt. Ltd. 1990) pp. 245-251.

Sam Laird and Andre Sapir, "Tariff Preferences" in Andrezj Olechowsky (ed;), "*The Uruguay Round; A Handbook of the Multilateral Trade Negotiations*", (Washington), 1987.

Sapir, Andre (1981), "Trade Benefits under the EEC Generalised System of Preferences", *European Economic Review*, (Brussels), 15, pp. 339-55.

Sampson, G. and Richard Snape, "Effects of the EEC's Variable Import Levies", *Journal of Political Economy*, Vol 88, No. 51, 1988.

Schuknecht I. and Stephen J., "EC Trade Protection Law : Pro-dumping or Anti-dumping", *Public Choice*, No.1-2, 1994, pp. 143-156.

Shibata, A., "On Equivalence of Tariff and Quota : Once Again", *Kyklos* 23 March 1970.

Shiela, A.B. Page, "Increased Use of Trade Controls by the Industrial Countries" *Intereconomics*, May/June, 1980.

Shobha Ahuja, "Liberalisation of Trade in Services : The Revealed Comparative Advantage Approach", *Foreign Trade Review* (New Delhi), 1993, pp.43-58.

Simpson, G. and Yeats, A.J., "Do Import Levies Matter? The Case of Sweden", *Journal of Political Economy* No. 84, 1976.

Stern, Robert M., (1976), "Evaluating Alternative Tariff Cutting Formulae", *Journal of World Trade and Law* (Geneva), (Jan.-Feb.), pp. 50-64.

Stern Robert M., "Evaluating the Consequences of Alternative Policy for Trade Liberalisation in The MTN" *University of Michigan Research*

Seminar in International Economies, Discussion Paper No. 15, (Ann Arbor, Michigan), 1977.

Stephen Magee, The Welfare Effects of Protection on US Trade", *Brooking Paper on Economic Activity* 3, 1972.

Swapan K. Bhattacharya, "Transition from MFA to WTO : Prospects for · the India's Trade in Textiles and Garments" in K.R. Gupta (ed;) "*World Trade*", (New Delhi, Atlantic Publisher), 1995, pp. 240-311.

__________, "Intellectual Property Rights : Implications for Indian Industries" *Backgrounder prepared for ASSOCHAM,* (New Delhi), October 1995.

__________, "EC's Non-Tariff Barriers and GSP; Implications for India", *International Industry Annual,* (New Delhi), 1990.

__________, "Final Act of the Uruguay Round of Negotiations : The Proposed *sui genris* system for India", in B. Bhattacharya and A. K. Sengupta (eds;) "*Trade in Agriculture : The Uruguay Round After*", Indian Institute of Foreign Trade, 1994, pp. 211-242.

__________, "Patenting Biotechnology and Micro-organism : Indian Position in the Post Uruguay Round in K. R. Gupta (ed;) *World Trade Organisation and India,* Atlantic Publisher, New Delhi, 1996, pp. 83-111.

__________, "*The Growth of Non-Tariff Barriers in Indo-US Trade*", paper presented at the ICRIER Seminar under USAID Project, (New Delhi), 1994.

__________, " .iT, the WTO and Social clauses", *International Industries, Annual,* (New Delhi), 1994, pp. 69-77.

__________, "WTO and Agreement on Anti-dumping Duties : The Casse of Indo-US Trade" in P.K. Banerjee (ed), *Indo-US Trade and Economic Cooperation*", (New Delhi) : IIFT, 1996, pp. 209-236.

__________ and Vijaya Katti, "EC's New GSP Scheme: Areas of Concern for India", *Business Line,* (New Delhi), 9 October 1995.

__________, "Rationalisation of Tariff Structure of Indian Consumer Goods Imports", Paper presented as a USAID Seminar on *Policy Implements to Trade and FDI in India,* at Indian Institute of Foreign Trade (New Delhi), 1995, pp.

__________, "India's Textile Agreements with USA and EC : Beginning of a New Era Competitiveness" Foreign Trade Bulletin, (IIFT, New Delhi), May-June 1995, pp. 10-13 & 22.

__________, "*Implication of the Uruguay Round of Negotiations on Small and Medium Enterprises (SMEs) : The Case of the Indian Textiles Industry*" Paper presented at a seminar in Delhi organised by Entrepreneurship Development Institute (EDT), Ahamdabad, 1994.

S.S. Saxena, "The EEC, GSP and the Third World" in K.B. Lall, H.S. Chopra (eds;) and "*The EEC and the Third World*", (New Delhi, 1981), pp.137-162.

Tharakan, P.K.M. Waelbrock, J., "Anti-dumping and Contracting Duty Decision in the EC and the US : An Experiment in Competitive Political Economy", *European Economic Review*, (Brussels), 1994(3), No. 1, pp. 171-194.

The Economic Times, "*The Overvalued Exchange Rates*", (editorial), March 3, 1970, (Bombay).

The Dilema of Rouble Conversion, *Times of India*, September, 1990.

Tracy Murray and Ingo Walter, "Quantitative Restrictions, Developing Countries and GATT", *Journal of World Trade Law*, Sept./Oct. 1977.

Tracy Murray, Wilson Schmidt and Ingo Walter, "Alternative Forms of Protection Against Market Disruption", *Kyklos*, Vol. 31, 1978.

Tracy Murray, "How Helpful in the Generalized System of Preference to Developing Countries?," *The Economic Journal*, (Blackwell, Cambridge) 1973, pp 449-55

Vasantha Bharueha, "Policy Liberalisation in India With Special Reference to Trade and Investment", in Karl Fasbender, Otto G. Mayer and Dilip K. Chatterjee (eds;), *Indian-European Trade Relations : Prospects of the Liberlisation process in India and Europe*, IIFT, GTZ and HWWA, Publication, (Hamburg), 1992, pp.15-18.

Vijaya Katti, "The Liberalisation of Indian Trade Policy", in Karl Fasbender, Otto G. Mayer and Dilip K. Chatterjee (ed;), *Indian-European Trade Relations, Prospects of the Liberalisation Process in India and Europe*, (Hamburg), 1992, pp.71-93.

Walter, Ingo (1972), "Non-Tariff Protection Among Industrial Countries : Some Preliminary Emperical Evidence", *Economic Internationale* Vol. 55 (May) pp. 335-54

Wolf, M., "Managed Trade in Practice : Implications of the Textile Arrangements" in W.R. Cline (ed), *Trade Policy in the 1980s*, (Washington D.C.) Institute of International Economics, 1983.

Yeats, A.J., "The Influence of Trade and Commercial Barriers on the Industrial Processing of Natural Resources" *World Development*, Vol. 9, No. 5, 1986.

——, "Effective Rate of Protection in the US, EEC and Japan", *Quarterly Journal of Economics and Business*, Vol. 4. 1974.

——and Vernon Roningen, "Non-Tariff Distortions International Trade Some Preliminary Empirical Evidence", *W. Archieves*, January 1977

Index